*

EDUCATION, POLITICS & SOCIAL CHANGE IN ETHIOPIA

*

*

EDUCATION, POLITICS & SOCIAL CHANGE IN ETHIOPIA

*

Edited by
Paulos Milkias and Messay Kebede

TSEHAI
Publishers & Distributors

TSEHAI
Publishers & Distributors

Education, Politics and Social Change in Ethiopia
Copyright © 2010 by Paulos Milkias and Messay Kebede. All rights reserved.

Tsehai books may be purchased for educational, business, or sales promotional use. For more information, please contact our special sales department.

Tsehai Publishers and Distributors
Loyola Marymount University
1 LMU Drive, UH 3000, Los Angeles, CA 90045

www.tsehaipublishers.com
info@tsehaipublishers.com

ISBN: 978-1-59907-043-8

First Edition: 2010

Publisher: Elias Wondimu
Cover Photography: Rachel Samuel [www.samueloverton.com]
Cover Design: Samuel Taye and Lisa Fang
Editorial Staff: James Mollison and Jacob Martin
Typesetting: Yoseph Wondimu

Library of Congress Catalog Card Number
A catalog record for this book is available from the Library of Congress.

British Library Cataloguing in Publication Data
A catalogue record for this book is available from the British Library.

10 9 8 7 6 5 4 3 2 1

Printed in the United States of America

Contents

List of Contributors .... *ix*
List of Acronyms .... *x*
Acknowledgements .... *xi*
Preface .... *xii*
Introduction *1*

1 | Tekeste Negash

The Curse of English as a Medium of Instruction in
Ethiopian Education System *9*

  Education Policy of the Imperial System of Governance, 1941-74 10
  The Socialist System of Governance and its Education Policy, 1974-91 ... 12
  The Federal System of Governance 14
  The Curse of English as a Medium of Instruction 17
  Replacing English with Amharic and Afan-Oromo as Mediums of
    Instruction 19

2 | Messay Kebede

Comparing Traditional and Modern Education:
the Decentering of Ethiopia *25*

  The Traditional Ethiopian System of Education 27
  The Drawbacks of Ethiopia's Modern Education 29
  Alienation and Radicalism 34

3 | Paulos Milkias

The Challenge of Modernity:
Western Education and the Demise of Feudalism In Ethiopia 39

Anatomy of the Ethiopian Revolution 40
Theories of Revolution 41
Linkage between Education and Revolution 45
Contraditions between Feudalism and Modernization 50
The Monarchy, the Church, and the Traditional Intelligentsia 51
The Modern Educated Intelligentsia and the Contradictions thereof 51
Cultural Penetration and the Ethiopian Revolution 53
The Objective and Subjective Conditions as a Backdrop to the
    Revolution 54
The Challenge of Modernity for Contemporary Ethiopian Youth 55

4 | Bekele Haile-Selassie Thomas

The Education System of Haile Selassie's Government:
the Roots of Political Fiasco 57

Foreign Involvement 59
Political Socialization 61
Concluding Remarks 64

5 | Maimire Menasemay

Towards A Critical Ethiopian Theory of Education 67

The Encounter with Modern Education 67
The Current Situation in Education 68
Current Critiques of Ethiopian Education 69
Traditional Education as History 71
Surplus-History: Towards a Critique of Homeless Education 74
Traditional Education and its Surplus Meanings 80
Daqiqa Estefanos, Ewqet, Mirmera, Tibeb, and Utopia 81
Concrete Utopia and the Tezeta of the Future 86
Educated Tezeta and the Limits of the Current Proposals 88
Against Education for Underdevelopment 91
Some Elements of a Critical Theory of Education 93

6 | Tibebe Eshete

Education, modernity and revival movements:
Making Sense of the Pentecostal Expansion in Ethiopia *99*

    Preliminary Notes on the Pentecostal Movement 100
    Origins: Historical Overview 100
    External influences 101
    Internal Dynamics 102
    The Harar Stream 102
    The Nazareth Stream 103
    The Addis Ababa Stream 103
    The Haile Selassie I University Stream 104
    The Rise of an Independent Pentecostal Church: Routinization and its
      Contexts 105
    Forming of the Mulu Wangiel Church 106
    The Pentecostals and their Persecution Experience 107
    Situating the Pentecostal Movement 109

7 | Data Dea

Governance, Language Politics and Education in Southern Ethiopia: the
Tribulations of Inventing WoGaGoDa *117*

    Governance and Ethnic Diversity in Southern Region of Ethiopia 118
    Co-opting Local Agents for the National State 120
    The Invention of WoGaGoDa, and its Use as the Language of
      Instruction in the South 121
    Teachers, Students and the WoGaGoDa Conflict in Wolaita 122
    Social Organization of the Resistance 124
    Issues and Interests Regarding WoGaGoDa: A Discussion 125

8 | Judith Narrowe

Development Policy, Education and Training: Women and Change in
Contemporary Ethiopia *129*

    Voices from the Fields: an Introduction 130
    Policy, Practice, Development, and Gender: the Scope of the Research ... 131
    The Conceptual Framework: Defining 'Policy' and 'Development' 131

'Gender' in Development Policies: Trajectories of Change 132
Women and Development in Ethiopia: A Cursory Review 134
Three Field Studies: A Comment on Methods 136
The Dodota Water Supply Project - 1988-89 137
The Women in Adult Education Pilot Project 1990 139
Gender and Affirmative Action: The Kotabe College of Teacher
    Education 2002-2004 141
What does Affirmative Action Affirm? Comments from Kotabe 142
Conclusion: from Learning Skills - How To Do - To Empowerment -
    How To Be 144

9 | Eva Poluha

Prevailing Over the Power of Continuity? *147*
Cultural Schemas, Continuity and Change 148
Peasants' Learning Political Behaviour 150
Children Learning to Become Good and Respectable Citizens 153
Cultural Schemas and Patron-Client Relations 156
Mechanisms and Processes Promoting Continuity 158
Preconditions for Change 159
Counter Discourses in the Ethiopian Context – Can They Prevail
    Over the Power of Continuity? 160
Children in the Birabiro School in Addis Ababa 160
Peasants in Ashena in Gojjam 162

Notes *165*
Glossary of Terms *190*
Bibliography *192*
Contributors Bio *204*
Index *206*

List of Contributors

Paulos Milkias Ph.D.
Professor of Humanities and Political Science
Marianopolis College/Concordia University
Canada

Messay Kebede, Ph.D.
Professor of Philosophy
University of Dayton
Dayton, Ohio

Maimire Mennasemay Ph.D.
Professor of Humanities
Dawson College
Canada

Eva Poluha Ph.D.
Professor of History
Dalarna University
Falun, Sweden

Tibebe Eshete Ph.D.
Professor of History
Michigan State University
East Lansing, MI

Data Dea Ph.D.
Professor of Anthropology
University of Northern British Columbia
Canada

Tekeste Negash Ph.D.
Professor of History
Dalarna University
Falun, Sweden

Judith Narrowe Ph.D.
Professor of History
Dalarna University
Falun, Sweden

Bekele Haile-Selassie Tomas,
Doctor of Juridical Science
Research Fellow
University of Wisconsin

List of Acronyms

BCMS — Bible Churchmen's Missionary Society
CRDA — Christian Relief And Development Association
CTSC — Community Skill Training Centre
DACE — Department of Adult and Continuing Education
EPRDF — Ethiopian People's Revolutionary Democratic Front
EUS — Ethiopian University Service
EUSF — Ethiopian University Students Christian Fellowship
FPM — Finland Pentecostal Missionaries
PA — Peasant Association
REWA — Revolutionary Ethiopian Women's Association
REYA — Revolutionary Ethiopian Youth Association
SEPDF — Southern Ethiopian Peoples Democratic Front
SNNPR — Southern Nations, Nationalities And People's Region
SPM — Swedish Philadelphia Mission
TPLF — Tigray People's Liberation Front
UCAA — University College Of Addis Ababa
WID — Women in Development
WoGaGoDa — "Wolaita, Gamo, Gofa, Dawro," a defunct Ethnic entity with its own language created by the EPRDF Government amalgamating four ethnic groups [namely Wolaita, Gamo, Gofa and Dawro].

ACKNOWLEDGEMENTS

In collecting the articles and publishing them here, the collaboration of many individuals was of major significance. First and foremost, we want to convey our gratitude for the enthusiasm shown by the contributors, many of whom are distinguished scholars in their own fields – in particular Eva Poluha, Judith Narrowe, and Tekeste Negash, all of Dalarna University in Sweden. With regard to the realization of the workshop, the editors would like to express their thanks to the Department of Philosophy of the University of Dayton and especially to its chair, William M. Richards, for their manifold and sustained support. They also convey their thanks to Amy Anderson, Director of the Center for International Programs, for financial assistance.

On an individual level, Paulos Milkias wants to extend his thanks to Dr. Margaret Gillett, former William C. Macdonald Professor of Education at McGill University and winner of the Governor Generals Award, who introduced him to the field of education; his office mate Dr. Nancy Berman, for her continuous encouragement; Professor Lise Winer, of the Faculty of Education of McGill University for inspiring him to work on the subject; Dr. Irene Moss, of the College of the Bahamas, who has been so kind as to lend her time to copy edit his work; Ms. Jeannie Krumel, administrator of the Department of Political Science of Concordia University, Professor Ted Vestal of the Department of Political Science of Oklahoma State University and Professor Jeffrey Rudolph of Marianopolis College who have been keen supporters of his academic endeavours.

His Excellency Mr. Aubrey Lawrence Morantz, former Canadian Ambassador Extraordinary and Plenipotentiary to Ethiopia [1981-1984], Dr. Laurie Betito of CJAD Radio Programme in Montreal, Quebec, Dr. Teshome Akalehiywot of Centennial College in Toronto and Prof. Tobby Morantz of McGill University deserve special thanks for being so generous as to show keen interest in his works. Distance notwithstanding, my friends Dr. Karen Ray and Dr. John hill have always given me support. My Ethiopian compatriots, Ms. Beth Woldegiorgis, and Mr. Abebe Brehanu, as well as Ms. Rahel Getachew are unending sources of inspiration. Last but not least, I express my deepest gratitude to my lifelong friend, Ms. Teobesta Tesfa Andreas, who employed her exceptional skill in word processing and separated this education section from the historical and political analysis in which I originally composed my essay.

PREFACE

The book is comprised of articles that were read and debated at a workshop on Education and Social Change in Ethiopia held at the University of Dayton on May 13 and 14, 2006. The idea of organizing the workshop came from the realization that Ethiopia's numerous problems were directly associated with a failed modernization and that the impact of the introduction and spread of an unsuitable system of modern education was an important component of the derailment. Both the contents of the education and its guiding principles were and still are not conducive to the nurturing of an educated elite capable of promoting economic prosperity, democratic values, and national integration.

While it would be wrong to ascribe the failed modernization to modern education if only because its contents and effects are rooted in the political and ideological needs of successive regimes, it remains a privileged avenue to understand the nature and the goals of the regimes themselves. Better still, its implementation has set a course of transformation fraught with autonomous and unintended outcomes. The articles gathered in this book analyze the various facets of the impact of modern education from different disciplines and theoretical premises. Their diversity exhibits the complexity and richness of the topic while their common focus shows the centrality of education to the understanding of the problems of modern Ethiopia.

INTRODUCTION

PAULOS MILKIAS & MESSAY KEBEDE

It was Aristotle who said 2,300 years ago: "All who have meditated on the art of governing mankind have been convinced that the fate of states depends on the education of their youth."[1] The dictum conveys an incontrovertible truth, yet succeeding regimes in modern Ethiopia have never learned a lesson from this cardinal insight. It was to underscore the seriousness of this problem that several Ethiopianist scholars met to discuss and ultimately produce a collected work that surveys problems and prospects in Ethiopia' education system

When one speaks of Ethiopia, the name immediately elicits visions of children suffering from endemic famine, visions that were particularly etched on the minds of people all over the world by media exposure of the drought of the mid-1980s. Yet exposure to famine was not what Emperors Menelik and Haile Selassie had in mind when they encouraged the introduction of modern education. Already quite aware of the importance of education, traditional Ethiopia had developed its own sophisticated and lengthy system of education. To the extent that this traditional cognizance of the value of education offered a guarantee of success, the failure of modern education is turned into a riddle. The various chapters of this book attempt to unravel some of the components of this riddle of analyzing the relationship of education with economic development, ideological and religious formation, gender equality, and political behaviour, with the view of assessing its conditioning effects on the destiny of the country.

A country of some 85 million inhabitants located in northeast Africa, Ethiopia has a profoundly unique historical background because it is one of the oldest nation-states with thousands of years of uninterrupted independence. As a result, the history of education in the country is immensely different from that of most third world countries. The conversion en mass of Ethiopians to Christianity in the fourth century A.D. and the translation of the Bible into Ge'ez—at the time the lingua Franca of the nation—led within the following centuries to the establishment of numerous religious schools. Not only did these schools train young Ethiopians for the priesthood, but they also made a coterie of the laity literate and preserved the country's spiritual and cultural heritage. This indigenous system of education had also a parallel development in Ethiopian Jewish [Beta Israel] schools as well as Koranic training centers in regions where the two religions predominate.

1

During its long history, Ethiopia evolved a unique phonetic writing system. It also spawned a class of scribes with distinctly home-grown characteristics known as the *Dabtaras* (or church scholars). Beside being the custodians of education, these traditional scribes constituted a privileged elite who played a pivotal role in the political life of the country.

The traditional education that evolved during the past millennia has been under the aegis of the Ethiopian Tewahdo Orthodox Church, an institution with strong political clout, since it required all emperors to take a solemn pledge to protect all the national spiritual organs of miaphysite orthodoxy and its religious schools as well as the economic interests of the Church. By the beginning of the 20th century, however, traditional education was found to be wanting in fulfilling the needs of the modernizing autocracies of Emperors Menelik and Haile Selassie.

The transition from religious to secular education required the utmost care, given that independent Ethiopia was totally surrounded by European colonial powers. After all, its past history is replete with attempts to interfere with its religion and education with the view of undermining its independence. Drastic measures were often necessary to stop these attempts, as shown by the expulsion of the Jesuits from Ethiopia in the 17th century. The problem that the country faced was thus how to introduce modern technology and know-how without falling under the control of European colonial powers.

The quest for modern technology started in the 1850's when Emperor Tewodros harboured the project of sending Ethiopians to Europe to train them in the manufacturing of cannons. At the end of the 19th century, Emperor Menelik sent off the first set of Ethiopian students to Orthodox Russia and Switzerland, which had no colonial ambitions in Africa. And in 1905, he commissioned Coptic instructors from Egypt to establish secular schools in Addis Ababa and other major towns.

The pioneering efforts of Menelik were continued by Emperor Haile Selassie who set up more schools and dispatched a troupe of students to Europe and America. Some mission schools were also opened in areas that were not steeped in the tradition of Orthodox Christianity, but they did not leave the same impact on the country as they did in the rest of colonial Africa.

Fascist Italy's occupation of Ethiopia from 1936 to 1941 interrupted Haile Selassie's reign. During that brutal occupation, Mussolini's cronies physically eliminated the few Western educated Ethiopians and attempted to introduce an apartheid system of instruction whose purpose was to inculcate Ethiopian pupils with a sense of inferiority in accordance with the Italian dictator's grand design of promoting the superiority of the Italian race. When the country was liberated in 1941 through the joint effort of Ethiopian patriots and British troops, Haile Selassie returned from exile and regained his throne. He subsequently resumed the expansion of modern education with some momentum.

The pedagogical system that emerged in Ethiopia was unlike the rest of Africa. It was more cosmopolitan in that instructors and teaching manuals were imported from various countries. In particular, the education was, to a significant degree, elitist: it placed more emphasis on the training of high level bureaucrats who would help run a modern state. As a result, unlike the rest of Africa, fewer resources were expended on teaching citizens how to read and write. While high schools mushroomed in the capital and a few select places like Harar and Asmara, 95% of the people remained illiterate even by the closing years of the Haile Selassie regime. This elitist system reached its crowning moment in 1950 when the Emperor commissioned a group of French Canadian Jesuits to establish the University College of Addis Ababa.

With the introduction of Western education at the beginning of the 20th century, a novel element was introduced into the country's body politic, namely, a new Western-educated intelligentsia progressively replaced the diehard *Dabtaras*. The latter were mostly of peasant stock, while the new intelligentsia was drawn from the upper echelons of the Ethiopian ruling classes. Not surprisingly, the new elite's relationship with the secular powers was non-antagonistic in the beginning. However, as the needs of the modernizing autocracy continued to grow, the secular state was forced into enlisting more and more children from the middle and lower echelons of society. Political agitation soon took root and in 1974 the age-old feudal order collapsed under the impact of the protests of the masses, affected by a series of chronic economic and social problems culminating in severe famine, and the political agitation of a second generation of highly radicalized Western educated intelligentsia.

A provisional military regime, which committed itself to a socialist platform, arose from the ashes of an antiquated political order. With a group of avant-garde civilian revolutionaries, the military committee known as the Derg set in motion far reaching socioeconomic, political and cultural transformations. The implementations of these fundamental changes portended the dawning of an entirely new era. But the military committee soon degenerated into a totalitarian and outrageously repressive power. Civil war raged all over the country and the brutal military junta was eventually overthrown in 1991, with its leader, Mengistu Haile Mariam, taking refuge in Zimbabwe.

From then on, political power went into the hands of the Tigray People's Liberation Front, [TPLF], a narrow ethnonationalist clique with an umbrella organization called the Ethiopian People's Revolutionary Democratic Front [EPRDF]. In addition to unfurling an ethnic oriented political system exclusively designed to assert its hegemony, the clique, contrary to the previous regimes, assigned to the educational system the task of furthering the ethnicization of Ethiopian society through the promotion of parochialism to the detriment of national integration.

Notwithstanding these changes, educational opportunities remain as scarce a commodity under the new regime as they were under the previous regimes. For instance, under the Derg, the ministry of education's long range plan had projected the country would soon achieve 100% literacy and would rapidly provide universal higher education for all pupils. None of these projections became even remotely true. The situation is not different today: despite the fact that hundreds of schools and a dozen of universities have been opened—partly because the population has doubled within the span of a single generation—the ministry of education of the present government has not shown a better result in terms of increasing educational opportunities for Ethiopians of lower classes.

The collection in this book emanates from many sources. As already indicated, contributors come from various disciplines; they are philosophers, political scientists, economists, historians, anthropologists, and university researchers. Just like their background differs, their analysis is also multidisciplinary.

Tekeste Negash's chapter attempts to revisit the predicament of contemporary education in Ethiopia. His analysis is based on the hypothesis that there is a causal link between the use of indigenous language as a medium of instruction and the general social development of a country's economic, political and cultural institutions. At the outset, the author provides a bird's eye view of the policy of education in Ethiopia as they were developed under the auspices of different regimes starting from the early 1940s. The study then elucidates the problems that have arisen vis-à-vis the employment of English as a medium of instruction in the schools.

Tekeste introduces the central issue of his paper with regard to the importance of replacing English by Afan Oromo and Amharic. He reveals that notwithstanding the extraordinary growth of enrolment over the years, the crisis of education in Ethiopia has grown by leaps and bounds and that the system is on the edge of total breakdown. This state of affairs arose, in his belief, from various mechanisms in place that are organically linked.

In the author's view, political and ideological transformations and their bearing on education policy can be explained with several episodes that have taken place. He stresses that the curricula, the medium of instruction, the resource base of the educational system as well as the notion of the role of education on the national level, comprise the key instruments of the process.

Tekeste employs Michel Foucault's "discursive analysis" in discourse and construes the problem of education in Ethiopia in terms of the political and ideological processes that have expired. He also envisages the dawning of a counter discourse. His ultimate aim in using this approach is to examine the shift in the concept of education on the continued existence of Ethiopian political and cultural roots. For him, the new counter discourse that has emerged is in the form of employing Ethiopian languages as mediums of instruction in the country's school system. Tekeste is convinced the persuasive value of discursive analysis is rooted in practice and the rendering of the language problem by the writer. As well, it emanates from an assemblage of stake holders such as political parties and professional organizations.

In the chapter that follows, Messay Kebede begins by associating the numerous problems bedeviling modern Ethiopia with the disastrous effects that modern education had on the country's youth. He directly draws the shortcomings of the educational policy from Haile Selassie's misguided socioeconomic policy of modernization. The educational system was alienating and devoid of national objectives because these characteristics were necessary to establish an autocratic rule which was at the same time dependent on Western support. Messay shows how the various facets of Haile Selassie's educational policy had uprooting effects. In particular, he systematically compares and contrasts the traditional system of education with the modern system with the view of showing the alien and denationalized orientation of the latter.

Messay argues the infatuation of Ethiopian students and intellectuals in the 60s and early 70s with the ideology of Marxism-Leninism has its root in the system of education devised by the imperial regime. The cultural tabula rasa resulting from the educational system has laid the ground for the attraction of an ideology whose essential feature was that it combined foreign origination with an extreme form of anti-traditionalism. Influenced by a radical theory of social change, the new elite developed a proclivity for polarizing political discourses with no middle ground. In thus turning its back on democratic values in favor of antagonism and exclusion, the new elite could not but fail to develop a sense of leadership intent on achieving national prosperity and integration.

Paulos Milkias traces the Ethiopian revolution of 1974 to modern education, modern educated elites, and the cultural penetration that came in its wake. For him, traditional power in Ethiopia involved a triple relationship of the monarchy, the church, and the church educated Dabtaras. The latter had an important role to play in the Ethiopian body politic, for dynasties had been created or decimated through their political intrigues. A new political picture emerged with the advent of modern education. Paulos argues the transfer of education of Ethiopian children from the church to the few western type schools became a turning point in modern Ethiopian history, for it produced an aristocratic cream of the crop whose perception of politics was distinctly secular. Furthermore, the new political order was based on a new ideology: *Zamanawi-seletane* (modernity), which implied modern institutions, modern schooling, and modern frame of thought.

Through modern education also came a very intense cultural penetration. The Americans who invested heavily in Ethiopian schools embarked on influencing Ethiopian politics, particularly its youth. Thus, the feudal regime, the U. S. and the first generation of Western educated elite became intrinsically tied.

The author argues there was a kernel of incompatibility in the alliance and the ideological link that tied the trio. American education, which shaped the new Ethiopian intelligentsia, is based on a liberal-utilitarian credo which upholds the values of metropolitan market economies. Autonomy and individual freedom—which is a mainstay of this liberal-utilitarian ideology—was accepted at face value by the new intelligentsia. However, these ideological standards could not be applied in Haile Selassie's Ethiopia. The contradictions involved are the liberal education disseminated through the Ethiopian school system and the political principles connected with it were annulled by the operating techniques of Haile Selassie's authoritarian system.

There was also further contradiction in terms. Since Haile Selassie's authoritarian system was steered by metropolitan capitalism, the alienated elite rejected the latter world view and turned to Marxism-Leninism, which it used to kindle a revolutionary tumult. All the military had to do in 1974 was to deliver a finishing stroke to Haile Selassie's feudal system.

In the next chapter, Bekele Haile-Selassie Tomas presents the thesis that the flaws in the public education policy of the government of Haile Selassie were at the root of its downfall. He argues the subjection of virtually the whole school system to overwhelming foreign influence and the failure to use education as a politically socializing mechanism were among the prime causes that led to the demise of the Ethiopian monarchy in 1974.

In closing, the author advances the view that the Ethiopia of today is in desperate need of what he calls "enlightened political socialization," which requires the interplay of informal and formal education processes focusing on the elements of its national foundation. The focus recaptures the pride in its heritage with the avowed purpose of raising nationally conscious, politically socialized patriotic civic generation.

Maimire Mennasemay's analysis uses the concept of surplus-history to bring out the internal contradictions of Ethiopian traditional education and their potential to provide criteria for reflecting on the crisis of modern education in Ethiopia. Drawing on some of the implications of the practices of the 15th century movement, the *Daqiqa Estefanos,* it argues that the distinctions and tensions between *temhirt* and *ewqet* [education and knowledge], *moya* [mastery of skills] and *tibeb* [knowledge of how things work], and *Mammar* [to learn] and *mirmera* [questioning what one knows and believes] in Ethiopian traditional education harbour possibilities for developing emancipatory and forward-looking conceptions of education. For Mennasemay, the mobilization of the imagination and utopian energies gestating in Ethiopian social practices, including traditional education is essential if Ethiopian education is to bridge the abyss between the actual and the possible and cast a liberating light upon the future.

The author's research suggests that to overcome the erosion of cultural confidence that modern education has spawned among the Western-educated elite, Ethiopia needs an educational system that resonates with her history, replaces imitation with imagination, and allows a fusion of historical consciousness and utopian energies. To reach this end,

Mennasemay argues, we need a critical Ethiopian theory of education that shows the way to an educational system capable of keeping the future open and of enabling us to trust ourselves again.

Tibebe Eshete, in his contribution on Education and Modernity, attempts to make sense of the burgeoning Pentecostal movement in Ethiopia during the crucial years of Emperor Haile Selassie's reign. As he points out, the 1960's is a generational divide in Ethiopian history because it was during this period that a novel awareness had sprang up among the youth. The new developments originated, according to him, mainly from national sources, albeit with limited foreign influence. This was a period when customary outlooks were cast aside and directing one's life through consensus was frowned upon. Traditional ethos faded as novel approaches surged. Modern education and western values had afforded the new generation new instruments of investigation/exploration. Now, they could clearly see the divergence between past glory which the old generation insisted on and the phenomenological outlook they had come to acquire. The air of complacency which guided those in position of power and influence was no longer a way to proceed. The youth had embarked on the search for some kind of redemptive uplift and their movement took two divergent routes. For one group, it was through the adoption of a Marxist-Leninist world outlook; for the other, it was advancing through a spiritual and transcendental renaissance.

The Ethiopian Pentecostal movement of the 1960's, driven as it was by the daunting life experiences of a society in transition, spread rapidly via personal interactions among peer groups. By and large, it was based on students in high schools and universities of the period and had a reactive characteristic; reactive because it challenged the traditional Tewahdo Orthodox church.

The Pentecostal movement's non-structured disposition allowed new forms of life experiences. Interestingly, the proponents of this new movement came from Tewahdo Orthodox quarters because its novel approach provided the members with relative autonomy and freedom to re-examine their life experiences. It also allowed them an opportunity of visualizing/conceptualizing things through a totally different lens.

For the Pentecostals, the traditional church lacked the capacity to stem the moral decay that was emerging among the youth and was too anachronistic to contend with a communist ideology that was surging among the youth of the period. The movement was also reactive in regard to foreign missionaries that limited themselves to the rural masses and lacked a national agenda. Pentecostalism was guided by the slogan "Gospel to Ethiopia by Ethiopians," interjecting into the field a form of spiritual nationalism. The movement's moral and political vision emanated from the youth's experience during a serious search for redemption and emphasized the importance of individual salvation that can be achieved solely by being born again.

Data Dea analyzes the ethnographic and pedagogical perspectives of discontinuity between the idiom of good governance and reality of a centralized administrative apparatus put into place in southern Ethiopia. In the chapter, the author scrutinizes the process of participatory democracy the regime claims it has introduced into post Derg Ethiopia. The focus of the study is the invention by the EPRDF regime of a hitherto nonexistent ethnic group named WoGaGoDa with a brand new language of its own culled from existing dialects. The introduction of new language into the school system of the North Omo region unleashed violent oppositions and protests among the populous.

Data acknowledges that the intention of the EPRDF state was to bring about regional ethnic integration, but he criticizes the government for adapting a faulty policy of inventing a brand new ethnic group with its own language of instruction since formulating and applying such a radical step without properly consulting the stakeholders—namely the people of the Omo region, who had to abandon their own languages for a new amalgamated one was highly unpopular and even infuriating. The editors would like to point out at this juncture that the EPRDF government happens to be the only one in the history of the world to ever attempt to invent an ethnic group with its own unique language. Not surprisingly, the imposition met with popular resistance and forced the authorities to acknowledge their errors and abandon the policy. But this was not before many people were shot dead and others incarcerated. Data closes his chapter with the observation that like all enforced unification attempts ignoring the views and feelings of the majority members of the society, the introduction of WoGaGoDa threatened the economic and political survival, the identity and the very humanity of its constituents. The ramifications are, as he points out, still reverberating since the event engendered animosities particularly among the Wolaita and Gamo ethnic groups of Southern Ethiopia.

Judith Narrowe, in a pioneering empirical investigation, analyzes discourses of development and social transformation as expounded by various Ethiopian women during the past two decades. The chapter holds public policy and implementation jointly and uses them as a common framework for analysis. It spotlights the ethnography engendered during the process of examining the implementation of three different development policies and how they regarded and indeed affected the status of women in two rural and one urban settings.

Narrowe's project involves diverse characteristics of the policies as they affect education and training. The investigation conducted and the discourses referred to by the participants in the evaluation process expose apparent variations in the substance of the policies with regard to the position of women in the development process. The variations in the policies are also heard in the tones of the women's narratives. Most significant is the critique suggested by young urban females at a teachers college regarding current affirmative action policies. Narrowe finds the policy differs in kind from previous policies in its emphasis on character change and individual development.

Whereas, for Narrowe, expressions of development maintain a pivotal spot in all of the discourses, recent narratives regarding development the young urban females appear to be influenced by debates that are raging regarding globalization. According to the author, the students' deliberations locate development and tradition in a single continuum and spawn a distinctive view of what they regard as "Ethiopian modernity" in today's Ethiopia.

In another pioneering empirical study Eva Poluha discusses the make-up of cultural schemas in Ethiopia, and its relationship to the question of change, asking if it is possible to distinguish cultural schema change, as expressed in a community's shared experiences and interpretations, from change in individual behaviour, attitudes or perceptions, resulting from experiences that affect the individual's feelings, motivations or understandings. Poluha bases her discussion on studies carried out on informal political learning by peasants in Gojjam and on formal and informal learning by school children in Addis Ababa.

During three consecutives regimes, that of Haile Selassie, of the Derg and of the EPRDF, peasants in Ethiopia learned representatives of the state should always be treated with respect and signs of submission, and acts by state employees or the official ideology should never be publicly questioned. This behaviour continued to be the same, even though incumbents of the state hierarchy themselves changed. School children also learned their elders should be respected, that this respect was reciprocated with protection, care and economic redistribution and that anyone, if endowed with *edel* (luck), could reach the apex of a hierarchy. Poluha's empirical study shows that regardless of age, profession and types of interaction, the children and the adults in the two divergent settings exhibited remarkably similar hierarchical, patron client relationships. On the basis of these experiences Poluha argues that this cultural schema promotes continuity rather than change and for change to occur it is not enough to change the persons in power.[2]

1

THE CURSE OF ENGLISH AS A MEDIUM OF INSTRUCTION IN THE ETHIOPIAN EDUCATION SYSTEM

TEKESTE NEGASH

Perhaps more than any other country in Africa, Ethiopia stresses a causal link between education and development. The faith on the schools to mould the new generation is an ever recurring theme. More often, the poverty of the country is explained as a result of high rate of illiteracy. Hence education is seen as the "single and most important change needed to hasten the socio-economic development of poor nations like Ethiopia" (Christian Relief and Development Association, (CRDA) 2004). The official view on education is based on an outdated knowledge (on the causal link between education and development) and on the belief that any kind of education could do no harm to its individual beneficiaries. Accordingly, issues about the relevance and quality of education were often interpreted by Ethiopian authorities as elitist and reactionary, until donors and the World Bank begun to show their concern. The crisis of the education sector is very much a result of the absence of a range of realistic assessments of the role of education in social reproduction. As things stand now, the great majority of those students who completed grade four failed to score a passing grade. One can indeed raise the issue as to whether these students have achieved permanent literacy. The examination results of those students who completed grade eight were not better. The decline of the quality of education is most acute at the secondary schools where all subjects are taught in English. The teachers lack proficiency to both understand the curriculum and teach it; their students are in a far worse position to follow their studies in English. The expansion of secondary education, the continued growth of vernacular languages (at primary schools) and the shortage of funds appear to lead the education sector from crisis to system collapse. This study reconstructs the growth of the crisis of the sector during the last three decades. It then discusses the implications of the crisis in

9

terms of communication breakdown; absence of analytical capacity at system level; the fragmentation of society; loss of political legitimacy and perpetuation of authoritarian power, and eventually political and social anarchy. By way of conclusion, this study argues, among other things, for the abolition of English as a medium of instruction in secondary schools and colleges and the overhaul of language policy in education.

The major focus of this chapter is to contextualize the dilemmas of education in Ethiopia. Its main purpose is to demonstrate that the crisis of education, despite phenomenal growth in enrollment, has deepened and the education system in Ethiopia is in fact on the verge of collapse. Crisis and system collapse are interpretations of the actual state of the education system and of the extent to which its various components are organically linked. A major methodological tool for such interpretation is a discursive analysis of relevant episodes and instruments. Political and ideological changes and their impact on education policy belong to the realm of episodes, whereas curricula, medium of instruction, resource base and views on the role of education constitute the key instruments. Discursive analysis is most often political as well as ideological. Hence discursive analysis as used by the founder of the concept, Michel Foucault, may be carried out within an established discourse or as a contribution to the evolution of a counter discourse.

The goal of this discursive analysis is to contribute to a shift in the discourse on the role of education on the survival of Ethiopian political and cultural society. The key instrument in the evolution of a new counter discourse, I believe, is the use of Ethiopian languages as mediums of instruction at all stages of the education system.[1] The persuasive value of discursive analysis depends on the experience and reading of the author as well as on the constellation of power holders such as professional organizations and political parties. The paper first introduces the education policy of the various systems of governance since the 1940s. It then discusses the problems around the use of English as a medium of instruction and finally introduces the central issue of the paper, namely the importance of replacing English by Amharic and Afan-Oromo.

Education policy of the Imperial system of governance, 1941-74 [2]

The golden age of modern education in Ethiopia is usually dated to the years between 1941 and 1970. The education sector with Haile Selassie as frontline minister was by far the best staffed and financed. With the Emperor at the helm of power, the Ethiopian government strongly believed in the centrality of education as a vehicle of progress. It is debatable as to what the Emperor meant by education and progress but, his numerous statements on the subject indicate that he believed education would enrich Ethiopian civilization.

The beneficiaries of modern education were those who were born from the mid 1930's until the end of the 1940s. Throughout the 1940s and 1950s, there were far more schools than students; and incentives such as clothing, school materials and boarding were quite common. Qualified students were enticed to join vocational secondary institutions such as agricultural and laboratory schools, as well as teacher training establishments through the provision of food and lodging. Throughout the 1950s and 1960s, the University College of Addis Ababa had to compete for students with the various vocational and technical secondary schools. Jobs were plenty and salaries were closely tied to academic qualifications. During this period, the return to investment in education was clear to grasp. After just few years of education, children from humble backgrounds found themselves in high positions with income that could have been more than 10 times the per capita income of their parents. Education was free and it appealed more to the poorer section of the population; the rich and the aristocracy were less enticed by the economic returns of education.

The Emperor and his government might have believed they were laying down the foundations for the modernization of the country but they did not pay enough attention to the communication gaps between the generations that modern schools were creating. In practice, the Ethiopian government had no coherent strategy. Curriculum was ad-hoc and left to teachers who came from different countries with different backgrounds. The first primers for primary schools in the official language of the country were first developed in 1955, nearly 15 years after the demise of Italian colonial occupation. As early as 1958, one of the pioneers in Ethiopian education pointed out that the curriculum in place was incapable of producing citizens who had the capability to interpret, enrich and adapt the heritage of the country to new needs and changing conditions. Though the curriculum may have been irrelevant, all those who went through the system could count on finding public employment with good remuneration.

The golden age when education was a profitable investment came to an end towards the late 1960s. The public sector could no longer absorb secondary school graduates produced by a continuously growing number of schools. As early as 1973, up to 25 percent of the secondary school graduates were unemployed. At the time, when so many secondary school graduates were roaming the streets of Addis Ababa and other towns in search of white collar employment, the country had a gross enrollment rate of about ten percent. In the 1962-63 academic year, there were about 8,000 students enrolled in grade 8, whereas total enrollment in grades 9-12 of public and private schools combined was 9,940.[3] During the same year, enrolment in grades 1-8 reached 304,138. Ten years later, (1974) total enrollment reached 1.1 million.[4]

The problem of widespread illiteracy and the anomalous situation of secondary school graduates roaming the streets in search of employment called for a series of education sector reviews. The modern economic sector was too small to accommodate the growing pool of secondary school graduates. There was a widespread dissatisfaction with the education sector from secondary school students who depicted the future in bleak terms. As an attempt of rectification, the first Ethiopian education sector review, made up of an international group of experts, was set up in 1971-2.

The first task of the Ethiopian education sector review of 1971-2 was the control of entry to secondary education. Fully cognizant of the social upheaval unemployed secondary school graduates were capable of inciting, the planners of the Ethiopian education system reasoned that secondary education need not grow beyond the natural population increase, estimated at 2.1 per cent per annum. Throughout the 1960s, the number of secondary school students has been growing at the rate of 12 percent per annum. As I pointed out earlier, although only 4 per cent of the appropriate age group attended secondary education, it was the wish of the Ethiopian government to try to think in terms of supply and demand. The implementation of the sector review would have gone a long way in solving the problem of unemployed secondary school graduates.

The second task of the 1971-2 education sector review was to make the rural population the main target of its educational policy. The slow pace in spreading education into the rural areas was deplored both by the Ethiopian government and its partners. The year 2000 was set as the year when Ethiopia would extend universal primary education to all its citizens. The experts who framed the sector review (51 Ethiopians and 31 international experts) argued it was the right of all citizens to get a basic primary education for a minimum of 4 years.

The recommendations of the Education Sector Review of 1971-2 would have had far reaching implications had they been implemented. It is interesting to note that there are great similarities between the 1971-2 sector review and the education policy of 1994 that is currently in use. I shall return to this topic later.

Here, it is important to notice the quality of teaching was far better during the imperial system of governance than what came to prevail in the succeeding years. At the secondary level for instance, most of the teachers were native speakers of English and Pupil-teacher ratio was below 40:1. It is another matter whether the subjects, especially those dealing with the human and social sciences were responsive to the history and culture of Ethiopia, which they were not. It is also notable that most of those who currently hold political power have gotten their training during the imperial era.

The Socialist System of Governance and its Education Policy, 1974-91

The Ethiopian political system that prevailed between 1974 and 1991 was the complete antithesis of the imperial one. Ethiopia was declared a republic and ruled by a socialist/communist workers party. The economy was socialized; urban and rural lands were put under state control. The path of scientific socialism was deemed the most appropriate strategy to bring out the country from its backward stage of development. The Cold War was indeed a decisive context which made the transition from the pro-west alliance of the imperial system to one that supported and protected by the Soviet Union. Buttressed by the ideological position of the Soviet Union and its East European allies, the Ethiopian government began to put more emphasis on the role of education for development. Socialist education stressed the inculcation of ideology as a prime objective within Marxism and the value of production as its main pillars. The United States of America, one of the main partners in the development of the Ethiopian education sector, was replaced by educational experts from Eastern Germany.

The disruption of relations with the western world in general and the United States in particular signalled the decline of English as a medium of instruction. At the height of the US-Ethiopian cultural relations, there were up to 400 Peace Corps teachers from the United States in Ethiopia. The entire Ethiopian society was in one way or another subjected to political indoctrination. The political economy of Marxism/Leninism was made a subject at all levels of the education system. From there on, the importance of English as the major language of instruction became unquestionable. But during the time of the Derg, the fundamental aim of education, as expressed by the Ethiopian government in the early 1980s, was to cultivate Marxist-Leninist ideology in the young generation, to develop knowledge in science and technology, and to integrate and co-ordinate research with production so as to enable the revolution to move forward and spawn productive citizens.[5] A new curriculum was duly produced where five new subjects namely, agriculture, production technology, political education, home economics and introduction to business were added. This meant Ethiopian secondary students had to follow 12 subjects. This was in sharp contrast to the format of the curriculum of the imperial period where students took no more than seven subjects. The inclusion of additional subjects without prior planning and adequate infrastructure led to the further deterioration of pedagogical conditions. [6]

Between 1975 and 1989, enrollment grew at a rate of 12 percent, thus covering about 35 per cent of 7-16 year school age cohorts. Table 1 demonstrates the rate of growth during the two periods. However, expansion of the education sector was not accompanied by a comparable increase in resources. On the contrary, the Socialist regime intensified the use of the shift system (where students follow all their studies either in the morning or in the afternoon) so as to maximize the utilization of school premises.

By the mid 1980s, the Socialist government could no longer ignore the widespread public dissatisfaction with the quality of education. As is often the case, the government and the bureaucrats within the Ministry of Education and the amorphous public had different understandings. For the government, quality issues meant the content "must fully prepare the students to meet the objective demands of the nation and the ideological needs of our society". [7] These needs and demands were to be fulfilled by "the implementation without delay the Programme for expansion of technical and vocational education in line with the manpower demands of the country." [8] For the officials of the Ministry of Education, teachers and university employees, the decline of quality was discussed in terms of the growing pupil-teacher and pupil section ratios as well as by the decline of the proficiency of teachers in the use of English as medium of instruction.

Yet, the manpower demands of the country for people trained in technical and vocational education remained extremely modest. The labour force of the industrial sector increased from 63,000 to 80, 000 between 1978 and 1984 or at the rate of 2430 new workers per year.[9] The private sector that could absorb educated labour continued to grow at a snail's pace. As late as 1990, the entire manufacturing sector (or modern sector) of the Ethiopian economy employed not more than 100,000 people out of a labour force of about 30 million.[10] Ethiopia was rural in the end of 1960s and still remains rural with an estimated 85 per cent of the population firmly engaged in agriculture in the year 2004.

In 1983, the socialist government commissioned an evaluation of the education system with a view of devising strategies for the "implementation without delay the objectives of education."[11] I have discussed elsewhere at great length the findings of the evaluating committee. The Ethiopian government hardly benefited from it. It is most probable that the evaluation committee failed to attempt to answer the shortcomings of the sector as perceived by the government. It is also possible that the committee perceived the decline of quality as of largely technical nature that could be resolved with the infusion of additional funds geared to the upgrading of teacher competence in teaching methodology and subject matter.

Although the rate of expansion of the education sector was uniform from the 1960s well into the end of 1980s, such expansion was carried out at the expense of teaching and learning environment. Very little resources were made available for the recruitment of sufficient teachers so as to keep the pupil-teacher ratio at the range of 40 to 1. Even fewer resources were made available to attain and develop pedagogical materials; most of the budget for education went to salaries. The non-salary component became even less during the socialist regime. The curriculum department, heavily dominated by expertise from East Germany, did what it could to develop text books designed "to meet the objective demands of the nation and the ideological needs of our society."[12] The curriculum was permeated with ideological texts as well as texts on agriculture and on the primacy of technology.

The progressive withdrawal of English teachers and the overcrowding of classes, led to the decline of language proficiency among teachers and students. By 1980, the Ministry of Education toyed with the idea of replacing English with Amharic for junior secondary (grades 7and 8). The problem of media of instruction was also confronted by the Evaluation Committee of 1983. The evaluation committee advised the government to study the issue further within the context of a new language policy. By 1990, one could say English had effectively ceased to be the language of instruction. Despite the fact that it remained the language printed in text books of all subjects for junior and senior secondary education.

The socialist government worked under the lie that education was the key instrument to inculcate Marxist-Leninist ideology and to produce productive citizens. It portrayed itself as a regime that has done more to spread the benefits of education compared to the imperial rule that it replaced. It is of course doubtful whether the socialist regime has achieved any of its objectives.

Although there might have been a broad consensus as to the shortcomings of the education sector, opinions were divided as to the implications of the crisis. The Education Evaluation Committee had, for instance, concluded its massive survey by identifying the bottlenecks in terms of resources and training. Others regarded the long term negative impact of an educational system that ignored the inculcation of values that keep a nation/ polity/society cohesive and forward looking.[13] While donors like UNESCO and SIDA were impressed with the consistent literacy campaigns carried out by the Ethiopian government, and the spread of primary education from about 10 percent of the age cohort to about 35 per cent by 1989, uncertainty remained as to the implications of the spread or expansion of education on poverty. For the great majority of the Ethiopian population, socialism is associated with the spread of the equality of poverty. The replacement of the private sector by state institutions made everyone, with the exception of high political functionaries uniformly poor. In 1991, the socialist system of governance was defeated by the regional/ethnic armed insurgents.

The Federal System of Governance (functional since 1991)

The ruling political cum military party (Ethiopian Peoples Revolutionary Democratic Front, EPRDF) that came to power in 1991 reconfigured Ethiopia as a federal state. According to the constitution that came into effect in 1994, Ethiopia is composed of nations and nationalities that freely and voluntarily adhere to it. All member nations have the right to opt out of the federation. At present Ethiopia is made up of nine federal states and two chartered cities. A new era dawned on Ethiopia that of the federal system of governance equipped with an appropriate educational policy that became operational in 1994. The educational policy of the new government is thus the third policy in the history of the country since 1945. The major feature of the new educational policy that became operational in 1994 is the introduction of ethnic languages as mediums of education for primary education. Overnight, more than a dozen languages were deemed fit to function as mediums of instruction. A similar feature related to the language issue is the choice by the Oromo Liberation organizations of Qubé (Latin script to write the Oromo language) instead of the Ethiopic script used to write Tigrigna and Amharigna. Since 1994, Ethiopia has had no constitutionally mandated official language; Amharic and English are considered as working languages.

The landscape of Ethiopian education has since 1994 changed dramatically. Gross enrolment ratio increased from 35 per cent in 1990 to 70 per cent in 2004.[14] The Ethiopian government in general and the Ministry of Education in particular have been extremely efficient in mobilizing external funds (bilateral and multilateral) for the expansion of the education sector. Most of the expansion is financed by the growing flow of foreign aid and loans as well by a growing contribution from the communities. However, the area of education where growth has been most dramatic is the tertiary sector. Enrolment in all sectors of higher education (diploma, undergraduate and post graduate) increased from 18,000 in 1991 to 147,000 in 2003.[15] This rate of increase is indeed impressive by any count. What has even been more impressive is the growth of the private sector in the provision of higher education.

In 1996, I attempted to argue the state ought to leave the formal education sector in the urban areas to the private sector. The underlying argument was that there were enough households who would and could finance private schools for their children. It is worthwhile to note I was referring to the primary and secondary sectors. I did not imagine the private sector could be an important partner in the development of higher education. In 1996, there were very few private schools in the country and none of them were involved in higher education. By 2004, however, more than 35 000 students were following their studies at the private colleges that had mushroomed since 1997. At the end of 2004,there were more than 37 such institutions in the country.

Another aspect that augurs very well indeed is the number of female students. In the private institutions of higher learning, more than 50 per cent of the students are women whereas in the institutions run by the state and the various regions, female enrollment is far below 20 percent. This is indeed a revolution that the EPRDF government has unleashed in the country, wittingly or unwittingly.

The main impetus for the rapid expansion of the education sector (from the primary to higher education) is the belief in the role of education in the alleviation of poverty and the flow of external financial assistance. The 1994 educational policy does not draw on close links between the provision of education and the alleviation of poverty. The aims of education as specified in the policy document are indeed modern in the sense that the needs and potential of the individual student are put in the centre.[16] It appears, rather that the inspirational ideas regarding the role of education for the development of society (and hence for the reduction of poverty) came from donors. More specifically, the Poverty Reduction Strategy Policy, that the Ethiopian government was obliged to submit to the World Bank as partial condition for continued loans and aid, lay behind the policy of rapid expansion. Another document that has provided a strong framework for the logic of rapid expansion is the United Nations Millennium Development Goals where the International Community is committed to assist poor nations to provide universal primary education to their citizens and reduce by half the number of people who live below the poverty line of one dollar per day.[17].

Even though the current government has succeeded very well to mobilize external funds for development (according to some sources Ethiopia receives aid to the tune of 2 billion US Dollars per year), most of the budget for the education sector has to come from internal sources. Parents have been partners in financing the education of their children, although the burden on some households is too heavy. Furthermore, as has always been the case, the allocated budget is far too small to manage the education sector.

It is debatable whether the rise in gross enrolment that Ethiopia has experienced since 1991 is significantly different from the rate of increase of the earlier educational regimes, i.e. 1941-74 and 1975-1991. Table 1 indicates that there was a predictable and uniform rate of expansion of the primary and secondary sectors since the 1960s. The major change is to be found in the field of higher education. Since 2000 the government has diverted a considerable amount of resources from the general education budget into higher education. Higher education, the World Bank study noted, takes up 20 per cent of the educational resources and benefits only 1.7 per cent of the cohort population.[18]

Ethiopia has now a comparable number of university students as many nations in Europe about a century ago.[19]

Whereas enrolment in urban areas is nearly universal, it is only about 45 per cent among rural children. Moreover, 25 per cent of newly enrolled rural children drop out before making it to the next grade and nearly 50 per cent of them hardly stay in school for five years.[20] With the exception of Addis Ababa, completion rates are very low in the rest of the country. According to the data assembled by the World Bank, for the country as a whole, it is only about 30 percent of school age population who complete the first four years of primary education. And about 20 per cent complete 8 years of schooling.[21]

In spite of the continuous polemic, the current government has done very little to expand and consolidate primary education in the rural areas. Rural Ethiopia is still short changed. Urban children, irrespective of their economic status, have a far greater chance of completing primary education than rural children. The disparity in schooling is much wider between children in urban and rural areas than between boys and girls or even between rich and poor.[22] In other words, the urban/rural divide is far more decisive on the educational destiny of children than gender or class.

The most important contribution of the federal government of Ethiopia is that it opened up education to private providers, a move that has proved to be extremely successful. Higher Education in Ethiopia is no longer the monopoly of the state. The private sector has made its presence felt by capturing more than 25 percent of all enrolments. What is even more remarkable is more than 50 per cent of those enrolled in private institutions of higher learning are women.

In public universities, enrollment is heavily skewed in favour of male students. Although there are more women in diploma programs (up to 20 percent) their number decreases drastically in degree programs. In 2002/3, there were 1,915 students enrolled in post graduate (Master of Arts and Master of Science programs) out of whom 135 were female students. Yet, I believe that the current government, compared with its predecessors, can indeed look back with justifiable pride for creating conditions for the economically well off households to finance the education of their children.[23]

The implications of institutionalizing private education are difficult to predict but could well be very negative on the political evolution of the society. Polarization of society may be one such negative effect. However, some of the negative effects could probably be offset by a comparable investment in the public institutions of higher learning accessible to disadvantaged groups in the society. It remains to be seen how the government would manage the emerging effects of such a revolutionary decision.

Taken as a whole, however, the Ethiopian education sector is on the brink of collapse. The rapid expansion of primary education was achieved at a heavy price. According to the World Bank study conducted in 2004, the Ethiopian education sector has signs of distress. A key indicator of this distress is the deterioration of pedagogical conditions as exemplified in the pupil-section ratio and in the real spending per student.[24] In 2001/2, Ethiopia's pupil-teacher ratio of 65:1 in primary education and 52:1 in secondary education were among the highest in the world. Pupil-section sizes have also risen extremely high, averaging about 75 and 82 students per section.

An achievement study commissioned by US AID among fourth and eighth graders showed the average percentage of correct answers for all was 48 percent among fourth graders and 41 per cent among eighth graders.[25] In 2001/2 the Oromo region eight grade students who sat for the regional examination managed to get 33 percent of the questions right.[26]

There are two lessons the current government could still draw from the experiences of the earlier educational systems. The first is the tendency of the education system to produce graduates that could not be absorbed by the economy. Policy makers of the imperial regime were indeed aware of this problem and tried to deal with it. The educational praxis of the socialist regime continued to pour out secondary graduates into an essentially stagnant economy. Most of the secondary graduates continued to be unemployed and we do not know the extent to which this collective mass of educated but unemployed and unemployable youth might have undermined the legitimacy of the socialist regime to rule.[27] Its appears the socialist regime tried to limit the damage by a firm commitment of providing employment to all those who managed to get a diploma or a degree from the institutions of higher learning.

The second lesson the federal regime could really consider is the relevance of English as a medium of instruction. The regionalization of education and the wide spread use of regional languages for primary education could have diverted the attention of the government at least during the first few years of its coming to power from appreciating the problems associated with the use of English. More than ten years later, the federal government either refuses to review earlier experience, or is completely unaware of the negative impact of the use of English as a medium of instruction.

The Curse of English as a Medium of Instruction

The fact that the use of English as a medium of instruction from grade 7 upwards was a problem both for students and teachers was noticed as early as 1983. The federal state did very little to confront the decline of the quality of education, mainly arising from the lack of proficiency of English among Ethiopian teachers. Anecdotal accounts tell about the arrogance of government officials treating quality as an elitist issue. The government told its critics wide and loud that it is busy expanding primary education with the implication that quantity would soon take care of issues/aspects of quality.

The pressure on the government to deal with the issue of quality of education in general and the quality of English as medium of instruction came not only from people outside the state such as parents, academicians, journalists, but more so from the teachers as well as the regional education bureaus. For instance, since 2003, the regional states of Oromo and Tigrai use only Afan-Oromo and Tigrigna respectively as mediums of instruction in grades 7 and 8. Textbooks for junior secondary schools (grades 7 and 8) are still written in English but they are taught in the regional languages. The reasons appear to be clear and simple. The teachers working in these regions lack proficiency to teach in English. Both teachers and students found themselves in a classical vicious circle. The students can not follow their studies in English because their knowledgeof it is poor and the teachers can not help their students since they themselves are not proficient in the language.

The nature of the decline of quality of education that prevails at secondary schools deals mainly with the capacity of students to follow their lessons in English. The education policy of 1994 and the subsequent growth of the use of vernaculars for instruction further weakened the position and status of English among teachers and students. Officially English is the medium of instruction from grade 7 on. But in reality, in many parts of the country, subject are taught in the vernacular both in grades 7 and 8.

In the study I wrote in 1990, I expressed my surprise as to why the Ethiopian governments did not make use of the country's rich tradition in literacy and develop the Amharic language to be used in secondary education.[28] The position of English as a medium of instruction was further affected by the modest expansion of the secondary school sector. In a period of ten years the number of secondary school students increased from ca. 450,000 to 620,000. The impact of such expansion was that few teachers teaching at the Secondary Schools are qualified to teach in English.

Fully cognizant of this precarious situation, the government resolved to introduce televised teaching as a solution. Hence, since the beginning of October 2004, Ethiopian secondary school students follow their lessons via satellite dish. The Programme commonly known as education by plasma is beamed from South Africa. The 491 secondary schools in the country are equipped with satellite dishes. Television (plasma) screens are installed in each and every class. The following subjects are taught by plasma: Chemistry, Physics, Mathematics, English, Biology, and Civics. The teachers were no longer required to lecture or even explain in English. Although it is too early to assess the impact of plasma education the evidence that can be gleaned from teachers and students are sufficient enough to hazard some remarks:

- The lectures though based on the Ethiopian curriculum are read too fast so students have no chance of listening and keeping notes at the same time.
- A lecture is beamed only once and is not repeated or repeatable. Students who miss a lecture due to illness or some other causes have no way of listening to the lecture.
- The lectures in biology and chemistry are so poorly organized that they do not exploit the virtual reality potential of the medium.
- Most of the lectures (with some exceptions) are read by people who are not themselves subject teachers.
- Plasma education is highly dependent on uninterrupted flow of electric power. Power cuts throughout the country are common so entire lectures are lost for ever. Power supply, quite precarious in semi-rural Ethiopia, is not entirely reliable even Addis Ababa, the capital of the African Union.[29] Student and teachers guides are available in CD ROMS. Student guides contain the entire lecture with all the questions and assignments. In addition to the lectures, teachers' guides contain answers as well. But printing and distributing student guides would involve the installation of thousands of copiers and the supply of millions of Xerox paper. Neither funds to buy paper and machinery nor the technology to run and repair the latter are available at the schools.
- Secondary school students have great difficulties to read, write and above all to listen to spoken English. There are no studies showing the level of proficiency of English among secondary school students. However, the sample survey I undertook indicates strongly that the proficiency is extremely low.
- A typical plasma education teaching room contains about 90 students (for grades 9 and 10) with very little ventilation. Teachers describe the teaching and learning environment especially for students who attend afternoon shift as quite discouraging.
- Student dissatisfaction appears to gain momentum day by day as many students find it more and more difficult to follow their studies. It is most

likely that this dissatisfaction could be translated to widespread acts of sabotage as a way of getting back the teacher.

- According to several teachers I spoke to, they express the opinion that it would have been better if plasma had not been introduced.
- Experience with plasma education would undoubtedly grow but it would be highly unlikely that such experience would be positive.
- The problem with English as a medium of instruction is even more complex. English is not only a language but it is a value system. Attending all classes in English is tantamount to the whole sale adaptation of the culture that the English language represents at the price of one's native language and the values such language contains. Moreover, the replacement of the teacher by a televised lecture is taking place in a context where the role of the teacher is being continuously eroded. Ethiopian teachers are told via regular seminars and the media that they have to implement the new pedagogy the prime features of which are: student cantered learning; self-contained classes during the first four years of primary schooling; and automatic promotion during the first four years of primary education. In fairness, secondary schools students are also told they have to do two thirds of the learning themselves and could only expect the rest from their teachers.[30] I do not see how English as a medium of instruction can be firmly established (with or without plasma) so long that the great majority of the Ethiopian people are so poor that annual per capita consumption of paper is not more than a couple of hundred grams. Even those who are well off do not have access to the language in such a way that it would enable them to make good use of it. The only exceptions are of course, those handful students who attend British and American schools in Addis Ababa.

Replacing English by Amharic and Afan-Oromo as Mediums of Instruction

Whereas the Ethiopian educational landscape bears no resemblance to what it was in the late 1950s, the poverty landscape is all too recognizable. There are certainly several reasons why countries like Ethiopia appear to develop backwards. However, one thing is certain. The role of education in the alleviation of poverty has not been significant at all. And part of the reason, as I argued in part two above, is that Ethiopian education has been based on false premises. The table on enrollment demonstrates the dramatic changes of the landscape of Ethiopian education during the last fifty years. The poverty landscape has changed for the worse during the last half century. Although, the statistical material for impact assessment is not as reliable as school enrolment, there is a wide consensus that poverty has not only persisted but continued to grow. Ethiopia is poorer now than it was fifty years ago. Ethiopia of today has an income of about 100 USD per head which is much lower than that of forty years ago. But the population has more than doubled during these years. Most of the studies on the state of poverty in Africa state in general terms that the majority of Africans are worse now than what they were on the eve of independence.[31]

Table1. Enrolment

Academic year	Primary (grades 1-8)	Secondary (grades 9-12)	Higher (post-secondary
1956/7	135,467	4,845	466
1974/5	1,042,900	81,000	6,474 (1973/4)
1990/91	3,926,700	454,000	18,000
2002/03	8,743,265	627,000	147,954

Sources: UNESCO, 1961; World Bank, 2004; Negash, 1990, McNab, Teshome Wagaw, 1990:167;

Enrolment in Public and Private Colleges and universities, 2002/03

Public institutions	90,687 male students	21,685 female students
Private institutions	20,828 male students	14,574 female students
Total	111,685 male students	36,269 female students

Source: Ministry of Education: Education Statistics Annual Abstract, for 2002/03.

A consensus appears to be emerging on the failure of the education system either in the reduction of poverty or in the country's enhanced capacity for survival. The few Diaspora philosophers who analyzed Ethiopia's enigmatic modernization appear to be merciless in their judgments. This section is greatly inspired by the philosophical enquires on tradition and modernity that are still being carried out by two Diaspora philosophers, Messay Kebede and Maimire Mennesemay. Here at the outset, I wish to bring to the attention of the reader on the considerable differences between the premises of both philosophers and my own. Whereas both philosophers call for a complete overhaul of the political and ideological premises of Ethiopian society,[32] I take my cue from the incisive remark of Karl Marx who said that man makes his own destiny but not the way he likes. Any substantial thinking on Ethiopian education has to take into account as its point of departure the current state of education. There ought not to be a question of systemic overhaul but rather a consistent and long term reform of the education system.

As Maimire puts it:

> It is precisely in regards to the capacity to enable the student to absorb Ethiopia's culture and to be absorbed into it that modern education has failed. It has deprived students of the opportunity to make the crucial transformation from the unhistorical consciousness of youth to the historical consciousness of adults who understand the man-made nature of their circumstances and recognize themselves as collective agents capable of changing these circumstances within the historical possibilities they share with their compatriots. Unlike modern Ethiopian education, that seems intent on cultivating a historical-cultural amnesia, traditional education accomplishes the task of enabling the student to absorb Ethiopian culture and to be absorbed into it. It is precisely when

this civilizing process broke down that Ethiopia became a prey to "educated" leaders for whom the life an Ethiopian has little value. The important challenge for modern education is then to awaken the civilizing process that church, mosque, Gada and other traditional education systems have already developed but that we have squandered in our blind compulsion to treat ourselves as raw material that Western Education transforms into a finished product. However to awaken this humanizing and civilizing process of traditional education means also to inquire into the reasons that prevented traditional education from bringing about productive social transformations in Ethiopia.[33]

The consequences of an education system based on imported Western educational practices have been catastrophic. "A century of thoughtless embrace of Western Education has left Ethiopia with more poverty, corruption, and tyranny than she has ever known before the encounter with this imported education.[34]

One can certainly argue it is only through and by language that collective life and the world could be interpreted in an integrative manner. So I believe the eventual replacement of English by Ethiopian languages is one of the factors that could strengthen the survival potential of the Ethiopian political community. An astute reader may ask: survival for what and what kind of survival? I understand survival as a term that encompasses well-being of the great majority of the citizens of a given community, as well as the capacity of a community to cope with internal and external challenges.

In the 1970s, the crucial role of culture and hence language for overcoming underdevelopment was put forward by leftist scholars who did not adhere to the main schools of Marxist political economy of development.[35] More recently, a powerful case has been put forward by Alamin Mazrui who associates the use of African languages with intellectual self determination. Alamin Mazrui is of the opinion that the wider use of African languages could be the basis for an intellectual revolution.[36] Such a revolution, I am tempted to add, if and when it happens, would have the goal of enhancing the survival of Ethiopian society and consequently several of its values.

With due respect to Amharic (as the undeclared official language) there are other languages as well that need to be considered. The choice of language within the context of a state is always political. In Ethiopia the role of the Oromo (or the Oromo question as it is sometimes called) has been greatly debated. In *Rethinking Education (1996)*, I discussed the value of indigenous knowledge systems and their role in rural development. More than 80 per cent of the Ethiopian people are fluent in one of the two languages, namely Amharic and Afan-Oromo. As an example I took the case of Oromo and concluded the challenge facing Ethiopian education policy makers was to create conditions for the modernization of the Oromo culture without the reproduction of its negative aspects.[37] Since then, the role of the Oromo in contemporary Ethiopian history has become even more pronounced with the growing pace of federalism. It is with pleasure that I quote Messay Kebede's appraisal of the role of the Oromo in the modernization of Ethiopia:

> There is no way by which Ethiopia can change unless it shows greater openness to a revived Oromo identity, for in so doing it will simply be evolving universalistic values and methods of work. In sum, the problem of its modernization boils down to a genuine form of national integration. Only when the Oromo together with the other Ethiopian peoples knuckle down to the task of creating a new trans-ethnic, national identity, can impersonalization, so vital to modernization, take root.[38]

The language policy as it currently operates in schools does not in any way contribute to the task Messay Kebede outlined above. On the contrary, the current language policy appears to produce citizens who would find it hard to communicate with each other. The fact that Amharic is taught in non Amharic areas only as a subject is not sufficient to make Amharic as a vehicle for a trans-ethnic media of communication. The unifying language is supposed to be English since it is the medium of instruction all over the country officially from grade 7 on. The discussion on the state of English above, has hopefully shown English would not and could not function as a unifying language in Ethiopia. Therefore, the only way that the Oromo could "knuckle down to the task of creating a trans-ethnic national identity" is when the Oromo language is widely available to non-Oromo citizens of the country.

The central thesis of Messay Kebede is that no country has modernized its culture and society by whole sale importation of Westernization. It also argues that the only way out for countries like Ethiopia is to anchor modernization on the traditional values and beliefs of the Ethiopian people. The survival of Ethiopia as a political and cultural unit over a very long period of time was due to values and virtues of the traditional system of governance. And yet Ethiopia failed whereas countries that had comparable political systems such as Japan succeeded in modernizing. The comparison with Japan, as the outstanding study of Bahru Zewde illustrated, was, an issue picked up by Ethiopian intellectuals from the 1890s until the 1930s, that Japan and Ethiopia were faced with the threat of colonialism.[39] However, whereas Japan, greatly due to its geography, had to reorganize its human and material resources with the expressed intention of protecting itself from colonial intrusions, Ethiopia used the option of territorial expansion. The territorial expansion to the south of the country (where Ethiopia became three times as big as it was in the 1860s) provided the Ethiopian state the resources it needed to purchase arms. Moreover, the victory of Adwa against the Italians in 1896 validated the option.[40]

"Thirty years after the downfall of the imperial system and what followed later," writes Messay Kebede, "the country has gone on to the bitter end of depersonalization and subsequent failings by adopting a radical socialism." Ethiopia mistook modernization for Westernization, that is, a process whereby the borrowing of Western technology and rationality meant the progressive dissolution of Ethiopian mentality.[41] Modernization was conceptualized in terms of conflict between tradition and modernity, not in terms of modernity going in for the revival and enhancement of tradition.[42]

Survival and Modernization is a huge book that deserves more commentary than what is appropriate in this essay. Here below I shall highlight some of the salient points. A theory of modernization of Ethiopia, argues Messay Kebede;

> must also detect which aspects of the traditional set up that favour or obstruct the process of modernization, with the view of strengthening the positive elements while suppressing - more precisely, sublimating – the negative ones. The force and validity of this theory stem from its promise of an inner, self-induced process of change, unlike acculturation or Westernization, whose failure originates with the imposition of an exogenous and inharmonious type of change.[43]

Although the present as I understand it is the most difficult moment to grasp, Messay Kebede defines the current situation in Ethiopia in quite bleak terms. He writes that socialism and its colossal failures have inflicted serious wounds on the Ethiopian personality robbing her of pride; moreover, the mess that socialism left behind appears to increase the dangers of an irreversible marginalization and perhaps of disintegration.[44]

Messay Kebede did not devote sufficient thinking on the crucial linkages between education and modernization. However, his thinking can certainly be interpreted to favour the widespread use of Ethiopian languages. If education is to prove relevant for the modernization of Ethiopian society, it has to be based on the positive elements of Ethiopian cultures. It is only when education is framed, planned and implemented in such a manner that it can contribute to a self-induced process of change. Such self-knowledge of ones cultural resources can only be reached when the discourse on education is conducted in Ethiopian languages.

Theoretically, of course, an extensive access to English as a medium of instruction and by implication as a medium of communication among the ruling elite, could lead to the modernization of a society in terms of the building of economic and social infrastructure in countries like Ethiopia. But such extensive access of English language requires a resource base in the form of huge abundance of highly coveted materials such as cobalt, uranium and oil. In so far as current appraisals are concerned, Ethiopia lacks the above resources and what it has in the form of thermal energy, important though for the country, is not an item for immediate export.

Education is only one of the variables needed in order to consolidate the development of any society. In most countries, the educational system is organically linked to the economy and society concerned. The educational content changes in tandem with the changes taking place at the level of economy and society. It is in developing countries where education and society appear not to meet. This I contend is due to the use of foreign language as media of instruction. The use of foreign language implies the absorption of values of the language in question. There is nothing wrong in encouraging as many Ethiopians as possible to study English as a means of connecting to the outside world. However, it is altogether a different matter to use English as a media of instruction for all subjects from grade 7 upwards.

At this stage of the overview, it is relevant to raise the question as to the feasibility and viability of Amharic and Afan-Oromo as mediums of instruction throughout the education system. In a review of an earlier discussion paper on the subject, Shiferaw Bekele commented that the scarping of English as a medium of instruction and its replacement with Amharic and Afan-Oromo all the way to graduate studies was tantamount to a choice between the devil and the deep sea because accepting this proposal would mean even more disaster as there is practically no scientific publication in Amharic [and Afan-Oromo].[45] I have great respect for his criticism partly because I am inclined to share the same views and partly because it would be counter-productive to introduce such radical changes without adequate planning and preparation. There are far too many examples of the disastrous impacts of radical changes from recent Ethiopian history. Moreover, any attempt at system overhaul is bound to fail if it is not firmly based on consensus among the major stakeholders, namely urban (teachers, parents, products of the education system with English as medium of instruction) and the political elite.

Yet I believe it is imperative that Ethiopia makes the transition from English into Amharic and Afan-Oromo by about 2025. To some readers of this paper, twenty years may sound a very long time; but 20 to 25 years is just enough to discuss the issue of the benefits of connecting to ones world view and of initiating the process of translation and reinterpretation of school materials as well the development of both languages. According to my reading of Ethiopian politics since the 1960s, any policy on the introduction of Ethiopian languages imposed from above rather than by long planning, long drawn negotiation and consensus, is bound to fail.

It is absolutely important that educational policies are anchored very well among all stakeholders. A common error committed by developmentalist states is a tendency to know all the answers to all the questions. The Ethiopian landscape was run by that ideology during the military/socialist regime that had power between 1974 and 1991. The situation since 1991 is slightly better as the policy of federalism inevitably deals with the decentralization of power. Yet a great deal remains to be done in opening major issues such as education to wide involvement of stakeholders.

One of the most important attitudnal changes the government has to encourage is the recognition that the main function of the government is to implement policies that have been developed together with all stakeholders in an open and transparent manner. Indeed governments do initiate policies and then seek support for such policies among the electorate. But rarely do governments combine both powers. In the case of Ethiopia, the practice of developing policies on the basis of expert opinions ought to be expanded so as to include parents, students, civic organizations, and, above, all the major religious institutions.[46]

The Ethiopian society of today appears to exhibit considerable internal strength as well as strong divisive features. Freedom of the press appears to be in the process of leading to a strong civil society; while the politicization of ethnicity bears with it a serious danger of political fragmentation that could lead to a debilitating civil war.

Ethiopia is once again at crossroads. In so far as modernization is closely linked to the capacity of a political entity for survival, the foundation for such capacity could very well be the values that encourage and privilege self-confidence. In this context, the education sector is crucial.

The realization that the Ethiopian state and society have to rely on themselves to find their place in this globalized world ought to create a series of conditions for taking a hard look on how to restructure the education sector. The decision to abandon English as a medium of instruction could undoubtedly lead to a cultural revival which in turn is a precondition for the modernization of Ethiopian society.

The obstacles to learning created by English as a medium of instruction have been recognized since the early 1980s. However, the issue has neither been studied systematically nor fully debated. This brief chapter would have amply fulfilled its objective if it contributes to a process of public debate and sustained research on the role of Amharic and Afan-Oromo in the revitalization of the Ethiopian education sector. And on a personal note, I find it most encouraging to observe that philosophers are giving considerable attention to the crucial role of an education system in harmony with its cultural and historical values for dynamic survival and development of a community.

2

Comparing Traditional and Modern Education: the Decentering of Ethiopia

MESSAY KEBEDE

Given that it is not possible to understand Ethiopia's continuous political crises and economic stagnation since the Revolution of 1974 without bringing into play the decisive role of its Western educated elite, the paper wonders whether the nature of the Ethiopian system of education was not an accessory to the gestation of these lingering tribulations. In particular, it inquires whether the infatuation of Ethiopian students and intellectuals with Marxism-Leninism and their propensity to opt for polarizing and confrontational methods of political competition are not the result of a decentering educational system that caused cultural cracks into which radical ideas, which were then in vogue, were injected. The paper attempts to validate the idea by showing how the introduction of Western education removed all the cultural hooks by which the traditional system of education had created a national clerical intelligentsia (Dabtara). It is not possible to understand Ethiopia's continuous political crises and economic stagnation since the Revolution of 1974 without bringing into play the decisive role of its Western educated elite.

Admittedly, students and intellectuals have spearheaded the uprising against the imperial regime; they have also been instrumental in the radicalization of the military junta, known as the Derg, which seized power and ruled the country for 17 years. The ethnic movements that brought down the Derg were also launched by intellectuals. The present rulers of Ethiopia are remnants of the Ethiopian student movement of the 60s and early 70s. In short, what happened in Ethiopia since the early 70s is largely the handiwork of Ethiopians educated in modern schools.

25

Seeing the incessant political instability and persistent economic inertia of the country, one cannot help but wonder whether the nature of the Ethiopian system of education was not an accessory to the gestation of these lingering tribulations. What else could explain the failure to stabilize and put the country to work but the emergence of an educated elite too prone to radical and oppositional views? True, the reluctance of the imperial regime to make the necessary reforms had polarized the country and created the conditions of class and ethnic confrontations. No scholar can seriously underestimate the impact of repression and lack of reforms on the radicalization of students. As Bahru Zewde puts it, radicalization reflected "the growing impatience with a regime which was not prepared to reform itself. As the century wore on, the medicine prescribed also grew in virulence."[47]

But the evil legacies of Haile Selassie's long reign do not fully explain the drift of the county into the path of radicalization and confrontation, given that reformist and less oppositional solutions were available. The venture into a revolutionary path is the direct product of the infatuation of Ethiopian students and intellectuals with Marxism-Leninism. Hence the assumption that the educational system may have caused cultural cracks into which radical ideas, which were then in vogue, were injected. The best way to validate the assumption is to assess the impact of modern education on the cultural setup of Ethiopian students by laying out the kind of thoughts it encourages. To weigh the cultural metamorphoses caused by modern education, a brief review of the traditional, pre-modern system of education is necessary.

The Traditional Ethiopian System of Education

Scholars who have reflected on the traditional system of education agree on its Ethiocentric orientation and contents. The Ethiopian Orthodox Church assumed the exclusive task of designing and propagating an educational system whose central subjects were the religious beliefs, values, and practices of the Ethiopian Church. In addition to religious instruction, the teaching had a secular component that dealt with Ethiopia's history and socio-political organization. Teaching was so tied up with the Church that scholars speak of "Church schools which bore the main burden of education for sixteen centuries," that is, until they were progressively supplanted by modern schools.[48]

A brief review of the curriculum is enough to show the Ethiocentric orientation of the traditional education. The system had three distinct and successive stages, which can be said to correspond to elementary, secondary, and higher levels. The first level "taught reading and writing in Ge'ez, and Amharic... and simple arithmetic. The emphasis was upon reading the Scriptures in Ge'ez, the original language of the Church ritual."[49] This elementary education was dispensed to students who became ordinary priests and deacons. Students who wanted to pursue higher levels of study had to go to the great churches and monasteries. Higher studies begin with the "*Zema Bet*" ("School of Music") in which students study the musical composition and the liturgy of the Ethiopian Church.[50] The next stage was called "*Kiné Bet*," which means "School of Poetry."[51] It focused on "church music, the composition of poetry... theology and history, painting... manuscript writing."[52] The *Kiné* level also added the teaching of philosophy whose "main text was *Metsahafe-Falasfa Tabiban* (Book of Wise Philosophers), with passages from Plato, Aristotle, Diogenes, Cicero, etc."[53] The third level, called "*Metsahaf Bet* (Schools of texts, or books)," provided an in-depth study of the sacred books of the Old and New Testaments as well as of books related to monastic life.[54] It also included the study of three major books of Ethiopian history and code of laws, namely, "*Tarike-*

Nagast (monarchic history), *Kebra-Nagast* (Glory of the Kings), *Fiteha-Nagast* (laws of the Kings)."[55] World history was taught at the third level: the ancient world and the histories of the Jews and the Arabs made up the substance of the teaching. The student who successfully went through the three stages earned the title of *"Liq"* or *"Dabtara."*

The focus on the Christian doctrine and values, the use of indigenous languages, and the extensive reading of books and textbooks all impregnated with native contents bear witness to the fact that the subject of study was Ethiopia, its legacies, characteristics, and history. Not only did the materials deal with Ethiopian history, customs, languages, and values, but the spirit of the education was also to produce scholars able to serve the Church and, by extension, the country with a sense of dedication to its characteristics and sense of mission. Describing the requirement of the school of poetry, Sylvia Pankhrust says: the teaching "must be rich in content, revealing a deep knowledge of the Bible, of Ethiopian history, and of the stories and legends which have gathered during the centuries around the great personalities and events of religious and national tradition."[56]

Take the Ethiopic text known as the *Kebra Nagast*: it establishes kinship between the rulers of Ethiopia and King Solomon of Israel, the favourite nation of God. The epic narrates the visit of an Ethiopian queen, Sheba or Makeda, to King Solomon and the subsequent birth of a son who became the king of Ethiopia under the name of Menelik I. Besides stating the blood ties of Ethiopian rulers with the Solomonian dynasty, the epic relates the transfer of God's favour from Israel to Ethiopia. Unlike the Jewish people, acceptance of Christianity promoted Ethiopians to the rank of God's chosen people. The bonus for being a country favoured by God is, of course, the assurance of the survival of Christian Ethiopia in a hostile environment dominated by heathens and powerful Muslim countries. The following passage taken from the book that glorifies the victories of King Amda Tsiyon gives a good idea of the deep and stubborn belief that allowed Ethiopia to resist for centuries against its non-Christian neighbours:

> As for us, we have heard and we know from the Holy Scripture that the kingdom of the Moslems, established for but seven hundred years, shall cease to be at the proper time. But the kingdom of the Christians shall continue till the second coming of the Son of God, according to the words of the Holy Scripture, and above all (we know) that the kingdom of Ethiopia shall endure till the coming of Christ, of which David prophesized saying 'Ethiopia shall stretch her hand unto God.'[57]

Clearly, the *Kebra Nagast* is a national epic: it lays the foundation for the merger of church and state as the best guarantee for Ethiopia's survival, and so "defines the secular and religious foundation of Ethiopian nationhood."[58] It also imparts a direction to history such that Ethiopia is where the sun rises and sets. The pervasion of students with the spirit of *Kebra Nagast* enabled them to see the world from the viewpoint of Ethiopia. In a word, the discourse cantered Ethiopia by endowing it with a specific mission, which became the repository of its national identity.[59]

The emphasis on serving the Church did not entail the exclusive confinement of the traditional system to the formation of priests, deacons, and church teachers. As stated earlier, the religious education extended to the secular realm, since "church education also produced civil servants... such as judges, governors, scribes, treasurers, and general administrators."[60] This extension to the secular society was a natural consequence of the basic and all-embracing cultural function of religion in Ethiopia. The religious instruction conveyed the norms of social behaviour, the meaning of the social hierarchy, and the rights and duties attached to the social status of individuals. The education was thus both mundane and spiritual: it taught a religious belief inextricably intertwined with a definite social system and a mode of life. According to the renowned Ethiopian novelist and essayist, Addis Alemayehu, the traditional education had served as "a powerful means to unite the spiritual existence with the secular mode of life."[61]

In addition to its highly integrative and nationalistic function, the other virtue of the traditional system was its freedom from political influence and vicissitudes. This freedom emanated from the complete autonomy of the Church from the state in terms of education. Because traditional schools were "run by the church without the intervention of the state," education was not politicized.[62] On the contrary, church education transcended political rivalries to concentrate on what was permanently Ethiopian, and so was an agent of unity and national cohesion. As one author writes: "acting as the sole repository of Christian culture and identity, an educated elite of priests and *Dabtaras* preserved a heritage which for fifteen centuries united the Christian community against surrounding alien cultural influences."[63]

Modern critics of the traditional system have, of course, no trouble exposing its severe shortcomings. Thus, Mulugeta Wodajo points out how the techniques and the contents of the education were not particularly apt to develop understanding; nor were they liable to cultivate the intellectual faculties of creativity, criticism, and imagination. These deficiencies sprang from the emphasis on "the role of rote memory" in the traditional educational system.[64] Worse yet, the teaching used a language that was not current and familiar to students, as "all the texts are in Ge'ez and hence are meaningless for the child."[65] However, Mulugeta tempers this negative evaluation by the recognition that the high level of poetry made "great use of the imagination and creative mind of the pupil" and that "it is a source of sorrow to see the decline of the *'Zema Bet'* without any worthwhile substitute in the Government schools."[66] Some critics have underlined the discriminatory nature of the church education, since only parents who were Orthodox Christian could send their children to the traditional schools. "Church schools did not serve the whole nation, therefore, and so cannot be considered impartial or democratic," says one critic.[67]

Where critics are unanimous and most vociferous is in their denunciation of the total expulsion of scientific courses from the traditional system of education. Being basically religious, the teaching had little inclination to include scientific and technological components. Reluctance changed into outright rejection as the religious doctrine progressively turned into a rigid dogma. The dismissal of whatever was not in line with transmitted beliefs was so endemic that Teshome Wagaw speaks of an approach to education that "became increasingly rigid, to the point of ossification."[68] The educational system simply stuck to the old belief according to which "as the heavens and the earth are ruled by God all enquiries into the working of the heavenly bodies and the laws of nature were and are regarded as sinful."[69]

As so rigid a system was particularly unfit for modernization, Ethiopia, like all third world countries, reached the conclusion that the best way to get out of the disabilities of the traditional system and catch up with the economic and social advances of western countries was through the resolute sidelining of traditional schools and the rapid spread of modern education. The latter is a shortcut to development: what Europe has achieved through a long and gradual process of evolution can be captured and rapidly disseminated by an appropriate system of education. And as science, technology, and enlightened beliefs and values are the distinctive features of modernity, no better means exist to effect a rapid modernization than through the adoption of the Western system of education.

For Ethiopia, the adoption of the Western system meant an abrupt shift from the religious content of the traditional system to a secular teaching, just as it implied the dissolution of the traditional conservatism by the inculcation of the innovative spirit characteristic of modernity. Accordingly, the formation of an educated elite entirely opposed to the characteristics of the traditional elite became the major goal of the new system. The task was particularly difficult: the traditional system directly counteracted the effort of modernization by its very purpose of producing a mind that repudiates whatever is not sanctioned by tradition. To show the extent to which the traditional system was diametrically opposed to the spirit of modernity, Wagaw writes:

> The purpose of church education is not to extend man's understanding of the world, but rather to lead men to accepting the existing order of things as it is, to preserve whatever has been handed down through the years, and in turn to pass it on unchanged to the next generation.[70]

Given its complete irrelevance and opposition to the modern world, the traditional system of education was beyond salvation. It had to be entirely rejected and replaced by modern schools. Before making a judgment on the wisdom of the decision to virtually eliminate church schools, we must reflect on the characteristics of the system that replaced the traditional education. Let there be no misunderstanding: my assessment of modern education in Ethiopia is not inspired by the argument that church schools should have been preserved. As Addis noted, given the realities of the modern world and the new challenges it poses, "it is very difficult to say that an education restricted to the teaching of religion and mode of life can fulfill the needs of the society."[71]

But it is one thing to say the system had to be changed, quite another to entirely throw away the old in favour of an alien system. The path taken by Ethiopia was not to update and modernize the traditional system; it was to erase past practices so as to implement a new system. The decision to leave out the legacy emanated, moreover, from an unfair criticism of the traditional system. Granted the traditional education had been quite reluctant to include scientific studies, the truth remains the indiscriminately negative evaluation of tradition by norms borrowed from another culture is a one-sided approach. Not only is such a criticism alien to the very notion of human pluralism, but it also promotes Western culture to the rank of universal culture. Such a Eurocentric stand naturally fails to appreciate the positive aspects of the traditional culture, just as it becomes headless of the accomplishments it achieved in accordance with its own norms and goals.

The question whether a tabula rasa policy was wise is all the more legitimate the more the expected benefits of the new system proved evasive. Indeed, so radical and rapid a shift was bound to encounter great difficulties. Even those who are very harsh about the traditional education admit that Ethiopia's modern education has lamentably failed. The causes of the failure are no doubt multiple. Some of them spring from a rapid change that failed to provide the appropriate material and human conditions. Others are products of misconceptions and policy impediments. We will examine these causes with some detail with the view of understanding how the deficiencies of the educational system have a hand in the radicalization of the intelligentsia.

The Drawbacks of Ethiopia's Modern Education

The late Emperor Haile Selassie is universally recognized as being the pioneer as well as the active and dedicated promoter of modern education in Ethiopia. With few supporters, he stood up to the stubborn opposition of the powerful Ethiopian Church and most members of the nobility. This is to say the inauguration of modern education in Ethiopia did not occur under favourable conditions. It had to be instituted against powerful conservative forces in a socio-cultural condition that completely lacked the necessary material and human requisites.

Sure enough, thanks to the effort of the previous emperor, Menelik II, some rudiments of modern education existed. Menelik had created one modern school in 1908, and some Ethiopians had become exposed to modern education. Unfortunately, most of these Ethiopians, who could have provided the necessary transitional administrative and teaching staff, were exterminated during the Italian occupation of 1935-41. According to the estimate of one author, "about 75 percent of those who had some modern education were wiped out during the years of occupation."[72] All the efforts of Menelik and Haile Selassie himself, first as regent and since 1930 as emperor, to provide a transitional staff were thus annihilated. As most of the pre-war educated Ethiopians combined traditional training with modern education, they could have secured a smooth transition. Because of their extermination, the post-war effort to establish and spread modern education had to rely exclusively on expatriate advisers, administrators, and teachers.

Before analyzing the downsides of the complete reliance on expatriate staff, we should note how the country's economic backwardness had severely hampered the spread of modern education and affected the quality of the teaching. One consequence of the scarcity of human and material resources was that "educational opportunity was not equitably distributed among the regions of the country, favouring instead only a few provinces and urban centres, and administration was therefore highly centralized."[73] Addis Ababa, Eritrea, Showa, and the most important urban areas took most of the students. This unequal distribution resulted in a very low level of enrolment in modern schools. Statistical data show clearly the extent to which imperial Ethiopia was behind most African countries:

> In 1961, when the average enrolment in primary schools on the African continent was estimated at over 40 per cent, the estimated primary school enrolment in Ethiopia was 3.8 per cent. On the secondary level, estimated average enrolment for the appropriate age group on the continent and in Ethiopia was 3.5 and 0.5 per cent, respectively.[74]

Equally low was the budget allotted to education by the imperial government. Thus, "in a comparison of 17 African countries' expenditure on education over a period of years in the 1960s, Ethiopia ranks lowest with 11.4 per cent of the national budget."[75] Some such low level of expenditure negatively affected the quality of the teaching. Even in the urban centres, such as Addis Ababa and Asmara, the paucity of teachers and teaching facilities was such that "extreme overcrowding in the class room" was the rule.[76] To these overcrowded class rooms were added the impediments caused by a lack of qualified teachers and the paucity of textbooks, which "severely lowered the standard of teaching in the schools and encouraged extensive copying and memorization as methods of learning."[77]

The sluggish economic progress of the country under Haile Selassie's rule and the restricted expansion of modern education contributed to the spread of social discontent. As the system was not expanding fast enough, especially to the rural areas, the opportunity for education took the form of a privilege with "the inevitable effects of accentuating class divisions and perpetuating the 'ruling class' idea."[78] In other words, the limitation became a source of grudge for young Ethiopians who could not continue beyond elementary education. What is more, unemployment became a primary concern for those who did enroll and reach high schools and even university level. The alarming number of graduates who could not find jobs in the cities was a clear indication that the educational system was producing more people than the economy could absorb. The promise of a better life, which was one of the arguments the imperial regime used to make modern education attractive, was thus flatly contradicted. Instead, schools and colleges produced disillusioned students who fell prey to false ideological notions.

On the severe material and human shortcomings was grafted an educational policy that lacked direction and national objectives. According to many scholars, the main reason for the lack of a national direction is to be found in the decisive role that foreign advisers, administrators, and teachers played in the establishment and expansion of Ethiopia's educational system. That the curriculum tended to reflect at all levels courses offered in Western countries was glaring proof of their harmful influence. As one author put it, "appointed foreign advisers tended to think that what had proved successful in their countries would also benefit Ethiopian development."[79] Moreover, the external teachers were neither fully qualified nor appropriately trained. They mostly came from India and the Peace Corps program, and as such "were not trained to meet with the specific needs and problems of the Ethiopian society."[80] Besides financial, infrastructural, and technical problems, the introduction and development of modern education thus faced the paramount issue of Ethiopianization. To quote one author:

> The most important characteristic of the entire set-up of modern education in Ethiopia was that it was imposed from Britain, the USA, and influenced by various other European countries and thus essentially constructed to serve a different society than the Ethiopian..... Curricula as well as textbooks came from abroad. There was little in the curricula related to basic and immediate needs of the Ethiopian society. To the average child the school was essentially an alien institution of which his own parents were entirely ignorant.[81]

Strange as it may seem, though Haile Selassie consistently presented himself as the active promoter and patron of modern education and supported this role by regularly visiting schools, handing certificates and prizes, sending students abroad, and stressing the importance of education to development in many of his speeches, he has never clearly fastened his educational policy to the goal of national development. This lack of articulation has been pointed out by an in-depth study of the entire educational system known as "the sector review" of 1971. In light of the increasing number of dropouts and unemployed and the glaring inadequacy of the educational system to the needs of the country, the Ministry of Education decided to undertake a review of the entire educational system. The project involved Ethiopian scholars and experts from Haile Selassie I University, Ministries of Education, Agriculture, Community Development, and the Planning Commission. It also included foreign members from UNESCO, the International Labour Organization, the Ford Foundation, and Harvard University Development Advisory Service. The final report of this serious and extensive assessment deplored "the lack of a clear statement of national ideology."[82]

Nothing could better illustrate the non-national orientation of the educational system than the manner Haile Selassie I University was founded and organized. The responsibility of supplying the necessary administrative and teaching staff to what was at first only a college went to American Jesuits. The Mormons replaced the Jesuits when "in 1961 a University of Utah survey team organized the graduation of the college into Haile Selassie I University."[83] The fact that the administrative and academic staff was predominantly American inevitably entailed the modelling of the University on American universities: teachings as well as organizational structures reproduced the American model, which also provided the textbooks.

Though the traditional and official religion of Ethiopia was Orthodox Christianity, it was not given a place at the University and Ethiopian students were placed under the influence of Catholic and Protestant academic staff. The dominance of expatriate staff with alien religious affiliations indicated from the beginning that the University had forsaken the goal of defending and promoting the national culture, which was interwoven with the religious legacy. Herein lies the main difference with the traditional education which, as we saw, was prompted by the goal of protecting and disseminating the national culture. Doubtless, Haile Selassie opted for a religious staff because he could rely on their political conservatism. Under their leadership, the University would not become a playground for radicalism. But this prudent policy backfired: the apolitical attitude of the staff drove students to read underground books and pamphlets. Because they were not offered a liberal alternative, neither could they develop a culture of openness, debate, and moderation. Not only did the University fail to defend students' traditional identity, but it also exposed them to the influence of underground radicals by not championing a culture of political debate and openness.

Let us ponder the Ethiopian paradox. The issue of endowing modern education with a national content and direction is a problem Ethiopia shares with other African countries. All studies in Africa deplore the irrelevance and alienating effects of the educational system. The appropriate solution, the studies suggest, is the Africanization of the system. According to Ali Mazrui, "first, the staff should be Africanized and secondly, the curriculum should be Africanized."[84] Only thus can the educational system become relevant and national. Whereas most African countries can impute the lack of national direction to colonization and its aftermaths, Ethiopia offers the unique case of failing to inaugurate and develop a national system of education while not being hampered by colonial rule. Beyond missing the opportunity of harnessing education to a national policy of development, the Ethiopian system took a turn that was even less protective of the national identity than the system prevailing in the colonized African countries.

Consider the study of history. Given the exceptional status of Ethiopia as an African country that remained independent as a result of pushing back colonial forces and the great pride the victory inspires to Ethiopians, one would assume an essential component of history courses at various levels would be devoted to explaining the reasons for Ethiopia's independence. Nothing of the kind happened: because history courses reproduced the scheme of Western history, there was no provision for the Ethiopian exception. Asked to give an idea of how history courses described Ethiopia, a former student said: "we were only told that she had preserved her independence."[85] And as the preservation of independence was not explained, it appeared as an aberration or an accident. This omission ceases to be surprising when one recalls that the history course for eight grade students used for many years a bulky textbook titled *"The Old World— Past and Present."* On top of designating Africa as 'The Dark Continent,' the textbook "mentions Ethiopia as Abyssinia in only one paragraph, referring to it as an 'Italian colony'."[86] Though Ethiopians are proud of their independence, much of the benefit of withstanding colonial powers was thus taken away from them by the introduction of a system of education that had a colonial character. We should speak less and less of independence and subscribe to the idea that Ethiopia, too, a colony. The introduction of Western education had accomplished what military means failed to achieve.

It must not be made to seem that Haile Selassie and officials of his regime were not aware of the serious shortcomings of the educational system. Official speeches repeatedly stressed the need to correct the system, "to Ethiopianize the entire curriculum."[87] But nothing substantial was done, true attempts were made to inject courses dealing with Ethiopian realities into the curriculum. Thus, at the university level, a noticeable place was progressively attributed to the study of Ethiopian history; courses on Ethiopian geography and law were given a much needed boost. Mention should also be made of the creation of "the Institute of Ethiopian Studies" with its museum and library in which researches and students could find appreciable documentations on Ethiopia.

Granting these efforts to Ethiopianize, the issue that needs to be discussed is whether the efforts successfully redirected the teaching. Indeed, the issue being one of ideological reorientation rather than of quantitative increase of courses devoted to Ethiopia, the proper question is "to what degree did [Ethiopianization] take place and to what extent did agreement exist as to the university's role as a force for change and development in Ethiopia?"[88] It is safe to say courses dealing with Ethiopian legacy, environment, and socioeconomic problems were simply appended to a curriculum that remained largely Eurocentric both in its inspiration and contents. Moreover, the University could hardly become an engine for change and development without a free and critical examination of Ethiopia's problems. Haile Selassie's autocratic rule did not grant such a right even to the University. This suggests the lack of national direction of the educational system may be due to the nature of the imperial regime itself.

How otherwise could one explain the apparent inconsistency of Haile Selassie's educational policy? Underlining the fundamental role of the University as guardian of Ethiopian culture, Haile Selassie said in his inaugural address:

> A fundamental objective of the University must be the safeguarding and the developing of the culture of the people which it serves. This University is a product of that culture; it is the grouping together of those capable of understanding and using the accumulated heritage of the Ethiopian people. In this University men and women will, working in association with one another, study the well-springs of our culture, trace its development, and mould its future.[89]

This major speech ascertains the connection between education and modernization: the fundamental goal of education is to modernize Ethiopia, but to modernize it in the spirit of its traditions and culture. The study of Ethiopian culture becomes essential because (1) the Ethiopian legacy is useful and galvanizing; (2) modern education is put at the service of Ethiopia only when it connects with the culture of its people. Education must serve the nation, and it can do so only by promoting its culture. Development cannot occur if the beliefs and traditions of the people are demeaned or ignored. Haile Selassie reiterates the need to base development on the legacy: "although such education may be technical," he pursues, "it must nonetheless be founded on Ethiopia's cultural heritage if it is to bear fruit and if the student is to be well adapted to his environment and the effective use of his skills facilitated."[90] One of the basic tasks of the University is, therefore, to ensure historical continuity by building bridges between the past and the new.

More yet, Haile Selassie recommends the study and development of Ethiopia's cultural heritage as the best way to fight iconoclastic ideologies. In an apparent reference to the socialist ideology, he says:

> These young people face a world beset with the most effectively organized Programme of deceptive propaganda and of thinly screened operations ever known; they deserve the best that can be taught by their parents, by religious institutions and by the university, to prepare them for a wise choice among contending ideals.[91]

The elaborate propaganda designed to mislead young and impressionable students into wrong beliefs and attitudes is effectively countered if they are taught the values they admire in other cultures are also part of their heritage. People desist from converting to alien ideologies once they are shown what they have is the best.

What is most baffling is none of these loudly proclaimed directives was applied. Though the speeches call for a syncretic approach to modernization, the real practice was to hand over Ethiopian schools and higher education to expatriate staff, thereby chasing the representatives of the traditional culture out of modern institutions. One way of achieving the proclaimed goal was to design a system of education that integrated the modern with the traditional. Scholars are unanimous: Haile Selassie never pushed for a serious effort to integrate, which alone would have provided modern education with a national orientation. "The greatest shortcoming of the educational system in Africa in general and in Ethiopia in particular is that it is poorly related to and interlinked with the traditions of education which predate the coming of the modern school," writes an acute critic of the Ethiopian system.[92] Let no one raise the objection the resistance of the Ethiopia Church made the integration impossible. The attempt to set church against modernity simply overlooks that "the Churches in Europe managed to lay down the basis for most of secular higher learning."[93] In Europe, modernity grew out of Christianity so that there was a historical continuity between the secular and the religious. Being ruled by a Christian elite, Ethiopia could have gone through the same kind of evolution.

The problem was not so much the resistance of the Church as Haile Selassie's reluctance to encourage its modernization. Rather than involving the Church in the process of modernization, he opted for a policy that blocked its modernization. The reason is clear enough: in his bid to establish autocratic rule, the aloofness of the Church from modern life was the best way to curtail its traditional authority. And indeed the appropriation of the monopoly of education by the state represented a great loss of authority to the Church. In order to curb opposition, Haile Selassie bribed the Church with land grants and other privileges, thereby transforming "her relative autonomy into dependency on the state's policies."[94] Unsuitability for modernization as much as the need to transfer the traditional authority of the Church to the autocratic state explains, therefore, the marginalization of church schools.

Alienation and Radicalism

In failing to integrate the traditional with the modern, the Ethiopian system produced students with a declining sense of national identity, nay, with a marked contempt for their own legacy. Without the involvement of the moral and cultural values and the specific features of the national heritage, the educational system cannot have a national goal. A draft paper on "educational objectives" by a task force composed of three Ethiopian experts who were involved in "the sector review" of 1971 prophetically stated: "an educational system that merely provides knowledge and skills without the essential blend of such [moral and cultural] values is in danger of producing soulless and rootless robots."[95] The Ethiopian educational system failed to accomplish the basic task of any education, namely, the transmission of the cultural legacy of the country to the next generation. Let us go further, by propagating the Eurocentric paradigm, the system was but denigrating the Ethiopian legacy. In so doing, what else could it produce but "a rootless social caste?"[96]

A comparison with Japan is most instructive. The way Japan introduced modern education is quite different from the Ethiopian experience. The difference does not lie in that Japan did not import or imported less from Western educational system. It borrowed from the West extensively, both through the use of foreign instructors and textbooks and by sending Japanese to Western countries for higher studies. As a Japanese scholar writes: "the methods of constructing a modernized curriculum were modelled after European and American schools, and necessary materials and tools for teaching were introduced from those countries."[97] The great difference, however, is that the Japanese ruling elite very soon realized the danger of alienation. Without a firm foundation in the traditional heritage, an educational system modelled on the West was nothing but uprooting. In effect, "the impact of foreign influences upon the traditional culture of Japan had resulted in a state of social disturbance and ideological confusion such as Japan had never before experienced."[98]

Unless Japanese students quickly countered the borrowed system with a commitment to their own traditions and values, modern education was going to give way to an imperceptible but forceful colonization. Hence the government decree known as "the *Kyôgaku Taishi* (Principles of Education) of 1879," which introduced the traditional Confucian philosophy and ethics into the modern educational system. The declaration emphasized the importance of "the virtues of benevolence, responsibility, loyalty and fidelity based on the precepts of [Japanese] ancestors" and added that "in the teaching of morality, the Confucian morality will be primary."[99] This interpenetration of the traditional and the modern inaugurated the appropriation of Western science and technology by a mind that remained Japanese, thereby investing modern education with a national foundation and purpose. In this way, introducing modern education amounted to the process of reforming and adapting the traditional teaching to the modern world. Unlike the path taken by Ethiopia, the Japanese understood the best way to counter the subversive influence of the West and other alien ideologies was by preventing the formation of an ideological vacuum among students. The more the educational system assumed the task of enhancing, glorifying the Japanese cultural heritage, the stronger the counter-offensive against the demeaning impact of Western education became. The display of the good things that tradition has to offer assured the success of the crusade against alienation.

The other important disparity of Japan is the use of the national language. Japanese leaders have encouraged the learning of foreign languages for the purpose of translating books and having access to Western knowledge. This strictly utilitarian function prevented foreign languages from usurping the traditional prerogatives of the national language. The preservation of the national language as a medium of instruction made modern knowledge easily accessible to a large number of people. More importantly, it provided a good basis for the defence of the culture itself by avoiding the expulsion of the native language from the realm of modern studies and researches. If "the Japanese borrowed more techniques than values from the West," unlike Africans, it is because they "undertook their modernization primarily through the Japanese language, and did not become linguistic converts to an alien idiom."[100] Though Amharic was given the status of a national language, it was used as a medium of instruction only at the elementary level. Could this limitation suggest anything other than the acceptance by the Ethiopian leaders themselves of the congenital inadequacy of the national language to express higher levels of knowledge?

The glaring inconsistency of the imperial regime was anything but innocent. Since official speeches stated the ideal formula while nothing was done to implement it, we can neither speak of mistake nor of lack of awareness. Tekeste Negash expresses the disparity between discourse and practice thus:

> The official policy during the period of Emperor Haile Selassie was that Ethiopia, as an ancient and civilized society, should opt for a carefully selected adaptation of European ideas and systems. In practice, however, the Imperial regime did very little to inculcate respect for Ethiopian traditions of social and political organization. It left the curriculum and most of the teaching in secondary schools to expatriates who quite naturally spread the gospel of modernization.[101]

Though many authors have reflected on the alienating impact of Western education, few actually link the alienation with the propensity to espouse radical ideas. In their eyes, repression and the lack of freedom are the primary causes of student radicalization in Ethiopia. Yet what else could the alienating impact of modern education induce but radicalism? What was taught was so disparaging to Ethiopian culture and history that it unleashed the desire to get rid of everything and start anew. It must be emphasized that what Westernized elite wanted was not mere change, but change that implicated a total break. The normal process of change reconciles novelty with heritage, and so achieves continuity. Different is the impact of Western education on natives; it causes "a fundamental rupture with the beliefs and outlook accepted by their family, their class, their society."[102] Because the teaching contrasts two societies one of which is taken as a norm, it does not plead for continuity with the indigenous legacy but for rupture, thereby creating a predisposition to revolutionary ideas. History is no longer the framework of continuity moving toward the future; it is how arrested societies, get towed by another history. The rise of radical intellectuals is thus part of the process of modernization of countries that are latecomers: the contrast of their society with those of the West produces a characteristic disenchantment and dissociation that set them as liquidators.

There is no denying the lack of national orientation of the educational system has greatly encouraged, not only the alienation of the educated elite from the traditional elite, but also the polarization of the educated elite itself. So uprooted an elite could hardly assume the task of unifying the country: subjected to various and contradictory external influences to the detriment of national norms, the educated elite could not produce any consensus about Ethiopia and its future direction. Unlike the traditional Dabtara who had subdued their ethnic and regional attachments to what permanently defined Ethiopia, the modern educated elite fell back on ethnic and regional ties because it had become alien to national mission. After the illusive and temporary unity provided by the adherence to Marxism-Leninism, which was itself, an expression of alienation, nothing was left but to adopt the even more divisive ideology of ethnicization.

The great tragedy of Ethiopia is, therefore, that it did not produce domestic, home-grown intellectuals, the very ones who would have conceived of modernization as an upgrading of the traditional culture. Such intellectuals could have easily grown from the traditional culture if the system of education had established some form of continuity between traditional and Western education. As we saw, the choice was to expel the traditional culture and its representatives from modern schooling so that a system of education committed to uprooting young Ethiopians prevailed in the end. Is it surprising if such intellectuals worked actively toward the dismissal of the traditional culture rather than its renewal through purification and reinterpretation? And in so doing, were they not curtailing their ability to achieve consensus, that is, to become a national intelligentsia by transcending particularism? Once national norms are put aside, the promotion of ethnicity is all that it is left. Just as the Marxist-Leninist notion of class struggle had divided the country, so too ethnicization continues the same polarizing policy.

3

THE CHALLENGE OF MODERNITY: WESTERN EDUCATION AND THE DEMISE OF FEUDALISM IN ETHIOPIA [103]

PAULOS MILKIAS

This chapter traces the Ethiopian revolution of 1974 to modern education, modern educated elites and the cultural penetration that came in its wake. The transfer of education of Ethiopian children from the church to the few western type schools became a turning point in modern Ethiopian history, for it produced a new aristocratic elite whose perception of politics was secular. Through modern education also came a very intense American cultural penetration. There was, the author argues, a seed of contradiction in the ideology introduced by the Americans and Ethiopia's feudal autocracy. The liberal education disseminated through the Ethiopian school system and the political ideals connected with it were negated by an authoritarian system and the autocratic political realities in Ethiopia. Ultimately, because of this paradox, the new breed of western educated intelligentsia, who were mostly students, kindled the embers of the revolutionary tumult and all the military had to do in 1974 was deliver a finishing stroke to Haile Selassie's feudal regime. The author suggests in the conclusion the Ethiopian intelligentsia of today imbued, as they are with modern education, will have to face the challenge of the onslaught of modernization and globalization with alacrity and prudence.

Ethiopia is a unique nation state; it is one of the oldest sovereign territories and one of the three countries with the longest uninterrupted independence in the entire planet.[104] Its continuous historical antecedents are much longer and much older than the annals of all African countries except Egypt and are indeed more ancient than those of most nations anywhere on this globe. The relationship between Western education and the Ethiopian revolution of 1974, which forms the core of this research, has to be juxtaposed against this unique historical background.

It has been generally recognized for several decades that Ethiopia's ancient polity had been straining under the load of a rigid feudal order trying to adjust itself to the modem world. But the fall of the ancient regime in 1974 and its political aftermath has been highly misunderstood in scholarly literature that has proliferated within the last few years. Too often, the entire event has been depicted as just another African military coup d' état.

Anatomy of the Ethiopian Revolution

According to most Western scholars who treated the subject, the only difference between the 1974 Ethiopian episode and other sudden illegal, often violent, taking of government power by an army was that whereas the latter are characteristically swift and dramatic, the Ethiopian coup was "creeping" led by faceless lower level military officers and N. C. O.' s. Blair Thomson is one of the authors who considers the 1974 upheaval as a coup d'état. Thomson even goes to the extent of hinting, although in a form of denial, he himself might have overthrown Haile Selassie! These kind of simplistic ideas originate from the well-known paternalistic attitude of Western scholars. It is based on the assumption that Ethiopians or any Third World people for that matter could not undertake such an important task as overthrowing a well-entrenched monarch so ingeniously (the "creeping coup" approach was a new phenomenon in political science) and thus they must have taken advice and direction from the West. However the idea of "advice and direction" is nothing but a total myth.[105]

Some have tried to show the Ethiopian revolution as part of a struggle for power by the different ethnic groups, especially the Oromos and the Tigrayans against the Amharas.[106] Others have tried to represent it as a nationalist revolution (similar to that of Algeria or Angola) which was pushed to the brink by the Eritrean revolt. This assumption is based on the wrong premise that the Amharas were imperialistic in a way similar to the French or the Portuguese. If one follows a classic analysis of imperialism, however, it does not take into consideration the fact that the Amhara nation is not developed enough to export finance capital like France or Portugal. It also fails to recognize that the Ethiopian ruling classes come from all major ethnic groups although they have adopted the Amharic language as their medium of communication.[107]

What has been overlooked in all these analyses is that the 1974 Ethiopian revolution was unique to the African continent both in depth and magnitude. It was a social upheaval of dramatic proportions which was a result of a historical process that had been unfolding over several decades. The upheaval was directly tied to education, modern educated elites and the contradictions inherent in a traditional polity that was attempting to survive with all its intrinsic characters even when modernization had introduced entirely new and different vistas to the country's body-politic.

This research attempts to prove Haile Selassie was not overthrown by the military; the 1974 revolution was not merely an ethnic revolt, although ethnic revolts did indeed contribute to its outcome. The analysis is based on the premise that Haile Selassie was overthrown by the students and the teachers who were the products of the modern school system. Hence, the author focuses on education and political processes in Ethiopia from 1905 to 1974.

The empirical research involved links education in Ethiopia with the educated elites' status and their own perception of the system at work. It also deals with the reciprocal and contradictory relationships which existed between the feudal regime, the metropolitan powers, and the modernization efforts.

It is known that the modernization of any traditional developing nation necessarily requires the introduction of modern education which is based on science and technology. This is what gave rise to a concerted move by international agencies to introduce massive aid money in development schemes which usually linked education with political and economic development. However, the campaigns, which aimed at producing more skilled manpower, have not succeeded in transforming Third World countries in the direction of the equitable distribution of resources. Even where industrial development had taken place and had created employment for a section of the urban population, labour in the market continued to increase at a faster rate than available jobs. The inevitable consequence is that the unemployed intellectuals, liberated from the constraints of past tradition, have rebelled against their Western educators and their own indigenous rulers who are, in most cases, autocratic, depending militarily, economically and politically on the metropolitan Western nations.

In spite of the above point, many Western scholars blame the systematic instability and underdevelopment problems of the Third World countries as emanating from the inherent backward nature of those societies themselves, not from their dependence on the metropolitan centres. This has been argued in many elite and modernizationist theories (e. g., Pareto, Rostow, Smelser and Lipset).[108]

A challenging view which blames the underdevelopment and the unstable nature of the Third World countries on the metropolitan nations has recently emerged. This model is commonly referred to as Dependency Theory (e. g., Baran, Dos Santos, Frank, Amin, and Wallerstein).[109] In both cases, however, there is as yet no in-depth analysis of the problem of underdevelopment and subsequent social upheavals in traditional modernizing autocracies such as Ethiopia and Iran, both of which fell in the decade of 1970. This research will try to fathom the Ethiopian episode and shed light on the anatomy of Third World revolutions.

Theories of Revolution

In the review of the literature, the author has focused on attempts to analyze and categorize revolutions of the last 300 years. Such phenomena may be studied under three major subdivisions.[110] In the early part of this century, Ellwood, Sorokin, Edwards, Lederer, Pettee and Brinton left their imprint on the crucial investigation of revolutionary phenomena. But since their preoccupation was with the identification of the main stages of revolutionary processes and a description of socio-demographic changes that took place after the change, their studies had numerous shortcomings. Ellwood, for example, tried to explain revolutions by what he called a breakdown in "social habits," LeBon, through "mob psychology," and Sorokin through the effect of "repression of basic instinctual needs."[111]

Since then, a second generation of scholars has arisen. This group, which has provided a serious critique of the first generation of Western studies of revolution, has attempted to advance new insights to develop theories that would explain why and when revolutionary upheavals arise. Davies, Gurr, Feierabend, Schwartz, Geschwender thus suggested revolution originates from the condition of the state of mind of the masses.[112] The critical moment is, according to their analytical framework, when the cognitive state of the masses reaches "frustration" or "deprivation" compared with some preconceived goals.

For Feierabend, "frustration" and/or "deprivation" originates during the process of urbanization and modernization; for Davies and Geschwender, from short term socioeconomic problems; and for Gurr, from denial of access to some groups' specific political and economic benefits. Smelser, Johnson, Tiryakian, Hart, Jessop and Hagopian, on the other hand, believe that revolution arises when a state of disequilibrium arises between the social system and its sub-systems such as the economic, political, social and cultural status of the country.[113]

Another group (Amman, Huntington, Stinchcombe and Tilly) traces the origin of revolutions to conflicts between competing interest groups.[114] Revolution arises, according to them, when there is lack of symmetry between institutions and mass mobility, and when normal political processes ultimately cease to function. The malfunction occurs when there is high intensity of conflict between the competing interest groups, when resolution and mediations fail, and when the political system is consequently ripped apart in a violent manner.

There should be two necessary conditions for the above phenomenon to take place. First, the differences between the interest groups must be irreconcilable within the existing system. And second, two or more of the competing interest groups must have sufficient resources organizationally, financially and politically to wield substantial control over the country's military and political machine.

All second generation theorists mentioned above agree on one thing. Once a revolutionary situation becomes ripe, any incidental reversal that societies could normally absorb, war, wrong and foolish steps taken by those in a ruling position, a mutiny or a riot or even crop failure and incidental famine, may trigger the final act of the revolution.

The problem with the second generation of revolutionary theorists is they all believe a country faces a revolution due to a variety of social changes: economic, demographic, military, cultural, technological, or organizational. But as Eisenstadt's study has shown, the great empires of the past, such as Rome, Byzantium and the Moguls had also experienced these changes, and yet the empires did not end up with a revolution but a gradual decline and decay.[115] One may, therefore, rightly ask, why these changes led to revolution in case of say, France, Russia or China and yet ended in gradual decay in the case of Rome, Byzantium or the Moguls in India. The problem with these theories is also the assumption that any society undergoing rapid change moves towards an inevitable violent revolution. But as Eckstein notes, the West has been subjected to rapid social change since the 1750s and with European contact other parts of the world since the 1850s and yet the systems have stayed in equilibrium.[116] One may, therefore, ask why violent revolutions have actually been rare. Why it was that revolution did not take place, for instance, in Britain, subjected to rapid social change since 1700, and Japan since 1875?

A third group of non-Marxist revolutionary theorists has also sprung up almost simultaneously with the second generation. The new group, unlike the first or the second generation theorists, considers four variables to be crucial for an understanding of the anatomy of a revolution. First, they feel the above-mentioned theorists have neglected the structure and priorities of the status quo state as a distinct variable. For example, Eckstein posits that only a particular kind of state that he dubs "feudal-imperial" may inevitably face a revolution.[117] This kind of state is prone to revolution, according to him, because it extracts resources from the society, permeates and mobilizes them for the benefit of a specific elite which monopolizes the political, cultural and religious institutions. Skocpol, who tried to understand, in her own words, "the logic of social revolutionary causes and outcomes from France in the 1790s to Ethiopia in the 1970s," points out that revolutions are enhanced in societies where the goals of a state, for example, industrialization or modernization, come into conflict with elite class privileges and resource capabilities.[118] Trimberger concurs with this stand.[119] Skocpol also suggests revolutions take place in "agrarian-bureaucratic" societies, where a centralized machine, and powerful landlords reap the benefit of a predominantly agrarian economy.

Another variable the third generation theorists consider important in deciphering the causes of a revolution is the effect linkage with international political and economic forces has on revolution. Neumann, Moore, Wolfe, Kelly, Miller, Rosenau, and Paige thus posit that revolutions are triggered by foreign military conflicts, or by the intrusion of international capitalist markets on domestic, agriculture and trade.[120]

Political linkage as a theoretical framework of political analysis has increased in importance since the 60s. But the study has been almost wholly confined to an explanation of the impact of external variables on domestic politics or of internal politics on foreign policy. Rosenau's Linkage Politics is the keynote of this move.[121] He distinguished between nine types of linkage, six aspects of international political behaviour, and twenty-four features of domestic political processes. This is all the more important because there is no lack of linkages between domestic conflict and domestic variables; indeed, almost all explanations of political instability employ this approach.

Armed forces' coherence is a third important variable cited. Chorley and Russell, for example, suggest revolution is not possible where the armed forces are loyal, intact and effectively used by the state.[122] However, in the author's view, this does not explain how, for example, the Shah of Iran or Somoza of Nicaragua fell despite unquestionable loyalty from the formidable modern armies they had created during the course of their autocratic rule.

The structure of rural societies or landlord-peasant relationships is a fourth important variable considered essential by the new theorists of revolution. This arises from their observation of the role of the peasants especially in the Bolshevik, the Chinese and the Vietnamese revolutions. Moore, Wolfe, Landberger, Migdal, Paige, Prosterman and Linz have attempted to analyze the role of the structure of agrarian communities in a national revolution.[123]

Skocpol goes to the extent of downgrading the effect of urban revolts on social revolution whether in initiating or determining its outcome.[124] Urban revolts, according to her, took place only in unsuccessful revolutions, for which she cites the Paris Commune and the German and Austrian revolutions of 1848. She also adds the outcome of a major social revolution transformed rural life by removing the powers and privileges of the landlords over the peasants in the countryside without any apparent change in the social organization of the cities. The crucial thing in a revolution, according to her, is a peasant revolt coming simultaneously with a breakdown in the power structure of a country's central government.

Finally, third generation theorists of revolution consider elites' relationships and elite behaviour as an important variable in precipitating not only a revolution, but also the type of revolutionary outcome. Skocpol, Eisenstadt and Trimberger have carried out a wide range of studies to explain this phenomenon. Eisenstadt, for example, suggests new elites with a close tie to old elites create "pluralist or "open" regimes whereas isolated or clandestine elites create what he calls "coercive" or "closed" regimes when their revolution becomes successful.[125] Skocpol also suggests that "marginal" or isolated elites are likely to adopt radical revolutionary policies while traditional landed elites tend to do just the opposite.[126]

Three major hypotheses have been advanced by scholars in the study of major world revolutions. These are: 1) the "increasing expectations" hypothesis, 2) the "relative gap" hypothesis, and 3) the "climb and fall" hypothesis, all related in that, according to their major premise, rebellion starts when there is a significant discrepancy between actual and anticipated circumstances or the perception that 'there is an intolerable gap between a state of affairs believed possible and desirable and a state of affairs actually existing."

The "increasing expectations" hypothesis goes as far back as 1856, the time of de Tocqueville, who wrote:

> Revolutions are not always' brought about by a gradual decline from bad to worse. Nations that have endured patiently and almost unconsciously the most overwhelming oppression often burst into rebellion against the yoke the moment it begins to grow lighter. The regime which is destroyed by a revolution is almost always an improvement on its immediate predecessor. Evils which are patiently endured when they seem inevitable become intolerable once the idea of escape from them is suggested.[127]

Edwards and Crane Brinton also concur with de Tocqueville's suggestion.[128] Their studies of the French, the Bolshevik and the American revolutions had indicated upheavals taking place when people experienced a period of improvement in their socio-economic conditions, were expecting more but further improvements came too slowly. Their main suggestion is that blockage in group mobility will enhance the movement towards social upheaval.

The "relative gap hypothesis" is traced to Karl Marx's study of the condition of the proletariat and his anticipation of a future revolution which he predicted would be caused by an inevitable class conflict. Marx wrote in *Wage, Labour and Capital*:

> A noticeable increase in wages presupposes a rapid growth of productive capital. The rapid growth of productive capital brings about an equally rapid growth of wealth, luxury, social wants, and social enjoyments. Thus, although the enjoyments of the workers have risen, the social satisfaction that they give has fallen in comparison with the increased enjoyments of the capitalist, which are inaccessible to the worker, in comparison with the state of development of society in general. Our desires and pleasures spring from society; we measure them, therefore, by society and not by the objects which serve for their satisfaction. Because they are of "social" nature, they are of a "relative" nature.[129]

Edward and Brinton, although arguing from a different perspective than Marx's conceptions, also agree it is not the actual deprivation of socio-economic status as such that matters in elite agitation but rather their perception of a relative gap where one group is unjustly deprived relative to another group at a specific space in time.[130] The "climb and fall" hypothesis is advanced by James C. Davies as follows:

> Revolutions are most likely to occur when a prolonged period of objective economic and social development is followed by a short period of sharp reversal. The all-important effect on the minds of people in a particular society is to produce, during the former period, an expectation of continued ability to satisfy needs-which continue to rise-and, during the latter, a mental state of anxiety and frustration when manifest reality breaks away from anticipated

reality. The actual state of socio-economic development is less significant than the expectation that past progress, not blocked, can and must continue in the future.[131]

Crane Brinton's study in the "Anatomy of Revolution" had identified some "tentative" uniformities in major world revolutions including the Bolshevik Revolution of 1917. These uniformities were: a) that the societies were somewhat advancing compared with the past, b) they had clearly identifiable class antagonisms, c) the government of the status quo were inept and inefficient, d) the ruling elites had lost confidence in themselves, e) the government was experiencing financial failures, f) the educated elites had deserted the system, and g) there was inept use of force to contain the growing rebellion.[132] The author considers it important to point out here that all these variables were present in Ethiopia in 1974; the country was thus ripe for revolution.

Linkage Between Education and Revolution

This study involves not only an explanation of why, when and how revolutions start and the role of educated elites in the revolutionary process. It also analyzes the relationship between education and political movements. Thus, the author believes a careful survey of the available literature which covers education and a country's domestic political processes would be useful.

By tradition, Western scholars have attempted to create a dichotomy between education and politics by advancing the view that the political system is a separate entity from the educational system and that, therefore, both practically and analytically, schools should be considered non-ideological and non- political. However, this view and its totally misleading premise had been challenged by a new generation of scholars who have come to appreciate the close and intrinsic relationship that has always existed between schooling and political processes. A concerted move towards explaining the phenomenon started in the 1920s and went through the 30s and beyond in studies of political education and training (Merriam and Pierce);[133] in the examination of acquired personality, politics and "national character" (Inkles and Levinson);[134] and in political behaviour development and "socialization" (Hyman and Easton).[135]

"Political socialization," which is nothing but a euphemism for "political indoctrination," has recently attracted a great deal of scholarly interest, especially in the political science discipline. Its analysis is rooted in communications theory (Lasswell):[136] a) who b) learns what c) from whom d) under what circumstances e) with what effects? Class and sex stereotyping is, according to Hyman and Easton, reinforced by political learning. For example, because of political socialization, most political participants are male. The upper classes are more active in politics than the workers. Schools, according to this view, therefore perpetuate social and political stratification and are, by design, the main pillars of the system within which they function.

Whereas all the above studies are Western-liberal in orientation, their detractors approach it differently. Karl Marx, for example, was clear when he said that "life [or actual material activity] is not determined by consciousness, but consciousness by life."[137] For him, human thought is rooted in human activity, not the other way around. In this concept, the way we are organized in our daily life is always reflected in the way we think about objective and subjective situations and the type of world we have helped to create. The institutions we build, the philosophies we advance, the prevailing ideas of the time, the culture of a group in question, all are, to a significant degree, a spin-off from the economic base of a given society. The political as well as the legal system, the family, the press, the education system are all rooted in the class nature of society, which in turn is a reflection of the economic base.

For Marx, the economic base or the infrastructure generates a superstructure that keeps it in place. The education system being part of the superstructure, is a reflection of the economic base and serves to reproduce it. In other words, the institutions of society that produce school curricula, are reflections of the world created by human activity and all ideas pertaining to it arise from and reflect the material conditions and circumstances in which they are generated.

In his book, *The German Ideology,* Marx maintained, "the class which is the dominant *material* force in society is at the same time its dominant *intellectual* force." What he meant is the ruling classes always determine the agenda of survival and control. They rule as sages and as manufacturers of thoughts that get noticed. They command and direct what we call "common sense." Ideas that are presented as normal reflections of human nature, and as collective belief system, are given a veneer of objectivity when, in fact, they are simply reflections of the superstructure of a class based society.

Marx also stated elsewhere:

> Each new class which puts itself in the place of the one ruling before it, is compelled, simply in order to achieve its aims, to represent its interest as the common interest of all members of society i.e. to give its ideas the form of universality and to represent them as the only rational and universally valid ones".

In a Marxist paradigm, ideas and ideologies are presented by the ruling classes as if they are universal and dispassionate. Durham & Kellner are even more brusque in explaining this phenomenon when they assert, "ideologies reproduce social domination, they legitimate rule by the prevailing groups over subordinate ones, and help replicate the existing inequalities and hierarchies of power and control."[138] All Marxists agree the types of education that are imparted to perpetuate a certain ideology serve as protective weapons of social interests. They are, in other words, kept in place to prop up the systems that create them.

For Marx, social knowledge, ideas and thoughts are never neutral. They are always determined by the existing relations of production and the economic structure of society. Educational ideas change according to the interests of the dominant class at a particular time. The Euro-communist theoretician, Antonio Gramsci has coined the phrase "ideological hegemony" to describe the power the ruling class has over knowledge.[139] For Marxists as well as neo-Marxists, the hegemony Gramsci mentions is exercised through the institutions of education or the media, which the neo-Marxist philosopher Louis Althusser calls "Ideological State Apparatus."[140] Unfortunately for the ancien regime, Haile Selassie had surrendered this important instrument of political socialization to the Metropolitan powers and had ultimately no choice but to suffer the consequences.

The question of alienation in school and society is one major variable to consider in other types of radical political analysis. The latter assumes that under a non-socialist organizational structure, man is separated from his activity, the products he makes and his fellow human beings. Potential human powers under feudalism or capitalism are made use of without being replenished and the schools neglect this potential and consider the student a mere commodity. Education, in this sense, becomes deified and is considered like a fetish. As time goes by, this would ultimately result in the total dehumanization of man.

Proponents of de schooling (Illich, Reimer, Postman and Weingartner, and Lister)[141] have tried to explain the root causes of these dehumanizing conditions in their studies. Ivan Illich, the main theoretician in that field, posits that man's apparent dehumanization is a result of the institutional frameworks spawned by a mass production and mass consumption society. The institutions, he argues, develop into a pervasive and powerful force. In the process they become anti-educational and anti-social.

Illich further argues that, in spite of the claim that Western schools are non-political and non-ideological, one of their primary aims is socializing the child to accept the existing basic tenets of the status quo political system. Western schooling, according to him, therefore has the subtle motive of internalization or the hidden mechanism for persuading children to accept prevalent political realities so that when they start work, they would be kept "democratically" in place.

For Illich, the socialization process in schools takes many shapes. First, children are initiated into the belief that everything is measured, which means that all kinds of values (e.g., happiness in democratic or dictatorial societies) can be measured and ranked like an ordinary commodity. Second, children are schooled into disciplined consumption patterns and, thus, start to entertain the myth of unending consumption. Third, and perhaps most importantly, schools legitimize the divine origin of economic, social and political stratification that exists much more vigorously and effectively than the Christian churches have been able to in the last couple of millennia.

The works of Paolo Friere mainly concentrate on literacy studies for adults but his major concern, just like the de-schoolers, is alienation and the pervasive, sterile education environment which arises due to lack of relevant and fulfilling political content in schooling.[142] Alienation is, in his view, born of the mentality of "consumerism."

Illich's and Friere's explanation are revisionist views and do not follow Marx's original explanation of the concept of alienation in political economy analysis. Marx had clearly described his concept of "alienated labour" which specifically deals with the worker as follows:

> According to the laws of political economy, the alienation of the worker in his object is expressed as follows: the more the worker produces, the less he has to consume, the more values he creates, the more valueless and worthless he becomes, the more formed the product, the more deformed the worker, the more civilized the product, the more barbaric the worker, the more powerful the work, the more powerless becomes the worker, the more cultured the work, the more philistine the worker becomes and more of a slave to nature.[143]

In Friere's analysis, "consumerism' is built into the school system a system that follows the example of "banking." Knowledge, in the traditional method, is consumed, not made and remade. Illiterates are treated like objects-oppressed and dehumanized. Friere therefore attempts to introduce a new teaching and learning system which creates "conscientization." The method, according to him, would liberate the learner. The major flow in this view is, however, the implied assumption that a new type of educational approach can redress society's ills regardless of the political system within which it functions. Whereas "conscientization" is his short term aim, Friere is also curiously silent on the long range goals of his method. In other words, "conscientization," instead of being a means to revolutionary change to combat alienation, becomes an end in itself.

Careful investigation of the literature on education and politics shows neither the political socialization scholars, nor the de-schoolers and the Friereans, have addressed themselves to the explanation of the relationship between education and revolution in which the author is interested. This analysis will, therefore, attempt to explore the role of education as an important variable in the socio-political transformations of Ethiopia which culminated in the far-reaching revolutionary upheaval of 1974.

This research was conducted with some, basic hypothetical assumptions in mind. In the study of revolutions which forms the crux of the problem, elites' perception of their status is crucial for an understanding of the root causes of social upheavals. All the scholarly works the author has investigated seem to agree that when rewards such as substantial earnings, property, fame, popularity, authority, power (none of them mutually exclusive), are forthcoming, educated elites could be, by and large, co-opted. These are, however, individual rewards.

There are other collective rewards which although not personal are nevertheless very crucial. Elites' perception of their country and the' condition of their own people in comparison with other's with similar resources and status in the international community are among these neglected variables. If they perceive the performance of the status quo regime as not contributing to the general well-being and socio-political development of their country and of their people compared with others with similar opportunities and resource capabilities, the elites' personal alienation from the established order would reach a crucial threshold and, thus, lead to an eventual revolution.

The author would like to stress his agreement with the already prevalent scholarly view that perceptions may be more important than realities. But if realities and perceptions correspond, the rationale and the success of an impending revolution becomes greater. For example, if Ethiopian educated elites perceived their government as slow moving in educational development process as compared with their African neighbours, their alienation would be crucial, regardless of whether the perception corresponded to reality or not. But if perceptions and realities corresponded, the chances for a revolutionary upheaval would be further enhanced. This would be so because while in the first instance the government may successfully defend itself with its records and stem the tide, in the second instance it could not possibly do so. Indeed, it would be an easy prey for attack since it could be politically disarmed. Even support from indispensable friendly governments would tend to wane.

In both cases, that is, in cases of added or reduced material and psychological benefits which are personal and collective rewards which emanate from the perception of one's own country in comparison with others, there are increasing expectations. But with increasing expectations, there may come a stage when both the individual and collective rewards become scarce. The educated elites then start to be fragmented. The established ones who have substantially benefited from the individual rewards would be either quiescent or openly attach themselves to the old order. But the new elites who have not benefited from these rewards and have therefore not been co-opted would be alienated from the established order. They would then start championing the causes of the masses by attacking the system's apparent socio-economic weaknesses.

Since economic development cannot take place in the absence of educational expansion, the regime's commitment or non-commitment in that sphere becomes detrimental to its very survival. But in both cases it faces a paradox. Too much educational expansion, which entails larger and larger numbers of educated personnel, makes material rewards by which the elites are co-opted dangerously thin (unless there is a regulated system of egalitarian distribution of scarce resources) thus increasing the chances of rebellion. Too little educational expansion also alienates the educated elites who have accepted the West's normative values [Fig. 1] and standards and thus opens the regime to severe criticism which is even more detrimental [See Fig. 2.] That this problem was acute when compared with Africa is very clear with the statistics this author analyzed covering a quarter of a century. [See Figs. 3, 4, 5, 6 7, 8 and 9.] Haile Selassie's feudalism opted for and suffered more from the second than from the first. But since educational expansion in Ethiopia in the decades of the 50s, 60s, and 70s favoured higher education in liberal arts and social sciences, [See Fig. 10] despite the fact that there were severe shortages of skilled manpower in technical areas,[144] there was also a certain amount of the first element. Lopsided elite production without concomitant rewards and even jobs had significantly increased the ranks of the educated rebels, especially in the late 60s and early 70s, thus enhancing opposition to Haile Selassie's feudalism.

The author believes the role of education and the educated students and teachers in precipitating a revolution in underdeveloped societies deserves close scrutiny, since in this particular aspect, the literature is, by and large, lacking. Indeed, in societies where serious socio-economic problems exist, even though the illiterate rural masses are quiescent, however miserable their condition, education acts as a stimulus for political upheavals, because the teachers and students always have increasing expectations that could not ultimately be fulfilled through a gradualist approach.

The role of students and teachers in the Russian, Chinese and other major revolutions was quite significant. That at a particular revolutionary period these societies had high proportions of alienated intellectuals and students was, therefore, not coincidental. The author also assumes that the role of the military in Third World countries with a revolutionary momentum have seldom been any different from the traditional bureaucratic elites that are status quo oriented and are strongly attached to the state machinery. At the most, their role in revolutionary situations had been either passive or playing "a waiting game." Their decisive involvement usually appears when the ruled rise en masse, join ranks with the small but highly committed civilian intelligentsia who are the vanguards of the revolution and defy the established order; and the rulers exhibit a tendency of crumbling under the new revolutionary onslaught. What makes them effective at that stage is that if there is not a well-established and well-organized party as in the Soviet Union prior to 1917 and China in the late 40s, the military establishment, being the only group with the most important physical powers in the entire society, could crush the revolution, subvert or co-opt it, or as in the Ethiopian case, jump on the bandwagon and adopt the radical programs championed by the civilian revolutionaries. They would then ultimately entrench themselves by neutralizing the revolutionary intelligentsia who had started to roll the ball of the revolution in the first place.

The author started the investigation of the relationship between education, educated elites and political processes in Ethiopia with the notion that Ethiopia has a unique status in the international community because of its long period of independence and the subsequent isolationism which shielded and preserved its age-old feudal system. Modern exigencies forced Emperors Menelik and Haile Selassie to introduce Western education into the country and set in motion the process of modernization from 1905 onwards. But the modernization they introduced was to run parallel to feudalism and was not aimed at supplanting the existing system. This inevitably created a clearly discernible dialectical process fuelled by the apparent co-existence of two contradictory social forces, namely, the new order and the old [Fig. 11].

Contradictions Between Feudalism and Modernization

The contradictions between these forces are not hard to observe. Feudalism, by its very nature, presupposes lord-vassal relationships where seigniorial and manorial rights of the lord are recognized and the property-owner is entitled by traditional conventions to exercise a high degree of authority over peasants farming his land. Modernization presupposes the creation of appropriate participatory institutions for channelling temporal power to be shared and channelled through a more efficient bureaucratic decision-making process. Feudalism as a political system is highly personalized and makes no divisions between the political functions of the institution of the monarchy at the apex of the political pyramid. Modernization requires the bridging of political communications from several quarters and the distribution of policy decisions through modern institutions; it also requires the transfer of ultimate loyalty from the monarch to the nation-state. Feudalism is characterized by huge land holdings of a powerful aristocratic class and the granting of fiefs to subjects in return for loyalty and service to the monarch. Modernization requires the creation of political legitimacy for new elites or a meritocracy who may not own land but who, nevertheless, draw significant benefits from their education and acquired skills. The list is by no means exhaustive.

That the stimulus for Menelik's and Haile Selassie's decision to introduce Western education into Ethiopia was spurred by the Japanese success in adopting Western methods and industrializing their country is clear. However, both emperors had missed the fundamental differences in the socio.-political traditions of these two old nation-states.

It may be useful to point out that in Japan, the industrialization drive and the introduction of Western education came about as a political revolution - state power being centralized in the Meiji court. Although Haile Selassie had also attempted to do just that, the structure and traditions of Ethiopian feudal society was fundamentally different from that of the Japanese. In Ethiopia, association with business as well as craft was despised and all those connected with these professions were looked down upon. It was in fact one of the anomalies Emperor Menelik tried to confront in his modernization drive, though unsuccessfully.[145] This explains why the country's first industries and business enterprises were almost wholly monopolized by people of foreign origin - Greeks, Armenians [many of whom were Ethiopian citizens], Arabs, and Indians. In Japan, on the other hand, there was a significant merchant class even before the 1868 Meiji Restoration. This class carried out inter-regional trade and produced and controlled a great deal of indigenous craft and business. Furthermore, it was drawn from the Samurai – a class highly respected in the society. Japanese modernization, therefore, depended on traditional business elite unlike that of Ethiopia which hinged on the gentry. In Japan, those who held prestige and power did not hold their property in land since the Meiji land settlement had freed the peasants of servitude to their landlords by compensating the latter with government bonds. The bonds were, in turn, heavily invested in banking and major industrial enterprises. The Japanese example, though, rightly chosen as a role model, evidently missed the fundamental difference between the two non-Western societies and only spawned unfulfillable hopes for Haile Selassie's Ethiopia.

Indeed, those who suggested, and this includes many Western-educated Ethiopians of the earlier generation, Ethiopian traditional rulers could modernize the country without serious societal strains that might lead to revolution were clearly wrong. Feudalism and modernization are by their very nature incongruous and cannot live side by side without creating fissures in the body-politic. Even Haile Selassie seemed to have realized the long-range consequences early in his reign when he remarked:

> You must bear in mind that Ethiopia is like a Sleeping Beauty, that time has stood still here for the last 2000 years. Therefore, in order not to overwhelm her with changes, we should be full of care now that she is beginning to awaken from her deep slumber! [146]

The Monarchy, the Church, and the Traditional Intelligentsia

The author would like to point out that the role of the educated intelligentsia in overthrowing a monarch or even a dynasty was not a new phenomenon, but rather a continuation of the role played by the traditional Ethiopian intelligentsia-known as the Dabtaras who were church educated.[147] Traditional power in Ethiopia involved the tripartite relationship of the monarchy, the church, and the Dabtaras.

By virtue of being the custodian of the institution of education, the church supplied the monarchy not only with its pen, but also with its interpreters and justifiers of political legitimacy. In this sense, the educated had dual dependence. On the one hand, they hinged on the ecclesiastical hierarchy as a conduit to the secular powers. On the other hand, they aspired to win the favours of the secular powers from whom they received land grants which, through its pecuniary and symbolic values, gave them better status than the peasants from whose ranks they were largely drawn. In turn, the Dabtaras served the feudal monarchs and aristocrats in interpreting to the masses of the uneducated peasantry, the rulers' actions in terms of customary, historical and religious ideas. This symbolic explanation assured the legitimacy of the feudal power structure.

Despite the fact that to a certain degree the triple power relationship between the monarchy, the church and the Dabtaras was asymmetrical in favour of the monarchy, the Dabtaras had an important ideological role to play in the Ethiopian body politic, for dynasties have fallen and risen through their direct political machinations. However, one very important point to bear in mind is that all the time, feudalism was untouched; a change in monarchies and dynasties did not mean a change in systems. This, the author stresses, was the fundamental difference. The 1974 event was a mass movement which challenged and succeeded to tear asunder a millennium-old system at its seams. The previous ones did not. In other words, whereas the former ones were coup d' états, the latter was a political revolution.

The Modern Educated Intelligentsia and the Contradictions thereof

With modern education came a new power relationship. If we refer to Ethiopian' political history, starting from Emperor Tewodros, whose experiment in opening Ethiopia to Westernization was cut short by his death at the battle of Makdala in 1868, Ethiopian monarchs had a strong desire to create a modernizing autocracy. The first ruler to embark fully on this road was Emperor Menelik, followed by Haile Selassie. Both relied heavily on Western type schools to produce a new type of intelligentsia and establish a modern state. With the new intelligentsia came a new type of power relationship, [See Fig. 12] By losing their traditional monopoly on education during the long reign of Haile Selassie, the church and the traditionally educated elite were, for all practical purposes, out of the political equation.

The aristocracy which was enfeebled by Haile Selassie's centralization efforts was later almost wholly liquidated during the Fascist occupation. The monopoly of education now passed mainly to Britain and the United States who used it as a conduit for cultural penetration. Thus, the modern power relationship included: a) the monarchy, b) the Western Metropolitan nations of Britain and the United states, and c) the new intelligentsia. The central assumption in this study is the intrinsic contradictions between the values of metropolitan political systems to which the Ethiopian intelligentsia were exposed and the political realities of a modernizing autocracy triggered the Ethiopian revolution and led to the fall of Haile Selassie in December, 1974.

There was, without doubt, a relationship between the economic structure and the social relations of education; the form and content of education and the mode of production in Ethiopia. The reason is there was no balance between social sciences and technical training [See Fig. 13]. The regime consistently favoured social sciences - disciplines that would create high level intellectuals to modernize feudalism from the top and not fundamentally transgress its character and structurally transform it.

Education in feudal Ethiopia was elitist, male oriented and attempted to Amharize the entire Ethiopian population. And as the "Education Sector Review" rightly pointed out, it also neglected eighty percent of the rural masses. When the authorities came to redress this problem, however, it was too late; the attempt to solve the problem at the expense of the Ethiopian teachers who were already alienated and were on the verge of revolt simply sharpened the existing contradictions. It neglected the fact that Ethiopian students' and teachers' struggle for educational reform was inextricably linked with the struggle to democratize the economic life of their country. This seems to prove that problems characterized as students' or teachers' revolt in Third World countries emanate not from the school as such but from the contradictions of the workings of the political system within which the institution itself is located. It also proves that an autocratic dependent state is not monolithic but contradictory since it also carries within itself progressive elements which may propel it towards an eventual revolution.

The supply side of education seems to indicate under certain conditions, the economic situation of the elites may have some correlation with the social upheavals that may erupt. The high level of unemployed intellectuals in Ethiopia preceded the widening rebellion of the educated; the less the expenditure as percentage of the national outlay [Fig. 14] and the GDP particularly when compared with Africa [Fig. 15 and the more the per capita expenditure per student decreased, [Fig. 15] [148] the more the students rebelled against the regime [See Fig. 16]; the larger the number of high school and elementary school failures,[See Fig. 17, 18 and 19] [149] the more the student agitation increased. All this seems to indicate intellectual rebellions are, to a significant degree, born of alienation which arises when self realization becomes unattainable. In other words, the process of "rising expectations" inevitably breeds the "Revolution of Rising Frustrations."

That students and teachers can play a decisive role in precipitating a revolution in countries governed by autocratic Third World regimes cannot be doubted. Also, contrary to popular belief, the Ethiopian military which was created as an arm of Haile Selassie's autocratic regime, was status quo oriented,[150] that it initially threw its weight behind the emperor and his throne,[151] and as the Ethiopian revolution kept on raging, it played a "sit and wait" game. It took a counter-establishment role only when the popular movement seemed to be succeeding. Even then, it started with the prodding, indeed, the attack and the strong influence, of the students who successfully infiltrated some sectors of the military establishment.[152]

The educated elites' perception of their own status and particularly the status of their country in comparison with their African neighbours undoubtedly fuelled their alienation from the established order and thus spurred them more and more to agitate for a revolutionary change in Ethiopia. In the 1950's, 60's and 70's, there was an extremely low level of Ethiopian progress towards the expansion of modern education compared with all countries of the world, the technologically advanced nations, the developing nations and particularly with the newly independent African countries [See Fig.20].[153] The fact that the alienated elites were alarmed by this huge discrepancy can be seen from the main platforms of the abortive 1960 coup d'état and the 1974 revolution in which the elites indicated their apparent shame at the status of Ethiopian education and called for an immediate redress.[154]

Cultural Penetration and the Ethiopian Revolution

The alienation described above was reinforced by the intense American cultural penetration which was channelled through the Ethiopian school system. Whereas Haile Selassie, hoping the American free enterprise system would absorb those his bureaucracy could not, gave free reign to the U. S. to influence the Ethiopian youth, the strategic position of Ethiopia, and the missionary zeal that guided America's global policy of "containment" combined to create a situation where the United States invested heavily in the ideological section (i.e., educational) of its "anti-Communists" campaign.

In the beginning, the American pedagogy did produce, as Haile Selassie had hoped, a different breed of educated people. Whereas the traditional educated class, the Dabtaras, were strongly attached to the people, their values and customs, the new elite tended to isolate itself from the mainstream and express its faith in the American way of life and ideology. It became the cerebral link in the metropolitan- client relationship that was taking shape through the material weight that American economic and military aid had created in the Ethiopian social fabric. But as long as the new elite had an unrestricted access to money and eventually to power, the imperatives of interest dictated that all three partners-Haile Selassie, the Western-educated elite, and the United states should construct a viable bond of interdependence and patronage.

Situations started to change rapidly starting in 1960 when the Americans clearly ranged themselves with Haile Selassie's loyalists. By that time, the new generation of students had discovered the level of American cultural penetration, and there came the first crack not only in the tripartite alliance of the monarchy, the Western-educated class and the United states, but also in the fragile co-existence of the *Adirbays* (careerists) and the still not co-opted young rebels churned out of the modern school system. The latter phenomenon then rendered a serious challenge to the ideological quietism practiced by the already integrated intelligentsia. A new. chapter was thus opened in the history of the educated youth - a chapter which made possible the mobilization of the students and the formation of a political front in a struggle against the feudal-client government of Haile Selassie, which by its intensity imposed itself as a trigger of the political consciousness of some of the important sectors of the power structure, especially the army, the air force and the police.

The Objective and Subjective Conditions as a Backdrop to the Revolution:

> For the new products of Western education, particularly the students and the teachers, who were caught up in the educational, social, and economic bottleneck of Ethiopia's modernizing autocracy, the process of funnelling radical political consciousness among the lower ranks of the military and

paramilitary forces - the only organized group in the country (other than the students, whose weapons were merely ideological) - was not a difficult one.[155]

The Objective Conditions as a Backdrop to the Revolution

There were internal wrangling among members of Haile Selassie's family, the aristocrats and ministerial factions as to who should control power once the aging Emperor had left the scene, either by abdicating in favour of one of his children or grandchildren, or through his natural death.[156] Despite spiraling inflation and outstanding grievances for higher wages, the government was threatening to produce only low paid teachers - thus raising the wrath of the country's educators. This was according to the recommendation of the "Education Sector Review," which was accepted· by the government, the projected date of implementation being 1973.[157] Other accepted recommendations were that the work year for teachers should be 48 weeks, with double shifts of five hours daily, and a class load of at least 67 students.

In addition, the failure rate in the entire pedagogical system was extremely alarming. In the high schools, for example, failure jumped from 10% in 1950 to a stunning 81% in 1970 [See Fig. 21].[158] Per capita expenditure per student was similarly on a continuous decline.[159]

In the social and economic spheres, the problems were no less acute. Taxi drivers could not absorb the sudden steep increase in gasoline prices.[160] Workers in the few factories could not democratically organize themselves to carryon genuine collective bargaining. Trade unionism was actually forbidden until 1962 and when later the Confederation of Ethiopian Labour Unions was established, the government put stringent controls on its activities. Strikes were regarded as insurrectionist in nature and mass dismissals were usually the result.[161] Unemployment was chronic and average worker salaries were less than U. S. $20 per month. Ethiopian peasants were still paying 50-75% of their produce to their landlords. Famine had laid its murderous hands on hundreds of thousands of peasant Ethiopians.[162] The feudal order at the apex of the political pyramid was in a state of irredeemable disarray, and the morale of the soldiers fighting in the north and the south of the country was at its lowest ebb due to deplorable living conditions.[163] The country was thus ripe for revolution.

To the extent that the objective realities mentioned above were facilitating the growth of radical political consciousness among the populace, the students and the teachers, imbued with Western liberal education, but now armed with Socialist and revolutionary ideological weapons, were taking the plight of their people to the political arena.[164] In short, the role of this new breed of educated youth was one of the necessary catalysts to enhance the pace of revolutionary ferment that ultimately sealed the fate of the feudal regime in December 1974.

This analysis has focused on the spectrum of the political face of the Ethiopian educational system because education in Ethiopia has been political. While the line of continuity between the traditional system of education and the modern one can only be drawn by a dichotomy of dialectically-related variables - conflictual/consensual - which have always existed between the political powers and the catalytic intelligentsia, the burgeoning conflict smouldering for over a decade ultimately superseded the tripartite consensus and hastened the revolutionary uprising in Ethiopia which culminated in the creation of a new political order.

One way or another, the fall of the Haile Selassie regime was inevitable not only because the objective conditions were leading towards that end, but also because his modernizing autocracy could not, by its very nature, accommodate metropolitan liberal values acquired by the new elite through the Ethiopian educational system.[165] A system seething in the dangerous atmosphere of an economic and political cauldron needs protection even from its own people. This leads to dependency. Protection is readily available owing the strategic, economic and political advantages accruing from such a relationship of crucial importance to the penetrating system. Whereas metropolitan guardianship is a precursor to cultural penetration, in the long run, cultural penetration breeds a condition which becomes a catalyst for an eventual social upheaval.[166] Hence, the author concludes an authoritarian, penetrated system that attempts to introduce Western education and all the accompanying values without changing the intrinsic character pertaining to itself, carries the seeds of its own destruction.

The Challenge of Modernity for Contemporary Ethiopian Youth

We are now beyond feudalism. For the first time in our history, millions of us have become exiles. Since 1974, Ethiopia has faced a bloody "Red Terror," and a divisive civil war that led to the dismemberment of Ethiopia. We are in the throes of "Ethnicity" that threaten to tear us asunder.

Furthermore, we are faced with the uncharted ways of globalization which has brought with it myriads of problems that we have to cope with if we have to survive in the 21st century and beyond. Whereas attitudes and behaviours are hard to change, we are, nevertheless, in the throes of globalization and "future shock" that do not spare Ethiopians at home or abroad.

Modernity incubated by Western education knocks on our doors gleaming in two faces, one positive and the other negative. The first feature is avant-garde, dynamic, progressive, guaranteeing to deliver free choice and personal satisfaction, unparalleled material abundance, autonomy and self-determination. Here, there are potentials of alluring accolades and rewards for those who strive for it and have the aptitude to attain it...

The other feature is blurred with environmental degradation that we clearly see when we look around Ethiopia, overcrowding as seen abundantly in Addis Ababa's shanty towns, catastrophic contagion, and the spread of communicable diseases such as HIV/AIDS that has not spared even citizens slogging on far off *ambas* and toiling on farms in narrow glens in this ancient land. A serene life, personal space, and privacy have all gone down the drain. Exodus from Ethiopia's rural tranquility to join the usual urban upsurge increases "anomie," personal and cultural alienation, loneliness, helplessness powerlessness, meaninglessness, anonymity, dehumanization and homelessness.

The school system, controlled by the Woyanes uses political socialization to keep people in their places. Mass media controlled by dictatorial rulers or unresponsive semi-private conglomerates try to shape our peoples minds, thus breeding conformity and passivity. What led to revolution during the period of feudalism is now moving in a new direction. The new socialization is leading towards the creation of an inward looking individual, an automaton with raging problems within thus multiplying the number of people suffering with mental disorders. Whether they are within or without the country, people tend to fall back on chemicals to escape roots [such as those found in chat or cocaine], committing bizarre slayings [e.g. sudden attempted or actual murder-suicides]. The fragility of the nuclear family has slowly crumbled under an onslaught of rugged individualism, narcissism, extreme materialism, the abandonment of religious precepts without any substitute.[167] All these direct individual Ethiopians and everybody else in the global village towards more hopelessness and meaninglessness opening the way for mounting conversions to bizarre cults or religious ecstasies created by Pentecostals speaking in "strange" tongues similar to the legend of the tower of Babel, that are attracting larger and larger numbers of Ethiopians from the formalistic Orthodox order both at home and abroad. This steers gullible individuals towards passively [many of the new ecstatic denominations teach their members not to fight against their country's enemies since they depict such action as transgressing one of the ten commandments!] thus allowing members to be victimized and be trampled upon by tin pot dictators masquerading as born again democrats.

The odds of defeating these negative developments are indeed exceedingly difficult. At the risk of being labelled overoptimistic, however, the author is inclined to suggest that the younger generation of Ethiopia not be left to the caprice of Western schooling controlled by the Woyanes who have their political axe to grind, but be inculcated with the age-old Ethiopian values of *Melkam Astedadeg* [good breeding.]. *Melkam Astedadeg* may not give them total shelter — not quite, but it will hopefully keep them grounded in their roots and provide them with some fundamental values that protect them from modern day "Anomie" which breeds the pathologies described above. It may also help them to love their country – a country that is currently in ethnic strife. There is a political spin here. As Lao Tzu put it in the 6th century B.C, it is "when a nation is filled with strife, patriots sprout." The more Meles' educational system and its political socialization spreads the venom of ethnicity, divisiveness and opportunism, the more Ethiopian nationalism flourishes.

4

THE EDUCATION SYSTEM OF HAILE SELASSIE'S GOVERNMENT: THE ROOTS OF POLITICAL FIASCO

BEKELE HAILE-SELASSIE TOMAS

In this chapter, Bekele Haile-Selassie Tomas narrates the sequence of events that led to the fall of Ethiopia's monarchy in 1974. He acknowledges this phenomenon has been analyzed by several scholars though only in relation to the conflict that arose between modernization and traditionalism, or between the hard realities of the socio-economic system of the period and the radicalism of the Ethiopian intelligentsia of the 1960s and early 1970s. The reasonings on which these analyses are based, though to an extent cogent, cannot be construed as conclusive. If one takes a fresher look, the thesis that the fall of the monarchy in Ethiopia was a result of the nihilistic nature of the ruling group is abundantly clear. With this in mind, the chapter scrutinizes the inadequacies and imperfections of the school system during the Haile Selassie period and ferrets out the major mistakes and final breakdown that engulfed the system thus leading to the fall of the regime. The author closes with the argument that a proper policy could have possibly averted the onset of the revolution of 1974.

It has now been a little more than three decades since the last royal ruler of Ethiopia, Haile Selassie, was deposed and the long history of monarchy in the country ended. But the question why it did so seems to be a recurring subject of scholarly debate. In the course of its existence that spanned over thousands of years, the monarchy had caused a complex tradition, i.e. "an interlocking system of ideas and attitudes," to evolve that influenced the views and behaviour of the people in various ways.[168]

The people held the crown as a symbol of national unity and territorial integrity. They believed the monarch was the sole guarantor of peace and prosperity. They perceived the sovereign as the single source of all legitimate authority.[169]

During the monarchic era, so overwhelming was the influence of the sovereign that it affected even private intercourses and social institutions. Uncommon was, for example, to hear individual's swear in the name of the sovereign when they committed themselves to an undertaking or they gave their word to do something.

"The monarch's very name," asserted one writer, "is very awesome." "There is no Ethiopian who will not keep an appointment or a promise after he has promised to do so upon oath saying 'let the king die!' "Even in the marriage contract, the last binding word of oath is 'let the king die!'"[170]

The Ethiopians of the past owed implicit allegiance to their sovereign. Being loyal to the king was equated with being loyal to the nation. The monarch's commands were obeyed without question. To carry this point, one could hear people say, if you entreat it in the name of the king, even flowing water will stop, let alone a man."[171]

The monarchic order apparently provided for a stable arrangement of political and social institutions wherein Ethiopians were able to interact and live together for millennia. It allowed them to establish social networks and evolve norms conducive to the pursuit of common interests and shared objectives.

However, that system of government could not withstand the 1974 social unrest and political upheaval which swept it away, culminating in a radical change of the Ethiopian social structure. The question under inquiry is then not how but why it did so happen.

The events leading to the downfall of the government of Haile Selassie I have been hashed and rehashed in numerous discourses. Much of the literature on the subject attempts to explain this historical accident in terms of the conflict between tradition and modernity, the widespread discontent with the harsh socio-economic conditions of the time and the spirit of revolution that haunted the Ethiopian intelligentsia of the 1960s and early 1970s.

Such explanations, though undeniably plausible to a lesser or greater degree, hardly tell the whole story. This paper seeks to look at the matter from what may be called "the inner perspective." It postulates that indiscretion in the conduct of national affairs on the part of Haile Selassie's government, rather than outright popular disaffection with the tradition of royal rule, was the root cause for the downfall of the regime.

The disappearance of the monarchy from Ethiopian society was scarcely a result of a concrete plan of political action. Doubtless, there was a persistent demand for the dismantlement of the noxious socio-economic structures of the establishment. True, there was an unrelenting voice of dissent advocating for the economic emancipation of the masses from the exploitation of the landed aristocracy. For sure, there was mounting pressure on the government of Haile Selassie to stamp out the malpractices and scandalous acts of its functionaries.

Nevertheless, no popular political design was at work to abolish the crown. No call emerged from a national consensus for the dissolution of the royal institution.[172] The injudicious statecraft that characterized the government of Haile Selassie was the prime agent of destruction that brought about the demise of the Ethiopian monarchy.

If only the government had good judgment in critical areas of national affairs and executed what itself had proclaimed, implemented what it had declared, carried out what had been positive and realistically possible within the constraints of the circumstances, it could have in all likelihood ensured the subsistence of some form of the monarchic order, withstanding if not averting the spontaneous socio-political upheaval of 1974.

One can furnish arguments in support of this viewpoint from diverse perspectives. Here the establishment of its validity is sought in the area of public education.

Jusitfiably, Haile Selassie took a special pride in the expansion of modern schools throughout Ethiopia under his initiative.[173] Ironically, however, it is in the field of education that the government sowed the seeds of its own destruction and brought about the disappearance of the monarchy.

The regime set the stage for the denouement by subjecting all major aspects of the Ethiopian school system to foreign influence thereby failing to use education as a tool of political socialization. This argument is further developed in the framework of a brief historical review of the role foreigners had in the public school system of the time.

Foreign Involvement

The involvement of foreigners in the field of public education during the reign of Haile Selassie was quite substantial. It encompassed the teaching, administrative, technical and advisory aspects.

Prior to the Italian Fascist invasion of 1935, with the exception to Amharic and Geez, elementary courses were offered in the French language, although English and Italian were used as a medium of instruction in small instances. Pupils at the Menelik II, Tafari Makonnen and Itege Menen schools had to take annual examinations for French certificate in primary studies.[174]

Men and women of diverse nationalities served as instructors in many public schools, teaching at both the elementary and secondary levels. They were also in charge of many government institutions of learning.

Nationals of different countries often ran the same schools at different times. This was the case, for instance, with Tafari Makonnen School, the Haile Selassie I Secondary School and the Itege Menen School, which were under the supervision of the American, Swedish, British and Canadian principals on different occasions.[175]

Foreign educators and advisers had an active role in the formulation of the directives that public schools had to follow. As a result, the ways in which lessons were offered tended to imitate those of other countries.

The teachers from different nationalities practiced the philosophy of their own native land in the Ethiopian public schools. Consequently, the students were exposed to varying methods of instruction.[176] Indeed, the situation hardly allowed for the development of a unified Ethiopian philosophical approach to education.

Following the restoration of the government of Haile Selassie I in 1941, first Britain and then the United states had overwhelming influence on the public education system that evolved in Ethiopia.[177] The British had considerable say on the organization and provision of the educational services until 1953.

In the early years, experts from Britain had great prominence in the Ministry of Education. In addition to acting as advisers, they held important administrative positions such as the inspector-general and co-coordinator of the curricula.[178]

At that time the British Council imported textbooks, teaching materials and supplies from Britain and its erstwhile colonies for use in the primary and secondary schools. It was heavily involved in the task of recruiting the persons who would serve as headmasters and teachers in Ethiopia.[179]

Under the sway of Britain, the British schooling system formed the basis of the education system in Ethiopia. Accordingly, proficiency in the English language turned out to be the ostensible, primary goal of the Ethiopian public education. Hence, English became the language of instruction from grade four onward.[180]

The Programme of learning developed for students in the erstwhile British colonies was adopted in the Ethiopian primary and secondary schools. For example, the flora and fauna of the British Isles and the history of western civilization formed the core of the social sciences, while the story of the Knights of the Round Table and the works of Shakespeare constituted the subject matter of literature.

The secondary school curriculum closely followed the requirements of the London University General Certificate of Education Examination. It was drawn with little regard to the needs of the students and the conditions of the country.[181]

The University College of Addis Ababa made its appearance in the Ethiopian educational scene in 1950. It was established as a two-year liberal arts college under a group of Canadian Jesuits. When the College came into existence, an approach was made to the British inter-University Council with a view to set up an evaluation system with respect to the quality of its courses and the qualifications of its staff.[182]

The implementation of President Truman's Point IV Programme of technical assistance to Ethiopia in 1953 helped the United States to gain prominence in the field of Ethiopian public education.[183] Indeed, the American predominance continued until the downfall of the Government of Haile Selassie in 1974.

The Point IV venture has been described as "the most influential single Programme after the restoration."[184] Upon the recommendation of the Americans, who replaced the British as policy advisers and technical experts, the Ministry of Education was restructured more or less along the lines of the national education Programme of the United States.[185]

The Point IV launched projects that sought to upgrade the quality and increase the number of the teaching staff at all levels. It imported school supplies and new textbooks, primarily from the United States, and engaged in the reproduction of teaching materials.[186]

Upon the recommendation of the American experts, a system of eight years of elementary and four years of secondary schooling was introduced. Students completing grade eight had to take a national examination to determine their fitness for secondary education. The British method of testing with subjective questions gave way to the American technique of testing with objective questions, generally consisting of multiple choice items.[187]

The education at the tertiary level also came under the American influence. The University College of Addis Ababa was restructured so as to comprise two faculties, one in arts and another in sciences. The College of Agriculture was established in 1953 as a branch of the Oklahoma State University.[188]

In 1960, the United States Agency of International Development took over the work of the Point IV establishment.[189] It continued to direct the American involvement in the field of education in Ethiopia. Once again the influence of the aid advisers brought about the restructuring of the learning Programme below the tertiary level in such a way as to comprise six years of elementary and six years of secondary education.[190]

The elementary schools featured the so-called self-contained classes where one teacher taught all the subjects. The secondary education consisted of junior and senior levels of two years and four years of instruction respectively.

The junior secondary level included grades seven and eight and was intended to serve as a stage where students could explore their aptitudes, interests and abilities with a view to identify and choose their area of study.

The senior secondary education system comprised grades nine to twelve and embraced the academic secondary schools, the comprehensive secondary schools, the vocational/technical schools and the teachers training institutes.[191]

As the name indicates, the academic senior secondary schools concentrated on purely academic subjects. The comprehensive senior secondary schools, on the other hand, taught commercial, technical, industrial and home economics courses in addition to academic ones. The vocational/technical schools and the teachers training institutes were approximately equivalent to grades ten through twelve.[192]

The review of the American influence on the pre-Derg public education would be incomplete without reference to the Peace Corps program. The introduction of the Programme to the country in the early years of the sixties markedly increased the involvement of the United States in the area of teaching.

Between 1963 and 1974, a large number of Americans came to Ethiopia under the Peace Corps Programme and served as volunteer teachers, especially in the secondary comprehensive schools. Their increased presence in Ethiopia was of particular significance as it exposed the students to the western liberal culture more than ever.[193]

As already indicated, the government of Haile Selassie heavily relied on foreign advisers and instructors to provide education for the Ethiopian students of the 1940s. This state of affairs did not seem to change significantly in the latter years, especially at the secondary and tertiary levels.

In 1955, a report concerning this matter was submitted to the Ministry of Education. The report indicated most of the secondary school teachers of the time were foreigners, and urged the reduction of the heavy reliance on expatriate staff as rapidly as equally qualified Ethiopian teachers became available.[194]

Ten years later, instructors of foreign nationalities still continued to constitute the bulk of the secondary school teaching staff. Nearly half of the expatriate teachers were volunteers from the United States and France.[195]

Most of the volunteers, especially those who came under the American Peace Corps Program, had little or no earlier teaching experience.[196] Nevertheless, the Government of Haile Selassie continued the practice of heavily relying on the service of foreign volunteers for the provision of education at secondary level and they remained to be in the majority until the eve of the 1974 upheaval that ended of the monarchy.[197]

Political Socialization

As earlier asserted, the failure on the part of the government of Haile Selassie to use education as a political, socializing mechanism was one of the major factors that led to the destruction of the Ethiopian monarchy. This matter is further explained below.

Political socialization may be understood as the process through which the values, beliefs and principles underlying a system of government are transmitted from one generation to another. It is a means of orienting the youths of a nation to its ethos, tradition and heritage – a way in which the political culture of a polity is handed down to posterity.

The starting point of this process is, of course, the family. But it is through the formal system of schooling that it is most effectively accomplished and the best tool to carry out the task is civic education.

The course of study on civics helps to create and develop social and political consciousness in the learner. It provides access to basic knowledge about the government and the political institutions of one's country.

Civic education helps one grasp the rudiments of the legal order in one's country. It helps one to learn about the law-making process, the court structure, the justice system and citizenship, too.

The study of civics affords students the opportunity to become familiar with the customs and ways of life of the various communities inhabited the different parts of their country. As such, it contributes significantly to the maintenance of national coherence and mutual trust.

The study has the potential to foster noble ideals such as unity, patriotism, equality and justice. Through civic education, moral virtues such as sincerity, honesty, compassion, and mutual respect may also be nurtured.

Because of its importance, it is imperative to ensure a course on civic education is incorporated in the elementary and secondary curricula. School children should have exposure to the basics of civics at the lowest level possible of the grade structure.

In order to be able to develop a course of instruction on civics, that has the potential to produce conscientious and patriotic citizens, one must absorb the ethos of a nation and have a thorough knowledge about its history and culture. In order to be able to teach it effectively, one must not only have mastery on the subject. One must be imbued with patriotism as well.

Indeed, it is not easy to find expatriate educators that fit the above description. Prudent leaders of nations, therefore, will ensure the availability of indigenous pedagogic expertise for the task. The Ethiopian rulers of the pre-Derg era, however, consigned much of the educational function to foreign advisers, administrators, and teachers.

There were several instances where concerns over this state of affair were expressed during the reign of Haile Selassie. For example, an Ethiopian observer of the 1940s remarked that a truly Ethiopian education could not be designed to produce American, English, Egyptian or any other national perspectives, but stalwart men and women with a healthy Ethiopian outlook.[198]

Again, in 1955, an advisory committee to the Ministry of Education, critical of the large proportion of the foreign staff in the secondary schools, stressed the necessity of developing a truly Ethiopian educational system relying on trained local personnel.[199]

At about the same time, Ma'aza Bekele, who was the head of the Curriculum Development Department of the Ministry of Education, urged a reexamination of the value of the imported learning that had been superimposed "on ancient and revered culture."[200]

The critique further questioned the adequacy of the, then public, education to nurture indigenous perspectives and asked whether the Ethiopian schools had the capacity to produce men and women that could appreciate the "valuable aspects" of their own communities.[201]

Finally, the report of the special committee that reviewed the Ethiopian education sector in 1971 and 1972 underscored that the teaching-learning process should aim at producing individuals with a firm sense of right and responsibility. It stressed that the country needed a system of education capable of building a society appreciative of its heritage.[202]

Despite the above critical comments, the government of Haile Selassie made the ostensible choice to perpetuate the preponderance of foreign influence in the teaching and learning environment. Indeed, it showed hardly any interest in introducing into the curricula civic instructions of far-reaching national effects.[203]

It is worth noting that, in the case of Ethiopia, there is a plethora of indigenous materials from which a course of study on civics may be developed: folklore, songs, poetry, anecdotes and adages of ethnic communities, historical records of foreign travelers, accounts of chroniclers of sovereigns, written and customary sources of law, as well as spiritual and secular literature of ecclesiastical origin are but a few of such materials.

The course may be structured in such a way as to help extract valuable lessons from past and present practices, experiences and institutions. For example, a study of the Feteha Nagast, other sources of law and traditional court systems, may serve to explore the importance of impartiality and equity in the administration of justice.[204]

An introduction to ethnology in the Ethiopian context may assist in understanding the need for a common language to facilitate communication and forge social cohesion among the different ethno-linguistic groups. The study may be a window on the historical processes that helped the Amharic language become the Lingua Franca of Ethiopia.[205]

The value of labour may be discussed in the context of what Tewodros II did in an attempt to encourage private initiative and the Decree that Menelik II issued in order to ensure respect for workers.[206] So illuminating is the latter that it is worth reproducing below:

> Let those who insult the worker on account of his labour, cease to do so. Oftentimes you call the blacksmith 'teib'; those who wrote you called 'tenquay.'

The farmers who produce our food and is known to be even better than the king, you call 'gabar.' The merchant who brought gold, you call 'gataba atabi' and insulted him on account of his trade. The lazy man whose son is ignorant causes trouble by insulting the clever man. All mankind is descended from Adam and Eve. There was no other ancestor. Discrimination is the result of ignorance. God said to Adam "in the sweat of thy brow shalt thou eat bread."[207] If we do not carryout this injunction, if one is idle, there will be neither government nor country. In European countries when people undertake new kinds of work and make canons, guns, trains or other things revealed by God, the people concerned are called 'mehandis' (engineers). They are praised and are given more assistance; not insulted on account of the craft. But you, by your insults are going to leave my country without people who work or make the plough. The land will thus become barren and destitute.

Hereafter, anyone who insults these people is insulting me. From this time on anyone found insulting another on account of his work will be punished by a year's imprisonment. If officials find it difficult to imprison such persons for a year, let the latter be arrested and sent before me.[208]

The exhortation in the order cited above may be used to discuss the negative social values associated with manual work and occupational skills and their harmful effects on economic development. It may also help to examine the social ills of discrimination and the virtue of equality.

The narratives and apocrypha in the Kebra Nagast (The Glory of the Kings) and other writings of yore may assist in developing appreciation of the Ethiopian literary tradition.[209] They may even be used as a tool to evolve an Ethiopian philosophical perspective through exploring connections of cross generation thought patterns.

The chaos and turmoil of the Zamana Masafint (The Era of the Princes) and the devastating religious conflicts of the medieval times may help to evolve instructions designed to develop and enhance an appreciation of political stability, tolerance and the virtue of peaceful coexistence.[210]

In his speech on the opening of the first Parliament in 1932, Haile Selassie declared his government would not destroy the tradition that had lasted for thousands of years. He affirmed it would ensure the preservation of the useful customs of the forefathers.[211]

Haile Selassie established a board of education in 1947 and placed its whole operations under his personal direction. He declared the administration, supervision, and guidance of all functions and controls of his government relating to education within the country would be under his exclusive authority.[212]

In spite of the foregoing, Haile Selassie and his government allowed foreign ideas and views to dominate the teaching and learning environment. They apparently left much of the responsibility to shape the education system in the hands of expatriates, who had no particular interest to see Ethiopian youths received civic instructions of national value.

Civic education in its proper sense had never been taught in the schools as part of the curricula during the reign of Haile Selassie I. Such being the case, it is hardly possible to say that the students of those days had adequate knowledge about the origin of the Ethiopian nation, the history of the monarchy, the formation of the Ethiopian modern state, the structures and functions of traditional socio-political institutions, let alone the customs, norms and ways of life of the diverse ethno-linguistic and religious communities existing in the different parts of the country.

Deprived of adequate knowledge about their country, society and heritage, it is not then surprising that the youths in the public schools of the 1960s and early 1970s saw nothing to be proud of in the Ethiopian polity. For a large number of them, even its existence as an independent political entity for thousands of years was something ridiculous.

Indeed, the students were in a state where they could hardly see anything worthwhile that deserved preservation in the tradition of the royal rule when they had been at loggerheads with the government of Haile Selassie. Even worse was that they could scarcely contemplate what the consequence of its abolition could be.[213]

The omission of basic civic instructions from the curricula meant the government of Haile Selassie hardly had any way to politically socialize Ethiopian youths through education. That was one of the most serious flaws of the regime and indiscretion was among the principal factors that set the monarchy on the course to its doom.

Concluding Remarks

Just as of old, the Ethiopia of today has a desperate need for political socialization, but of an enlightened type whose primary goal is to ensure the continued existence and well-being of the nation rather than the preservation of a system or structure of government.

Enlightened political socialization aims at recapturing the pride in the heritage of Ethiopia. It has in view the reinforcement of the safeguards against the threats that threaten its survival as a state.[214]

Nothing seems to be more important to Ethiopia at this juncture than the pursuit of enlightened political socialization through a process of informal and formal education that focuses on the elements of its national foundation.

The ultimate objective of the whole exercise will be to foster in succeeding generations:

> The kind of nationalism that causes the heart to burn with indignation against insults to the honor of the country; the kind of nationalism that makes it impossible to remain indifferent and unresponsive to the denigration of its history, cultural legacies and ways of life; the kind of nationalism that nurtures, rather than negates, the enjoyment of the richness and beauty that

lie in the ethno-linguistic and religious diversities of its inhabitants; the kind of nationalism that creates the irresistible impulse to answer its call for help in time of need and distress, transcending narcissism and parochialism.[215]

Indeed, the task is quite formidable under the existing ethno-federal political order, which has apparently become a breeding ground of ethnic distrust. However, there is a call for all conscientious citizens, responsible families, broad-minded interested groups, visionary private institutions of learning and patriotic ecclesiastical establishments, to rise up to the occasion and take on the challenge. They should join hands in the venture of raising a politically-socialized, nationally conscious, Ethiopian civic generation.

5

TOWARDS A CRITICAL ETHIOPIAN THEORY OF EDUCATION

MAIMIRE MENNASEMAY

By utilizing the theory of surplus-history, this chapter scrutinizes the fundamental nature of Ethiopian pedagogy. It attempts to pin point the dialectics involved in conventional Ethiopian educational experience and their prospective status to illustrate the root causes of the crises modern education in Ethiopia has faced. It argues at the centre of Ethiopian traditional education exist different concepts. These concepts are recognized under the rubrics of education, knowledge, profession, wisdom, as well as the process of learning and scholarly investigation. It is argued that knowledge, wisdom and scholarly investigation exhibit a liberating and positive notion of education. Furthermore, the nostalgia of education reflected among the learned elite point to an imaginary concept that is part and parcel of Ethiopian social milieu and traditional pedagogy. The analysis concludes with the observation that the beliefs, values and traditions reflected in education, knowledge, profession, wisdom, the process of learning and scholarly investigation and the nostalgia of education have the capacity to spawn historically based criteria that can evolve a critical theory in Ethiopian pedagogy.

The Encounter with Modern Education

With the opening of Menelik II School in 1908, a state-sponsored western style education made its official entrance into Ethiopian history. The purpose was to promote the acquisition of skills Emperor Menelik felt necessary for confronting the colonial ambitions of European powers as well as for giving himself some additional tools to administer the Ethiopian state he had rebuilt through his various campaigns.[216] Between

1929 and 1935, Ras Tafari, who, after 1930, reigned as Emperor Haile Selassie, expanded modern education and opened schools in Gore, Jijjiga, Neqemte, Asbe Teferi, Jimma, Gojjam, Gondar, Selale, Adwa, and Mekelle.[217] By 1935, there were fourteen schools in Addis Abeba alone with about "4000 pupils, one-fourth of whom were girls."[218] Together with students going to Europe for further studies, the number of Ethiopians with western education was sufficient to give rise to a small intelligentsia that was aware of the country's vulnerable position in the face of a militant Europe intent on dominating Africa.

Concerned about the weakness of Ethiopia in the emerging world order, these intellectuals articulated the idea that western education is necessary for Ethiopia's survival. Gabre Heywat, an early member of the intelligentsia, compared the Sudan and Ethiopia, and lamented the dangers that face his country: "All around us colonies are marching ahead undeterred by any obstacles ... Woe, then, to a people that persist in its ignorance for it is ultimately bound to perish."[219] Tekle Hawaryat, another member of the intelligentsia, went even further and ruminated, "Sometimes I ask myself, would it have been better, if the civilized nations had colonized us for a short period of time?"[220] The pre-1941 intelligentsia, "among the most articulate group of intellectuals that Ethiopia has ever seen," according to Bahru, "advocated a multifaceted programme of reform, including the expansion of education."[221]

Many of these intellectuals were aware of the risks of alienation if western education is not rooted in the love and knowledge of Ethiopia.[222] There were however differences among them about how to implement western education. Some, such as Sahle Tsadalu, proposed that Ethiopians should be introduced to western education only after "a ten-year educational programme" based on "a standardization of traditional church education."[223] Others, such as Gabre Heywat, dreamt of quickly opening "Western-style schools in all the provincial capitals" in order to ensure a more rapid development.[224] However, there was a consensus that, Ethiopia's development depends on being, in the words of Tamrat Ammanuel, "self-sufficient in all fields of education."[225]

In making self-sufficiency "in all fields of education" a requirement for Ethiopia's development, these intellectuals laid down the foundation for a critical reflection on education. However, subsequent Ethiopian generations failed to rise up to this task. The result is the current exocentric system based on western education, which, oblivious to the processes that constituted Ethiopia as a unique society, treats students as a *tabula rasa* on which one could write imported knowledge. The consequences have been catastrophic. A century of thoughtless embrace of western education has left Ethiopians with knowledge that in most cases is alien to and often counters their aspirations for freedom, prosperity and justice.

The Current Situation in Education

With one of the lowest literacy rates in the world, the situation of education in Ethiopia in these opening years of the twenty-first century is tragic.[226] Ethiopia's gross enrolment ratio for primary and secondary schools stands at approximately 51%, "smaller than the corresponding averages for Sub-Saharan Africa." [227] Compared to 20 low-income Sub-Saharan countries, Ethiopia has the lowest cohort survival rate to grade 6; only "60 percent in each age cohort ever enrol in grade 1, and barely 60 percent reach grade 4." [228]

Moreover, the burden of educational injustice is not equally borne. In rural areas, "less than half the children in each age cohort enter grade 1, and of those who do, only 55 percent survive to grade 4 and only 19 percent, to grade 8," in the agricultural sector, "nearly 80% of the workers are illiterate."[229] The gender gap is higher in Ethiopia than in other African country.[230] In parts of Ethiopia, women describe themselves as the "forgotten on earth."[231] Only 25% of women, as compared with 46% of men have achieved literacy.[232] Nor is women's access to higher education any better. They account "for only 16% of degree enrollments in regular and evening programs of public institutions," whereas only "7% of graduate students are women" as compared to the 35% sub-Saharan average, and "barely 7% of academic staff in public tertiary institutions are women". In comparison, "the Sub-Saharan average for women's participation in degree programs is roughly 35% and the proportion of women academic staff is about 20%."[233]

In addition, the cost of education weighs more heavily on the poor than on the rich. Public sector spending on education is inequitable. The "poorest 20 percent of households account[ed] for 15 percent of public spending on all levels of education, while the richest 20 percent receive[d] 29 percent."[234] Often, "hunger and insufficient food" are reasons given "for not enrolling children in school."[235]

Ethiopian education does not fare any better in the tertiary sector. Ethiopia's "tertiary level gross enrollment ratio is around "0.8%," with "62 tertiary students per 100,000 inhabitants."[236] This places it below the tertiary level GER for Sub-Saharan Africa, which stands at "4% with a regional average of 339 students per 100,000 persons." Not surprisingly, Ethiopia suffers from an acute shortage of "professional and technical capacities of all types," creating a serious impediment to economic and social development.[237] Currently, the shortage of qualified personnel in education is extensive, a shortage exacerbated by the EPRDF policy that gives primacy to ethnic identity over competence. There is a "lack of sufficient qualified teachers" and the increasing de-professionalization of school principals and directors makes it even more unlikely that the situation could be improved.[238] In addition, the brain drain that started during the Derg regime continues unabated with "half of all academic staff ... lost to brain drain during the 1990s."[239] In the health sector alone, where the availability of both preventive and curative care is one of the least developed in the world, approximately "one-third of Ethiopian physicians" have left the country.[240]

Not surprisingly, the World Bank study concludes its report on a depressing note: "At the start of the 21st century," it states, "Ethiopia's population is among the least educated in the world, averaging fewer than two full years of formal schooling among the adults."[241] The main price for the lack of commitment to make education equally and universally accessible across gender, rural-urban and class divides is paid by children: 3, 355,382 children aged 5 to 9; 4,078,991, aged 10 to 14; and 2,049,237, aged 15 to 19, are obliged to work in order to survive.[242]

Current Critiques of Ethiopian Education

There are different approaches that try to account for Ethiopia's educational failure; the World Bank, the non-formal education, the cultural, and the pragmatist approaches.

The World Bank puts the emphasis on inadequate investment, inappropriate policies, administrative shortcomings, and lack of resources. According to the Bank, recurrent spending on education is "insufficient for achieving the goal of universal primary education" and the current 4-4-2-2 schooling system is unproductive in that the "completion of the first cycle [the first 4 years] may be insufficient to insure...literacy". Other problems it identifies are: the lack of access to schooling in rural areas, the high gender gap, the shortage of space in schools, the high pupil-teacher ratio, the high drop-out rate, the high cost of schooling for poor children, the scarcity of competent teachers and pedagogical materials, the deterioration of teaching conditions, and the inefficiency of school management.[243]

It is the Bank's view that the Ethiopian government could overcome these shortcomings if it were to increase investment in education, and adopt market-oriented curriculum development, as well as business-inspired management of educational institutions. It recommends "labour market conditions" be allowed "to guide the pace of expansion" of the school system, that "the role of private sector providers at the post-primary levels" be enlarged, and that "household contributions for education needs … be part of an overall strategy for the education sector." [244]

The non-formal sector perspective relates Ethiopia's educational failure to the exclusive emphasis on the formal to the detriment of the non-formal sector. "It is morally wrong and economically unjustifiable," writes Tekeste, "to invest scarce resources on the formal education system whose contribution to the development of society is at best tenuous and at worst irrelevant."[245] The dependence on external resources for curriculum development, teaching and pedagogical material is so pervasive that one could speak of a system designed to divorce students from their social and historical roots.[246]

Tekeste argues it is imperative to acknowledge Ethiopia's heritage as a launching pad for an educational Programme that is meaningful to the majority of Ethiopians. He contends the non-formal systems of knowledge transmission, located in institutions such as churches, mosques, and *Gada,* offer "a better alternative both as regards the expansion of literacy and the fulfillment of educational needs than formal education."[247]

The cultural approach suggests that we revive Ethiopian traditional values and integrate them into our educational system.[248] Elleni claims the main site of non-formal education is the village itself, which she distinguishes from Church education. She points out, very few children attend Church education, whereas village education is the location of the most formative education. She enumerates some of the Ethiopian ("Amhara") traditional values that are acquired, admired, or validated in village education: *chewanet* (politeness), *sena ser'at* (right conduct) *gubzenna* (bravery), *haqegnennet* (honesty), *tehetenna* (humility), *moya* (mastery of skills), and so forth.[249] The implication is the recognition of the village as a site of education and that the inclusion of traditional values in the current educational system would help alleviate the current crisis.

Finally, the pragmatist approach suggests we disaggregate traditional education into discrete elements and choose those that are functional for "modernization." Levine advances such an approach. He identifies five possible patterns of the encounter between traditional and modern cultures—"(1) the Traditional, (2) the Modernist, (3) the Skeptic, (4) the Conciliatory, and (5) the Pragmatist"—and opts for the latter, which he describes as a commitment "to the optimum realization of all values in a given historic situation."[250] According to him, the pragmatist "would sustain traditional values wherever possible; would modify them where feasible; and would reject them where necessary."[251] The failures of modern education would then be the outcome of an educational system that, in failing to be pragmatic, has lost its way.

David Bridges *et al.* hold similar views. They point out traditional education does offer a model of "rich relationship between teacher and taught"; that it develops a "kind of argumentation, improvization and public defence of one's position, which is education in the *Qene* School," and it offers a model that emphasizes "the intimate connection between learning and doing."[252] They go over the traditional values Elleni identifies, and suggest "this kind of thought contains both considerable wisdom and matter for consideration in contemporary educational debate." They conclude: "Our approach to educational development is primarily a pragmatic approach." [253]

Traditional Education as History

The above considerations show the problem of education in Ethiopia is complex. Therefore, a critical reflection on education in Ethiopia must take these critiques into account, but without falling into an eclecticism that would only compound the existing confusion about the meaning and purpose of modern education.

According to John Binns, whereas "modern education seeks to develop the capacities and abilities of the child," Ethiopian traditional education does the opposite: it "seeks to enable the student to absorb the culture and to be absorbed into it" and Binns' citations indicate that this is a criticism made not only by westerners but also shared by some Ethiopian educationalists.[254] However, this is a curious criticism. If one observes American, European, Japanese education systems, they seek to do what Binns criticizes as the defect of Ethiopian traditional education. They "enable the student to absorb the culture and to be absorbed into it"; and, to judge by the depth and intensity of patriotism in these countries, their education systems successfully accomplish the mutual absorption of "culture" and students. They have thus succeeded in making education a process that ensures that children, in becoming educated adults, become conscious historical subjects of their society. It is indeed in the educational system's capacity "to enable the student to absorb the culture and to be absorbed into it" that resides the civilizing or humanizing potential of education.

It is precisely with regard to the capacity to enable the student to absorb Ethiopia's "culture" and to be absorbed into it that modern education has failed.[255] It has deprived students of the opportunity to make the crucial transition from the unhistorical consciousness of children to the historical consciousness of adults who reflectively understand their circumstances and recognize themselves as agents capable of changing these circumstances from within the historical possibilities available to them. The failure of modern education to bring about this transformation is one of the reasons for the cultural disorientation of those whose education is "modern." They are often depicted in contemporary Ethiopian literature in terms such as "purposeless... faceless... restless... aimless... unsteady... undecided... confused."[256] This disorientation has facilitated the rise of destructive ideologies that spawned the Red terror and ethnic politics, while generating, at the same time, rootless knowledge that continuously misses its purported aim of throwing light on the ways for overcoming endemic poverty and oppression. The result is the decline of social hope and the erosion of our cultural confidence in our capacity to cope with our country's problems through our own understanding and imagination.

Yet, it is precisely where modern education has failed that traditional education has been remarkably successful. Unlike modern Ethiopian education, which cultivates historical amnesia, traditional education accomplishes the civilizing process that enables the student to absorb Ethiopian culture and to be absorbed into it. Let us not forget, Ethiopians, formed by traditional education, successfully defeated Europe's colonial ambitions. It is precisely when modern education robbed us of our self-intelligibility as Ethiopians that this civilizing process broke down and Ethiopia became prey to "modern" leaders for whom she became a laboratory for experimenting their ideological fantasies of "socialism" (the Derg) and "ethnic democracy" (the EPRDF). The important challenge for modern education is then to awaken the civilizing process that church, village, mosque, *Gada* and other traditional education systems harbour but that we have squandered in our compulsion to treat ourselves as unformed matter for western education to transform into a finished product.

However, to awaken this humanizing process of traditional education means also to inquire into the reasons for the failures of traditional education to initiate emancipatory social transformations in Ethiopia.[257] To repudiate traditional education *in toto* because it has failed to transform Ethiopian society is not to overcome it but to occlude its historical contradictions and perpetuate unwittingly into the present and the future the forces that stifled its transformative potential. This is why it is dangerous to consider modernization as a process of sloughing off one's traditions. One way to avoid this danger is to approach traditional education from the perspective of "the word that wounds is the word that heals" and enucleate from within traditional education itself the emancipatory potential the authoritarianism of the traditional order asphyxiates. To accomplish this, we need to consider traditional education as a historical process.

To consider traditional education as a historical process means to see its subject matters, its pedagogy, its practices and its institutions as historical phenomena formed and informed by the social and political contradictions that animate Ethiopian history. Such a historicization reveals traditional education is internally conflicted, and bears within itself the hegemonic meanings that validate the existing order, while secreting and repressing at the same time surplus meanings that point to an alternative social order and educational practice. The purpose of identifying these surplus meanings is to excavate and examine the emancipatory potential that gestates within traditional education in order to develop an internal critique of Ethiopian modern education.

An interpretative approach helps us excavate the surplus meanings of traditional education, which are critical of the hegemonic meanings that it transmits and of the order it serves. For example, *chewanet* (being polite) is one of the values traditional education tries to inculcate in students. However, this value does not stand alone. It is part of a network of social practices. The meanings and surplus meanings of *chewanet* arise from the way it is connected to, differentiated from, and conflicts with the other social practices in this network. *Chewanet* and *rassen makber* (self-respect), both highly valued, are interconnected, whereas *rassen mawwared* (demeaning oneself) is considered incompatible with *chewanet* (being polite). But how does one interpret a person's *chewanet* to his oppressor and his *chewanet* to an equal? The two *chewanet* could not have the same worth. The first could be interpreted as involving *rassen mawwared* (demeaning oneself), but not the second, for the latter implies *rassen makber* (self-respect) in that the *chewanet* takes place in a relationship of equality. One could then argue that, although those who have power impose the hegemonic meaning of *chewanet* (being polite) to one's oppressor as right conduct, from the perspective of the oppressed, such *chewanet* (being polite) could be seen as confirming one's status as an oppressed person and, therefore, as *rassen mawwared* (demeaning oneself). That is, *chewanet,* a highly valued social practice in Ethiopia, bears surplus meanings that are critical of the hegemonic meaning of *chewanet,* for the latter excludes the value of *rassen makber* without which *chewanet* lacks substance. In other words, the conflict of meanings that traverse the practice of *chewanet* indicate is a sense in which the authentic fulfillment of *chewanet* requires the abolition of the circumstances that impose *rassen mawwared* as a condition of being *chewa* (polite). The contradictions between the hegemonic and surplus meanings of *chewanet* reflect an aspect of the social contradictions that drive Ethiopian history. The traditional educational values Elleni enumerates, ostensibly transmitted to ensure the reproduction of the hegemonic social order, harbour similarly conflicts of meanings that secrete surplus meanings subversive of the established order. When we consider these internal conflicts of meanings, we see we are neither hermetically enclosed in our tradition nor are we completely outside it. When historicized, our tradition itself has the potential to enable us to step out of it and make such a stepping out meaningful; that is, our tradition itself has the internal resources that make possible and make sense of emancipatory transformations.[258] Indeed, one of the beliefs of traditional Ethiopia— that "knowledge corrupt[s] the heart"[259]—suggests a tacit awareness of these conflict of meanings and, thus, of the subversive surplus meanings of knowledge.

The main obstacle in historicizing traditional education is the divorce between history and culture that the social sciences have imposed on African studies. Auguste Comte's injunction that history should deal with "the development of the most advanced peoples" and shun those societies "whose evolution has so far been…at a more imperfect stage,"[260] saw its implementation with the invention of the colonial discipline of anthropology as the science of "people without history."[261] As an approach that purges history from African social practices and institutions, it represents what it names traditional cultures as static social practices without internal transformative potentials.[262]

It is of interest to note the concept of culture does not have the same connotations when used in Ethiopian and European studies. In European studies, culture has both philosophical and sociological meanings. From the Enlightenment onwards, culture in the West is related to the ideas of freedom and progress. Cassirer captures this transformative understanding of Western culture: "Human culture taken as a whole may be described as the process of man's progressive self-liberation. Language, art, religion, science, are various phases of this process. In all of them man discovers and proves a new power—the power to build up a world of his own, an 'ideal' world."[263] This philosophical meaning ensures that the transformative significance of culture is present in studies of Western societies even when used as a sociological category. Not so in Ethiopian studies where the conception of culture is devoid of comparable philosophical underpinnings and is understood as an ensemble of immutable ideas, values and practices with no future-oriented transformative potential.[264] Indeed, one is hard pressed to find in the anthropological literature a "native" described as "cultured" though he may be described as "wise." The use of the qualifier "cultured," is reserved for westerners. This difference in use points to the differing connotations the word culture has when used in describing Ethiopian and European social practices. Whereas considering a "native" as wise fits the presupposition that his culture is static, since wisdom is seen as timeless, describing him as "cultured" would undermine the very premise that the native's culture is static and backward looking.

Critiques of Ethiopian culture write, "qualities such as curiosity, creativity and critical analysis are not valued in traditional education," and that "obedience is valued above creativity."[265] According to Haile Gabriel Dagne, traditional education "contributes little to the spiritual and mental development of the child."[266] Levine writes that Ethiopians (the "Amhara"), have "a preoccupation with private interests that leaves little room for the consideration of communal needs," that "there is little spontaneous co-operation in Amhara life" that "aggressiveness is further encouraged by the Amhara ego ideal," that "argumentation, litigation, insulting, and revenge comprise the hard core of social interaction among Amhara," and that "the most characteristic form of interaction among the Amhara is that of domination."[267] He asserts traditional education "is based on repetition and memorization," that "obedience and politeness [are] the overriding goals in bringing up children," and claims that the "Amhara child is conditioned to become, for the rest of his childhood, and to a large extent throughout his life, taciturn, fearful, and slightly morose."[268] If these critiques were right, Ethiopian culture and its educational institutions would have no redeeming meanings and values within them. Indeed, how a people with such a frozen culture have managed to defeat so many efforts to colonize them becomes a mystery. What frames the critiques' claims is a radical de-historicization of Ethiopian culture that congeals it into a homogeneous ensemble of timeless practices. In forgetting that a living culture is internally conflicted, incomplete, and in motion, however slow this may appear to the hurried observer, such a perspective erases a crucial question: i.e., do Ethiopian culture and its educational institutions also harbour meanings and values that point to an emancipatory potential and, thus, contradict the critiques' claims?

To unpack the contradictions embedded within traditional education and explore the possibilities it offers for developing a critical Ethiopian theory of education that could help us Ethiopianize modern education, we have to historicize Ethiopian culture. The concept of "surplus-history" offers this possibility.[269]

Surplus-History: Towards a Critique of Homeless Education

Surplus-history is the ensemble of subjugated meanings, values and practices—surplus meanings, in short—that expresses and articulates the emancipatory dimensions and utopian energies that inhabit Ethiopian social practices and culture as the repressed other of the hegemonic order and its history. Traditional education—church, mosque, *Gada,* village—is an aspect of Ethiopian culture. It is an ensemble of social practices made up of the values, subject matter, pedagogy, and institutions engaged in the transmission of inherited knowledge and a way of life. I will argue the social practices constitutive of traditional education have surplus meanings critical of the hegemonic meanings that traditional education transmits. To make this point, however, a brief clarification of the nature of social practices is required, which I will do by first making a short detour via some ideas from the hermeneutical tradition, both Ethiopian and European. This will elucidate what I mean by surplus-history and bring out its relevance for historicizing traditional culture and its educational practices.

As writers in the hermeneutical tradition have argued, social practices are historically formed; they are not transparent, homogeneous, discrete, brute data.[270] They arise from and are interconnected through shared common, inter-subjective and background meanings. These are their conditions of intelligibility. Since social practices are inherently historical. They are not identical to themselves; no conceptual determination can exhaust their meanings.[271] This is also true of events and institutions, for no event (e.g. the Adwa victory) or institution (e.g. traditional education) is a finished work, in a state of a harmoniously balanced equilibrium, at one with itself.[272] This draws our attention to two important issues. First, an adequate understanding of Ethiopian social practices requires recognition of the existence, density and interconnectedness of background meanings. Second, the meanings of these social practices go beyond their immediate or hegemonic determinations. Understanding social practices requires that we recognize their polysemous nature and unpack their contradictory meanings through interpretive work.

The Ethiopian hermeneutical tradition, embodied in the literary trope of *Sam enna Worq* (Wax and Gold), leads us to similar conclusions. This hermeneutical tradition rejects the transparency of discourse. According to *Sam enna Worq*, discourse has manifest meanings that convey the hegemonic understanding (the *sam* or the wax), while, at the same time, it harbours hidden meanings (the *Worq* or the gold) that are qualitatively different from and in contradiction to the manifest meanings the hegemonic understanding imposes. These hidden meanings (the *Worq*) could be revealed only through interpretative labour. This *Worq* is the surplus meaning, critical of and in tension with the hegemonic understanding of the discourse. My contention is the trope of *Sam enna Worq* could be applied also to social practices. As I have indicated above in the brief discussion of *chewanet*, social practices are not transparent. They articulate multiple meanings that are in tension with each other. True, the hegemonic powers impose one of these meanings as "the" meaning of a given social practice. However, this does not entail the non-existence of surplus meanings—the *Worq*: critical and subversive of the hegemonic understanding of social practices. From this perspective, one could speak of Ethiopian culture as *Sam enna Worq culture*, as a culture whose manifest meanings are the *Sem*, and whose surplus meanings, constituting surplus-history, are the *Worq*. Surplus-history, the ensemble of the *Worq*, is the dynamic "historical unconscious," as it were, of Ethiopian culture; the "mole" that burrows tenaciously through the subterrane of the hegemonic order. This *Worq* is what is missed by those who de-historicize Ethiopian culture and generalize, based on an empiricist understanding that reduces meanings to observables, that is, to that which the hegemonic order makes visible.

It is crucial then to recognize Ethiopian culture as a historical process producing plurivocal social practices. Understanding these as historical phenomena requires unpacking the various meanings that traverse them as symptoms of the social contradictions of Ethiopian society. In this sense, social practices secrete surplus meanings that undermine the legitimacy of their hegemonic meaning. Indeed, the coherence of the latter depends on the exclusion of surplus meanings. Take, for example, the current ethnic liberation fronts in Ethiopia. Their hegemonic meaning, enshrined in the 1994 Constitution, is that they express self-determination. However, ethnic liberation fronts secrete a surplus meaning that implies that to be free is to overcome ethnicity, for, if ethnicity is the source of oppression, then liberation could come only by going beyond ethnic divisions. The creation of ethnicstans and the inclusion of article 39 in the 1994 Ethiopian Constitution, which equates ethnic secession with self-determination, appear then as impediments to liberation. It is this surplus meaning that plays the role of the historical mole. It undermines the coherence of the ethnic discourse of the current regime and emerges unexpectedly in the May 2005 general election as the victory of the forces opposed to ethnic politics, leading to massive government repression. The maintenance of the hegemonic interpretation of ethnic politics as an expression of self-determination generates the repression of the surplus meaning that points to the abolition of ethnic politics.

Surplus meanings may be subjugated, but they do not disappear. They form a polyphonic subterranean world of repressed ideas, values and practices that incubate new forces, identities, hopes and ideals that mature imperceptibly, and some of which burst to the surface in certain situations. Thus, one discovers in our history, *inter alia*, the sudden rise of Queen Gudit (10th century), Lalibela's utopian vision of a second Jerusalem (1190-1225), Tekle Haimanot's vision of a restored Ethiopia (1215-1313), the unexpected emergence of *Daqiqa Estefanos* (15th century), the rapid success of Ahmed Gragn (1527-1543), the meteoric rise of Tewodros II in 1855, the surprising victory of Adwa (1896), the swift demise of the Imperial regime in 1974, the sudden collapse of the Derg (1991), and the eruption of democratic forces in the May 2005 elections. The problem here is that the conditions out of which these events emerge seem to be somewhat inadequate to account for their emergence. Indeed, one could argue there are certain historical events, such as the unexpected victory of democratic forces in the May

2005 elections or the Adwa victory (1896), that no amount of empirical description of the historical context can explain.[273] Such events overflow the sum total of the causes one may use to explain them. The only way of apprehending them would be then as supplements to the situations out of which they emerge. There are two points here. First, there are surplus meanings one cannot grasp through causal explanations, however complete these may be, but that participate in making the event possible. Second, the event itself produces surplus meanings such that no causal explanation could have predicted them. In short, one's understanding of events or social practices is inadequate, incomplete, or even wrong, if one does not grasp through an "interpretative confrontation" the surplus meanings that precede and emerge from social practices and events.

Surplus meanings are constitutive of surplus-history. I suggested earlier that we consider surplus-history as the dynamic historical unconscious of Ethiopian culture. But we have to understand the "unconscious" in the Blochian and not the Freudian sense. In his critique of Freud, Bloch points out that the Freudian unconscious "is solely the forgotten" or the "No-Longer-Conscious," that it is a "backward…disposed darkness" that "merely send[s] a neurotic symptom of itself into consciousness."[274] For Bloch, there is a forward-looking "non-repressed unconscious" or a "Not-Yet-Conscious" made up of historical and social material committed to the concrete hope of achieving humankind's dream of emancipation. The Not-Yet-Conscious is "the preconscious of what is to come… there is within it a content of consciousness which has not yet become wholly manifest, and is still dawning from the future."[275] That is, it is a dynamic historical unconscious, with a three-dimensional temporality, wherein "the rigid divisions between future and past themselves collapse, unbecome future becomes visible in the past, avenged and inherited, mediated and fulfilled past in the future… [and] true action in the present itself occurs solely in the totality of this process which is unclosed both backwards and forwards." [276]

It is in the Blochian sense that surplus-history (the *Worq* in the interstices of Ethiopian culture) is the dynamic historical unconscious of Ethiopian culture. It is its critical and subversive dimension, subjugated but active silently. It deploys a three-dimensional temporality: it harbours the memories of the aborted hopes of our past, keeps these memories active in the present, foreshadows a different future that redeems the struggles of Ethiopians, and illuminates the injustices they suffer in the present. Surplus-history is "unclosed both backwards and forwards." In it, the past, the present and the future are alive in each other, conjoined in pulling forward "to overturn all circumstances in which a man is a degraded, a subjugated, a forsaken, a contemptible being."[277] Surplus-history inseminates the present with the "militant hope" that a different Ethiopia—one without poverty and oppression—is possible.

This does not mean surplus-history stands outside history. Rather, the split between surplus-history and history is internal to Ethiopian history itself. One could speak of Ethiopian history as *Sam enna Worq* history wherein hegemonic and surplus-history imbricate in each other, with the former as *Sam* and the latter as *Worq*, or with the former as manifest history and the latter as its unconscious—in the Blochian sense. Though surplus-history is internal to history, it is a critical rather than a descriptive category. It throws light from within on the arbitrary and oppressive nature of Ethiopian social reality and expresses the refusal to accept the ruling elite's appropriation of Ethiopian culture—past, present and future. It bears within itself latent emancipatory anticipations that challenge the despotic closures that the reigning order imposes on aspirations, ideas, and actions. Surplus-history is the effect of the unresolved contradictions of Ethiopian society.

Recognizing surplus-history historicizes Ethiopian culture. Consequently, it has important implications for understanding traditional education, for we can now comprehend traditional education as a historical process traversed by the unresolved contradictions of Ethiopian society, generating surplus meanings. Since education takes place in the context of everyday life as an activity that forms students' understanding of the past, their relation to the present, and their vision of the future, it is crucial to bring out briefly the critical significance of surplus-history in their education. Two angles of inquiry—the conflict of historical subjects in Ethiopian history and the conflict of meanings that inform daily practices—throw light on this issue.

The hegemonic historical narrative affirms the ruling elite as the historical subject—the "national we"—of Ethiopian history. This hegemonic "national we" imposes itself through oppression and exploitation and treats its interests as the universal interests of Ethiopians. At the same time it constitutes Ethiopia as a shared space, even if unequally, for all Ethiopians. This historical process has two outcomes: the creation of competing ethnic identities, creating ethnic "we"s, hegemonic within each ethnicity, and the formation of the emancipatory "we" of surplus-history that cuts across ethnic identities, opposed to both the hegemonic "national we" and the "ethnic we." The historical processes that form Ethiopia as a shared space create shared trans-ethnic identities such as being a peasant, a labourer, a pastoralist, a student, a trader, an artisan, and so forth, subjected to the same trans-ethnic conditions of exploitation and oppression, in resistance to which emerges the "we" of surplus-history. Thus, peasants in Wallaga and Wallo, labourers in Jijjiga and Gondar, students in Makalle and Jimma, have shared identities in addition to their ethnic, religious, gender, regional identities. In this sense, there is an Oromo peasant in every Amhara peasant, a Jijjiga labourer in every Gondare labourer, and a Makalle student in every Jimma student, and vice versa. Thus, from the perspective of the "we" of surplus-history, every Ethiopian has a complex identity. We have thus three competing visions: that of the hegemonic "we," of the ethnic "we," and of the "we" of surplus-history. The question then is: since education embodies a vision of the future and forms the subjectivity of youth, and since youth are "the architects of the future," which historical vision should inform education if emancipation is the goal?

Moreover, whereas the hegemonic "we," both national and ethnic, imposes a homogeneous linear time that reflects the established system's belief that there is no alternative to its order, the "we" of surplus-history, embedded in its tri-dimensional temporality, tacitly asserts that there is a qualitatively different alternative to the established order. In this sense, everyday life is the domain where the surplus meanings constitutive of surplus-history are engaged in a subterranean struggle against the hegemonic order.

From the angle of everyday life, surplus-history is the sanctuary of emancipation denied. In Ethiopia, one of the ten poorest countries in the world, the daily acts necessary to survive poverty and oppression are daily "acts of resistance."[278] The established order condemns these acts as irresponsibility, deception, disloyalty, disrespect of property, ignorance, impoliteness, procrastination (*eshi nege*). It interprets these actions, whose emancipatory possibilities are invisible to it, as "lacks" in the moral character of peasants, the oppressed, the exploited and the poor. However, from the perspective of surplus-history, one could see these acts as "weapons of the weak,"[279] whose surplus meanings are critiques of freedom trampled, of prosperity denied, and of justice corrupted. Unable to actualize themselves in the public realm, the aspirations for freedom, prosperity and justice escape the network of oppression that constrains daily life and become the constitutive elements of surplus-history. Let me take a popular weapon of the weak, *eshi nege* (translated as "I will do it tomorrow"), to illustrate this point.

The hegemonic understanding of *eshi nege* is laziness or procrastination. However, if we consider its use in its context, we discover it has surplus meanings that exhibit their characteristic three-dimensional temporality. *Eshi nege* secretes meanings that refer to the past, for what provokes it as an answer is the complaint that a task that should have been done is not yet done, and that it should be done today. The response *eshi nege* excludes today, as a time unfit for doing the not-yet done task, and postpones it to tomorrow (*nege*), which is the time appropriate for doing the task. The socially acceptable reason given to justify such an answer could be something such as "I have too much work to do it today." But in the context of poverty, exploitation and oppression, *eshi nege* has surplus meanings that indicate resistance to the injustices of the established order. The identification of *nege* (tomorrow) as the right time for doing the task signifies multiple critical judgments. It connects the past (the origin of the unfulfilled task) with the future (the promised time of completion of the unfulfilled task), in a way that implies the present is still an extension of the past obstacles that prevented the task from being accomplished. Thus, *eshi nege* creates a time warp where the past and the future overlap and throw light on the present as the abode of conditions that prevented and still prevent the task from being accomplished, intimating that overcoming these conditions is a prerequisite for completing the task in the future. The demand that arises from these surplus meanings is that we must start instituting today (*zare*) the freedom, equality and social justice that are already present, though repressed, in the actual as possibilities, thus making the task doable. Otherwise, the conditions that prevented the fulfillment of the task in the past, and still do in the present, will extend themselves into the future, and the task will remain unaccomplished. Thus, *eshi nege* is a critique of the unfreedom, the inequality and the injustices that permeate the past and the present; it is a refusal to conform to the homogeneous linear time of the hegemonic "we," and thus, it is an act of freedom, a weapon of the oppressed, an act of resistance. It secretes as one of its surplus meanings a demand to transform the present conditions so that the qualitatively new *nege* (tomorrow), gestating as the possibility of freedom, equality and justice within the *zare* (today), starts actualizing itself today, thereby creating the new conditions that will make the task achievable. If, as mentioned earlier, education is an important activity that forms the historical subjectivity of the young, education for the future cannot afford not to awaken the young to the surplus meanings that overflow everyday life both as critiques of the dark present and as promises of a bright future.

What surplus-history thus indicates is there is an antagonistic split between the historically actual - the established order - and the historically possible, a split buried in the actual. The historically actual represses the surplus meanings that undermine it. But, in being pushed out from the actual, these surplus meanings do not become inert; they incubate and generate new possibilities and the "possibilities of new possibilities," waiting, as it were, for historical subjects capable of seizing and actualizing them. Nor does Ethiopian social reality become homogeneous in repressing the surplus meanings that contest it. Rather, as Ethiopian history shows, the more ideas and values disappear into surplus-history, the more Ethiopian society becomes uneven, fragmented, and unstable. This is visible in modern Ethiopian education. The more it has repressed traditional education, the more modern education has contributed to the erosion of social confidence and social hope, spewing in its wake unreflective knowledge that made possible the Derg and ethnic politics, cynicism, and a massive brain drain. Recognizing surplus-history thus opens the door to the exploration and harnessing of emancipatory ideas, values and alternatives that are already in the bowels of Ethiopian culture and its traditions of education. It creates new possibilities for the eruption to the surface of some of the repressed ideas, values and practices. As Marx puts it, "the world has long since dreamed of some of which it needs only to become conscious for it to possess it in reality. It will then become plain that our task is not to draw a sharp mental line between past and future but to complete the thought of the past… [to] consciously bring about the completion of its old work."[280] Modern education will fail to meet the emancipatory aspirations of Ethiopians if it ignores what Ethiopians have "long since dreamed."

Treating traditional education as a historical process allows us to appropriate reflectively its surplus meanings. This has a number of ramifications. First, Ethiopian traditional education is not homogeneous in that it is intertwined with the contradictions that drive Ethiopian history. Consequently, it is, on the one hand, conservative as far as it expresses the meanings and values of the established order; and, on the other, progressive in so far as it harbours surplus meanings that express a repressed knowledge of the unjust conditions of life and, thus, articulates ideas and values that anticipate the reversal of the existing relations of domination. That these forward-looking and transformative dimensions—its surplus meanings—are not immediately accessible to our understanding does not mean that they do not exist. Rather, it means that discovering them demands that we consider Ethiopian traditional education as a historical process and adopt an interpretative approach to excavate its surplus meanings. These surplus meanings could indicate the directions and goals of emancipatory educational practices.

Second, the historicization of the defeated hopes of the past, of the subjugated present aspirations and of the anticipated future enables us to conduct a reflective excavation of the surplus meanings of our traditions, thus awakening our critical capacities, our imagination and our utopian energies. One of the most deleterious consequences of imported education is the excision of imagination and utopian visions from Ethiopian education. Yet, from Plato to the present, including hard-nosed materialists such as Marx, imagination and utopian visions play important roles in thinking about our conditions, in the generation of anticipatory concepts, and in disclosing a different future. The presence of forward-pulling emancipatory aspirations in surplus-history empowers our imagination, our utopian visions, and critical capacities.

Third, traditional education does not divorce education from everyday life. Consequently, it harbours the surplus meaning of what we could call praxis. This suggests a critique of modern education that reveals it as homeless education—an exocentric education that produces dehydrated knowledge whose shriveled arteries and veins have squeezed out all traces of historical consciousness, of the memories of defeated hopes, and of the possibilities of an alternative future. Homeless education has no roots in our past, present or future; it is incapable of redeeming our aborted hopes, of grasping our present aspirations, and of foreshadowing the future anticipated in our past and present struggles; it cannot lead to a liberating praxis.

In the rest of the paper, I will develop the ramifications of such a reflective appropriation of the surplus meanings of traditional education and draw the implications for developing a critical Ethiopian theory of education.

Traditional Education and Its Surplus Meanings

Let me start with some of the common terms associated with traditional Ethiopian education. *Mammar* is a verb that refers to the process of learning, *mastemar* to the process of transmitting knowledge, *astemari* or *memher* to the teacher, and *temari* to the student. *Mammar* is seen as successful when *temhirt*—a term that refers interestingly to both education and to what one learns—transforms the *temari* into what the community recognizes as *yetemare sew* (educated person). The *dabtara*, a graduate of the church-based education system, is the main figure of the educated person in traditional Ethiopia. In addition, we find the word *moya,* a term that describes the mastery of time-honoured skills in performing certain tasks. At first blush, traditional education appears to be limited to the transmission of inherited knowledge and way of life.

However, traditional education, being a historical process, is not a homogeneous practice. It harbours tensions and contradictions out of which emerge surplus meanings that are critical of it. Thus, we encounter four additional terms: *ewqet*, which is the knowledge of *ewnet* (the truth or the right order of the world) as the surplus meaning of *temhirt; tibeb*, which is the knowledge of how things work, as the surplus meaning of *moya; awaqi*, which means he who knows *ewnet*, as the surplus meaning of *dabtara* or of *yeTemare sew;* and *mirmera*, which means curiosity, questioning and investigation into the working of things, as the surplus meaning of *Mammar.* Moreover, memorization plays an important role in traditional education. It anchors students deeply in their lifeworld and provides them with the inner resources and rootedness necessary for self-affirmation and for confronting the adversities of life with tenacity and resourcefulness. Though memorization appears to the superficial observer as a process of mindless repetition, it has the crucial surplus meaning of inwardness. As such, it has the potential to provide a fertile ground for the exercise of the imagination and for mobilizing utopian energies. Imagination and utopian visions are the surplus meanings of traditional education that some fail to grasp. Levine, for example, dismisses the capability of Ethiopians to imagine new ways of relating events as telling "preposterous fictions."[281] One way of bringing out the surplus meanings that critiques who disparage traditional education fail to see is to ask the question Rubenson raises: "How did it happen that Ethiopia…preserved its independence throughout the era of European colonization?"[282] One cannot neglect the manifestation, however fleetingly, of the surplus meanings of traditional education—emancipation, imagination, utopian visions—in traditional Ethiopia's successful defeat of European powers despite their superiority in arms.

Whereas *temhirt* does not include *mirmera* and is more conservative rather than creative, *ewqet* submits traditional knowledge and its objects of knowledge to *mirmera* and tries to gain *ewnet* or a deeper insight into the world. Whereas the goal of *temhirt* is the acquisition of functional literacy and the goal of *moya* is to master tradition-honored skills, the goal of *ewqet, tibeb* and *mirmera* is to go beyond the given in order to achieve intellectual and moral sovereignty. It is for this reason that the *awaqi* is accorded more respect than the *dabtara*, who is generally considered a sophist. However, any *dabtara* could become an *awaqi* if he adopts *mirmera* and pursues the goal of *ewnet.*

Ewqet, tibeb, awaqi, and mirmera are the *Worq* of traditional education. One way of grasping their significance is by looking at the difference between *dabtara* and *awaqi* in terms of their relation to knowledge and the world. The *dabtara* is a graduate of church education and a master of what the church tradition has accumulated as theological knowledge, rituals, *Qene* (religious poems) compositions, hymns, and techniques of argumentation. His education is premised on preserving rather than on questioning what he learns. Whereas *Mammar* is the foundation of the *dabtara's* learning, *mirmera*—doubting and questioning what one knows and believes, venturing into new territory unknown to existing knowledge, or investigating the workings of the world—is not part of his repertoire of *temhirt.* The *mirmera* of the *dabtara* is limited to the exegesis of existing knowledge within the boundaries set by traditional rules of interpretation. The *dabtara* is mostly engaged in using his knowledge to facilitate the functioning of the established order: he writes magic scrolls or *kitabs,* works as a chronicler for secular or ecclesiastical institutions, writes letters and *abetutas* (petitions) for the illiterate, and, generally, confirms the legitimacy of the existing order. The *dabtara* is the "organic intellectual" of the traditional social order. Unlike the *dabtara,* an *awaqi* endeavors to reveal *ewnet* (truth) and to expose the falsehoods and injustices that nourish the existing order. [283]

Temhirt, moya, Mammar and *dabtara* are the dominant tropes of traditional education. They signify meanings and values that are consistent with preserving the existing order and its legitimating beliefs. *Ewqet, tibeb, mirmera* and *awaqi* are the manifestations of the repressed dimension of traditional education, internal to it but subjugated, and whose meanings are available only through a labour of interpretation. These surplus meanings signify that the things of the world are subject to *mirmera,* and, thus, to the judgment of *ewnet* acquired through *ewqet.* The surplus meanings that differentiate *temhirt* from *ewqet, moya* from *tibeb, Mammar* from *mirmera,* and *dabtara* from *awaqi* have been smothered by the hegemonic order as if activating them would have traumatic social implications. Indeed, the second term in each pair is practically absent from the discourse on traditional education. For example, in *A Social History of Ethiopia,* Pankhurst gives sixteen entries for *dabtara* in the index but none for *awaqi, mirmera, tibeb,* or *ewqet.* [284] Levine has in *Wax and Gold* five entries for *dabtara* but none for *ewqet, mirmera, tibeb,* or *awaqi.* [285]

However, like all the surplus meanings the existing order renders invisible, the critical meanings of *ewqet, tibeb, mirmera, awaqi* gestate in surplus-history and erupt sometimes as ciphers of a possible alternative education, and indeed, of a qualitatively different future. I would like to examine one such case—the *Daqiqa Estefanos,* a reformist movement that emerged in fifteenth century Ethiopia—from within the realm of traditional education and see how the surplus meanings of traditional education could contribute to a reflection on a critical Ethiopian theory of education.

Daqiqa Estefanos, Ewqet, Mirmera, Tibeb, and Utopia

Daqiqa Estefanos, founded by Abba Estefanos, was a movement of reformist monks that arose from within the Ethiopian Orthodox Church around 1406 and was active until at least 1460, though remnants of the movement are discernable after this period. [286] The movement started in Tigray and expanded to other regions of Ethiopia. Its membership included Amharas, Wolaitas, Gamos, Agews, Boshas, Hadiyas, and others. The *Daqiqa Estefanos* were persecuted for their ideas. Many of them were flogged, stoned, their limbs chopped, their bodies lacerated with razors, their eyes gouged, their ears and noses cut, their tongues torn out; some of them were even burnt alive and murdered. [287]

On the surface, the conflict between the *Daqiqa Estefanos* and the secular powers appears to be about theological matters. However, one perceives in the discourse and conduct of the *Daqiqa Estefanos* the gestation of new ideas about law, justice, power, and nature, implying new conceptions of knowledge and education.

The *Daqiqa Estefanos* approach to knowledge is aptly and metaphorically summarized by the founder of the movement. "Of what use is the sun," he asks, "if it cannot give light and warmth?" [288] Though the specific issue raised in the passage that contains this comment is a theological one—the nature of the Trinity—the question applies to secular matters, especially when articulated with the *Daqiqa Estefanos* critiques of the conduct and governance of Emperor Yesehaq (1406-1421), Emperor Zara Ya'iqob (1426-1460), and the various local rulers. These critiques draw their sustenance from the understanding of knowledge as the sun that throws light on the right relation between ruler and ruled, men and women, knowledge and life, knowledge and nature. The *Daqiqa Estefanos* understand knowledge as *ewqet* and *tibeb,* and *mirmera* as the way to knowledge. They see knowledge as the sun that sweeps away the night of ignorance and exposes the true nature of reality.

Throughout their brief existence, the *Daqiqa Estefanos* challenge important pillars of the existing order. Whereas laymen, nobles, priests, and *dabtaras* address the Emperor by using the respectful "You," the *Daqiqa Estefanos* refuse to follow this practice and address the Emperor using the familiar "you." When the Emperor demands that they, like everybody else, should use the respectful "You," they respond that since they use the familiar "you" when they address God in their prayers, there is no justification for using the respectful "You" when they address a human being.[289] Why this issue became a major cause of conflict cannot be understood if we skate over it as an idiosyncrasy that concerns only the relationships between the Emperor and the *Daqiqa Estefanos.* The issue here is that the justification they give for using the familiar "you" is one any Ethiopian could give, since Ethiopians address God in the familiar "you" in their prayers. The implication here is that, as a human being, the Emperor is not above his subjects. This is a challenge that de-sacralizes the Emperor, a mortal threat to a ruler who sees himself as anointed by God. This challenge bears within itself the notion of equality between rulers and ruled and excludes the idea of privileged knowledge gained through anointment.

The second challenge accentuates this de-sacralization. The *Daqiqa Estefanos* refuse to prostrate themselves before the Emperor.[290] Prostrations have profound political and social meanings in traditional Ethiopia. Not only do they express one's unquestioning obedience to the ruler, they also symbolize the unbridgeable gap between the Emperor and his subjects. The upright position of the Emperor signifies his power of vision and speech and his capacity of determining the life-horizon of his subjects; whereas the prostrating person has his face stuck to the ground, his eyes deprived of vision and his voice of its dialogic intent, thus acknowledging his powerlessness to determine the path and destination of his life. In rejecting this bodily posture, which replaces the God-given uprightness of man with the animal's position of a head confined to the ground, and in deciding to stand upright when talking to the Emperor, the *Daqiqa Estefanos* state in their conduct that the Emperor and his subjects are equal as human beings, and that the difference between him and his subjects is contingent. Their challenge proclaims his vision of things is but one of many possible visions, his voice is but one among many, and each person could make his voice heard, determine his horizon, and choose the path that leads to it. In this stand inheres a democratic, conception of knowing, deciding and interacting.

The third challenge concerns the relation between the ruler and the ruled. Abba Estefanos tells the Emperor that to rule means to govern with truth and justice, and that the law matters more than rulers do. It is quite striking to see the insistent manner with which the *Daqiqa Estefanos* refer to law (*heg*) as the basis of the relations between the powerful and the powerless.[291] The expression "*amlak,*" with its interesting double meaning of the "God of law" and the "law as God," encapsulates the *Daqiqa Estefanos* idea of the primacy of law: the law, like God, is above man. Such a conception of the primacy of law secretes the notion of the equality of all Ethiopians before the law, and thus, to use a modern expression, the notion of inalienable rights. In this way, it opens the door to the idea of individual autonomy, the right to know and to express freely one's convictions, as indeed the *Daqiqa Estefanos* did.

In addition, the *Daqiqa Estefanos* recognize women as having the same capacities as men. In a phrasing that is surprising in its modernity, the *Daqiqa Estefanos* acclaim Negesta Mariam, a nun, as "deeply learned, courageous and beautiful," and praise another nun for courageously standing up to and challenging a man.[292] The women followers of the movement were also targets of persecution, suggesting the rulers recognized the fatal consequences to their powers of the notion of "gender equality", as we would call it now, that the participation of women in the *Daqiqa Estefanos* movement signifies.

The words and actions of the *Daqiqa Estefanos* announce the possibility of a new framework of understanding and indeed of an alternative society. When a *Daqiqa Estefanos* is asked by his interlocutors, "With whom are you debating?" he answers the question in a way that situates the debate within society-at-large. He responds, "My debate is with Ethiopia."[293] This answer, suggesting Ethiopia as a forum for and a topic of debate, intimates that the focus of the challenges of the *Daqiqa Estefanos* is not the ruler as a person, but the justness of the relations between ruler and ruled. In this answer, then, there is already the germ of the idea of public debate or public reasoning as the way of dealing with issues. The surplus meanings of this answer have not only political implications but also educational ones in so far the notion of public reasoning presupposes a subject educated to be autonomous and to reflect critically.

What needs to be emphasized is that the *Daqiqa Estefanos* emerge from within traditional education. One wonders how a system decried as conservative, authoritarian and non-creative could produce such persons with ideas centuries ahead of their times, unless there are emancipatory ideas and values existing as surplus meanings within traditional education that make such radical outcomes possible. Though graduates of traditional education, the *Daqiqa Estefanos* distinguish themselves from the *dabtaras* whom they criticize for serving the interests of the established order.[294] They argue the *dabtaras* have only *temhirt* but lack *ewqet* or an understanding of the true order of things; for, if they had *ewqet*, the *dabtaras* would have refused, as *Aba Estefanos* and his disciples did, to be subservient to the Emperor.[295]

The *Daqiqa Estefanos* do not minimize the importance of *temhirt*. Rather, they see it as a stage one must traverse in order to reach the level of *ewqet*. Only through *mirmera* could one advance from *temhirt* to *ewqet*. In the framework of understanding that the teachings and the actions of the *Daqiqa Estefanos* secrete, *mirmera* is a practice that creates a critical space that allows independent reflection and right action, endows one with the discernment and courage to recognize injustice and to reject it publicly, even if the price incurred by such defiance is very high.[296] Indeed, one of the qualities Aba Estefanos is known for is "*mirmera.*"[297] It is interesting to note here that, unlike the *dabtara*, who reduce knowledge to an instrument for doing things, the *Daqiqa Estefanos* establish an inner link between knowledge and virtue. For them, *ewqet* is virtue, for *ewqet* is committed to *ewnet* (truth), implying that learning is a virtue if *ewqet* is its guide. Their refusal to prostrate themselves before the Emperor and their obstinacy to address him as a common man, their claim of the equality of rulers and ruled, their defence of the primacy of law, their recognition of "gender equality," and their call for "public reasoning," are all rooted in the critical consciousness gained through *ewqet*, but attained through *temhirt* alone. The latter limits itself to the acknowledgment of the given. The implication is that though *temhirt* is part of the process of education, it is not its final goal. *Ewqet* is the *telos* of education.

Moreover, the *Daqiqa Estefanos* promote *tibeb,* an understanding of and relation to nature that goes beyond the established understanding of *moya* (skills). *Moya* is an aggregate of time-honored skills one learns through repetition. Its practice reflects a static view of nature that limits innovation for fear of disturbing the existing balance between man and nature and provoking harm. There are certain similarities between *moya* and *temhirt:* both are oriented towards conserving rather than towards questioning and innovating; both are acquired in similar ways, through repetition; both are rooted in a conception of the world that prohibits venturing beyond the known. Thus *mirmera,* as an activity that questions the already known and ventures into territory unknown to existing knowledge, has little place in *temhirt* and *moya.* Even though *moya* expresses the desire to put nature's resources at the service of human purposes, the uncertainties of outcomes implied in venturing into unknown ways of dealing with nature leads to the repression of this desire. *Moya* is thus limited to being a set of skills whose executions and outcomes eliminate risk-taking by making every step and its outcomes predictable.

Tibeb, on the other hand, accepts *moya* but sublates it from within through the practice of *mirmera* (questioning and research), transforming *moya* into *tibeb* (*ewqet* about the workings of nature). It thus gives free reign to and actualizes *moya's* surplus meaning—the repressed desire to master the forces of nature. *Tibeb* is internally related to *ewqet* in that in both cases one finds the urge to go beyond the already known, to understand why things are the way they are and work the way they do. Both use *mirmera* to respond to this urge, making questioning, creativity and innovation central to one's acquisition of knowledge. In a passage that is instructive, Abune Ezra, a follower of the *Daqiqa Estefanos,* is described as "a man of *tibeb* filled with *ewqet,*" thus linking *ewqet* to *tibeb.*[298]

The principal reason why Abune Ezra is described in this manner is because he is a man who challenges the passive understanding of the world embedded in *temhirt* and *moya.* He demonstrates that men could overcome the limitations of *moya* through *mirmera,* and understand and use the forces of nature to serve human purposes. Abune Ezra conducts *mirmera* to construct windmills, water mills, animal driven mills, oil pressing machines, water-pumps, and so forth, and shows how the forces of nature could be made to respond to human purposes. Asked to demonstrate his *tibeb,* he builds a mill, which evokes "fright" and "wonder."[299] We see in these twin reactions to the results of *mirmera* and *tibeb* the ambiguous relation of traditional society to nature. The "fright" brings to the surface traditional society's alarm that the social order might crumble with the collapse of its static understanding of the world transmitted through traditional education; hence, the marginalization of *tibeb.* The "wonder," on the other hand, gives us a glimpse into the repressed surplus meaning of traditional education: the desire to use nature's forces to serve men's purposes.

The idea of the de-sacralization of nature that one discovers here is visible in Abune Ezra's rejection of the deep-rooted belief in miracles that characterizes Medieval Ethiopia. Questioned as to why he does not recognize miracles, he answers, miracles are necessary only to pagans.[300] It is significant to note, on the one hand, this new approach to nature emerges in 15th century Ethiopia from within the traditional education system, and, on the other, the *tibeb* challenge to *moya* disappears into the realm of surplus-history and has barely emerged from it even today. Indeed, there is something enigmatic in the eclipse of the ideas of the *Daqiqa Estefanos* from traditional education. It is as if their ideas were too traumatic for the Ethiopian social order.

Finally, the *Daqiqa Estefanos* bring to light two important ideas absent from the discourse on education in Ethiopia—imagination and utopia. The *Daqiqa Estefanos* profess ideas and beliefs that are out of joint with their times and are the fruits of their imagination and utopian visions. The violence with which the rulers reacted to their ideas suggests they provoked real fear, as if they expressed a historical possibility of an alternative order that, in exposing the inequity of the existing order spells also its demise. True, given the conditions of the era, the *Daqiqa Estefanos* were bound to fail. Still, one cannot help but acknowledge their ideas are the pulse of a better and different future beating in the heart of Medieval Ethiopia. The "non-synchronicity"[301] of their ideas with their times, indicate the presence of a powerful imagination and a utopian vision. It is their utopian ideas that exposed the gap between what is and what could be, and infuriated the Emperors. Despite their failures, what their actions illuminate is how imagination and utopian ideas are necessary to reveal the gap between the actual and the possible and the alternative futures therein.

The emergence of the *Daqiqa Estefanos* shows traditional education is not homogeneous: it produced the *dabtaras* and the *Daqiqa Estefanos*. Traditional education impedes and facilitates the birth of new ideas, utopian visions, and the exercise of the imagination. The ideas and practices of the *Daqiqa Estefanos* point to an education that cultivates reflective actions: actions for which one could give defensible reasons to justify them, and, as their practice illustrates, whatever the cost may be. They also suggest an education that creates a certain distance between oneself and one's actions, one's society and its dominant beliefs, in order to open up a critical space for knowledge and reflection.[302] Their critiques of the *dabtara,* their rejection of non-justified authority, their skepticism about miracles, point to an understanding of knowledge as an outcome of human questioning, creativity and effort, and, thus, of learning as a process of *mirmera.* Their conceptions of equality and public reasoning suggest an understanding of education as a non-authoritarian process and as an acquisition of a critical spirit. In all the ideas and actions of the *Daqiqa Estefanos*, one sees the gestation of a novel understanding of education, which could help us reflect, in a way that is rooted in our history, on the kind of critical Ethiopian theory of education that is possible.

Moreover, the utopian dimension of the teachings of the *Daqiqa Estefanos* offers an important idea for reflecting on education. If education is to escape asphyxiation from society's dominant ideas and values, it needs to have a utopian dimension that cultivates the imagination and creates the intellectual space necessary for teachers and students to step back from the given so as to be able to see critically the potentialities that lurk in the present. In other words, utopian thinking is indispensable for developing a critical Ethiopian theory of education. What is instructive about the *Daqiqa Estefanos* is that they were the subjects of Medieval Ethiopia who were able to grasp the utopian emancipatory meanings that lurked in the interstices of their historical period. Here lies an important lesson: it is possible to find within Ethiopia's traditional education surplus meanings that orient our attention to the importance of imagination and utopian ideas in education. Retrieving these surplus meanings contributes to the development of a critical Ethiopian theory of education, providing ways of Ethiopianizing modern education, which is now rooted in the utopian imagination of the West rather than in ours.

However, the claim we need a utopian dimension to develop a critical Ethiopian theory of education raises the question of the meaning of utopia. Given the absence of explicit utopian thinking in our history of education, I will first articulate what utopian thinking could mean in the Ethiopian context, and indicate its relevance to our discussion. To do so, I will appropriate a term, *tezeta,* from Ethiopian traditional music.[303] The traditional understanding of *tezeta* is nostalgia. What I want to excavate from this traditional understanding is its surplus meaning as it relates to the idea of utopia. *Tezeta* has sufficient depth and multiple dimensions to allow us to elicit from it a concept of a historically rooted utopia, or a "concrete utopia" in the sense of Bloch.[304] Such a concept of utopia could provide us with resources for developing a critical Ethiopian theory of education.

Concrete Utopia and the Tezeta of the Future

The absence of utopian thinking in Ethiopian education is intriguing. Yet, as noted earlier, since at least Queen Gudit (10th century), we see periodically the eruptions of events that overflow the conditions out of which they emerge and suggest the presence of utopian ideas. In all these cases, one has to ask: From where comes the hope that drives Ethiopians to desire something is absent, often at tremendous risks to their lives? To raise this question is to recognize that "somewhere" in our history there are powerful utopian yearnings that imperceptibly force us to project ourselves beyond what we experience and what we are at a given historical moment. This "somewhere," where Ethiopian utopian visions dwell, is surplus-history.

Utopia, commonly identified with Thomas Moore's 1516 book with the same title, describes a perfect society. Such a society is an abstract construction, justly described as daydreaming. This kind of utopia is detached from historical processes and possibilities and is of little use for developing a critical Ethiopian theory of education. There is, however, another kind of utopia, one rooted in the real possibilities present in history. This is the utopia that Ernst Bloch calls "concrete utopia," anchored in the historically articulated aspirations of men and women. Bloch convincingly argues we should make a distinction between "abstract utopia"—the futile project of drawing detailed blueprints of the future—and "concrete utopia," which he identifies with "the historical content of hope."[305] Concrete utopia "draws its images from What Has Been which is not obsolete, in so far as they are capable of future… and it makes them suitable for the expression of What Has Still Not Yet Been."[306] Concrete utopia is therefore the "real possible" inhabiting the present as the "Not-Yet-Become."[307] It is a historically rooted anticipation of an objectively possible future. It expresses what Bloch calls *docta spes* or "educated hope" which he defines as "the concretely and utopianly comprehended correlate in real possibility" that expresses "concrete ideals" that are "mediated in terms of history and tendency."[308] From the perspective of this paper, surplus-history is the abode of "concrete utopia" and the "educated hope" it generates.

The Amharic term *minab* corresponds to abstract utopia; it describes wishful thinking and daydreaming. Though there is no specific Amharic word that refers to concrete utopia, I will borrow, as indicated earlier, a term from Ethiopian traditional music—*tezeta*—and reinterpret it to refer to "concrete utopia." One may be surprised that I am referring to a traditional musical motif (*qegnit*) to discuss the possibility of a critical Ethiopian theory of education. As discussed earlier, the divorce of our culture from our history has occluded our culture's emancipatory dimension—its surplus-history. When we recover our music as an integral part of our history, we rediscover in it the voice of the unfulfilled hopes of the past, the sufferings of the present, and the promise of the possible bright future. Ethiopian traditional music is one of those areas of our culture where the peasants and the dispossessed express themselves fully, giving voice to the sorrows of life and anticipating joyfully a life without sorrows. It is the site where the aspirations inscribed in surplus-history erupt metonymically, for the significance of Ethiopian traditional music goes deeper than the surface meanings of its lyrics: it arises from its non-representational components and its performance. One cannot witness a *zefen* (a traditional song) accompanied with *eskesta* (traditional Amharic shoulder-based dancing) and not see the radical discontinuity between the bareness of the life of the singers and the joy that exudes from their performance.[309] For the poor, the majority in Ethiopia, music is a sanctuary of hope, a reprieve from the crushing effects of poverty and tyranny, and a promise of a better future. Ethiopian popular music is both a social mirror and prophetic.[310] Bloch expresses this idea in a way that brings out the emancipatory surplus meanings of music rooted in one's history. Music has "the quality of incorporating the numerous sufferings, the wishes and the spots of light of the oppressed class...It is the surplus of hope-material."[311] The surplus meanings of traditional Ethiopian music announce the victory of hope over poverty and oppression, and anticipate a future liberated from the shackles of the present.

I single out *tezeta* from within traditional music because it is probably the most popular musical "*qegnit*" in Ethiopian history.[312] It is "the real musical soul of the Ethiopians...full of symbolism and allegory" and enthralls them—irrespective of class, gender, religion, age, and ethnic differences.[313] It signifies the bittersweet nostalgia of aborted hopes, audibly paints the present as exile into desolation, and evokes "an active memory," or a *tezeta,* that resides in the past, inflects the present, and projects itself into the future. It is a militant promise embedded in a restless memory that urges one to live forward.[314] It touches the "something that is missing" but that is ardently desired, has deep roots in our lives, and beckons from the future.

Tezeta is the song of suffering and hope, intertwining the past, the present, and the future. It has thus a tri-dimensional temporality. Experientially, it refers to real events that happened, to the passions they ignited, to the desire they left unquenched; but it affirms simultaneously that the happiness experienced fleetingly is both a promise of better things to come and an invitation to make it a reality. It establishes a dialectical relation between the past, the present and the future that pulls forward and embodies "a militant memory" that professes that the obstacles of the present could be overcome and the aborted hopes of the past redeemed. Recovered as a historical concept, *tezeta* has the temporal complexity—the dialectical relations it weaves between the past, the present and the future—and the experiential density and intensity to capture the tri-dimensional temporality of "concrete utopia" and its "educated hope." To express this connection between education and concrete utopia and its content of "educated hope," I will call it "educated *tezeta.*"

Educated *tezeta* expresses the sufferings and hopes of the "we" of surplus-history: the peasantry, the unemployed, the poor, the marginalized, the workers, the excluded, and the oppressed. It expresses the "historical content of hope," the critical voice of the militant desire for emancipation that manifests itself in Ethiopian history as peasant rebellions, regional uprisings, *shiftanet*, workers' strikes, and student movements, and even as religious movements, as we have seen in the case of the *Daqiqa Estefanos.* Educated *tezeta* captures that which in the past is not obsolete and is alive in the present. It casts itself forward and throws back from the possible future a revealing light on the inhumanity of the present. It thus reconstitutes what look like disparate acts of resistance and rebellions scattered over the Ethiopian historical landscape as internally connected quests for emancipation that transcend ethnic, religious, gender and regional differences.

Being historically rooted, educated *tezeta* articulates a concrete and not an abstract utopia. This concrete utopia points to the future society more in terms of what it is not— a society without oppression and poverty, without ignorance and exploitation, without inequality, injustice and unnecessary sufferings—rather than in terms of a blueprint of what it should be. The reason is historical. We Ethiopians know concretely what we have suffered from and against what we have struggled, but our knowledge of their opposites—freedom, democracy, prosperity, justice, knowledge, equality—are abstract in that they are still part of our unfulfilled aspirations. We have not yet given them form and content that speaks of us and to us in our own voice. From the perspective of educated *tezeta,* the future is ours to build; it is an open future, albeit rooted in our history. Educated *tezeta* is a call for imagining a new society that embodies emancipation and that defeats not only the inherited but also the new sources of oppression, inequalities and injustices. Education is the primary medium of educated *tezeta.*

To the extent that modern education is deaf to educated *tezeta,* it will continue to fabricate Ethiopians trapped in an egregious misunderstanding of themselves and their society, unaware of the real possibilities of transformation gestating within surplus-history. Though, children are supposed to be "educated, not for the present, but for a possibly improved condition of man in the future,"[315] modern education in Ethiopia is surprisingly dystopian. It is a prisoner of an inauthentic conception of the future, generated partly by aid agencies and partly by education experts, that is at best an extrapolation from and at worst an imitation of the West. Modern education, deaf to educated *tezeta,* is all *Sam* and no *Worq.* It generates and accentuates the erosion of our historical consciousness, cultural confidence, social hope, imagination and utopian energies, rendering us incapable of conceptualizing, understanding and resolving our problems through our own critical reflections on our history and life-conditions. This erosion has a double effect. First, every time Ethiopians try to overthrow tyranny, they recreate it, as one could see from the deadly routine of repetition compulsion of 'oppressive regime-revolt-oppressive regime' in which Ethiopia has been trapped since 1974. Second, this erosion is in part responsible for the flight of educated Ethiopians from the problems of their country, resulting in a quadruple brain drain—from rural to urban areas, from Ethiopia to the West, from critical self-reflection to dehydrated knowledge, and from imagination to imitation. Thus, modern education that is deaf to educated *tezeta* deprives us of the intellectual and affective resources we need to create a society that redeems our past sufferings.

Educated Tezeta and the Limits of the Current Proposals

The effort to extricate modern Ethiopian education from its crisis cannot take place in a vacuum. It has to take into account the critiques already made of the present system and reflect through them in order to keep in sight the various dimensions of the crisis.

The World Bank's proposals for reform embrace the notion of a linear development that forecloses the future as a fixed agenda, not of our own choosing. Since this linear development is situated within the framework of ends as currently defined by the international economic and political order, education in this framework amounts to adapting ourselves to the current international division of labour and to functioning at the lowest possible layer of the new globalized order, providing cheap labour, if and when needed. This proposal instrumentalizes education and reduces it to a survival kit for subsisting in the hostile world of neo-liberalism. This is a recipe for permanent dependency and poverty. The instrumentalist conception of education the World Bank espouses may "cure" the symptoms of the current dysfunctional system without however overcoming the source of its disfunctionality: the reduction of modern education to *temhirt* and *moya* in the pursuit of "development." As the history of modern Ethiopia attests, the instrumentalist conception traps education in a social logic that integrates it as an element of the system-maintenance of repressive regimes. An instrumentalist conception of education may provide the skills and knowledge necessary for what one may call 'modernization for the poor. However, it will not make available the kind of knowledge that *ewqet* and *tibeb* require—knowledge will give Ethiopians the intellectual and moral sovereignty that enables them to construct the emancipated society their educated *tezeta* foreshadows.

Tekeste's and Elleni's arguments in favor of non-formal education underestimate the internal contradictions within traditional education. It may be true, modern education has created an educated class submerged in a historical-cultural amnesia, which accounts largely for the failure of modern education to meet the aspirations of Ethiopians.[316] But reintroducing traditional values and falling back on informal education without eliciting why, in the first place, these failed to bring about an emancipatory transformation is a cure worse than the disease. Traditional education transmits mainly the values of the dominant social forces and legitimates the reproduction of poverty and inequalities, exemplified by its almost total exclusion of women from educational institutions. It reduces education to instruction, literacy to naïve reading, and knowledge to *moya* and *temhirt,* all in the service of the established order. True, there are, within traditional education, surplus meanings—*ewqet, tibeb, mirmera*—that undermine the hegemonic values, goals and methods of traditional education. However, unless we reflectively enucleate and liberate these subjugated meanings from the crushing weight of hegemonic traditional education, and critically appropriate them to overcome the internal and external adversities we face now and are likely to face in the future, non-formal and village education will reinforce and perpetuate the conservative and authoritarian strands of Ethiopian education and society. From this perspective, one must question Tekeste's explicit call for "the establishment of two separate education sectors, i.e. one sector for formal education and the other for non-formal education."[317] Tekeste's proposal, curiously reminiscent of the Platonic idea of qualitatively different education for the different social classes, goes counter to the democratic convictions that motivate his proposal. It is of interest to note, the idea that education should be tailored to the social destination of the individual is a view that has a long, anti-democratic history.[318] This dualist approach reinforces the current logic of oppression: it forecloses the recognition of emancipation as a commonly shared objective of the education of both rural and urban Ethiopians and intensifies the present urban-rural relations of domination.

The pragmatist approach, premised on the idea that if it works it is right, combines elements of the World Bank approach with elements of the non-formal and culturalist approaches. It thus concentrates within itself the shortcomings of both. Though Dewey links pragmatism and democracy, the link he makes presupposes the background meanings of a society already committed to the democratic way of life.[319] Where these background conditions do not exist, as is the case in Ethiopia, what we need is not something that works within the existing framework of oppression, but something that changes this framework itself. In the current Ethiopian context of ethnic politics, pragmatism could divert education from its task of emancipation, sow the seeds of political cynicism and moral nihilism, and distort education into learning how to survive in a corrupt society.

Finally, it is important to look closely at the kind of educated Ethiopians the application of the above proposals will produce. Given the ahistorical and instrumentalist conception of education that undergird the above proposals, the kind of educated persons their implementation produces will not differ from the ones produced now. That is, in the absence of the guidance of educated *tezeta,* the educational system will continue to produce Ethiopians trapped in a cognitive dysfunction that renders invisible the future-oriented emancipatory possibilities that throb in the interstices of the Ethiopian past and present. Let me examine this from the angle of the *mehur* and the *dabtara.*

Currently, the term *mehur* designates the modern Ethiopian intellectual, and I will use it here as an "ideal-type." In certain respects, the *mehur* is the modern *dabtara.* However, whereas the *dabtara* is versed in the knowledge and beliefs of traditional Ethiopia, the *mehur,* more often than not, knows more about the knowledge and beliefs of the West than of Ethiopia. This seems inevitable, for the young who go to school in contemporary Ethiopia are plunged into an education that gives scant place to Ethiopian social practices and history and are more likely to be acquainted with the values and practices of the West than with educated *tezeta.*[320] As a result, to be educated is to be captured by a process that considers knowledge as exocentric *temhirt* and establishes an external relationship to one's own society and to oneself. It directs the arrow of understanding from Western knowledge to Ethiopian realities and conceives change (reform, revolution) as an imitation of the historically antecedent reforms and revolutions of others. Education as the pursuit of *ewqet,* as an understanding that creates knowledge capable of grasping and transforming Ethiopia's unique circumstances from within, disappears and slides into surplus-history. Even when the *mehur* adopts a "radical" stand, he acquires it as an exocentric *temhirt,* as a patient who receives medication. A telling example is the introduction of "socialism" in Ethiopia "as an imitation of the Soviet or Chinese model of socialism."[321] This kind of exocentric *temhirt* is the paradigm for every level of education in contemporary Ethiopia. The outcome is historical amnesia, self-opacity, and inauthenticity—in a double sense: a distorted understanding of oneself, and of Ethiopian society. Here lies then the radical difference between the *mehur* and the *dabtara.* Since the *dabtara's* understanding of himself and of his society is rooted in internally developed schemes of interpretation of social practices, he suffers less from self-opacity than his modern counterpart. The *mehur,* on the other hand, is the product of a homeless education that produces dehydrated knowledge, unirrigated by the history, imagination and utopian visions of Ethiopians. Hence, more often than not, the *mehur* suffers a loss of cultural orientation that inhibits his capacity to produce knowledge that grasps Ethiopians morally, affectively and intellectually and inspires them to overcome the present destitution. That Alaqa Tayye's description of Ethiopia as a "broken car" and as "the citadel of bloodshed, injustice, evil and shame,"[322] made at the beginning of the twentieth century, still resonates true attests to the failure of a century of modern education. No wonder, then, that the *mehurs* became the architects of oppression: their ideas and actions gave birth to political monstrosities such as the Derg's "socialism" and the EPRDF's "ethnic politics."

Modern Ethiopian education is blind to the crucial point educated *tezeta* makes: that the question of education in Ethiopia is not only a question of means, but it is also, and more importantly, a question of ends. We cannot derive the end of education from the abstract utopia of the kind involved in considering the Western paradigm of our future, nor could we conceive the end of education in terms of solving "underdevelopment." The former crushes us under the deadweight of 'modernization for the poor' and renders us impotent to master our future; the latter is no better than shining an old shoe: it may look new, but it is still an old shoe, varnished with Western paint. Bloch's claim that "true genesis is not at the beginning but at the end" is pertinent to our case here.[323] Education is the site of the struggle for the future, and if educated *tezeta's* anticipated society of freedom, prosperity and justice is not internal to the educational system as its end, what we produce is homeless education: a propitious condition for tyranny and poverty. If it is the case that the pathologies of a practice reveal its truth, then modern Ethiopian pathologies—the Derg and ethnic politics—reveal the bankruptcy of modern education.[324] To avoid these pathologies, the strengths of Ethiopia and not so-called "underdevelopment" must be the premise of education.

Against Education for Underdevelopment

What is striking about Western education in Ethiopia is its failure to contribute effectively to the creation of a free, just, and prosperous society. Why is Western education, which has impressively contributed to the positive transformation of its originating societies, the purveyor of alienation, poverty and tyranny in Ethiopia?

I would like to emphasize I am not arguing from the perspective of cultural relativism and ethno-centrism and claiming Western knowledge has no relevance to Ethiopian issues. The Indian poet Rabindranath Tagore is right when he declares, "Whatever we understand and enjoy in human products instantly become ours, wherever they might have their origins... Let me feel with unalloyed gladness that all the great glories of man are mine."[325] The crucial terms here are "understand and enjoy." To "understand and enjoy" knowledge created independently of our agency is impossible if we receive knowledge as a patient receives medication. Knowledge is not consumption or imitation. To "understand and enjoy" the knowledge we received from Western education requires we be active agents who consider this knowledge as a raw material to be inseminated with our educated *tezeta*, so that we will Ethiopianize it, and thus "understand and enjoy" it. In our situation, it may be the case that we have sometimes no choice "but to borrow knowledge"; but why must we borrow unreflectively?

There is no doubt that the transformation of Ethiopia requires more than what traditional education has to offer. But it also requires more than what the present modern education provides. In terms of Ethiopia's present conditions, both are in fact abstract educational systems, detached from our defeated hopes and emancipatory interests, and isolated from each other: we have confined the first to the past and prevented it to catch up with the present; and the second is rooted in the West and is not yet inseminated with our educated *tezeta*. Ethiopia needs "context-transcending knowledge" capable of bridging the gulf between these two solitudes—traditional and modern education. Without an education that cultivates such a context-transcending knowledge, we will be deprived of the understanding, cultural confidence and social hope necessary for climbing out from the present pit of destitution. But context-transcending knowledge cannot emerge from a stand that completely objectifies our traditions and confines them to the past; it emerges only from a modern education that connects to our traditions and is ensouled by the educated *tezeta* they harbour. Otherwise, we are stuck with homeless education, and as we can see now from its fruits, violence and failures are its inevitable outcomes, because one cannot successfully promote political and economic visions that have no roots in the history of a people. Inevitably, this failure leads to violence as a response to the resistance of Ethiopian society to being changed from without.

Western education embodies within itself the contradictions of the history within which it developed. Its organization, means, and goals have been subject to debates, controversies, reforms, innovations and revolutions for centuries.[326] In the course of its history, Western education has been an accomplice of diverse policies: it has produced knowledge to support authoritarianism or to subvert it; to strengthen class domination or to weaken it; to justify peace or to undermine it; to justify colonialism, slavery and sexism, or to thwart them. When we adopt Western education, we adopt a variant of it which is dominant in a particular historical period of the West and which mainly serves its dominant interests. As such, there is no guarantee that the education system we borrow from the West serves also our educated *tezeta*. Since how we understand ourselves delineates the kind of possibilities open to us, we cannot blindly embrace imported knowledge without misunderstanding ourselves and thwarting these possibilities.

On the other hand, given our historical situation, we are bound to interact with and borrow from the West. The age of isolation is gone forever. The dilemma here is the Ethiopian educational system cannot simply echo the education of the West without falling into a linear conception of "development" that will leave us forever dependent on and trotting behind the West-as-history. Nor could our educational system be an arbitrary amalgam of Western and our traditional elements, for such eclecticism will create confusion and disorientation instead of enriching the semantic contents of Ethiopian culture. To harness to our purposes our borrowings from the West, we need a common ground shared by Ethiopia and the West, where we could meet each other on an equal footing as historical societies, each engaged in the quest for expressing its full potential. We need such a common and shared ground so what we borrow from the West could be Ethiopianized. The issue that confronts us then is to discover a ground that could mediate our inevitable borrowing of knowledge.

The relevant common ground between the West and us is the quest for emancipation.[327] Westerners have lived through oppression and adversities and have been able to eliminate to a certain extent the sources of overt oppression and widespread poverty. We Ethiopians have also experienced and still experience tyranny and poverty, and we have tried to free ourselves from them, even if our efforts have failed and our aborted hopes have slid into surplus-history. However, through our failed struggles and aborted hopes, we have caught glimpses of the values and ideas necessary for our human flourishing. Though we tend to forget it, we Ethiopians have come upon the modern ideas of equality, justice, freedom, *ewqet, tibeb* and *mirmera*, at least as early as the *Daqiqa Estefanos*. True, we have failed to institutionalize these ideas; but they are already present in our surplus-history and are part of our educated *tezeta*. Historically then, the quest for emancipation is the shared common experiential ground the West and we share. For us, then, the mediating ground is our educated *tezeta*. Since educated *tezeta* expresses our historically founded quest for emancipation, it can link up with the experiences of the West in terms of emancipatory interests, and mediate borrowed knowledge reflectively through this common ground. Such mediation implies considering borrowed knowledge as 'raw material' that must be reworked through our educated *tezeta* so we will have at our disposal modern knowledge that espouses Ethiopian aspirations, needs and interests.

Modern Ethiopian education is not based on such mediation. On the contrary, it is rooted in the problematic of Ethiopia as an "underdeveloped" society. International institutions, Western governments, aid agencies, educational consultants, and Ethiopian governments have made modernization the problematic of educational thinking and reform. Such an approach reduces Ethiopia to her weaknesses and occludes her strengths.[328] The modernization problematic articulates an instrumentalist conception of knowledge that reduces the Ethiopian situation to an aggregate of lacks called "underdevelopment" that modern knowledge is assumed to resolve. But knowledge and truth are not identical.[329] That is, resolving the problems of underdevelopment is not necessarily meeting the truth that our educated *tezeta* expresses: freedom, prosperity, and social justice as the stuff of our unrealized dreams, present aspirations and anticipated future. Educated *tezeta* demands social practices express this truth. Development or modernization, as practiced now, is not the fruit of our reflectively exercised agency; it is something that happens to us. Its *raison d'être* is repairing the defects—dubbed underdevelopment—of the present reality with imported knowledge-kits. Such an approach, makes underdevelopment—our weakness—the framework of our self-interpretation and the interpretation of our future. Indeed, the problems of "underdevelopment" could be solved and Ethiopia's survival as a subaltern in the modern world—the best we could hope for within the modernization problematic—ensured without overcoming social injustice and tyranny, thus betraying the truth of our educated *tezeta*. True, we have no choice but to modernize; but why must we modernize unreflectively?

Modern education that makes "underdevelopment" the condition of intelligibility of the Ethiopian situation and of ourselves as Ethiopians prevents us from reflecting critically on our history and cultures, of analysing our needs and imagining our future, of exploring our aspirations and utopian dreams. It drives us into abandoning to others the intellectual, moral, and affective resources we need to interrogate, understand, judge and transform ourselves. Unlike educated *tezeta,* that sees education as a condition of possibility for becoming self-affirming Ethiopians and masters of our destiny, modern education framed within the problematic of underdevelopment reduces Ethiopians to recipients of 'knowledge welfare' from the West, with deleterious effects comparable to those that international social welfare, euphemistically called foreign aid, has on its recipients. Since the opening of Menelik II School in 1908, modern education has been performing the euthanasia of our critical thinking, of our imagination and of our utopian visions, thereby perpetuating our current destitution. As a result, modern education has become an exocentric practice that forecloses our possibilities rather than a possibility-disclosing practice we ourselves bring into existence. If the current understanding and practice of "development" continues, one could legitimately ask: can Ethiopia survive "development?" To counter the dangers of "development," educational theory inspired by educated *tezeta* cannot but be a sustained critique of educational practices whose visions are blinkered and whose goals are shrunk by the problematic of underdevelopment.

Some Elements of a Critical Theory of Education

One could suggest, based on the arguments developed in this paper, the following general ideas for developing a critical Ethiopian theory of education.

First, from the perspective of educated *tezeta*, education is not a social service, a mere instrument for solving underdevelopment, or a kit of survival tools. Education is one of the most important ways for Ethiopia to experience herself as a strong, capable society with a historically generated objective—the free, prosperous and just society prefigured in educated *tezeta*—she should accomplish. Education is a social practice devoted to the exploration, evaluation and implementation of this objective and the means for reaching it. We could create an educational system that is up to this task only if *ewqet, tibeb* and *mirmera* rather than *temhirt* and *moya* become the regulative principles of education and supplant the present reduction of education to instruction, of literacy to naive reading and writing, of knowledge to the handmaiden of underdevelopment.

Second, what is characteristic of traditional education is that it is a collective enterprise related to human needs, both material and spiritual, expressed in the belief, prevalent in traditional Ethiopia, in learned magic, practiced by the *dabtara*, and in the power of words (*asmat, ketab*). In addition, the traditional student not only studies but also participates in the activities of his community. Education and knowledge are social practices traditional Ethiopians experience as ways of acting in their lifeworld, of overcoming internal and external adversities. The surplus meaning of this experience is the appropriation of knowledge for changing the world. The recovery of this surplus meaning could usher in, under the guidance of educated *tezeta*, a dialectic between knowledge and social practices that facilitates the concretization of the aspirations for freedom, prosperity and justice. Moreover, as we have seen above in our discussion of the *Daqiqa Estefanos*, one of the surplus meanings of traditional education is that learning is a virtue and to be educated is to acquire a manner of being in the community that contributes to social and personal emancipation. Reducing education to an instrument for solving "underdevelopment," as is currently the case, is to lose this emancipatory dimension. Within traditional education lies therefore a suppressed emancipatory dialectic of knowledge and practice that needs to be retrieved, examined and developed.

Third, traditional education shows in the figure of the *dabtara* the possibility of creating intellectuals who are historically rooted. This point is crucial for giving flesh to educated *tezeta*. Educated *tezeta* is not spontaneous consciousness and has no truck with populism and ethnicism, two common modes of spontaneous consciousness. Enucleating educated *tezeta* from our surplus-history is a hermeneutical activity that requires a "conscious element" or, in Gramscian terms, "organic intellectuals." Here, we meet one of the most crucial questions of contemporary Ethiopia—the nature of the education that creates the educated class—a question whose importance cannot be overstated in light of the destructive imported ideologies the educated class has inflicted on Ethiopians since the 1960's. The existence of an educated class is an indispensable condition for articulating our aspirations for a free, just and prosperous society in a way that is rooted in our historical conditions. We can here gain from the experience of the *Daqiqa Estefanos*. Their very existence shows traditional education has surplus meanings that make possible the emergence of "organic intellectuals." What makes such an outcome possible is the mediation of education through the history and background meanings of the Ethiopian lifeworld, which traditional education accomplishes admirably. Traditional education, which the hegemonic order used to create its own organic intellectuals—the *dabtaras*, generates surplus meanings that suggest how we can ensure the birth of modern Ethiopian "organic intellectuals" committed to emancipation. As noted earlier, Ethiopian traditional education draws its strength from the way it establishes deep connections with the background density of the students' lifeworld. Modern education that establishes similar deep connections with the background meanings of the Ethiopian lifeworld, could successfully Ethiopianize borrowed educational systems and knowledge, and create the appropriate conditions for the emergence of modern "organic intellectuals" committed to advancing the alternative future that informs educated *tezeta*.

Fourth, to meet the goals of educated *tezeta*, one must make a distinction between literacy as *temhirt* and literacy as *ewqet,* right from the start. The former confines literacy to the ability to read and write, whereas the latter transforms reading and writing into a process of *mirmera* that reveals to learners new horizons that pull them forward and enable them to self-consciously articulate and pursue their aspirations for a world without oppression and poverty. Literacy reduced to *temhirt* limits the learner to reading existing society as an immutable natural order, making literacy an instrument of mystification and domination in the service of the hegemonic power. One could see such an instrumentalization in the Derg's and the EPRDF's efforts to use literacy as a transmission belt of their "socialist" and "ethnic" propaganda, respectively. Such instrumentalization of literacy is incompatible with educated *tezeta*. Literacy must be subject to the regulative principles of *ewqet* and *mirmera* in order to liberate the surplus meanings of the "weapons of the poor" and of their daily "acts of resistance" and make them available as forces of social and personal emancipation.

Fifth, traditional education considers memorization as an achievement. The surplus meaning of memorization is, as suggested earlier, inwardness in that it enables students to connect themselves deeply to their lifeworld and allows them to gain a certain clarity about themselves and their communities. This clarity produces the sense of individuality for which Ethiopians are well known and that some misread as "egoism" and "weakness of attachment to symbols of local community."[330] Such clarity liberates the imagination and critical reflection, essential for mobilizing the utopian energies of Ethiopians, something necessary for overcoming the present destitution. The cultivation of inwardness, in the dual sense of exercising one's imagination and of retrieving through self-conscious critical reflection the emancipatory meanings embedded in educated *tezeta*, is antithetical to the current catastrophic treatment of students as a *tabula rasa*. Inwardness in this sense is a powerful defence against historical-cultural amnesia that the problematic of "underdevelopment" secretes; it liberates us from the cynicism and moral vacuum that exocentric *temhirt* breeds. To the extent that we lack inwardness, our relation to modernization will be external and imitative. Inwardness grasps modernization, not as something to be imitated but as something to be conquered from within. Only then will our modernization be authentic, because it will no longer be external to us, nor would we be external to it. We would then have a modernization as Ethiopian as the tradition through which we would have conquered modernization by mobilizing our educated *tezeta*. The inwardness that connected us to our tradition so deeply has the potential to connect us as deeply to modernization.

Sixth, traditional education—be it village, church, mosque, or *Gada* based—plays a crucial role in the identity formation of youth with the perspective of integrating them into the established order. The strength of traditional education lies in its capacity to "enable the student to absorb the culture and to be absorbed into it." As we saw earlier in our discussion of British, American, French, Japanese educational practices, to name a few, have mastered this capacity, whereas modern education in Ethiopia has miserably failed to do so. Educated *tezeta* retrieves the surplus meaning of identity formation in traditional education. However, unlike both traditional and modern Ethiopian education, educated *tezeta* draws our attention to the importance of relating emancipation to education and identity formation. To ensure education fosters an identity formation that integrates emancipation, educated *tezeta* offers the universal aspirations of the "we" of surplus-history as a guide. As discussed earlier, this "we" cuts across ethnic, religious, gender, and regional differences, and its goal is emancipation from the oppressive rule of the hegemonic "we," be it national or ethnic. Education guided by the "we" of surplus-history establishes universality—the recognition of the dignity of every Ethiopian—rather than a prescriptive criterion as the mediator of the identity formation of youth. Such an education is open to the complexity of Ethiopian history. From the perspective of the "we" of surplus-history, nationalism and ethnicism are the recto and verso of the identity formation secreted by imported educational practices. Not being rooted in educated *tezeta,* modern education treats students as a *tabula rasa* and leaves them at the mercy of spontaneous consciousness, i.e., nationalism, populism and ethnicism.

The issue of the relation between identity formation, education and emancipation has some crucial ramifications for a critical Ethiopian theory of education. If we reflect on Ethiopia in terms of its own history rather than in terms of the European theory of nation, and let our arrow of self-understanding travel from our history to theory rather than from the European theory of nation to Ethiopian history, as modern Ethiopian education does, we discover the historical uniqueness of Ethiopia. As discussed earlier, the resistance to the hegemonic "we," be it national or ethnic, is an affirmation of the "we" of surplus-history as the agent of emancipation and not an expression of ethnic, regional, or religious particularities. Historically, then, the conjugation of the activities of the hegemonic "we" and of the resistance of the "we" of surplus-history has given rise to an Ethiopia that is neither a mono-nation nor a multi-nation, but a "composite nation," with complex identities.[331] The question then is: what kind of education advances the articulation of identity formation and emancipation in a composite nation?

The process that formed Ethiopia as a composite nation is characterized by its tendency towards a double openness, manifested in the creation of intra-ethnic regions (Wallo, Shoa, Harar, Sidamo, Wallaga, and so forth) and in the historical emergence of an intra-ethnic Ethiopia. These intra-ethnic regions exemplify the openness of ethnicities to other ethnicities leading to the emergence of commonly shared territories and social practices, giving rise to a composite nation, Ethiopia, which, in turn, is characterized by an openness created by the transformations brought about by the interacting ethnicities. Educated *tezeta* recovers this double openness—the openness of ethnicities and the openness of Ethiopia—as a work-in-progress, making it our historically generated horizon to which we are pulled forward. That is, schooling premised on educated *tezeta* reflects this double openness in projecting education as a process of universalization— the passage from primary to secondary identification—and the maturation of students into adults who recognize themselves as historical subjects with common and shared universal objectives. The transition from primary to secondary identification is neither the erasure of ethnicity nor the homogenization of Ethiopia. From the perspective of educated *tezeta*, education does not seek a unity that leaves no space for diversity. Rather, it sees in the reciprocal openness of ethnicities and of Ethiopia a dialectic that enriches social practices at all levels, making the full development of Ethiopia the condition for the full development of each ethnicity, and the full development of each ethnicity the condition for the full development of Ethiopia. However, at least two conditions must be met to have an educational system capable of articulating this double openness of our history: every Ethiopian child must learn more than one Ethiopian language; and there must be a national language. There are two emancipation-oriented reasons for this: one pedagogical, the other historical.

Pedagogically, the existing evidence shows "instruction in the mother tongue is beneficial to language competencies in the first language, achievement in other subject areas, and second language learning."[332] Instruction in the mother tongue is then a prerequisite for a successful pursuit of the aspirations that educated *tezeta* projects. But this is not the end of the story, for the knowledge of more than one Ethiopian language is also a process that has deep historical roots, reflecting the emergence of Ethiopia as a composite nation. However, the mastery of more than one Ethiopian language by every Ethiopian is a task that is yet unfinished. From the perspective of educated *tezeta,* the mastery of more than one language is imperative, because it creates at least one condition that allows each student to discover that the others (in terms of region, ethnicity, or culture) are historically constitutive elements of his/her self-understanding. The awareness that every Ethiopian has thus a historically formed complex identity that includes the others as a necessary condition for self-understanding makes it possible to recognize the oppression, exploitation or suffering of one as an injustice that weighs on all Ethiopians. The forward-pulling emancipation that animates educated *tezeta* will thus find a fertile ground for fulfillment in an education premised on the recognition that overthrowing the inequities of the past and of the present and creating a free, just and prosperous Ethiopia is a responsibility shared by all.

However, the above condition—mastering at least one Ethiopian language in addition to one's mother tongue—is incomplete without the existence of a national language as an expression of Ethiopia's historical uniqueness as a composite nation. The existence of a national language does not preclude the development of other languages. On the contrary, it ensures the vitality of the double openness of our history, for it preempts the erection of linguistic barriers in the name of ethnic identity and its false premises of ethnic purity. A national language confirms the trajectory from primary to secondary identification already inscribed in Ethiopian history and enriches the density and intensity of dialogue among all Ethiopians on all issues.

To conclude, the challenge for a critical Ethiopian theory of education is to retrieve the educated *tezeta* that inhabits our history. Educated *tezeta* could then ensoul modern education, repatriate it from its present exile in exocentric *temhirt,* and rescue it from continuing to be the purveyor of poverty and tyranny. Only then could modern education be at a home in Ethiopia and give life to the aspirations of Ethiopians for freedom, prosperity and justice. Only then could we achieve self-intelligibility as Ethiopians; otherwise, we will indefinitely suffer "development" as something that happens to us, making us unintelligible to ourselves. Homeless education has made us aliens to our past and future and configured our history as a dead end. It has degraded our aspirations for freedom, prosperity and justice to a modernization-for-the-poor that cynically labels tyranny as democracy, poverty as development, and a survival kit that makes us subalterns in the neo-liberal world as knowledge. It has made Ethiopians sick of Ethiopia and engendered the illusion that ethnic politics (the 1994 Ethiopian Constitution) and foreign aid are the recipes for emancipation. That there are so many ethnic liberation fronts and so little freedom in Ethiopia shows the failure of modern education. It is thus an urgent task to reflect on an alternative to the present homeless education. True, educated *tezeta tells* us that currently we are born neither fully free nor fully Ethiopian. However, both being free and being Ethiopian are goals that our predecessors have already identified and pursued for centuries, at a heavy price. The dreams and hopes that nourished these efforts are in our educated *tezeta,* urging us to fulfil them. As it should become clear by now, from the perspective of educated *tezeta,* we are responsible for our past as much as for our possible future. We become free and Ethiopian thorough social practices that recognize our past failures as hopes we have yet to achieve fully, and must achieve in order to redeem the sacrifices of past generations. As a social practice, education has a crucial role in fulfilling these hopes. "The tomorrow in the today is alive," writes Bloch,[333] but the question is: do we now have the education that enables us to see it and grasp it?

6

EDUCATION, MODERNITY & REVIVAL MOVEMENTS: MAKING SENSE OF PENTECOSTAL EXPANSION IN ETHIOPIA

TIBEBE ESHETE

The 1960's marks a significant watershed in modern Ethiopian history in more ways than one. During this period, complex forces were putting pressure on the emerging consciousness of young Ethiopians. Education, which Haile Selassie considered a major tool in modernization Ethiopia, brought into existence a new social force that saw itself and the nation differently. The 60's, one of the most open and tumultuous times in Ethiopian history, was also an era that saw a number of jarring developments, some internally induced, others exogenous. It was a time that saw the collapse of conventions and consensus wisdom among the rising Ethiopian elites. Consequently, the elite were questing for new galvanizing ethos to remap their lives and organize their experience along new lines. The period represented that phase of in-betweens, in the ebbing of traditional values and the surfacing of new sensibilities that allowed new religious movements such as that of the Pentecostals analyzed herein to flourish. In hindsight, the epoch can aptly be characterized as the era of the ending and the beginning.

This chapter will record the history of the Pentecostal movement from the time of its inception in the 60's up to the period of the 1974 Ethiopian Revolution, by pulling together the religious and socio-political stirrings that led to its emergence and its expansion. I try to situate the rise of the Pentecostal movement within the larger socio-economic, religious, and political conditions of Ethiopia, the encounters of diverse forces in the 60's, and the responses of the youth to these encounters. This perspective helps us to view and analyze the movement not as a localized incident instead to understand it from its multi-discursive, national and global context.

The thesis I would like to propose is the Pentecostal movement in Ethiopia was a manifestation of a deep religious yearning demonstrated among young Ethiopians whose religious convictions were being tested by the rising secular thinking that engulfed their generation in the 60's. Those embracing the movement perceived "something" was lacking in their inherited faith traditions as the result of their encounters with modern education and an alternative variant of Christianity introduced by the Protestant missionaries. The challenge of modernity and the inability of the historic church to be alive and be relevant to the youth who lived in a tumultuous period lent the soil in which the seeds of the movement nourished. I argue young educated Ethiopians, predominantly from the Orthodox Church background, pioneered Pentecostalism provided the tour de force for the rapid expansion of the movement and the vital élan for its current national visibility.

Preliminary Notes on the Pentecostal Movement

Pentecostalism, which according to some scholars, originated in US at the turn of the 20th century, has become a global religious movement. Its rapid expansion, especially in the Third World countries, is increasingly attracting the attention of a wide-range of scholars.[334] Yet, the Pentecostal movement is one of the least understood and most understudied phenomena in modern Ethiopian history.

The current popular appellation of the term "*Pente,*" referring to all the denominations of various Protestant backgrounds in Ethiopia, is too confusing to be employed in any scholarly work without major qualifications. The designation "*Pente,*" has now become a rubric to non-Orthodox and non-Catholic brand of Christianity in Ethiopia and to its followers, as if they form a monolithic block. The term came into public usage as an aftermath of an episode that occurred in Dabra Zeit in August 1967 and remained lodged in public parlance, albeit erroneously.[335] The incident that attracted even government newspapers is tied to a clash between adherents of the faith and the Orthodox public. *Addis Zemen* reported the people of Dabra Zeit took action to punish those practicing "unknown" religion (*Yaltaweke Addis Haymanot*).[336] Soon the incident became an issue in the media and other public fora as a result of which the term entered into the public usage.

The term *Pente* initially referred to the new "religious outsiders" as a shortened allusion to their Pentecostal faith experience, the most salient aspect of its expression being speaking with tongues as an evidence of the "baptism of the Holy Spirit."[337]

Origins: Historical Overview

There are various historical locales from which the Pentecostal movement in Ethiopia drew its origins. Like all movements of political, social or, cultural origins, religious movements have soils and roots from which they germinate and find nourishments. Pentecostalism in Ethiopia sprang against the backdrop of evangelical Christianity that stressed personal salvation, the presence of a tiny segment of Pentecostal missionaries, who, albeit low key, highlighted the Holy Spirit dimension of the Christian faith, and the strings of youth-oriented movements within the Orthodox experiencing religious reawakening.

External influences

The first Pentecostal missionaries to have come to Ethiopia were three ladies from Elim Bible Institute. Bertha Dommermuth, Ruth Shippey, and Ellen French were missionaries from the Assembly of God Church of New York who came to Ethiopia in March 1934.[338] The missionaries started a weekly English class accompanied by Bible studies and prayer programs at their residence from which a language school, called the American Grade School and Mission, evolved.[339] Original participants included young men such as Worqu and Haile, members of *Serawite Kirstos,* a revivalist group affiliated with the Bible Churchmen's Missionary Society (BCMS),[340] and Fiqre Badma, the daughter of *Qes* Badma, a noted priest from Gojjam who was also a founding member of the Makana Yesus Church.[341] In fact, Dommermuth mentions Fiqre as one of the first young Ethiopians to have received the power of the Holy Spirit.[342]

Reports the missionaries sent indicate there was a growing congregation of young Ethiopians eagerly seeking to learn about the secret of miracles and healings. From this beginning, there appeared to have emerged a small community of Christians who could perhaps be dubbed as the first proto-Pentecostal congregation in Ethiopia.[343]

Unable to perform their activities due to increased hostilities from the Italians, the missionaries discontinued their operation in the turbulent years of the occupation period. The departing missionaries expressed their laments and hope as follows:

> Deep, deep sadness accompanied us as we left Ethiopia in May of 1938. What established work had we left behind? None that we could see. There had been so many tight restrictions placed upon us with very little freedom to do anything much; we had to leave everything in the hands of the Lord. The only thing we could do was accept our whole mission to Ethiopia as a precious treasure and, bury it, and expect God to bring it up resurrection life.[344]

The Italians took their houses and converted their School into barracks for the Italian soldiers.[345] Most of the members of the fledgling movement were hunted by the Italians and eliminated, as they were suspected of working for the patriotic forces under cover, while some joined the rank of the patriots and died resisting the occupying forces. Ethiopian Pentecostals of the latter generation do not seem to be aware of the existence of a Pentecostal cohort, albeit short-lived. [346]

The next likeminded missionary group that entered the country in 1952 was: Mrs. J.C. Jane Daoud and her husband. During their six-week undertakings, the missionaries highlighted in bold feature healing services, a crucial element of the Pentecostal practices in Ethiopia. The missionaries left a deep impression among a wide section of the populace in Addis Ababa. The lady who led the healing service is remembered to this day as "*Ya Cambologiwa Mariam.*"

The event was well reported even in the media, where sensational accounts were presented about the large turnout of people attending the services of "the faith healing missionary" at the national stadium and Jan Meda. The newspaper, *Addis Zemen,* recorded accounts of daily testimonies to miraculous healings. The list included names of high officials, army officers and dignitaries including members of the royal family.[347]

In this connection, it is also worth mentioning the "crusade" organized by the American evangelist, Billy Graham, at the National Stadium in 1960.[348] The Emperor not only approved the program, but also encouraged public attendance. In fact, schools were closed for the occasion to boost the turnout. Consequently, a large crowd of people attended the event. Billy Graham's "crusade" lent significantly public visibility to the obscure Evangelical faith in Ethiopia.

Two Nordic Pentecostal missionary groups arrived almost simultaneously in Ethiopia in the 1950's. The first were the Finland Pentecostal Missionaries (FPM), who arrived in Ethiopia in 1951 and set up a station, in Merkato. Mr. Sanfrid Mattson, the first missionary from the FPM, had prior contacts with Emperor Haile Selassie during his exile in England.[349] It was his previous acquaintance with the Emperor that gave the missionaries the entrée to open up a station. The Swedish Philadelphia Mission (SPM), which arrived in 1959, was the second company to make its way in Ethiopia.[350] The government allowed the SPM missionaries to establish mission stations in Awasa, a newly established modern town in southern Ethiopia.

The Nordic missionary groups had some influences upon the development of Pentecostalism in Ethiopia, at least, at its initial phase.[351] They were the first to capture active recruits from the capital city who received their Pentecostal experience through literature and direct exposure as interpreters and aides to the missionaries. The young Ethiopians, who embraced the newer forms of spirituality, exerted a measure of influence in the budding movement as it reached the students of the Haile Selassie I University in the late 60's.[352]

The Pentecostal movement also received some impetus, at least at its incipient phase, from Indian school instructors. According to informants, in the early 1960's, there were three Indian Pentecostals: Daniel Paul, Simen Stanley, and Paul Somngel, who were teaching in Harar, Dire-Dawa and Asmara, respectively. The Indians formed close links with those drawn to Pentecostalism in the mentioned areas, and gave added strength to the movement through their involvement in teaching and preaching.[353]

Internal Dynamics

According to early participants of the movement, it is hard to assign an original location to the rise of Pentecostalism in Ethiopia. In their views, the movement sprang like "a stream with many tributaries," where the "manifestation" of the power of the Holy Spirit occurred in multiple places at almost the same time.[354] According to their testimonies, the sites where the young people claimed to have experienced this encounters were mainly: Harar, Nazareth, Awasa, and Addis Ababa. The settings that provided the context for the encounters were, in most cases, high schools, teacher training institutes, and colleges. Also, a key element of the setting was the evolving of new informal associations such as Bible study groups, prayer and witnessing gatherings, and the availability of a wide variety of Christian literature, including the Bible.

The Harar Stream

The city of Harar, located in the eastern part of Ethiopia, is amongst the first centres of origin of the Pentecostal movement in Ethiopia. In its neighbourhood, Harar hosts major training institutions, such as the Harar Teacher Training Institute, the Harar Military Academy, and the Alemaya College of Agriculture. The Harar Teacher Training Institute was one of the few places where students had their first Pentecostal encounters in the form of the "baptism of the Holy Spirit" followed by speaking with tongues. According to informants this happened in 1964. The students, who claimed to have experienced the "supernatural" encounter, were mostly Orthodox Christians.[355] Along side with their Bible study and prayer gatherings, they began to investigate more on the working of the Holy Spirit and its power in their lives through rigorous reading of Christian literature dealing with the Pentecostal faith. Among the materials the students read were the works Oral Roberts, a leading proponent of faith healing and T.L Osborn, a Pentecostal minister with global influence.[356] The names often associated with the new faith movement in Harar were: Asefa Alemu, Betta Mengistu, and Zeleke Alemu.

The Nazareth Stream

The story of the Nazareth chapter of the rise of the Pentecostal movement is connected to the high school students of the *Atse* Gelawdewos Secondary School. In the early 1960's students from this high school formed a Bible study club, which later acquired the name, *Ye-Semay Birhan*, literally, "The Heavenly Light/Sunshine." Among those who were actively involved in the club, were members as well as leaders of the *Haymanote Abew* Christian youth association.[357] In their Bible study sessions, they often engaged in intense reading and discussions. Their extensive studies on the Scriptures, particularly the Book of Acts, led them to a passionate search of the nature and works of the Holy Spirit or how they could tap into the power of God to revitalize their Christian lives. Those who participated in the event stress that their experience of the "baptism" of the Holy Spirit was the result of fervent prayers and fasting, which in practice meant, abstaining from any meal for several days.[358] Many of the leading members of the *Ye-Semay Berhane* group joined Hails Selassie I University and later became influential agents in the dissemination of Pentecostalism.[359]

The Addis Ababa Stream

In considering the third constituent of the origin of the Pentecostal movement, we need to pay attention to developments in Addis Ababa. The story of this chapter, however, has two interrelated dimensions. It would be more appropriate to start with the group that had its roots in connection with the Finland Pentecostal Missions.

The Finnish Pentecostal missions established their station at a residential site in Merkato, a strategic commercial location in Addis Ababa. Their work in the Merkato neighbourhood attracted young students who through the literature and teachings of the missionaries embraced the Pentecostal faith. Among the most prominent of the students were Melese Wegu, Kebede Wolde Mariam, Fantahun Gabre, and Argaw Neda.[360]

Addis Ababa being the capital city, the group had the added benefit of being highly exposed, not only to Pentecostal literature, but talks offered by guest speakers from other countries. One such a speaker who left an indelible mark upon the group was the Kenyan Pentecostal preacher, Omaha Chacha, who visited Ethiopia in 1965.[361] The itinerant evangelist preached to the young Ethiopians congregating around the Merkato mission compound on the nature and the power of the Holy Spirit. Informants strongly agree it was the Kenyan preacher who gave the Pentecostal movement a solid ground among its Ethiopian adherents.[362] In the opinion of Kebede Wolde Mariam, a man who witnessed this development, Omahe Chacha's role could be compared to that of a matchstick who sparked light to the wood sticks waiting to burn.[363]

Some time after the visit of Omahe Chacha, a schism developed between the FPM missionaries and the Ethiopians. Various explanations are offered for the split. The main source of conflict revolves around the issue of leadership, strategy of evangelization, and modality of the exercise of the "gifts of the Spirit." It appears the inspiring preaching of the Kenyan evangelist brought fresh revelations about their faith, thus accentuating their differences with the missionaries.[364]

In 1966, the young Ethiopians who separated from the FPM mission started to meet at a rented house in the Messalemia area of the city. Shortly afterwards, they were joined by Harari Pentecostals, like Assefa and Zeleke, a dynamic blending of two streams forming the nucleus of a budding religious force that soon crystallized into an indigenous Pentecostal movement.[365]

This brings us to the last and most momentous phase of the development of Pentecostalism in Ethiopia, the event relating to the religious stirrings that transpired among the students at the national university in Addis Ababa.

The Haile Selassie I University Stream

It seems the Pentecostal movement began to reach university students in the early 1960s, mainly through the entries of students from Pentecostal backgrounds. Informants hold a somewhat divided opinion as to how Pentecostalism found its way in Haile Selassie I University. There are those who suggest the first group of students to have undergone Pentecostal experience were fresh returnees of the Ethiopian University Service (EUS). The returnees encountered their Pentecostal experience through long searches of the Bible accompanied by intense prayer at a shared rental house near the University.[366] There are, however, others who claim that Pentecostalism reached the campus though the Nazareth Pentecostals who joined the university in the 60's.[367] Bekele Wolde Kidan provides a more conciliatory and inclusive perspective. Under the heading "All roads lead to Addis Ababa," he concludes small tributaries from Asmara, Awasa, and Nazareth converged at the University to form the bigger river that flowed in other directions.[368]

The formation of a prayer and fellowship group in the rented house in Arat Kilo near Menelik II School that brought together the fledgling group was a decisive event for it laid the seed of a vibrant spiritual movement among the Ethiopian youth. The university students, namely Philipos, Teka Gabru, Iqube Igzi, Berhane Abreha, and Girma Demissie, joined by Kebede, began meeting in 1966 for fellowship at the rented room. They soon began to have steady prayer and Bible study programs, which gradually attracted others joining the national university. The increase in the number of visitors created the need to look for a larger accommodation, which they acquired by renting a bigger house in the neighbourhood of Sedest Kilo campus, the hub of activities of university students.[369] The students christened the new facility, chapel, a euphemistic version of a church. The chapel's foundation was another momentous landmark in the history of the expansion of Pentecostalism.[370] The chapel served as the nucleus of the embryonic movement and a forum for students craving for similar spiritual pursuits. Within a few months of the setting up of the chapel, the number of people joining them rose steadily.[371] The Pentecostals were very aggressive in intentionally communicating their faith to others through an evangelistic tool, which they commonly describe as, *memesker*, sharing personal testimonies to others and inviting them to attend chapel services. Those serving in the chapels were dedicated volunteers who had a strong desire to impact their generation and make a difference in their society.[372] The chapel provided amenable services that partially addressed the needs of students, mainly those coming from different provinces for higher studies. The groups also set up mutual aid programs to support one another reciprocally in terms of material exchange, sharing of ideas and helping one another as needed including in the area of academics to cement their solidarity as a community.

There were other factors that facilitated the work of the Pentecostal Christians in the University, one which was the establishment of a Christian Youth Centre with the permission of the Emperor and recognition of the Ministry of Education. The Youth Centre set up in 1960 by the SIM in the strategic area between Arat Kilo and Sedest Kilo campuses deserves special mention. The Centre was running multi-track activity, such as recreational, library, and counselling services. They also held lecture series in which they invited guest speakers on topics most pertinent to university students including faith and science.[373] Informants attest that the Centre was influential in winning some students from the University to the evangelical faith. There were also students of other persuasions visiting the Centre, albeit for some other reasons. Radical elements of the university from the Crocodile group, who viewed the Centre as a CIA project, also visited the site with the intention of disrupting its activities.[374] In the ensuing years the Crocks and the Pentecostals had bitter contestation over the fate of the youth and campus politics.

The Rise of an Independent Pentecostal Church: Routinization and its Contexts

Bolstered by the sense of confidence that the Pentecostals had reached a critical mass due to their rising number, interested leaders who were co-ordinating the activities in various chapels in Addis Ababa felt the need to form some kind of structure to conduct organized programs and consolidate the movement.[375]

The Addis Ababa Conference of August 1966 marked a watershed in the history of the Pentecostal movement. The four-day Conference, attended by more than 200 participants, was significant, for it brought together Pentecostals from all over the country to deliberate on the destiny of the new spiritual wave and the role of their generation in catalyzing its advance at the national level. The various teaching and prayer programs organized and run by Ethiopians emphasized the need for bringing the movement into a higher level by lending its sound leadership and guidance. Their guiding motto, "the Gospel for Ethiopia by Ethiopians," not only inspired many, but it also spelled out its national agenda.[376]

An important outcome of the national conference was that it hastened the channelling of the various Pentecostals into a common stream. It created the context for the shading of Pentecostal identities developing along residential, regional and personality lines and helped to pull able leaders under one umbrella. The major Conference in Addis Ababa was a sequel to an earlier gathering in Awasa in 1965.[377]

Informants note the Awasa Conference had rallied Ethiopian Pentecostals across the empire and it created the synergy necessary to launch a collective new beginning. In the two-week long educational and prayer sessions, students had the opportunity to learn relevant teachings by Pentecostal scholars on the varied aspects of the doctrine of Pentecostalism, evangelistic strategies, and church governance.[378]

The very fact of assembling in one place in such a large number infused among participants the sense that the movement has gathered a critical audience capable of taking it to the next level. Solomon Kebede, a participant of the Conference noted, "the thrill of being together and the powerful insight gained from the teaching ignited in us zeal and a messianic spirit that our generation was destined to impact the nation."[379]

The two conferences gave the young Pentecostals new impetus to reach their generation with their new found faith by conducting a massive campaign based on sharing testimonies as explained above.[380] Out of this new fervour grew an abiding interest among students to set up an inter-denominational organization, which later coalesced into the Ethiopian University Students Christian Fellowship (EUSF).[381] The Fellowship played a decisive role in bringing ecumenical awakening among various believers and recruiting new converts through its diverse outreach programs like retreats, drama shows, revival meetings and attractive seminars dealing with faith, career development and politics.[382]

EUSF also became one of the few associations that openly challenged the new Marxist ideology that was making inroads increasingly into the university system. The Pentecostal group daringly confronted those individuals who were promoting Marxism by taking time to study it so they could task the student radicals both at the intellectual and spiritual front.[383] The student activists who embraced the Marxist ideology saw the Pentecostals as a danger to the student movement and feared the vigour they displayed for their faith left no room for participation in student politics.[384] According to Solomon Lulu, a serious point of departure between the two groups was the Pentecostal's philosophical and theological contention that only a spiritually "regenerated" person had the moral authority to call out for actions that would engender community/social transformations. The Pentecostals' idea of the conversion of the "self," which in their perception begins with the individual heart, as micro-model of revolution, definitely clashed with the student radicals' macro-historical model that took Marxism as it centrepiece.[385]

Forming of the Mulu Wangiel Church

The Awasa conference of 1965 and the one that followed it in Addis Ababa in August 1966 set the tone for the vision of having a united Pentecostal church in Ethiopia. The necessity of carving a common religious identity and a common structure, coupled with the need to hold out persecution that its members were beginning to face, set the imperatives for speeding up the process. Soon after the national Pentecostal conference in Addis Ababa, co-ordinators of the various chapels operating in the Capital City took steps towards instituting some kind of formal leadership and an ad hoc committee was set up representing the various chapters.[386]

Confronting pioneers of the movement was the issue of designating a name for the future church. There were two names that competed for attention: namely, *Ye-Semay Berhan*, literally, Heavenly Sunshine, and *Tintawi Ye Egziabher Beta Krestian,* literally, the Old Time Church. After minor squabbles, the latter was adopted as the official name of the church. However, upon a formal request for a legal permit from the government, the leaders were told they had to drop the name for the term *Tintawi*, suggested a claim of primacy viewed against the national Church's long-running history. The Pentecostals renamed their institution *Ye-Mulu Wangiel Amagnoch Andenet Mahbar* (the Full Gospel Believers' Association), shortened to *Mulu Wangiel,* signifying the fullness and richness of the power of the Gospel.[387]

The newly established church set a new precedent of being a national mission sending agents "to all corners of Ethiopia" independent of any foreign financial assistance.[388] Some of its members volunteered to become evangelists with a monthly pay of 50 Ethiopian dollars. Among those who first served as evangelists were: Zeleke Alemu and the late Haile Wolde Michael.[389] Many others like Asefa Alemu, Ashennafi Zemat, Merid Lemma, Tsadiku Abo, Taye Takele, Seifu Kebede and a host of others, followed in their footsteps.

The Pentecostal movement developed a compulsion to create a contagious community of faith, which they sought to bring about with consuming passion. Embedded in their belief was the conviction that they had truly rediscovered their faith and that it was incumbent upon them to engage in spiritual rescue operation. This claim not only imbued the Pentecostals with a sense of collective entitlement, but persuaded them that Ethiopia needed a religious revolution that invoked the power of God, through the power of the Holy Spirit, as a sin qua non for its socio-economic and political transformations.[390] The motto, "The Gospel for Ethiopia by Ethiopians," the unwritten manifesto of the Pentecostals, proved to be the driving force behind this new spate of interest to go out and reach others, just like, "Land to the Tiller" (1965), was the driving slogan of the radical students of their generation in the national university.

As a result, the Pentecostals expanded their sphere of missionary activities from areas like Dabra Zeit, Nazareth, Ambo, and Dabra Berhan to parts of Wallaga, Bale, Gojjam, Arsi, Eritrea, Tigray, Jimma and Illubabor.[391] They accomplished this by mobilizing local missionaries, mostly men and women serving as government employees in different parts of Ethiopia and by organizing revivalist "spiritual conferences."[392] This "geographical peel off," to use Gerlach's expression, is one of the most important key elements in the dynamics of the expansion of the Pentecostal movement in Ethiopia.[393]

The Ethiopian Pentecostals right from the beginning made it a point that their movement was autonomous and free from foreign influences. The Pentecostals felt keeping the Western missionaries' influences at bay would partly help to allay the suspicion that the faith is an imported religion, a view which has been deeply engrained in the psychic of most Ethiopians.[394] The guiding philosophy of the *Mulu Wangiel* was the principles of the "Three Self" (self-supporting, self-propagating, and self-governing church). The Ethiopian Pentecostals supported their church by increasing their financial commitment through tithes and what they called love offerings.[395]

From the very outset, the Pentecostal movement attracted members of the emerging elite, enthusiastic about their faith and confident in their own inherent gifts. Very soon, there appeared not only talented preachers but also gifted musicians such as Addisu Worqu, Legese Watero (later Professor), and others who emerged afterwards, like the nationally acclaimed singers, Tesfaye Gabiso, Tamrat Welba, Atalay Alem (later Dr.), and Tamrat Haile.[396] These young musicians composed songs carrying theological as well as existential messages with personalized meanings and themes. The songs had strong appeal to the youth since they incorporated modern musical instruments such as accordions and guitars. Pentecostal music diffused through the conduits of soloist and choir singers, as they gradually became an integral part of the new worship practices of most evangelical churches. Significantly contributing to the diffusion and popularity of gospel songs was the availability of tape recordings and their increased use both for production and listening purposes. Gospel songs gained public visibility as they were regular transmitted through Radio Voice of the Gospel, established in 1963 with the aid of the World Lutheran Federation. [397]

The Pentecostals and their Persecution Experience

Ethiopian Pentecostals have gone through a series of persecutions since the August 1967 Dabra Zeit incident. In fact, persecution forms one of the main narratives and constant refrains of their Jeremiad songs.[398] In the main, expressing hostility toward the Pentecostals were those who saw the movement as a cult and a deviant form of Christianity that has corrupting influence on Ethiopian society. Official publications like *Addis Zemen* and *Ethiopian Herald* use flippant words such as "sect" an "unknown religion," and "foreign virus" and *Pentecosti,* to characterize the movement.[399]

Facing ill-treatment and persecutions largely from the Orthodox public and local officials, the Pentecostals took their case to the Emperor on April 26, 1972. The Emperor gave an audience to select members and allowed them to present their pleas. After listening to their impassioned speech as well as the response of the Minister of Justice, the Emperor advised the Pentecostals to work out their problems with the Ethiopian Orthodox Church.[400] The Pentecostals accused the Emperor of violating his most famed dictum, "*agar yegara new haymanot yegel new,*" literally, "the nation is for all, religion is private."

Some of the leaders of the Pentecostal movement made attempts to dialogue with the leaders of the Church including the Patriarch but in vain. Philipos Kemere, one of the early leaders of the Mulu Wangiel church, recalls that he met the Head of the national Church but without any success. He expressed his dismay by the Patriarch's insistence that the Pentecostals had better abandon their pursuit and his sarcastic remark, "why do you seek to open a *kiosk* (a small shop) when the there is already a large mall?" [401] Kebede Wolde Mariam, a prominent leader of the movement, also recalls his persistent efforts to open dialogue with the Patriarch and other lower level officials came to naught for lack of sympathy and understanding.[402]

Among the persecutions the Pentecostals underwent the one that occurred in August 1972 captured media attention both locally and internationally.[403] It began by the sudden arrest of Pentecostals by members of the police forces in Addis Ababa and elsewhere imprisoning them under the allegation of conducting illegal meetings *(beheg yaltefeqede sebseba.)*[404] Though estimates of arrests vary from source to source, they range in number anywhere from 165 to 480.[405]

Addis Zemen and *Ethiopian Herald* wrote articles providing explanations as to why the government cracked down on the Pentecostals. In fact, the *Ethiopian Herald* contained an article titled, "Newsweek's Report on Pentecostalists (sic) Unfounded," in response to the comments made by *Newsweek* and other foreign magazines, by dismissing any link between the suppression of the movement and religious freedom.[406] The view of the official newspaper was the Pentecostal movement was a sect that promoted anti-social practices contrary to the Ethiopian culture such as engagements in sexual misconduct and hooligan behaviour inimical to long established Ethiopian custom.[407] The newspaper reiterated that it was in the interest of the public to reprove those whose "malpractices" brought demoralizing effect upon the youth. In what it refers as "rubrics of the Pentecostal faith," the paper identified: the mixing of young girls and boys in night prayer meetings and their indulgence "in certain detrimental acts," "incest," and "blasphemous teaching that encouraged lustful desires" as dangerous traits of the new movement. The article critiqued Pentecostalism, saying its "teachings create a disruptive gap in the social life of the people by teaching the young not to obey their superiors and elders and to disregard patriotism, emphasizing in particular to despise the teaching of the Orthodox Church." The paper concluded the state rightly intervened to arrest "this foreign virus coming from an illegal association that flouts the laws of the land and teaches dissention among its people." [408]

Bedru Hussein, one of the pioneers of the Pentecostal movement from the Muslim background, bemoaned the government position and the complicity of the national Church. In his opinion, the national church should have empathized with the youth and its perplexing dilemma rather than misconstruing the movement and using its influence to curb it.

Messay in his recent book dealing with modernization makes a scathing remark that supports Bedru's view. Messay summarizes the problem as follows:

> Being so religious, the Ethiopian should have been keenly interested in new religious ideas if for no other reason than to fight them. Also periods

of purification, reform and renewal or religious commitments, would have been quite normal. Astonishing as it may sound, however, despite the long duration of the faith and despite the constant challenge by Jesuits, Protestants, and Muslims, Ethiopia has never known a period of religious purification and reform. Characteristically, the western religious challenge was handled not by means of reform and theological development, but by prohibition and expulsion... The response was not but still further isolation.[409]

Overall, it can be summed up that the persecution experience added a new dimension to the process of identity formation at this stage of the Pentecostal movement in Ethiopia. It strengthened the perception of the Pentecostals that they were messianic communities called out of the world by God to witness and for other proclaim to the Gospel. This conviction, not only added potency to the process of interiorizing existing self-perception, viz.-a –viz. with others, but heightened their sense of marginality which they sought to overcome through redoubled evangelistic efforts.

Situating the Pentecostal Movement

A fundamental question that needs to be addressed concerning the Pentecostalism in Ethiopia is: where do we situate the movement in Ethiopian history and in the larger socio-political contexts of the country?

Locating the rise of the Pentecostal movement in Ethiopia requires careful analysis of its contexts in the 60's, one of the most exceptionally open times in our history. The 60's was the time when the Ethiopian society was experiencing major transformations due to the increased pace of the process of modernizing, largely commencing in the immediate post-war period. The pivotal decade not only constitutes a great divide, but it provides the template to understand the context of the complex condition of contemporary Ethiopia.

Haile Selassie's modernization envisaged raising Ethiopia's reputation as a present day nation among the West through the promotion of technological and economic progress. It seems that in the Emperor's imagining of modernization, what featured prominently high was Ethiopia's advancement along the western lines. In his book, *My Life and Ethiopia's Progress,* the Emperor indicates his desire was to gradually improve the nation by initiating changes modelled along western ways of civilization so "the people may attain a higher level" of advancement. [410] According to Harold Marcus, as early as during his regency the Emperor "believed that Ethiopia could learn much from western lore and life, which fascinated him."[411] Perhaps, his exile experience during the Italian interlude and the need to suppress the conservative forces by creating a countervailing force might have been significant factors influencing the Emperor's decision to adopt the ideas of modernization.

Thus, from the very start the vision and inspiration as well as the manner of its adoption demonstrated a high dose of externality as was evidenced in the leaving out of even a giant institution like that of the Orthodox Church from the process.[412] As a result, the Church, which in the past had created a culture of consensus by its long history, national influence, and its privileged position, lost control and influence over the "mind and soul" of the youth.[413]

A study conducted in 1953 indicated the tradition of going to church and the observance of food taboos was showing signs of decline in urban areas and evidently so amongst the emerging elite.[414] By the 1960s, the generation of students of Haile Selassie I University believed the values and beliefs held by their older generation served a traditional conservative society and were jettisoning them out of their daily lives.[415] Cherished values informing codes of conducts (*Haymanot,* religion/faith, *feriha Egziabher*, fear of God, *chewanet/megbar*, gentleness, *sinesreat*, discipline/manner, *akbrot*, deference, *bandira*, the flag, *ager feqer,* love of the nation, etc.) were steadily loosing steam.

Randi Balsvik points out that, as of the late 60s radical university students were lodging scathing criticism of the role of the national Church by asserting that it contributed to the under-development of Ethiopia and hence was no longer a useful institution.[416] She further explains, "student criticism of the church was profound, whether it came from the minority that supported it, students of the College of Theology and the Haimanote Abew Association... or, from the majority who were estranged from the church."[417] Sandra Rickard, who made a survey of student attitudes in 1966, also observes students found the Church "not only irrelevant to their generation, but a political block to progress."[418] Similarly, Milkias notes, some members, if not all, of the rising generation viewed the traditional church as anachronistic with mere ceremonial functions.[419]

Basically, these developments stemmed out of the want for expanded discourses on past religious values, symbols, and rituals, and the lack of fitting arrangements to transpose them in tangible and meaningful manners. Conspicuously, missing in the encounters between the forces of tradition and modernity was a negotiated space. Hence, the generation felt the need to look for "something else" and crowded itself with radical ideologies, whether they were inspired by religious or secular thoughts.

Emperor Haile Selassie's modernizing Programme was an enterprise that issued from his personal aspiration and perceptions of the goal of his nation. The project, therefore, was more of a self-directed exercise involving minimal participation from the public. It was a top-down phenomenon emanating from what, Rickard described as, "a big man complex."[420] Indrias provides a succinct commentary when he stated, "The many introductions to Ethiopia, the various 'firsts,' such as Ethiopian Airlines, a university, modern schools, theatre, stadium, and television all occurred under the imperial brand. All was bestowed upon the people through his personal command and beneficence."[421]

A number of scholars who have closely studied the Emperor's modernization Programme stress that Emperor facilitated the course of modernization with the view of strengthening royal power without taking a hard look as to the wider ramifications.[422] McClellan shares the view that modernization is more of a super-structural development, and, as such, was largely a process that impacted the state and not the society as a whole.[423] Messay Kebede considers the modernization process as a phenomenon deriving from the Emperor's intention to consolidate his autocratic rule and scathingly adds, it "has no salvational purpose." According to Messay, modernization for Haile Selassie was, "nothing else but the use of modern means to assert his complete power over the nobility." Therefore, in his judgment, the Emperor used modern means to achieve a primitive goal.[424]

One of the principal venues for promoting progress and modernization, according to Haile Selassie's perception, was education. He had an almost religious belief in the modernizing effect of western education on the nation's youth.[425] The Emperor introduced a free, but not necessarily obligatory school system, beginning from elementary school up to the university level. Among some of the many actions the Emperor took following his return from exile in 1941 was the call to Ethiopian parents that stated, *weldo yalastemare indegedele yikoteral,* or, roughly translated, "parents who do not educate their children are effectively killing them."[426] While the Ethiopian nationals and

Indians served as teachers at the local elementary levels, secondary and college levels had European and American staff.

Higher education began with the founding of the University College of Addis Ababa (UCAA) in 1950, consisting of the Faculties of Arts and Science. By 1952 the Engineering College had been opened, and the Public Health College and Training Centre opened in Gondar in 1954. The College of Agricultural and Mechanical Arts was founded in 1952. In the late 50's the 60's more educational institutions were founded in Jimma, Ambo, and Harar. The Haile Selassie I University, amalgamating the Gondar Public College and the Alemaya College of Agricultural, was formally instituted in 1961. Though the Emperor recruited its administrative and teaching staff for UCAA mainly from the Canadian Jesuits and the Sudan Interior Mission, the college was a secular institution, modelled on foreign ideas and staffed by expatriates who offered instructions primarily in English.[427]

The university system was largely a foreign transplant in its general set up and orientation and its content as such remained so for a long time. Preparations were conspicuously lacking to sufficiently anchor "the end product" in indigenous soils.[428] Hence, the critical comment of Daniel Lemma that the Ethiopian educational system has not focused on the most serious business of educating the man, as it did not embody the requisite frameworks that would have allayed its fragmenting and de-linking influences upon the Ethiopian youth that went through it.[429] Rickard's study of the conditions of the college students, and the youth in general, in 1966, indicates the youth was virtually alone, uneasily straddling its traditional ethos and emerging sensibility. [430] Teshome Wagaw, a noted scholar on the field of higher education in Ethiopia, aptly remarks it is this fissure and discontinuity that lay at the intellectual root of the 1974 Ethiopian Revolution which brought demise to the old regime.[431]

A sizable number of students who entered the national university in the 60s to pursue higher education were without significant material and immediate emotional backing from their close relatives since they came from remote rural areas.[432] Their entry into colleges led them to go through a robust process of secondary socialization and exposed them to new ideas, habits of thinking, and ways of life, which in a sense, made them inhabit the bifurcate zone of socio-cultural liminality. Besides the concentration of students in same campuses and dormitories that allowed the contagious diffusion of ideas, the heterogeneity of the social mix and the adjustment skill it required, the challenges of rigorous academic life, all introduced their own stresses. Higher institutions also provided the ambience for the permeation of activated consciousness, the creation of a freed up space, "relative autonomy," that lent young students the liberty to think, speak and act either individually or corporately. It was this frontier situation, an area of porous boundaries lacking delimiters where the old and the new values encountered each other, that set the context for new conversations.

Broadly speaking, the expansion of western education, a key feature and a principal avenue of Haile Selassie's modernization policy, and the accompanying process of secularization, created among the emerging Ethiopian elite a sense of dissatisfaction and a climate of social dissonance that impinged both on their faith and persona. Modern education spawned a new set of experiential input that lent the Ethiopian youth of the 60's the lens to question dominant meaning systems and keenly notice the discrepancy between the new style, which tended to be more secular and western, and their traditional ways of life. Confronting the task of negotiating the space between "modernity," *zemenainet,* and traditional ways of life, sometimes misconstrued as *"hualaqernet,"* and living in the midst of the two zones not only fostered bouncing identities but also presented a monumental paradox, which Daniel describes as a serious disorder in normative behaviour.[433] Trapped in the social drama of varied levels of "encounters" and prolonged "conversation" entailing a cacophony of competing voices, conflicts, ambivalences, etc. the Ethiopian youth responded, proactively or reactively, depending on their assessments of the danger they sensed and the resources they had at their disposal.[434] As early as 1961, Donald Levine captured the perplexing conditions of the youth and its time as follows, "Ethiopia, like all other countries today, is in the throes of a dilemma, or serious dilemmas that stem from certain conflicts of values."[435]

This quandary of the emerging elite expressed itself in several metaphysical pursuits. For instance, certain students in the university made decisions to terminate their education and join the ranks of the monks in the monastery of Dabra Libanos to place themselves away from the world, which they perceived was pervasively infested with secular thinking. While this group chose a more pacifist a path of least resistance, there were others who opted for the path of active involvement through voluntary social and religious services. Examples of these groups include students like Negussie Ayele (later professor) and Daniel Lemma (later professor) who discontinued their university education and went into the countryside with the intention of serving as conscientizing agents to bring public enlightenment and spiritual revival through Biblical teachings and active service.[436]

Hence, it can be surmised that the alienation of the youth, the tensions and conflicted identity engendered by the combined process of modernization and secularization, and the overall rejectionist mood of the youth against their past traditions constitute the most crucial contextual elements within which to situate the rise of the Pentecostal movement in Ethiopia.[437] This does not presuppose Pentecostalism is the only response to the stress of modernization. Neither does it assume the convergence of the above events associated with modernization could perforce, eventuate such a religious movement or similar ones. But, in the context of Ethiopia, the social and intellectual context of modernization, nonetheless, provided the material for the emergence of a revitalized faith movement under the rubric of Pentecostalism.

A crucial element that could not be slighted in the study of the Pentecostal movement in Ethiopia is the influence of the Scriptures and related literatures. This is glaringly so in light of the rising culture of reading among the emerging elite. The Bible, which was translated in Amharic in 1962 under the auspices of the Emperor to help people learn about their faith, was becoming increasingly available among the youth in the 60's. Though not appreciated, this was one of the most critical factors contributing to the rise of revival movements and the resultant articulations of new religious experiences. This development impacted particularly the educated youth who tended to investigate and pick up new ideas at an impressionable age.

Early participants in the Pentecostal movement admit the Bible had been a major source of inspiration and constituted the central part of their faith and daily life. In fact, carrying the Bible around became a badge of their new identity by which others distinguished them.[438] Ethiopian Pentecostals claim Biblical studies and preaching have not been common practices among ordinary men in the past and maintain that, more than foreign missionaries, it was their generation that enhanced its wider use as well as raise its public prominence. [439]

In affirming the Bible as a guidebook and sole authoritative reference for the church and its missions, the young Pentecostals reverberated the plea of the Estefanites of the 15th century, who suffered severe persecutions under Emperor Zara Ya'iqob, for holding similar convictions.

The influence and impact of reading the Bible and other related materials upon the generation which passionately engaged in rescuing vital truth, as they interpreted their collective quest, and their counterpart's romantic zeal to discover truth from Marxist literature, is an intriguing phenomenon of the times, one which requires further comparative research.[440]

In laying out the macro-context of the socio-political conditions within which to locate the rise of the Pentecostal movement, we need to also consider the political terrain of the country in the 60's. The abortive coup d'état of 1960 carried with it a mixed feeling of anticipation and failure. Modern education had brought new consciousness among the students. It had brought to their attention the modern achievements of the west and challenged their pride as citizens belonging to a country, which had one of the most ancient civilizations. Support for the coup by the students, though largely uninformed, came from the expectations that a new system of government may usher Ethiopia into a new era. Failure brought despair and gloom among those who greeted the coup with a sense of anticipation.[441] One can describe the overall mood of the students in higher education in the 60's as swinging between gloom and anticipation, the latter gradually outweighing the former.[442] It is in this fault line that Marxism took grip of an idealist youth, short-changed and short-ended.

Most of the pioneers of the Pentecostal movement in Ethiopia admit politics was not within their immediate circle of concern. It was not a favourite topic for most of them.[443] Yet, most of them admit, in their own terms, they were trying to turn the country towards a new era and direction. As a professor from the faculty of science and a former active participant of the movement noted:

> We were filled with a new wave of consciousness, purpose and destiny, we were messianic in our new ventures and endeavours, we did not want to let go of things we wanted to involve in the country's fate in the way we saw fitting. For us, religion was the most fundamental issue on which all others things hinged upon.[444]

To conclude, it is tempting to consider the Pentecostal movement in Ethiopia as a revitalization movement, or to be more specific, reformation from without, though the reformers bypassed the historic Ethiopian Orthodox tradition as they looked for a New Testament Apostolic model to re-centre and resituate the foundation of their faith. The Pentecostal movement in Ethiopia was a spontaneous stirring of a grievously disturbed youth who were yearning for spiritual transformations. Its pioneers concur they did not initiate a movement with the intention of creating an oppositional culture, though the manner in which they conducted their faith conflicted with and presented counter-culture to prevailing religious norms. The church was so much of their mind and mood as scarcely to warrant a revolt. They had felt needs not met by the established Church, their earth while spiritual home base. In this respect, Paul Gifford's comment that Pentecostalism is answering needs not sufficiently addressed by mainline churches has some relevance to the Ethiopian situation.[445]

By choosing to form a non-hierarchical religious association, embracing a belief that affirms the centrality of the Bible, and practicing a form of spirituality that is more experiential than liturgical, they created a new model that stood in sharp contrast to the national Church. Hence, Pentecostalism in Ethiopia should not be seen as a discontinuous movement divorced from its past. This is a crucial issue, which both the Orthodox Christians and the current generation of Pentecostals, fail to see and appreciate.

Pentecostalism in the Ethiopian situation demonstrated a call for a radical faith commitment at the personal level holding the individual believer to live a life accountable to his Christian faith both privately and publicly. This individualized/personalized dimension of the faith conflicted with the national church's stress on the harmonial and the collective sense of Christian identity and worship practices. This paradigm difference could partly explain the tensions between Pentecostals and adherents of the Orthodox Church.

The faith of most young Ethiopians was tested by the convergence of many factors to which they had to react without the benefit of experiential preparedness and a properly relay received wisdom.[446] Ensuing from this, there were a variety of kickbacks and cultural rebounds expressed along different lines and outlets. Some young Ethiopians tried to accommodate the change by trying to create a niche within the historic church through some reform initiative. Witness the case of *Haymanote Abew*, while others who perceived the opportunity was closed to them, reconfigured the space and reconstructed a new zone of spiritual reality without intentionally negating the old.[447] In fact, the name they originally adopted to get legality, *Tintawi Ye Egziabher Beta Krestian, is* suggestive of the Pentecostal's desire to invoke the past along fresh lines.[448]

It should also be emphasized that in the context of Ethiopia, Pentecostalism was not an exogenous religion dumped upon passive recipients. Looked closely it is not plausible to view the faith movement as a western invasion, for it did not develop with a pervasive outside missionary effort. Nor did it sustain itself by resources gained from external sources. This is attested by reports of several Pentecostal missionaries who were very much intrigued by the youth's assertiveness and their longing for autonomy. In fact, it was a self-initiated, spontaneous, socio-religious movement accomplished in a situation of considerable isolation. All things considered, it can be safely surmised that its embrace emanated from the depth of an internal spiritual quest and consciousness, rather than from an external input.[449]

The Ethiopian Pentecostals should also be credited for setting a good example of standing for religious and civil liberties and sustaining alternative expressions of Christianity often facing formidable resistance. For the young Ethiopians, Pentecostalism was a vernacularized accent of their faith that gave them the autonomy to exercise it in a more expressive and participatory manner. In short, the shared experiences derived from the Pentecostal faith not only met the spiritual needs of the youth, but had other existential dividends. They provided them the glue to solidify generational strength and camaraderie, power to overcome transitional crisis, and a leverage to forge a sense of collective entitlement.

A crucial point is often overlooked is the Pentecostals increased the visibility of the evangelical faith in Ethiopia by gradually diffusing it across the nation through committed indigenous missionaries, thus extricating the popular imagining of evangelical Christianity from a rural religion and a mere southern phenomenon.[450] Not only that, the renewal movements, which many of the mainline movements are currently experiencing in Ethiopia, a phenomenon that has been described as the charismatic movement, is closely linked to the spread of Pentecostalism.[451]

Finally, it should be noted that the Pentecostal movement in Ethiopia did not evolve from a disinherited constituency. It sprang from the emerging elite questing for progress. That was a big plus for the movement, for it drew its strength from this elite avant-garde, gifted with relatively high intellectual tools, which they readily used for expanding the faith. Members of the Pentecostal faith also passionately invested their generative impulses: talents, resources, skills, and networking capacities to spread the Gospel across the country. Peer ties, interpersonal connections, and social networks offered the fodders for spreading the faith. They carried on their zeal and commitment through the period of the revolution by creating vast underground structures often at great odds thus presenting a strong counterpoint against Marxism. Witness their gospel songs that reflect the theme of suffering and victory, which constituted a rich heritage of people facing the tyranny of an oppressive regime.[452]

7

GOVERNANCE, LANGUAGE POLITICS AND EDUCATION IN SOUTHERN ETHIOPIA: THE TRIBULATIONS OF INVENTING WOGAGODA

DATA DEA

The chapter is an ethnographic and pedagogical analysis of a pervasive disjunction between the rhetoric of good governance and the reality of top-down policy processes as experienced in southern Ethiopian schools. It also deals with the associated discourse of participatory democracy and groups' rights. The study specially focuses on the WoGaGoDa conflict that plagued the schools in the Omotic speaking region of Ethiopia in the late 1990s. An empirical study shows even though the state's attempt was to address a real problem related to issues of language policy, managing diversity, and governance, it followed an excessive top-down approach and went to the extent of 'inventing' and imposing a new language on the people against their will. The act was clearly in contradiction of the new constitution that was promulgated during the post Derg era. The event in question ignited a popular resistance that forced the authorities to abandon the faulty policy. Though the government admitted to making a mistake after a tragic loss in human life, it never took responsibility for what happened. This study highlights the nature of the current governance, its flawed pedagogical setting and the enduring issues in state-society relations in Ethiopia.

The paper examines issues around a conflict that emerged in the context of a politico-linguistic concoction referred to as *WoGaGoDa* that plagued the schools and the society at large in the Omotic speaking region of Southern Ethiopia in the late 1990s.[453] Although *WoGaGoDa* was a particular historical experience, it is of general interest because it is

117

a specific manifestation of the general predicament of Ethiopia.[454] Part of what makes this case of general interest is that *WoGaGoDa* instantiated a practice of excessive policy imposition by the ruling party that provoked citizen anger and resistance. The creation and imposition of *WoGaGoDa* was yet another form of "top-down" approach to integration. Like many such imposed projects, *WoGaGoDa* failed tragically, after series of violent conflicts, lose of lives, destruction of property, leaving behind some painful memories.

The making and unmaking of *WoGaGoDa* prompts one to ask questions that throw important light on recurrently problematic issues in state-society relations in Ethiopia. Some of the specific questions that could be asked in relation to *WoGaGoDa* include: why did it prove to be a political nightmare to unite even such a closely related and relatively small groups of Omotic speakers? What is the limit to the power of the state and its local agents when it comes to deeply emotional issues such as language and identity? What does it take to successfully resist state malpractices such as exemplified in *WoGaGoDa*? How the resistance against WoGaGoDa was socially organized? The ruling party admitted to have made mistake in the process of creating *WoGaGoDa*. Was this "mistake" distinct from any other mistakes contemporary African states make?

WoGaGoDa affected the entire former North Omo zone. But the most violent conflict instigated by the imposition of WoGaGoDa took place in Wolaita.[455] This author observed directly some of the events related to the protest against *WoGaGoDa*. A large part of the ethnographic material presented in this chapter was collected during the year 1999/2000.[456] The author did additional field research in the area in 2004 and 2005.[457] The most recent field visit gave the researcher an excellent opportunity to follow up some issues including how people reflected on their experience with *WoGaGoDa* and the consequences of its unmaking. We will start by considering a historical background under which creating something as imposing as *WoGaGoDa* could be conceived--of in the era of participatory democracy, good governance and group rights so passionately advocated by the new government.

Governance and Ethnic Diversity in Southern Region of Ethiopia

The Southern Nations, Nationalities and People's Region (SNNPR) is the third largest (after Oromia and Amhara) of the ten regional states that constitute the Federal Democratic Republic of Ethiopia. In its recently released figures, the Central Statistical Authority' has asserted the population of Ethiopia has reached 79, 221, 000 by 2008. Of this, the SNNPR comprises 15,745,000 (about 20 percent of the national population).[458] The SNNPR is a region where over 45 "ethnic groups" live in close proximity.[459] This makes the region the most diverse region of Ethiopia and one of the most disparate localities in Africa. The diversity of this region is usually conceived of in terms of ethnicity, language, and particular local histories. After the southern region was incorporated into Ethiopia towards the end of the nineteenth century, the question of how to govern (in reality, how to control) these "disparate peoples" of the south has engaged the various agents of the central government.

Since the early 1990s, the "peoples" of southern Ethiopia have been administered under a hierarchical political construct referred to as the Southern Nations, Nationalities, and Peoples Regional State (SNNPRS). It is hierarchical because what are referred to as nations are considered to be 'more developed' than the nationalities who are in turn considered as more developed than "peoples." However, it is never clear what constitutes a nation or a nationality and what is meant by "people" as used by state authorities. While all the major groups have a separate zonal administration status under the SNNPR, not every group is happy with the current administrative structure. At the same time as there are some who want a separate regional state, there are also many who demand a distinct administrative status within the SNNPR. One way or another, the rise and fall of *WoGaGoDa ought to be understood in the context of popular demands. It also needs to be seen within a broader historical context of the administrative restructuring of the country.*

When the South was incorporated into Ethiopia towards the end of the 19th century, political systems in the region comprised of highly complex arrangements ranging from the Gada system of the Oromo to the Halaqa system of the Gamo to the highly centralised kingships of Kaffa, Wolaita and Jimma.[460] The autonomy and formal authority of these indigenous political systems in the South were brought to an end through forced incorporation into the Ethiopian empire under Emperor Menelik II. Menelik's conquest was ideologically justified as a reunification of an empire that disintegrated following the Moslem invasion of Gragn [El-Ghazi] in the 15th century. For southern nationalists, however, what Menelik's supporters referred to as "Ager Maqnat" was simply a form of colonization that came in tandem with the scramble for Africa unleashed by the European states that subdivided the continent at the Treaty of Berlin in 1884-85. Regarding this development, Ståhl notes: "in the early 1890s an economic crisis in Shoa made access to the resources of the South a pre-requisite for survival [of the Shoan dominated Ethiopian empire]."[461] Thus, the political/ administrative arrangements put in place subsequent to the conquest of the south were to be informed by a consistently narrow interest of the ruling elite steering the Ethiopian empire state.

How to administer (in today's parlance "govern") the diverse but somehow interrelated communities of the newly conquered regions engaged the "experts" and administrative bureaucrats of the state. This effort manifested itself in an endless reshuffling and redrawing of administrative maps. In a paper entitled, "A Nation in Perpetual Transition..." Daniel Gamachu describes at least eight major redrawings of administrative boundaries of Ethiopia during the last 100 years.[462] Accordingly, Ethiopia was divided into about 15 administrative units towards the end of Menelik's era: 32 provinces, in early 1930s, 12 in the 1940s, 13 in the early 1960s, 14 in the early 1970s, 30 in late 1980s, 14 in the early 1990s and 10 regional states at present.[463] Note that some opposition parties are calling for yet another redrawing of administrative boundaries. Given the history noted here, there is no guarantee there will not be yet another redrawing of the country's map.

Concerning the sub-region to be analyzed in relation to WoGaGoDa, this paper primarily focuses on the process of redrawing the administrative map of the country, which engendered the shifting of various sections of Omotic speaking areas between different administrative centres. By the end of Haile Selassie's era, the Omotic speaking groups were clustered into three different administrative provinces: Kaffa, Sidamo, and Gamo Gofa. Towards the end of the Derg regime in 1991, in recognition of the cultural history and psycho-ethnographic unity of the people of the Omotic speaking area, some of the former political units were dissociated from their imperial provincial administrative centres and were reassembled as North Omo, South Omo and Kaffa. For instance, Wolaita was detached from the former Sidamo, Dawro and Konta were separated from the province of Kaffa, and Gamo and Gofa were disengaged from the Gamo Gofa province thus constituting the Derg's North Omo administrative region.

The government which overthrew the Derg in 1991 drew the administrative map of the country predominantly along ethno-linguistic lines. Accordingly, the Derg's regions of North Omo, South Omo, and Kaffa were redesigned as three new regions: Wolaita, Omo, and Kaffa. In 1992, when the entire southern region was "brought together" as Southern Nations, Nationalities, and Peoples' Regional State (SNNPRS) it included five regions (7-11), the Omotic speaking area being restructured as North Omo, South Omo, Kaffa–Sheka and Bench-Maji zones and Yem special *Woreda*.

The redrawing of the map and subsequent formation of the SNNPR solved only some of the ruling party's governance challenges - that of having too many small political units to deal with - but it did not solve the problem of regional languages. While the SNNPR adopted Amharic as an official language of the regional state, subunits (which are organized mostly at zonal level) could still decide on their own specific language. North Omo was especially problematic in this regard. On the one hand, Wolaita, Gamo, Gofa, Dawro, Konta, and other smaller units were put together as one administrative unit (zone) partly in recognition of close affinity of these communities and their languages. On the other hand, they did not agree on which vernacular was to be used or what name they should give it.

This new phase of language controversy in North Omo started as early as 1992. On technical linguistic grounds, the Wolaita dialect could have easily been taken as the standard dialect and hence the written form.[464] But for political and symbolic reasons, it was not adopted as a benchmark by the constituents of North Omo. Therefore, between 1992 and 1998, different Ometo dialects were used in different parts of the zone. Among other things, this was found to be too expensive for the state. At the same time, there were increasing discontents with North Omo as an administrative unit and thus increasing demands to have it dissolved into separate zones for Wolaita, Gamo, Gofa and Dawro and special *Woreda*s [or districts] for smaller units. The ruling party rejected this popular demand and invented a language called "WoGaGoDa." This soon led to a bloody conflict in the region.

Following the *WoGaGoDa* debacle which took place in the year 2000, the North Omo zone was split into Wolaita, Gamo-Gofa and Dawro zones and Konta and Basketo were made into special *Woreda*s. But to the dismay of those who fought for the restructuring, the ruling party loyalists from the respective localities were put in charge of the new administrative units without any meaningful reform of the general policy or the way in which the states' administrations were to be run.

Co-opting Local Agents for the National State

What goes hand-in-hand with perpetual redrawing of the administrative map of the country is the staffing of the administrative machinery. A salient feature of manning state bureaucracy in the South since imperial times has been the co-opting of local agents who would mediate between their people and the national state. Even during the horrendous years of immediate post-incorporation period of late 19th century, many local persons (mainly men from locally dominant families) in the South were co-opted to be in charge of lower positions of the state machinery. That practice continued until the dawn of the socialist revolution of 1974.

In most parts of Southern Ethiopia, the typical pattern during the long stretch of the "feudal era" was some people from the former royal lineages and locally dominant clans were put in charge of the local administrative offices at or below the *Woreda* (district) levels.[465] With the socialist revolution, some fundamental changes were introduced to the principles of recruiting local agents of the state. At this time, the former locally dominant families were openly challenged. Some persons from lower status groups, such as occupational specialists and people from formerly enslaved families, seized the opportunity to take charge of political affairs, a role which was hitherto closed to them. With the introduction of the federal system and regional states in 1991, things seemed to have changed further. Donham describes the nature of this change as follows:

> If, then, the Derg's explicit project of *encadrement* [incorporation into structures of control] has been rejected at a national level, this does not mean that the Ethiopian state's fundamental project of 'capturing' its citizens has ended. Rather this undertaking has changed character in the 1990s. In converging with international expectations and rhetoric of democracy, it has come to mirror global discourses on rights, reparative group rights in particular. What this mirroring allowed, in many cases, is a co-optation of local (male) elites. In this new context, political leaders—even at the village level have become increasingly conscious of acting upon a stage in a kind of theatre of 'ethnicity.'[466]

In many parts of Southern Ethiopia, the co-option of local elites by the national state has increased rather than decreased the intrusion of the state into peasant life.[467] Without going into the detailed analysis of the actual practice of co-opting in specific places, this author shall only note the following. First, though the current state's bold acknowledgment of making ethnicity part of the principle of governance (as opposed to former regimes, which simply pretended ethnicity was not relevant in their functioning) is noted, it is not an entirely new development. Daniel Gamachu writes "the territorial distribution of ethnic groups in Ethiopia, in addition to the natural physiography of the country, has always been one of the main criteria employed in the past in subdividing the country for political and administrative purposes."[468] What needs to be emphasized is that as in the post Derg period, ethnicity had always underpinned who could be entrusted with political and economic leadership in southern Ethiopia.

Alsp wprth noting is the current political practice of power delegation to the regions, which is again not entirely new though practiced somehow differently. Despite the decentralization rhetoric, the central state still maintains tight control over the devolution process and there is a great deal of continuity in power disparity between the centre and the regions.[469] At least in the areas where this author has done field research, the current arrangement has a structure in place that makes the local agents of the regions more accountable to the state and far less accountable to their own constituency. However, it is also important to note in this connection that the local situation of diversity of interest groups and internal stratification within local societies plays a part as factors that make some individuals prone to state manoeuvre. Where it becomes extreme is when the central state considers only its local agents as *the* legitimate voice and dismisses everyone else as "the few," anti-peace, anti-democratic elements. In the case of *WoGaGoDa*, the state primarily consulted with its cadres and then until the popular movement forced it to reconsider its decision, all those who resisted *WoGaGoDa* were dismissed as "the few" and "anti-peace" elements.

The Invention of WoGaGoDa, and Its use as the Language of Instruction in the South

In the years spanning from 1992 to 2000, the EPRDF was in its formative stage. During that time, the North Omo zone was intact. Then, the ruling party of Ethiopia recognized the Ometo territorial units such as Wolaita, Garno, Gofa, Dawro and Konta as separate nationalities (or nations) in Southern Ethiopia and each was represented by a separate political organization such as the Wolaita People's Democratic Organization. The criteria used for determining what constitutes a national includes: occupation of a specific territory; speaking a common language, having a common culture or sharing similar customs and a belief in common identity.[470] Following this provision, local elites from different Ometo units, like elsewhere in the country, emerged as representatives of a distinct people, nation or nationality.

In the move Vaughan calls "repacking Pandora's box," in the late 1990s, the ruling party seemed to have reversed its position, and sponsored the task of "uniting" the people of North Omo.[471] Accordingly, step by step, it merged the separate territorial wings of the ruling party such as the Wolaita People's Democratic Organization, Gamo, Gofa, Dawro, Konta peoples Democratic organizations. By taking the first Amharic letter (first phonemes) of each of the four major Ometo groups (Wolaita, Garno, Gofa and Dawro) the ruling party created WoGaGoDa Peoples Democratic Organization. However, creating a merged new language for these groups was not as easy as merging the political parties.

Ever since the new government advocated the idea of using a local vernacular as an official language and medium of instruction in primary school, the North Omo experts never agreed on a common language. The experts first met in 1992 but could not deliver the common language desired by the central government. Consequently, between 1992 and 1998, the time of introduction of WoGaGoDa, different dialects were used at different times in different parts of the zone. But the ruling party was not happy with that state of affairs and thus instructed "a team of experts" to produce a common language which was ultimately called WoGaGoDa. Concurrently, the acronym WoGaGoDa was transformed by the ruling party into becoming an ethno-linguistic name of the area.

It was advocated that WoGaGoDa was no longer an acronym that stood for Wolaita, Gamo etc. but a new name of the peoples of North Omo. Henceforth, WoGaGoDa as an ethno-linguistic category was to replace North Omo units, which had till then been recognized as distinct ethnic groups. An ideological campaign was soon launched to strongly advocate that the groups that constituted North Omo were not distinct; they were members of the same ethnic group called WoGaGoDa. The ruling party cadres argued the peoples of North Omo were connected through clans, spoke dialects of the same language and that they were socially, economically and historically interrelated.

School texts were published in the new language as it was declared the official language of North Omo. The books in WoGaGoDa were introduced to North Omo in 1998.

No matter the propaganda the cadres made for the acceptance of WoGaGoDa, it was not accepted in any part of North Omo. In Wolaita citizens organized protests against WoGaGoDa. More than anything, it was the involvement of students and teachers that gave the resistance a particularly dramatic intensity.

Teachers, Students and the WoGaGoDa Conflict in Wolaita

In the weekend preceding November 8, 1999, the cadres in Wolaita Soddo imprisoned two teachers who opposed WoGaGoDa. In the morning of Monday November 8, 1999, the Soddo high school students after learning that two educators - one of them a high school teacher - had been imprisoned, marched to the police station and freed them from police custody. The angry students did not stop there. They marched to the store of the Ministry of Education where the books in the new language were stored broke it open and burned down the books.[472] On this day of angry protest, a significant number of citizens joined the student protesters. The town went out of control for a few hours.

According to the government account, on the day of the riots, two people were shot dead, five hotels and shops, and several residential houses as well as the store of the Bureau of Education were looted.[473] A few days later, on another "crackdown" on the student protesters, the police beat to death one female student and wounded over 150 school children.[474] According to the Ethiopian Human Rights Council report a total of 5 people were killed, 11 were shot and wounded, 2 disappeared, 78 were detained, and 10 were suspended from work. Twenty-nine were later released from detention, and 136 teachers were transferred from their work place to areas, which were defined as remote.[475] According to the author's informants, some 140 people who opposed WoGaGoDa were imprisoned for 4-6 months, 16 were incarcerated for 14 months each. The informants estimate at least 1,000 people were detained in Woreda prisons for from a few days to a month. The forced relocation of civil servants that began with the teachers reached many other government offices throughout Wolaita.

Though the most violent manifestation of the Soddo protest was put down in one day with the deployment of special army units and the local police force, the general resistance quickly spread into other Woredas and villages. Schools were closed down for almost two months in most parts of Wolaita. When the violent rebellion subsided in most parts of rural Wolaita, the cadres and the Kebele officials had to go into hiding for fear of reprisals.

It is important to note that in Soddo, even though the government poured a heavily armed *fetno-derash* (commando force), it was far from scaring the protesters who had poured into the streets. During the skirmish, the author remembers overhearing young protesters saying that "if we could die for Badime (referring to the place where many Ethiopian soldiers lost their lives in the then ongoing Ethio-Eritrean war), we should be ready to die fighting against the wrongs meted out to the people of Wolaita?" In one remote village the author saw young elementary school children march to the house of a school teacher who was a cadre and thus was engaged in propagating WoGaGoDa. This was the time when the fervent ethnically fueled conflict reached the level where the government would state the protesters had taken the matters into their own hands. It is not surprising that this violent crisis succeeded to attract the attention of national and international media.[476]

One of the formally organized aspects of the resistance against WoGaGoDa was the setting up of the Wolaita chima (elder) representative council, which appealed the Wolaita cause at various levels of the government bureaucracy up to the Prime Minster's office and to the national parliament demanding reinstatement of their language and at least a zonal level "self-administration" for Wolaita. The two simple questions put in a straightforward language were: While the new constitution entitles every nation, nationality and people of Ethiopia the right to use their own language, why was Wolaita denied this basic constitutional right and pressured to adopt WoGaGoDa as an official language? Secondly, in a country where less than 130,000 people were granted their own regional state (referring to the Harari region), why does the state deny over 2 million Wolaitas a status of at least zonal administration, if not regional state? Though these two questions seem simple and straightforward, the social constitutions of the group that formulated them and their feared political consequences were not.[477] Ultimately, the opponents of WoGaGoDa also demanded that those state agents who were responsible for such an unconstitutional act be removed from their offices and be brought to justice. In an interview with a BBC reporter, one of the Wolaita elder representatives stated "We were forced to accept 'WoGaGoDa' which was an insult to our culture... Why should we accept being ruled by a group of people we did not elect?"[478]

Social Organization of the Resistance

This conflict involved a number of social groups: state agents, students (from elementary school to higher level institutions), intellectuals (not just from Wolaita but from diverse backgrounds), elders, businessmen, religious leaders, ordinary peasants. Put otherwise, all the existing structures of the society including clan networks, religious institutions, schools and village institutions such as *Eder*, were mobilized in protest, as of course the state structure was also mobilized to its capacity to suppress the protest.

At this juncture, it is interesting to ask how the successful campaign was organized. The protest "officially" started when eight Wolaita elders submitted a letter to the Prime Minister's office dated 22/9/1991 (May 30, 1999) pinpointing the two main questions posed above. A month later, on June 29, 1999, the elders wrote to the Prime Minister demanding a reply to their earlier letter and at the same time repeating the same questions. This letter was also sent to the House of People's Representatives (the parliament), the House of Federation, the central office of the EPRDF, the Federal Minster of Education, the SNNPR council, the Regional Education Bureau, the North Omo Administrative Council, the North Omo Education Bureau, the administration of the seven Wolaita districts and the respective Education bureau of the seven Woreda of Wolaita. Until December 1999, the elders filed altogether six applications at the Prime Minister's office. But none of the applications were answered. In the end, most of the elders were imprisoned on charges of organizing looting and trying to overthrow the government. Most were incarcerated for about 14 months nad were released on bail and with the case still pending in 2005.

The state agents questioned the legitimacy of the "elders" as representatives of Wolaita. How did the chima (elders) get elected and who elected them? The "social construction" of the chima started with a few people in Soddo. And then they called in some handpicked elders from all the Wolaita districts who finally chose their chima (elder) representatives. In one of their applications to the Prime Minister's office, the elder representatives attached the minutes of a meeting in which they were elected. Whether this process was legitimate by a certain objective standard or not, the protesters took for granted the legitimacy of the elders. For example, the student demonstrators who took to the streets of Soddo on November 8 were shouting "we demand the questions asked by our chima be answered!"

The demonstrators accused the agents of ruling EPRDF of trying to discredit the "elders" by claiming they were mostly from one clan named Wolaita-Malla, which used to be the ruling clan of the kingdom of Wolaita before the Tigre clan of the Wolaita kingdom. It was true; more than half of the "elders" were from the Wolaita Malla clan. But as far as the author could observe, this was rarely raised as an issue by the people other than the party cadres.

The protesters accused the ruling party cadres for mobilizing an internal agitation to divide the opposition movement. Like many other societies of Southern Ethiopia, Wolaita was formerly stratified into the ruling lineage, free landowning citizen/ farmers, slaves, and artisans.[479] Though some social stigmas and even social discrimination emanating from this stratification is still affecting the lives of many people to a varying degree in various parts of the country,[480] it is not easy to tell how much role the lingering legacy of this stratification has played in the Wolaita resistance against WoGaGoDa. [481]

Another aspect of the social organization of this protest and the attempt to subdue it was how the issue of WoGaGoDa reached the ordinary peasants of Wolaita and how they reacted to it. The example for this can be found in the context of a funeral. In the middle of the WoGaGoDa conflict, I happened to attend a "Protestant funeral" in a relatively remote village of Wolaita which I have referred to earlier in the paper. As is customary in Protestant Christian way of organizing funeral rituals, a preacher read some verses from the Bible. It is also not uncommon that preachers often refer to outstanding contemporary social problems. The preacher in this particular funeral asked his listeners to pray for peace in the area which was disrupted because of WoGaGoDa. His diagnosis of the problem was the devil had made the government impose a strange language on the people of Wolaita and North Omo. In a discussion that ensued after the formal aspect of the funeral ritual was over, WoGaGoDa was the main subject of the talk among people. The mood was clearly agitated. A story was being circulated that in other parts of Wolaita, farmers had started chasing away the Kebele leaders, who were the nearest representatives of the government. Even in this Kebele, a high ranking zonal official who came to visit his family the previous evening, had to run away at night to the Woreda town after sensing "bad mood" in the area. It was also reported that some farmers from close by Kebeles poured into Soddo town at different point of the protest. In short, the peasant farmers were vital parts of the popular resistance.

Teachers and students were the most important channel through which the information about and against WoGaGoDa was disseminated. This was partly because they were the people immediately affected by the introduction of WoGaGoDa. Especially for elementary school teachers and their students, the introduction of WoGaGoDa meant some practical instructional difficulty since the "new language" contained some words which were not familiar to the speakers of Wolaita dialect. However, their protest was not limited to these immediate "practical reasons." The teachers and students were part of the whole community of intellectuals including university students who were highly discontented with WoGaGoDa and much more! What more was at stake?

Issues and Interests Regarding WoGaGoDa: A Discussion

Even the pro-EPRDF political scientist Vaughan calls WoGaGoDa a spectacular demonstration of political shortsightedness of the ruling EPRDF.[482] But by this, she refers only to the government's decision to give the "new language" the same name as the new EPRDF local wing, WoGaGoDa Peoples Democratic Organization. As she put it,

> The hostile reaction to the distribution of WoGaGoDa textbooks to the zone's [North Omo] schools in 1998 was rapid, widespread, and extreme. In failing to secure the support for its introduction even of the teachers who were responsible to inculcate the new language, the zone government had created a highly effective vehicle for the communication of discontent throughout both urban and rural areas of the zone. If teachers across the zone were unhappy, those in Wolaita Sodo town and its environs were furious.[483]

Here the author would like to stress the issue of "communication of discontent." What was held in common among all the protesters against WoGaGoDa was discontent with state misconduct. However, analytically, it is unhelpful to lump together issues and interests, though the two often crisscross each other's boundaries. For the intellectuals, WoGaGoDa was an imposition that disregarded too many local issues and interests. It was an outrageous decision to dissolve an identity category of groups of people without even properly consulting with them. To do so, the WoGaGoDa way was a gross underestimation of the kind of emotion ethnicity engenders and the fallout from its associated symbolic meaning. This was widely shared across the protesters including thw peasant farmers I talked to. The author disagrees with Vaughan who reduces the resistance against WoGaGoDa to a reflection of the material interests of Wolaita elite who, according to her, would benefit from budget injection if Wolaita becomes a separate zone. It may be obvious that the Wolaita elite, like elites elsewhere in the contemporary world, do have material interests to pursue in a way they deem fit. Where disagreement arises strongly is when Vaughan asserts "the Wolaita cause seems to have been of only indirect or marginal interest to the majority of its peasant farming population. Indeed one can make the case that, had the cause been designed in the service of the 'real' interests of this majority, it might in fact have favored their continued administration as part of a larger unit."[484]

Vaughan did not indicate her awareness of the fact that during the early 1990s, the strongest support to be part of the larger unit with the Omotic neighbours came from Wolaita elites. But nearly a decade later many of the Wolaita elite worked against that larger unit in the name of North Omo zone when they realized this was a unit of political mismanagement. Thus, it was an empirical experience with governance failure of this larger unit that led many Wolaitas to opt for further administrative reformulation within Omotic speakers. Besides, in themselves, larger units do not achieve anything if the subunits are pitted against each other and are thus obsessed with the suspicion that other sub-units only want to "snatch," as it were, one's resources.

These observations also contradict the claims of EPRDF cadres, that are echoed by Vaughan:

> A significant trigger of Wolaita insecurity was the dismissal and imprisonment in 1998 on corruption charges of Tefera Meskele, the powerful Chairman of both the Wolaita ruling party and the SEPDF [Southern Ethiopian Peoples Democratic Front], and a former Derg solider and TPLF POW. During Tefera's prominent reign as SNNPNRS Secretary, Wolaita had rested secure in the knowledge that their interests were more than well represented.[485]

The author's interviews with a cross-section of protesters and his own experience of Wolaita during Tefera's time in office as the regional secretary are contrary to Vaughan's claims. During that time period, Wolaita was not in turmoil not because people were contented with what was happening but mainly because Tefera had highly efficient repression apparatus in Wolaita, so many people who tried to resist state malpractice in one way or another were treated with characteristic harshness. After Tefera's removal from office, there seemed to have expired a short period of a let up in the party control machinery, at least in Wolaita, seemed to expire. Thus, open resistance against an imposed state policy seemed to have taken advantage of this window of opportunity (relapse in the control structure) than being a fight to reinstate any former cadre. One of the Wolaita chima (elders) the author interviewed reflects: "When I decided to join the chima (elder representatives) in protest against WoGaGoDa, I did not really think about Tefera's removal from office. But as I think about it now, I feel that had Tefera been in office, we might not have achieved what we have."[486]

The author was in Soddo town when the members of the ruling party held a meeting to decide whether or not to go ahead with WoGaGoDa. Party representatives were called in from the seven Woredas of Wolaita. The town was still extremely tense with a heavily armed special army unit cruising around the town in the beds of Toyota pick-up trucks. Notwithstanding this, the protesters took the chance to get across their message that there will not be any let up in the protest, should the party members continue with their earlier position of WoGaGoDa and reject the Wolaita question.

This meeting ended rather dramatically. The ruling party decided to abandon its earlier position on making WoGaGoDa the official language and thus decided to reinstate the "previous languages." The news was read on the national Ethiopian radio at 8:00 p.m. The effect was immediate. People were so happy that they poured into Soddo town at that late time. A few days later, the Prime-Minster went on the national TV admitting the leaders of the area (*ye akababiwu meriwoch*, who were the local agents of the ruling party) had made mistakes. But he still accused the political opponents of misleading "innocent citizens."

It is interesting to note, the agents of the ruling party seemed infuriated because opposition against WoGaGoDa was not about language per se but about politics. They accused the Wolaita elders and all those who were against WoGaGoDa of engaging in politics as though people are not supposed to engage in politics, not to mention accusations of opposition facing them.

Indeed, the agitation against WoGaGoDa was about politics. The impression the author got after observing some of the events related to WoGaGoDa and talking to varied actor groups is that opposition against WoGaGoDa was not politics in the paranoid sense of the party politicians. It was and continues to be politics of demanding an absolute minimum of rights, that people should have a say on matters affecting them directly, matters such as language and identity; a politics that demands the state to stop reducing the entire society to a few cadres and thereby requesting the state to stop thinking the view of these cadres is the only view that matters.

Having admitted its local agents had made a mistake, the government entrusted the same agents with the running of local affairs. While it is commendable that the government admitted having made mistakes and in the end stopped unduly punishing the victims of its flawed policy, the ruling party, by and large did not take responsibility for what had gone wrong, nor did it take sufficient measures to heal the social and psychological traumas sustained by victims. Thus, though a tradition of officially admitting being mistaken is a significant step forward, the culture of taking responsibility for one's mistakes is yet to emerge.

In conclusion, this empirical account of the making and unmaking of WoGaGoDa exemplifies how a top-down imposition of a 'unification project' has undermined an actually existing unity among the peoples of the region in question and the resultant resistance that for a while destabilized the region. At the end of the WoGaGoDa conflict, the real problem that needed a policy attention was left even more complicated. The author suggests one look at the conflict as a state-society conflict where the former came to be confronted with the majority members of the latter. At the root of this conflict is the state's failure to consult with the majority members of the society in favour, reliance on the opinions of its paid cadres. Thus, although WoGaGoDa appears to be an extreme case of policy imposition, it is not an exception. It is a particular manifestation of an enduring culture of power that characterizes generations of people who have come to dominate the Ethiopian national state.[487] A resistance against such state practice should therefore be looked at as a civil resistance against state misconduct.

The state 'invented' and imposed a language of instruction in schools reignited an enduring tension between the state and the society that has sediments from a long history of authoritarian rule. Against this background the author suggests one look at the WoGaGoDa conflict as state-society conflict. The conflict had indeed dragged a range of social groups and individuals. The school community had shown they are a critical agency able to use their strategic location between the state and the society. The state sought to utilize the potential of education as an instrument of governance that would ensure the state's control of the society. From this perspective, the fact that the school community stood against the state and in support of the society's cause is significant, though not so surprising, evidence attesting to the failure of the state to penetrate into the consciousness of the people it governs. In Foucaultian parlance, this is a failing of governmentality.

Finally, looking at WoGaGoDa as a unification project of a kind, highlights an important dilemma faced by all plural societies. It is not uncommon that such societies pursue unity as a desirable goal and one way of going about it might be progressively unifying the constituent subunits.

Knowing the deep interconnectedness of the communities of this region of Ethiopia, one cannot in principle object to the idea of promoting communalities in order to address some of the complex challenges faced by the people of the region and indeed by the nation at large. From this perspective, one would think the construction of something like WoGaGoDa would have been positive, in fact, an innovative, bold step forward towards politically/administratively managing diversity. In other words, as Abbink notes, "there is an objective need in this multi-ethnic and diverse Southern Region to sustain commonalities and shared institutions which facilitate the bridging [of] ethno-cultural and linguistic differences and define common issues and interests of efficient governance and economic development."[488] But WoGaGoDa simply added more to the problem than to the solution and thus prompted a fundamental question: is the state really addressing the issues or is it complicating the matter further?

In this particular case of Omotic speakers, the state policy clearly complicated the problem of an apparent diversity and micro-political boundaries. In fact, the particular policy of the state grossly misunderstood the historical, emotional, symbolic, economic and political dimensions of interconnectedness and distinctness and how either of these could be made relevant depending on the context. Thus, what was supposed to be a unifying project of small ethnic groups ended up undermining the existing ties. Like most integrationist attempts from above, in addition to ignoring the views and feelings of the majority members of the society, WoGaGoDa threatened the economic and political survival, the identity and the very humanity of some of its constituents. Hence, it was bound to fail; and left behind a painful legacy.

Although the processes of the resistance against WoGaGoDa stopped short of growing into an all-out ethnic conflict, tension (particularly between Wolaita and Gamo) escalated to a level not experienced within the last 100 years. As always, the real victims of these ethnic politics of opposition are ordinary citizens from all sides whose lives were torn apart or whose livelihoods were jeopardized by the government's faulty policy of inventing a new ethnic group with its own language of instruction. Not surprisingly, that callous action infuriated the stakeholders.

8

DEVELOPMENT POLICY, EDUCATION AND TRAINING: WOMEN AND CHANGE IN CONTEMPORARY ETHIOPIA[489]

JUDITH NARROWE

This chapter scrutinizes discourses of development and social transformation as expounded by various Ethiopian women during the past two decades. The chapter holds public policy and implementation jointly and uses them as a common framework for analysis. It spotlights the ethnography engendered during the process of examining the implementation of three different tasks revolving on the status of women in rural and urban settings. The projects involve diverse characteristics of education and training. In their import, they exhibit an expressed target that tries to uplift the status of women in Ethiopia. The investigation conducted and the discourses spawned by the participants in the evaluation process expose variations in the substance and the appearance of the narratives. Whereas, for Narrowe, expressions of 'development' maintain a pivotal spot in the discourses, thoughts in recent narratives regarding 'development' of young urban females at a teacher's college appear to be influenced by debates raging regarding globalization. According to the author, the deliberations involved locate 'development' and 'tradition' in a similar continuum; and as a causus beli of modernity in today's Ethiopia, they also spawn sharp perceptions of national as well as individual distinctiveness.

In looking at Women's education in Ethiopia, it is important to examine aspects of the dynamics of the encounter between centrally directed, international, development co-operation policies on the one hand, and local responses, on the other. Most generally, the author's analysis is influenced by the traditional anthropological concern with everyday life in local societies as well as with the on-going discussion of globalization and its effects on local communities.[490] Thus, the focus of the study is based on changes which occur at the nexus of the global-local connection. The specific concern of the author is with the variety of development aid policies which have been implemented in the course of several decades by two governments of Ethiopia and which are particularly directed toward women. The chapter will review some of the 'classic' development policies intending to teach skills, alleviate poverty, and/or provide basic needs and will argue that these differ in kind from more recent so-called affirmative action policies. The position taken is the affirmative action policies, while indeed promoting education and skill training, also purport to influence women to contest not only traditional women's roles but to urge them to change some ways of presenting themselves in social life.

Voices from the Fields: an Introduction

I begin with three incidents which took place over the course of some fifteen years in the context of women-oriented development programs in Ethiopia. Each resonates with comments on some of the changes experienced by these women both in their personal lives and in the lives of their communities.

In 1988, I participated in the final evaluation of an Ethiopian-Swedish water project. One afternoon, after I had spoken at length with one of the women who was employed by the project and had participated in the project's training program, I got in my car and was about to drive to another section of the town to interview one of her colleagues. Somewhat impetuously and spontaneously, I asked her whether she knew how to drive. "No," she said, but added with a vaguely aggressive tone in her voice, "but all you have to do is teach me." [491]

Some years later, I attended a meeting in a training centre in a village near the city of Jimma with twenty women, all of whom had participated in a project which involved training in income-generating skills. We had spent some hours discussing their views of the project. Just before we parted, I wondered whether we could discuss just one more question. "If you don't mind" I said, "can you tell me how your lives differ from your mothers' lives?" One young woman stood up and exclaimed, loudly and happily: "Oh Yodit, there is big difference. My mother was just like that stove over there. You didn't even see her. She just cooked and … she just was. And I… well, look at me; I'm sitting here discussing ideas with you! That's a huge difference…"[492]

More recently, in 2003, I sat in a dormitory room at a teacher's college in Addis Ababa with some female students. We were discussing the current government's affirmative action policies. I asked them to try to evaluate its effects:

> Girls: "Well, you know, there is still a gender hierarchy here; boys have more power,"
>
> The author: "Where? In the classroom?"
>
> Girls: "Well, the class representatives are usually boys. If the girls are elected, the boys dominate. Ok, it is true that there are some changes in the traditional gender structure, but the boys don't accept the change, though they think they have changed. The talk is ok, but not the practice. "[493]

All of these women participated in projects which had been initiated in the context of 'development' and development aid. Two of the policies and ensuing programs included education and training components and were intended most generally to improve women's lives, to provide women's basic needs and/or to include women as specific actors in the development process. The third reflects the so-called affirmative action policy originating in the United States, and focuses on 'levelling the playing field' by privileging disadvantaged and/or disabled minorities, specifically 'women' in this case, by admitting them to institutions from which they have traditionally been excluded.[494]

No doubt, all of the policies and associated programs have initiated a process of change in the lives and thoughts of the women participating. But what I will argue here is that the affirmative action policy introduces a radically different discourse, one which specifically proffers gender equality in addition to 'development' as its goal. Rather than focusing on organizing projects which intend to improve skills and job-related competencies, affirmative action policies begin with an acknowledgment of power structures characterized by hierarchy and inequality and encourage women to consciously and purposefully devise and implement personal and communal strategies to resist and/or counteract these structures. In this sense, affirmative action can be seen as more intrusive than other development interventions in that it openly supports empowerment and intends to counteract traditional gender-related norms.

Policy, Practice, Development, and Gender: the Scope of the Research

To place my argument and the accompanying ethnography in a broader context, I will first briefly define what I mean by the concepts of 'policy' and 'development.' I will then review several of the types of policies which have characterized international development co-operation programs since the 1970s. Where necessary, I will include how these policies affected or included 'women.' I will then move to Ethiopia and will very briefly summarize some of the major themes which have framed the Ethiopian gender discussion since 1974. Finally, I will introduce the particular projects in which I participated and will provide a forum for some of the women who participated in the programs or projects to comment on their experiences. I conclude with an analysis of their comments and will argue the most recent policy of affirmative action differs in kind and purpose from previous policies. My point is that in addition to providing education and training programs, the current affirmative action programs in Ethiopia, while by no means universally appreciated, have broadened the focus of gender-oriented policies from job-oriented skill training for women to a concern with gender equality more generally with a specific strategy to achieve this. Affirmative action would thereby seem to depart from a more critical view of the social organization of society and to promote an essentially new view of self.

The Conceptual Framework: Defining 'Policy' and 'Development'

By policy I mean "a more general notion than a decision [which] involves a predisposition to respond in a specific way."[495] This 'predisposition to respond' or, more simply, to act, is promoted, articulated and implemented by some rather specific directives which openly purport to affect some aspect of the society and/or the respondents' lives.[496] It is this aspect of policy-- how it changes lives and how the participants of policy describe these changes-- which is my concern here. This view of policy is most closely related to that of Shore and Wright, who have suggested, somewhat radically, that policy "shapes the way individuals construct themselves as subjects." [497] Viewed this way, policy is more than a "technical, rational, action-oriented instrument that decision-makers use to solve problems and affect change." [498] My argument is that in the long run, policies, in the course of being implemented and practiced in the form of programs, can and do also function as instruments which not only create competencies but also generate ideas and ultimately, as the women above point out, change perception of self. [499]

'Development' is more difficult and far more contentious to define. As will become apparent in the short summary of development policies I present below, the term is intimately linked with Western governments' views of the need for particular types of change in post-colonial states as well as the implementation of specific policies and programs to effectuate these changes. [500] For the sake of this discussion, I will regard development a powerful set of ideas which has guided thought and action across the world ... It involves deliberately planned change and continues to affect the lives of many millions of people world over." [501] Here, note that the definition avoids any mention of the power of 'the West' or the' North' as the necessary source and the standard of 'development.' What the 'powerful ideas' consist of, where they come from, and how they change become an ethnographic question which needs to be examined in particular contexts.

'Gender' in Development Policies: Trajectories of Change

Policies targeting 'women' have been present in one form or another other in development co-operation programs since some time in the early 1970s. when development policy makers saw fit to disaggregate the phrase the 'rural poor' and officially recognized women as actors and stakeholders in the development process. [502] In the decades that followed, we can identify several different discourses and related policies all of which can be seen in the context of the somewhat lopsided dialogue between external macro institutions such as the World Bank, the ILO and aid-dependent governments, and internal movements propelled by feminist organizations and local NGOs. [503] In the paragraphs that follow, I will briefly describe these policies and where and how they affected women.

At the close of the Second World War, national and international agencies initiated widespread development aid programs for the new states in what was the former colonial world. The definition of 'development' was then synonymous with economic growth and the transfer of commodities. This was to be accomplished by 'aid' in the form of large infrastructural projects and the provision of investment capital. The hoped-for resultant wealth was expected to 'trickle down' to the populace. The assumption or expectation was that higher rates of productivity, coupled with industrialization and modernization would lead to needed change. By the 1970s, however, it became clear that the expected 'trickle down' did not happen and poverty remained. We can thus identify a new tone in the development discourse whereby development was disassociated from growth and development policies focused directly on addressing the 'basic needs' of the poor, including women. Priority was now given to "poverty alleviation as an overriding development priority and the emergence of a more coherent call for an alternative development paradigm that places human well-being and agency at the centre of the development process." [504] Somewhat later, at the close of the 1970s and well into the 1980s, in conjunction with the rise of neo-liberalism and the ensuing structural adjustment programs, the focus shifted once again from addressing 'basic needs' of the poor, including what were often thought of as women's basic needs, to what have been called 'efficiency' arguments. Again, the focus was women. The efficiency arguments maintain, in general terms, that attention to and support of women are important components in development programs and attention to women will result in more efficient development. Its proponents maintain, in short, that in order to make development work, women are necessary participants in development schemes and projects. The approach, termed Women in Development (WID), is essentially market oriented and is characterized by a clear emphasis on production and productivity and on providing the training or education components needed to make participation in production possible.[505] Characteristic of projects associated with this policy, two of which I mentioned about and will review below, were extensive programs for skill training for productive jobs as well as formal and informal educational programs for girls and women.

No doubt, the most ideologically irrefutable of these policies is the gender equality or human rights approach launched by feminists many decades ago and still present as a dominant discourse. Put somewhat simply, the dominant position held by them was/ is women would have and could have contributed more to development had they been faced with fewer social and cultural constraints. What they more openly propose is to identify and mitigate the gender-based hierarchies which prevent or hinder women's participation in development programs. Advocates of this view, often sought and supported official legislation which could promote these changes.[506]

It is in this context, one which promotes gender equality and admits or acknowledges the existence of constraints of all kinds on the participation of women in development activities, that the concept of empowerment becomes relevant. While I do not doubt the emphasis on needs and efficiency remains, what is more central is the acknowledgment of the "nebulous territory of power and social injustice."[507] In these 'territories,' policies, programs and projects can be seen as frameworks or structures which probably promote possibilities for change, but what matters more in the long term is the change in participants' perception of their selves. In other words, empowerment implies some modicum of self consciousness and an acknowledgment of the presence of choices; "thus refers to the expansion in people's abilities to make strategic life choices in a context where this ability was previously denied them."[508] Defined this way, empowerment implies not only recognizing the need to initiate and implement changes in overall social and cultural systems but it more specifically implies the need to effect changes in individual consciousness. It is here, I contend, that the basic needs and efficiency policies differ from affirmative action: the first emphasizes training and income-producing jobs; the second promotes a critical view of the social organization of society. It acknowledges inequality and intends to 'level the playing field' by women moving themselves in, up and out.[509]

To summarize, gender policies in development co-operation contexts have moved in any or all of three directions: toward the market and skills-based production, toward meeting basic needs and alleviating poverty, and towards self realization and empowerment. The first policies emphasize efficiency and market-oriented production and are perhaps most succinctly expressed in programs for job-specific training. The second are policies which focus on providing basic needs and on recognizing the constraints within social, economic and cultural systems which prevent the satisfaction of basic needs. The third, and most elusive, are policies which encourage empowerment and are most heavily directed toward urging individuals to recognize their choices or lack of such and recognizing and realizing their power to change. It might be that affirmative action policies have this effect.

The remainder of this paper will be concerned with exploring how these several policies have been pursued, practiced and understood in Ethiopia. My particular concern is three women-oriented projects in which I have actively participated, both as an external evaluator and as a researcher. The first project took place in the late 1980s in the area of Arsi, some 100 kilometres south of Addis Ababa, and had as its goal the construction of a gravity-fed water system. The project was somewhat unusual in that the entire community identified the need for the system and participated in its construction. The project might probably be placed as focusing on both basic needs and efficiency. The second project, somewhat similar to the first, took place in the early 1990s in several areas of rural Ethiopia. The purpose was to train women to improve their income-generating skills and to then market their locally-made products. The third project - more a well-defined policy as well as concrete Programme was the most recent and is related to the Ethiopian government's affirmative action policy. Quite like the previous projects, it is also a policy which focuses on bringing women into the development process but it includes, as I have argued above, an extra dimension, indeed a new discourse. It not only involves training for a job but also openly encourages the participating women to change some aspects of traditionally normative behaviour. I thereby want to steer the argument to my original question: in the context of these several policies, how do policies "shape the way individuals construct themselves as subjects?

Women and Development in Ethiopia: A Cursory Review

Certainly, the inception of the Mengistu government in 1974 and until the present, there has been a constant and conscious acknowledgment of the problems of women in Ethiopia, most particularly on their subordinate status and on ingrained traditions of discrimination. Official attempts have been made on the part of governmental as well as social, legal and educational institutions to alleviate these problems and to bring women into the development process. The Revolutionary Ethiopian Women's Association, REWA, one of three mass organizations formed by the Derg government in the late 1970s, sought to activate women in local communities by establishing Women's Associations in all Peasant Associations (PA's).[510] When the Derg was disbanded in 1991 and the current government was established, a multi-tiered structure of women's offices was constructed, topped by the Prime Minister's unit and creating offices in all zones and woredas.[511]

Most significant in this context is Article 25 of the present constitution which specifically outlaws discrimination on all bases. Article 35 focuses specifically on women and equality and mandates affirmative action policies to ensure that women will be able to enter Ethiopian society on an equal status with men.[512] The current government has also supported a Programme to outlaw what are called the 'harmful traditional practices' such as early marriage, female genital mutilation, removing the epiglottis and marriage by abduction.[513] Thus, in today's Ethiopia, there is an audible formal discourse as well as a formal structure whereby women's problems and legal rights are recognized, if less often respected.[514]

How successful these policies and structures have been is a moot point. The Ethiopian historian Bahru Zewde has argued "gender discourse in Ethiopia could be said to have barely begun…It is still at the stage where the all-important thing is the liberation of women from legal and social oppression."[515] The emphasis is placed on 'women' rather than 'gender' and men are, to date, rather passive actors in this process. Thus, not surprisingly, Tsehai Berhane-Selassie points out that these official structures and policies have had a minimal effect on women's possibilities to gain real power in

Ethiopia.[516] She adds neither the REWA during the Derg or the current government's women's offices "have truly addressed the needs of rural women."[517]

The reasons for this are several and interrelated. The young student teachers at the teacher's college point out the policies originate with Western donors and are mainly 'tokens' to please them. This is one reason, they maintain, why local personnel currently employed in the several levels of women's offices receive little funding, little training and have very little local clout. Related to this might be the well-known divide between top-down policies which encourage change and socially ingrained local practices and/ or traditions which incur resistance and/or act as constraints.[518] One recurrent theme mentioned by many of the students is that these policies, specifically those working toward gender equality, are very much imposed on "beggar Ethiopia" by the hegemonic 'West' and take too little cognizance of Ethiopian traditions and values.[519] While they admit the need for change with regard to the perception of women and men and their relationships, they insist that the West's concept of gender equality is "not our culture" and that this kind of change will have to be defined and effectuated within a specifically Ethiopian cultural framework.

In this context, the possible influence of cultural ideas or 'schemes' on views of change, I find the work of the Swedish social anthropologist Eva Poluha most significant. In the course of her thirty years of conducting research in Ethiopia, Poluha has attempted to understand some of the underlying reasons for women's subordinate status in Ethiopian society. In one important article, she focuses on women's participation - or lack of such - in political life in a village in Gojjam.[520] She points out women are largely silent in the political sphere, and attributes their silence to traditional socialization practices and domestic relations whereby women are expected to be obedient, silent and compliant. Thus, while the present constitution explicitly promises legal equality between men and women and the present government and other bodies make conscious, if often faltering, attempts to uphold these rights, customary domestic practices reinforce these traditional hierarchical gender structures in everyday life. Men are formally heads of households. Men may criticize wives but not the reverse. Girls still marry younger than boys and girls spend much of their time inside their homes, while boys are outside. Boys are expected to take initiatives and to speak up, while girls' knowledge is mainly related to how it promotes their chances for a good marriage. Girls are encouraged even exhorted to stay behind.[521] She concludes: "Growing up in such an environment has implications for boys and girls and how they view themselves and each other when young and later as adults as for how they will behave in different contexts, private and public."[522] It is thus the social organization of the rural village which inhibits political participation. Rural women lack regular contact with non-kin social groups, their social lives are restricted to family. There are no institutions or organizations in which they can become aware of, say, political issues and their rights to participate. Thus "rural women in Ethiopia lack structures to create a common consciousness."[523]

Convinced the possible roots of women's silence lies in child socialization practices, Poluha conducted a one-year ethnographic study of daily life in an urban school in Addis Ababa and in a village school in Gojjam. In her recently published findings, she argues two basic 'cultural schemes' continue to characterize life in both schools and, by implication, in Ethiopia: the first is a respect for hierarchy and the second, an unwillingness to question those whose status is higher. Thus she finds women submit to men, children to adults, adults to government officials, etc. Not surprisingly, these gender roles and perceptions of self are implanted, praised and reinforced during childhood and are powerfully carried over into adulthood.

Poluha's portrayal of 'women as silent' in political contexts raises an important issue with regard to gender policies. It points toward the need to train women both to enter the job market and to effectuate an inward personality change to become, as I was told time and time again during my research at the teacher's college, less 'shy' and more 'assertive.' It is exactly in this context that the affirmative action policy would seem to be different in kind from previous job and needs oriented policies. Policies and programs which train women to work and/or improve their work-oriented skills are mainly concerned with entering the job market; the programs make no mention of inequalities in the social structure or women's 'innate' disability or 'culture.' Quite the contrary, it is in this context that I suggest that affirmative action is different and promotes a different message. Affirmative action provides a discourse as well as concrete opportunities to 'level the playing field' and creates or seeks to create concrete opportunities whereby women and men can start from a position of equality.[524] In the Ethiopian context, it also implies women need to change, become 'different,' more assertive, less shy, less 'silent'.

Two Plus One Field Studies: A Comment on Methods

The comments given above will suffice as a general political and social context for the projects I describe below. I now turn to the projects themselves but will first briefly position myself as participant-researcher and describe the methods used to collect information. As mentioned above, the first took place in the mid-1980s and involved training local women to manage and administer a water project in the woreda of Dodota in Arsi.[525] The second was completed in 1990 and intended to provide training for rural women in marketable skills which would help them increase their incomes. The third project, more specifically a study, was conducted between 2002 and 2004 and was different in kind from the others. Here I concentrated on very directly on social relations at the teacher's college and, most specifically, on teachers and student views of the affirmative action policy.

Each of the studies was conducted using qualitative methods in the form of semi-structured interviews with both groups and individuals. The third study included eight months of participant observation. All of the interviews took place in contexts familiar to the respondents – in their homes, in village meeting rooms, and on the lawns and paths of the teachers' college. In the first and second studies, I was a newcomer to Ethiopia and clearly an outsider who was recruited by a foreign funded agency to quickly evaluate the education and training aspects of the projects.[526] In the third study, I was not only older and perhaps a bit wiser but my role was different. Because I had been a visiting lecturer at the college for five weeks and had spent eight months over a period of three years at the college as an active fieldworker, I was known as a teacher, a social anthropologist and a long term fieldworker. Not quite a stranger or an outsider, in time I became a fixture on the college campus, participating in daily life and observing and discussing social life and gender relationships at every opportunity.[527] I attended class with the students, sat in the girls' dormitory rooms for hours, and with students in the college dining room and went to their parties. In addition to this extensive participant observation and constant group and individual interviews, I collected students' life stories and conducted several surveys. The comments I refer to below are the result of many relaxed conversations about gender and equality and social relations at the college.[528]

Two questions were asked of all respondents—village women and urban students. The first involved a comparison between the respondent's life and her mother's life. I have found this question to be a good one; it often prompts a quiet moment of wondering, a modicum of reflexivity, sometimes a bit of pride and/or anger, and leads easily to other change-oriented questions.

The second question related more directly to the specific Programme or project and concerned the effect of the training programs on the women's lives. Here I must insert a caveat: in the evaluation studies, I suspect my presence as an outsider and one who clearly represented the funding agency, introduced some kind of bias in their answers.

I contend, somewhat hesitatingly, that no such bias intruded in the teacher's college study. There, I occupied the comfortable, in-between or neutral position of the anthropologist, not for or against anything. There were no donors around and the students soon discovered there were no right or wrong answers and that they were, indeed, actively participating in research which they found important.

The Dodota Water Supply Project - 1988-89

The first project was a gravity-fed water system which was constructed with the combined efforts of the REWA, thousands of local villagers in the woreda of Dodota in Arsi, and Swedish Sida. The construction of the system coincided with the Mengistu government's villagization policy, the government moved people who had lived in isolated farms into villages or Peasant Associations, and provided them with new homes, a school and a medical clinic, and close-by neighbours.[529] Members of the villages participated as well in three national organizations - The Peasant Association (PA), the women's Association (REWA) and the Youth Association, (REYA) as well as several community-wide organizations, most particularly the Producers Co-operatives.

The water project/system can be seen as one outcome of both the basic needs and the efficiency policies which were propagated and legitimated by the overall ideology and concomitant political Programme of the Marxist government. The Programme mandated frequent meetings and encouraged discussions of the importance of development, local input and job-oriented training, and emphasized the responsibility of local people to participate in development-oriented activities.

The water system was a good example of this; it was one specific outcome of many discussions with women in the area who unequivocally identified lack of water as their greatest problem and the main hindrance to development.[530] When the water system was completed in 1986, it brought piped clean water to taps near the homes of the residents of three towns and nineteen villages, and thereby rather drastically changed the lives of women and men in Dodota; they now had access to clean water close to their homes, their children's health had improved, some village women were working and getting paid. The project was deemed successful in several evaluations and its general procedures have been used as a model for other Sida-supported water-centred projects in Ethiopia.[531]

The comments which follow below were made by women living in the midst of obvious change, some of which they themselves suggested, influenced and implemented. Most of the women I quote in the interviews below were 'water ladies,' women who had been trained for several weeks to manage and administer the water project and who were currently employed by the water system. I and my interpreter conducted most of the interviews in the women's homes, at the water taps where the women were working or walking home with the 'water ladies' after work.

The following comments were made in response my question, "What do you see as the difference between your life and your mother's life?" The question encouraged comparison and reflection and was always preceded with a noticeable moment of thought-filled silence. Three themes emerge to differentiate their lives from their mothers' lives: improved technology has made their lives easier, their job and salary have meant more independence for them as individuals, and education is the key to improvements in life and is crucial.

> "During my childhood, I was responsible for the landlord's cows. Now I am responsible for my daughter and she will go to school." T, 35.

> "My mother was a farmer's wife but I get a salary. My daughter will lead a better life. She will serve her country and herself." S, 28

> "There's a big difference. They were olden times when ground grain by hand, fetched water from the pond and crushed barley in hollow pits. Now we are partly idle, we are sitting. Women now must learn all things, to read and write." T, 64.[532]

> "They were in the house; they didn't go out like we do. We are out and do what we want. My mother was economically dependent, we are independent we buy what we want, and we make plans."

> "I am trained, salaried; my mother didn't get the chance."

> "The job changed my life. Now I get a salary, now I buy what I need."

> "My mother didn't go to literacy class and when I was little I was a shepherd. Now I am not in that position any more."

> "I was in the PA and in the fields. Now I am in an office and it is better."

> "My life is different from my mothers because I am an employee." W, 26.

> "I am trained, I get a salary, and I have a chance my mother didn't get."

Shewaye summarized her situation more fully:

> I like my work [as a 'water lady]. I have seen an improvement in my life. I have a salary. Even to work with people like these is an improvement… Formerly we had no relationships with people. We were sitting at home and had no public relations with people. Now I work with people every day and have relationships with them. This is a great improvement. People in the village say: "you supply us with water." I like that. No other people have such job.

I conclude with the remarks of Woizero Daro, 23, the mother of one child whose husband was away at the front at the time. I asked her how the water system affected her life. She looked at me for a long moment and said:

> With the time we save [by not having to fetch water from the river] we do many things. We work in our fields and gardens, make baskets… but this is nothing, not like carrying a water jug, an insera on your back for three hours. When we had to get water from the river, we killed time. Now we save time. Before, things went down not up. Now things are going up.

The optimism expressed by Woizero Daro is one outcome of the success of the Women in Development policy. She and her fellow villagers acknowledge the introduction of new technology and the opportunities for training and education have changed their lives for the better. But the responsibility aspect of empowerment is absent; in the evaluation report of the water project, while highly positive with regard to the procedures used and the outcome of this particular project, the team concluded somewhat paradoxically, that "the [mass women's] organization had not been able to strengthen the involvement, initiative and responsibility of women for matters of concern to them."[533] Put in the context of my question in this paper- how do policies "shape the way individuals construct themselves as subjects?"- this skills-oriented policy, as it was implemented in Ethiopia in the early 1990s, certainly motivated and, indeed trained women to participate in projects which satisfied felt or basic needs. But the women seemed to stop there: perhaps 'tradition,' perhaps the pressures of the political system in which this project took place, did not encourage women to move into the centre of development issues. They seemed to remain grateful participants and recipients rather than initiators of change.

The Women in Adult Education Pilot Project 1990

I turn now to a project which had a similar emphasis - an attempt to include women in the development process by training them for a job and/or income-oriented skills. The project was managed by the then Department of Adult and Continuing Education (DACE) and provided training for women to improve their income-generating skills and thereby improve their living standards and increase their contribution to development. The more general goal of this particular project was to strengthen the adult education infrastructure and to sensitize adult educators at all levels to the importance of women's accessibility to education and to skill-training programs. Conducted in the final years of the Mengistu regime (1989-90), the project utilized the woreda-based Community Skill Training Centres (CSTC's) and conducted courses which would train women from local Peasant Associations in skills for income generation, in mud technology and Family Life Planning. The course trainees would then return to their PA's and train local women to do the same - one example of the oft-used 'multiplier effect' is in training programs.

In the evaluation of this project, the participants identified a perceptible personal gain but a less positive general outcome of the project than that which occurred in Dodota. The evaluation suggested several reasons for this: first, too little attention was paid to involving the women in the goals of the project and encouraging them to identify their needs.[534] Problems, Progress and the Next Phase of the Women in Adult Education Pilot Project, and, second, too little emphasis was given to concrete skill-training. [535] More problematic, I think, was the gradual weakening of the political organizational structure: the PA's were no longer obligated to provide food for the trainees at the CTSA's and REWA could no longer demand women in the village provide money for training materials. Still, conversations with many women in two of the project sites indicated a strong interest in the training aspects of the project and in the possibilities it gave the women to increase their incomes.

The positive tones of the women's views are very audible in the following excerpts from the evaluation. We had begun our discussions with a rather general appraisal of local resources. They quickly changed the topic and spoke about their views of the training, the courses and their work, and the needs of their community. Here are some of the things they said:

> "What we need is a kindergarten [because] our children prevent us from working."

"We like the courses in soap-making; we will the children and we will sell it. We have many things in our homes that we made and can use and can also sell."

"Every training we got at the CTSC was new for us. We never had any training before…The candle and soap-making was best. We need light here."

"Soap and candle-making, tie and dye, rope and bag-making. Now we have to buy everything from the market. If we get training, we save money because soap is scarce and expensive. We will use what we make at home."

I wondered how the agricultural calendar affected their participation in the training. Again, they insisted that training is primary:

"We are busy but we will always have time for training. There will always be someone left here when the rest of us go to the fields. I will even carry my child on my back to come for training."

I wanted to focus on how they perceived changes in their world. I began by asking how they defined the Amharic term for development, *lemmät:*

"It is planting with irrigation, it's digging a well. They used to call it work (laugh), now they call it *lemmät.* …Training is also *lemmät* but *that is* a new thing for us."

We all laughed. Planners always find new words for old phenomena. The women again pointed out that training was new and valuable for them. One woman then referred specifically to my question about the difference between their lives and their mothers' lives as an example of change:

"Our mothers had huge workloads in the house and on the farms. They ground their own grain and they never went to meetings with men. Now we have mills and we go to gatherings and meetings and we discuss with each other."

An elderly woman concluded:

"I am sorry I am getting old. Between my time and today there is a great difference. When I was young, our husbands didn't allow us even to go out. Now we sit and discuss everything, even with men."

What emerges in the statements of these women as well as those of the women in Dodota is an awareness of the great changes in their lives. No doubt some of this awareness and accompanying rhetoric derived from the Mengistu government's outspoken ideology which was propagated in every possible context and which condemned the "oppression of women" and the "oppression of the feudal system." Again and again, the women refer to their "better lives" and their newly-found ability to discuss "ideas," There is however another message which is less politically motivated and more long lasting, and which lauds the importance of education: "we will always have time for training," and, "every training we got at the CTSC was new for us. We never had any training before."

Throughout the discussions, both the WAEPP and the Dodota women referred rather constantly to the practical results of the projects. There are also hints of a market orientation and a loud acknowledgment of the value of training as a means of making or saving money. What becomes clear here is that the distinctions between policies which are so easily drawn in policy-making circles become quite blurred in the real world. The women refer to the importance of 'markets,' to the provision of resources connected with their basic needs, and to their power to (somehow) accomplish their goals. The various policy discourses thus merge very comfortably in their comments.

Gender and Affirmative Action: The Kotabe College of Teacher Education 2002-2004

My focus in this study was quite different from the first two. Here, I was formally concerned with analyzing the implementation of a policy which was not connected to development co-operation or to a particular 'project,' but was rather specifically meant to increase the numbers of female students at Ethiopian institutions of higher learning. The policy, which is officially termed 'affirmative action' is widespread throughout the world and intends to redress the effects of discrimination and to improve the subordinate status of subaltern groups by introducing preferential treatment for member of these groups. The policy has been applied at many institutions of higher learning in Ethiopia and is based on Article 35 of the Constitution of Ethiopian which outlines the government's responsibility and women's rights to affirmative actio - openly legitimating preferential treatment in order to achieve de facto equality.

With this policy as background, my particular concern was everyday social life and social relations at the college. I intended to explore whether and how the female and male students reacted to the presence of increased numbers of female students at the college and whether the widespread rhetoric about 'gender equality' affected social life. What whetted my interest when I began my field work at the college was the one-day workshop in 'assertiveness training' which was obligatory for all first year female students.[536] The workshop focused on three themes: the importance of learning good study habits, the dangers of HIV-AIDS and the need for the girls to learn to become less shy and more assertive. The assumptions of the workshop were clear from the outset: the girls were thought to have problems at the college which clearly related to the fact that they were girls: their poor study habits were a result of too many duties in their homes; they were assumed to know too little about sex and HIV-AIDS, they had a culturally acknowledged tendency to be 'silent' and shy.

What was new here, and indeed different in kind from the typical development-oriented policies in which I had previously participated was the girls were to learn not only new skills as students but a new way of conducting themselves socially, as well as a rather new personality- to become more assertive, *defar,* and less shy, *aynafar.* The content and structure of the workshop seemed to relate specifically to the recent discourse in feminist as well as development co-operation contexts where empowerment seen as personal choice-making a new view of self is emphasized. Here, it seemed to me, the thrust of the hoped-for change was different from other policies; the girls were presented with a new person-oriented discourse where *change was seen as cultural as well as structural.* The goal was not only training for jobs and higher incomes but training for a new way of acting, a new view of self and a new way to conduct oneself socially. Rather than goal-oriented training, the Programme seemed to edge toward the 'changed behaviour' goal reminiscent of the classic definition of 'education.'

What does Affirmative Action Affirm? Comments from Kotabe

The students' views of affirmative action varied: some girls pointed out that 'it's not so great but we wouldn't be here without it,' others were less sure. I discussed the

Programme with Segenet, a very articulate second year student of English and Amharic. She was less than positive:

> "The 2.6 [entrance points] make people think we are weak. OK, I know that the government allows us to enter college with lower marks to encourage us, but people, some boys and some girls, take this to mean that our ability is less. We are always defined as less. In high school, we are kicked and harassed, but look, we have challenged them and we are here, but they don't know how much we are done. That is the major problem with gender – It is always the girls' fault."

I turned to her male classmate, Fish; he agreed:

> "Of course it is good because men and women must be made equal but the reason is not good. Because women are given affirmative action, they become dependent and they rely on the men and the system to help them. It doesn't give them self confidence…The policy has to be seen in practice. It is like the don't discriminate' policy; it is not practiced."

Blen, a first year female student, wanted to broaden our focus and made some more general statements about Ethiopian women. She looked annoyed:

> "Look, even if women work very hard and if no one supports them – like the government. It is meaningless and we won't have change. Women have many problems in the house, that's why we must let them join a college with lower marks.

Blen's comments were repeated by many girls: 'our position is difficult; we needed this help' she continued:

> "We must work hard." Menelik's wife, Taytu said, 'I will fight against the colonialists.' My task is to work, to fight for instance against poverty and HIV by not discriminating against People Living with AIDS."

The Author: "and povery?"

> "By working hard. I have to use my time to work, not to talk about just anything."

The Author: "your future?"

> "To be a teacher of English at the university... We are strong and equal because of education. Our mothers did not go out, they thought God made them inferior, but God made me from the middle, not the foot nor the head… I am not inferior."

I turned to a male student, then president of the Student Council, and began by asking about social life at the college. The conversation revealed his ponderings - elicited probably by my question about social life but focusing very specifically on 'culture:'

The Author: "We were talking about social life here…What has happened?"

Fikadu: "Last year, we were not intimate. We didn't say hello to girls because of the culture. Now because of our intimacy we are like sisters."

The Author: "What do you mean by 'the culture?'"

Fikadu: "We are shy. In our families when the elders talk, they told us to go away. We were not allowed to speak with elders. Now I have my own ideology – if this culture won't get up, I'll go my own way. I'm not shy now."

The Author: "and the girls?"

Fikadu: "They are more extroverted, that is good. Why? Because the environment backs them up. Boys are more exposed but the girls are becoming extrovert. This environment at KCTE makes us equal. We share ideas; we like to express what we feel. Nowadays the government and the college emphasize girls because people thought the girls are oppressed by men in the past. In Ethiopia, women are not equal; in Addis Ababa, they are becoming equal; at Kotabe, we are equal."

Finally, I relate a conversation I had with five second-year girls in their dorm room, which they named, in the best traditions of modernism, the 'room of promises'. The conversation touches upon themes of 'development,' culture and equality. We had been discussing the topic of gender equality:

The Author: "So what do you think about gender equality here?"

Azeb: "We think men are superior because they work hard. Not only that: they joined [the college] with 2.8. We had fewer points."

The Author: "So why do you think the government did it - admit women with lower marks and fewer points?"

Azeb: "Because there are not enough educated women."

The Author: "But why admit women with lower marks?"

Azeb: "Because we don't have enough time to study when we are at home. Our families give us more work than boys because in our culture, the women have to do the housework. That belief makes us feel inferior, and we don't score high scores."

Azeb's opinions were not shared by her roommates.

Selamawit: " I don't agree with this belief. There are girls who don't work at home and still score low on the exam."

Tiyint: "And it's not like that in my home. I do things and my brother does things."

Azeb insisted that these girls were exceptional: "There is still a belief in our country that boys are better. We hear that from our childhood, and we feel inferior, that's all. We develop this belief and it doesn't leave us in one night."

I find Azeb's comments about 'beliefs not leaving us in one night' reminiscent of Rao and Walton's concept of 'constraining preferences,'[537] These 'preferences' are the many tenacious habits and world views which certainly affect, if not always limit, the possibility of change. Like Rao and Walton, the girls infer that some aspects of "culture [can] affect their sense of the possible."[538] Azeb conceded and concluded: "We know we must change, Judi, but.... the culture is heavy," she said.

Conclusion: from Learning Skills - How To Do - To Empowerment - How To Be

I thus return to my question: how do the 'targets' of policy, here, several cohorts of women in urban and rural Ethiopia, speak subjectively of the effects of policy and of the specific programs in which they participated. From what we have heard, we need to qualify the question: there is policy and policy. No doubt participation in all of these programs, whatever the specific type of policy and specific context, initiated a change-oriented process; each project and Programme has generated some amount of self-consciousness as well as some very strongly held beliefs in the value of training and education. But I detect a significant difference between the messages of the needs-based policies and affirmative action. In the former, the needs and development oriented policies and programs, the focus is on learning and doing: women are selected to receive relevant training and to move into development projects, none of which seem at all problematic. In the latter, the affirmative action policy and its program, certainly as it is understood in Ethiopia, the focus is ultimately on changing social behaviour, becoming more assertive, perhaps becoming more conscious of self. The discourse is different: efficiency and needs based policies focus on training; affirmative action acknowledges 'women' as subordinate, perhaps weak, and in need of help to become equal.

I find this quite a different kind of message from 'you need training to get a new type of job, increase your income,' etc. Affirmative action openly assumes women's subordinate status in society; it both acknowledges and attempts to change some basic aspects of social organization in order to reverse the structure. The policy thus invites reflection and self consciousness and taking a stand on its suppositions: is it true that we are weak? Is it true that we need help? The students at Kotabe answer both yes and no: 'yes, we wouldn't be here without affirmative action; yes, we didn't get a chance to study, yes, our academic performance is not as good as the boys;' 'no, we are not weaker; no, we don't need special privileges; no, we are equal anyway.'

What I want to suggest here is: women are referring to two aspects of change, both of which might relate to the beleaguered influence of modernity. While I hesitate here to plunge into the morass of definitions of modernity, in the context of this paper I will contend that 'change' and 'modernity' are somehow related. Whether the modern involves a "rupture" from the past, as Harris (1996:3) has rather dramatically suggested, or whether it involves a gradual shift into a more pronounced emphasis on 'a better life,' more labour saving technology, more education and more individual choice is probably dependent upon the context and the perceived gains. Still, all of these projects and their underlying policies, indeed, ideologies have affected some measure of a shift from what we have done to what we will and can do. The change was perhaps less threatening in the case of the Dodota and WAEPP projects. In both projects, the women indicated the change was not a rupture: 'we women have always worked and we have always worked with water, we have always made and sold wares.' What was new was formal training - becoming part of a context where new skills were being taught and very happily practiced.

In the affirmative action policy as it is being implemented in the teachers college, the required change was more drastic, more personal, perhaps more difficult. Change now involved personality, being *defar*, assertive, and less *aynafar*, shy. This kind of change challenges some well-known rules of social interaction, perhaps some basic understandings of 'being a proper woman.' Azeb put it so well: 'we know what we should do, Judi, but the culture is heavy.' Nowadays, in the eyes of these young, urban educated student-teachers, the enemy is no longer ignorance; the enemy is shyness, *aynafar*, aspects of traditionally normative gender roles. My point is there is a perceptible difference between the train-and-get-a-job policies and those which encourage or advocate internal change and promote empowerment. The first result in training and jobs and salaries; the second move toward more subtle changes in views of self, perhaps a change in personality, all summarized in the emphasis on becoming assertive.

To conclude, if we return to the women and the water and skill-training projects, change was almost universally welcomed, there were virtually no complaints against working with the water system, certainly no complaints about working and earning a salary. But when we move to the college and introduce the Ethiopian variety of affirmative action, with its open and outright focus on gender equality and the encouragement to 'be assertive,' we meet with more contemplation, more reaction, more resistance: "It's not part of our culture," "it's you in the West again," "it's good but the culture is heavy." For the women in Dodota, the change brought on by the training and the acquisition of new skills was welcomed, not threatening. For the young students, the change demanded learning essentially new and not always attractive social skills, changes which are undoubtedly more complicated, more controversial, more difficult to accomplish and perhaps threatening.

I return to Azeb's awareness that the 'culture is heavy.' My feeling is in the course of identifying, acknowledging and labelling this cultural schema in the context of affirmative action, the 'culture' becomes less 'natural,' less 'heavy.' By focusing on it and questioning its prevalence, the shyness, *aynafar* that she now refers to has become less than 'natural,' and assertiveness, *defar*, has become not only more attractive but (in time) attainable.

9

PREVAILING OVER THE POWER OF CONTINUITY?

EVA POLUHA

In this study, education not only refers to what goes on within formal institutions of learning but encompasses those experiential processes of gaining information and skills that people undergo as part of their daily living and coping with the world. The study deals with the learning processes of two sections of the Ethiopian population: the political learning of peasants in Gojjam when dealing with representatives of the ruling elite, and the social and cultural learning of a class of school children in Addis Abeba interacting with teachers, parents and peers. Despite differences in age, occupation and forms of interactions, a comparison of the experiences gained by peasants and children yield similar results, namely an emphasis on hierarchical, patron-client relations. Status, position, gender and age proved to be decisive criteria for how people/ children interacted with each other. Those in a subordinate position were expected, and expected themselves, to show deference, obedience, and, at least a semblance of respect to those above them, while those in a super ordinate position showed a recurrent need to control and cross-check the allegiance of those below them. The discussion will focus on three aspects of these learning processes: the implications of hierarchical relations for processes of change; the mechanisms that promote the reproduction of hierarchical relations; and the preconditions for counter discourses to develop and counteract this continuity

This paper focuses on the learning processes of two categories of Ethiopians, peasants in northwest Ethiopia and school children in Addis Ababa. The descriptions and analyses deal with how they, as individuals and as members of a specific community, gain information, process it and adapt to it. Their learning processes are thereby seen as an integral part of their daily living and coping with the world. The political learning of the peasants in Gojjam focuses on how they deal with and relate to officials of the state while the learning of school children in Addis Ababa concerns the education process taking place between adults and children and how teachers and parents try to make children into "good citizens." Both cases are based on studies,[539] for each case I shall emphasize what the parties involved in the process learned, and how or the ways in which they learned. I refer to what both parties learned as cultural schemas (see also below), or cultural models in the sense of embodied yet flexible patterns for action, thinking and interpreting the world.[540] The cultural schemas of peasants and children are then related to what I call a dominant schema in Ethiopian history and society, namely patron-client relations.[541] The whole endeavour aims at getting a better understanding of how cultural schemas are constituted and if, and then how, change in and of schemas can be distinguished from change in the individual.

To widen the scope for the discussion about social change, as well as about continuity, I shall take recourse to some pertinent anthropological works that deal with the issue. Focus will be on what aspects or preconditions seem to promote the reproduction of cultural schemas and what preconditions might facilitate their being questioned and maybe even changed. Toward the end of the paper I shall present one example of a somewhat contradictory discourse from the school in Addis, another from some peasants in Gojjam, and discuss possible interpretations of these examples. The question to which no clear answer can be given is, whether we can see these counter-discourses as examples of schema change or whether they should rather be discussed in terms of individual experiences without a great impact on the dominant cultural schema.

Cultural Schemas, Continuity and Change

To start with, I want to give a brief outline of what is usually meant by cultural schemas or models. The concept of culture was originally developed within anthropology at the end of the 19th century but has, for the last decade, tended to be avoided by anthropologists mainly for the ways in which the concept has been misused.[542] Interpreted as the way of life of a people, their attitudes, values, modes of perception and habits of thought, culture (and the plural cultures) has, in many contexts, come to misrepresent the relationships between the individuals and groups that it wants to describe. Through essentializing the concept and making it into a thing, culture has been interpreted as something homogeneous as if every member of a group adhered to the same principles, felt the same degree of belonging and had the same amount of influence in defining what the group stood for, which they definitely do not. Power relations within groups, whether based on gender, class, age or other factors are often concealed when culture is taken to be their common denominator. Similarly, by fixing the stamp of culture on people's behaviour, changes in values and practices taking place in subgroups are not observed and culture came to be represented as static, impervious to change.

Yet, there is no denying that there are groups of people who share a language, norms and a way of life and if we do not call what they share culture, a new concept would have to be invented for it. Thus I agree with Hannerz who argues for" keeping the concept of culture to sum up the special capacity of human beings to create and uphold their lives together."[543] The point is, however, how to avoid the traps into which some previous users have fallen. To overcome these drawbacks with the culture concept, a more complex understanding of what people shared and why, entitled cultural schemas, has been developed.[544] The cultural schema approach has allowed researchers to study what individuals share and how the sharing of norms and values comes about, but also to depict great variations in a group with regard to access to power as well as to show that individuals can subscribe to dominant values to quite different degrees.

The use of cultural schemas thereby implied a move away from a preoccupation with either structure or agency to allow for both to be studied at the same time. Agency could, in this context, alter structures already in existence, even change them and promote the growth of new structures, while, at the same time, agency itself could be circumscribed, limited by the framework provided by existing structures, thereby promoting a continuity with what is in existence. Already in 1977 Bourdieu discussed this relationship between agency and structure in terms of internalization, stating that we are never completely free in our actions since they always relate to and are limited by previous experiences.[545] Anything new that happens to us is thus sorted and interpreted through a screen or schema established by prior knowledge. In this vein, the cultural schemas as discussed by Strauss and Quinn[546] are based on connectionism as a way of understanding ideation, or the mental process of learning, forming and using ideas, including culture.

Important in the way Strauss and Quinn use the concept of cultural schemas is the distinction they make between "intra-"and "extra-personal" cultural knowledge. They define the "intra-personal" as "the interpretation evoked in a person by an object or an event at a given time,"[547] adding that "a person's interpretation of an object or event includes an identification of it and expectations regarding it, and, often, a feeling about it and motivation to respond to it."[548] This "intrapersonal" cultural knowledge is, according to Strauss and Quinn, made up of flexible and adaptable interpretations rather than unchanging rules. It is therefore exposed to change, although, for various reasons, it might not change much.

All these interpretations, Strauss and Quinn argue, take place in each individual separately, although in constant interaction with others, like family, friends, and relatives who represent the 'extra-personal.'[549] Cultural schemas thus become all the interpretations an individual more or less shares with others with whom she/he communicates on a regular or not so regular basis and, or with whom she/he shares a language, religion, national media like TV and so on. A cultural meaning therefore becomes the similar interpretation evoked in a number of people who share life experiences. In this way, cultural meanings are no separate things but become shared experiences and interpretations. They are not bounded since when the sharing diminishes or stops, for example due to migration, different interpretations tend to develop.

Strauss and Quinn mainly discuss change with reference to what may happen to or in individuals, paying less attention to change of whole cultural schemas. With regard to individual change, they mention four centrifugal tendencies that may occur. The first refers to the fact that cultural understandings can change in persons across generations, because the ways in which for example parents worked or shared labour in the house might no longer be possible for their children to uphold, circumstances having changed. Secondly, existing cultural understandings can be unmotivating especially when new knowledge, information or experiences motivate new thoughts and acts. Thirdly, old cultural schemas can be contextually limited thus when people gain new knowledge or experience the interpretations that existing schemas offer might not cover the new information. Fourthly, they say that cultural understandings can sometimes be shared by relatively few and when new economic opportunities or technological innovations are faced, new interpretations will be required.[550] I shall come back to the issue of continuity and change on a larger scale, especially in relation to organizations after having presented the cases.

Peasants Learning Political Behaviour

The information presented about peasants learning political behaviour[551] is based on fieldwork in a village outside Dangla, which I call Ashena, but which has a different name. My contacts with the people in this village, administratively entitled a peasant association, started with a minor study in 1979. I then carried out extensive fieldwork in the area between 1980 and 1981, after which I have made repeated visits lasting a couple of weeks, and sometimes a few days at a time, to the community. The last visit took place in March 2006.

In the Dangla area peasants are basically aware of two different kinds of organizations, those which they consider private, *yegel*, and those which are public or organized through the government, *yemengist*. The private organizations are organized locally for spiritual, social and economic purposes. Examples of such organizations are the *Eder*, for burial support, the *sanbaté*, to cater for the church and to meet socially, eat and drink, by the church, the *mahaber*, a social organization where friends meet to celebrate a saint, and the *wubera*, a work organization through which labour is exchanged. All these private organizations are horizontal, and the leadership is accountable to the membership. Government organizations, on the other hand, are organized by state officials for purposes of the state. Examples of such organizations are the Peasant Association, which is the smallest administrative unit in the countryside, and the Service Co-operative. These organizations are vertical and accountability is to those above you. While the local organizations can be said to be egalitarian and democratic, the government organizations can be called hierarchical and also authoritarian.

The political learning process of the peasants in *Ashena*, whose lives I have had the possibility to follow for almost 27 years, cover both the Derg and the EPRDF regimes. If statements of older peasants are included, the regime of Haile Selassie (from which I only have older people's reminiscences) can be added to the other two, and three different regimes can be said to be represented in the study. The content of the learning process is in short as follows: In the beginning of its rule, the new government, i.e. both the Derg and the EPRDF, listens to the people and tries to frame its policies according to their wishes. People are encouraged to speak out, "from their stomachs," and inform the government of their grievances and their priorities. This period is like a kind of honeymoon for government and people. It does not last long though. Slowly, the government approach changes and from encouraging free speech and telling people to take their own initiatives it starts controlling them, especially those public acts and speeches which imply disrespect or criticism of the government and/or its employees. This is done through the use of various forms of punishments, like threats of loss of land, not having the right to food aid or even imprisonment.

In the beginning of the Derg era people felt that the government had really come to help the poor and the rulers wanted economic change and a better living standard for the needy. Peasants also appreciated self-government. The control they were given over the redistribution of land and other administrative decisions was a completely new and a very positive experience to them. Poor people also appreciated the land reform through which they got more land. Several peasants also joined a Producers' Co-operative since it provided a solution to some of their most urgent problems, such as lack of oxen or of labour. The Women's Association, in turn, provided the women with an arena where they could discuss their problems and look for both common and individual solutions. Through its activities and discussions, the Women's Association thus promoted both the self-awareness and self-esteem of individual women. Freedom of speech was in this way encouraged in the beginning of the Derg regime.

When change, although not of the whole cultural schema, came about, a number of things happened almost simultaneously, but slowly. One aspect of this change took place in the socialist language used by the Derg. After the take-over of power from the Haile Selassie government, the Derg solicited people's support through promising them a new economic era, announcing the time had come when at long last the Ethiopian people were going to obtain a better standard of living. All, government and people, were going to struggle together to reach this goal, the slogan said. Slowly, however, the inclusive "all" stopped referring to all the people and instead, through various innuendos, it was indicated that there were some individuals and groups who in actual fact were the enemies of the community. The "us," in the form of the government and the majority of the people, still existed, but there was now also a "them," enemies who, according to government employees, were against the government and thereby implicitly against the people. Since it was difficult for the Derg to promote development together with individuals who were against it, everybody was asked to take a stand against the enemies of the government.

Another change under the rule of the Derg concerned the PA executive committee. In the beginning those who were elected to the committee were individuals, mostly elders, much respected in the neighbourhood. Then, election procedures were modified, regulated from above and the persons to be elected were decided on beforehand. Thus, when individual peasants were asked to suggest names for positions to the executive committee, some had been prompted to give the names that government employees had told them to present. These names did not refer to people the community considered to be the best men and women in the PA, but were names of individuals who had started to co-operate with the government.

Towards the end of the 80s the content of and work load carried out by the PA also took on a new appearance. The committees were given ever more responsibilities and tasks to fulfil, jobs which previously had been carried out by the local administration. Much of this work was quite unpleasant because it forced committee members to act against the interests of their own relatives and neighbours. They were, for example, asked to select individual men to participate in the war against Eritrea, as part of the quota of soldiers the PA had been given by the government. The problem was nobody wanted to participate in the war. Another such task was to order households to deliver grain quotas to the government. These were fixed at a very low price and the farmers preferred to sell the grain at a higher price in the private market.

During this process, when the government increased its demands on the peasant leadership, threatening they would be severely punished if they did not provide all they had been asked for, the peasant leaders themselves started to change, as one of them told me several years later. They came to accept the use of violence even against their neighbours when the latter could not pay what was expected of them. Bribery also spread during this period and PA leaders accepted bribes from individuals who wanted to be exempted from the war. As a consequence, it was mostly sons from poor households, those who could not afford to pay bribes that were sent to the warfront.

In 1991 the Derg, with its large military apparatus, disintegrated and the Ethiopian People's Revolutionary Front, the EPRDF, took power. To start with, members of the peasant community experienced a positive relationship with the new government employees. Most important to people in *Ashena* was that the war with Eritrea stopped and there was no more recruitment for the warfront. Furthermore, peace was promoted in the countryside where lawlessness had reigned in the time gap between the Derg administration's disappearance and the establishment of the new government. Thieves who had stolen oxen and cows were now imprisoned. Peasants were allowed to sell grain at market prices instead of at the low, fixed government prices, which had previously been enforced. Extra taxes were also abolished and people were encouraged to talk freely and come out with their grievances. Nobody was forced to come to meetings or participate in local PA elections.

What was less positive was the whole new leadership, from PA level and above, were made up of comparatively young men. Older, more mature adults, who generally were considered to have better experience and were less easy to fool, were not allowed to be elected according to the new government, the reason being that they had worked in such positions during the Derg. These people were excluded from all administrative positions because, it was said, they had "rubbed shoulders" (*Nekiki*) with power during the Derg. Later people were again forced to take part in the elections and those who refused to register were threatened with the loss of land or with not receiving any food aid, even if they qualified for it. So they felt they had to obey. "We went and did what they wanted us to," I was told. "*Bedergamaw temirenal,*" they said, with the double meaning, "we learnt" but also "we were chastened during the Derg." While previous administrators had encouraged peasants to give their opinions at meetings they were now discouraged both from speaking or giving suggestions about what they thought ought to be done. Interventions in the daily lives of people in Ashena, which had been lifted after the fall of the Derg, were reintroduced. Peasants were again given a quota of work days when they had to labour for their community on projects designed and decided upon by government representatives. The peasant community's ideas about "development" and what activities that needed to be carried out were no longer called for.

During all three regimes, retaliations against those who had opposed, or just questioned the acts or ideology of the government, had been swift and severe. At the same time, however, it was difficult for all parties involved to know what the rules for their interactions were. Government officials tended to act according to their own, individual interpretations, of what their leaders wanted. Often the action of these officials contradicted what they said in public, which made it difficult for ordinary citizens to predict the consequences of their own acts or statements. Officials' access to various kinds of sanctions could, for peasants, imply beatings, loss of land or house, imprisonment and even death. At the same time, the officials were only accountable to those above them, never to those whom they were supposed to represent or serve. The government system was, in this sense, strictly hierarchical.

To summarize *what* the Ashena peasants learned during these regimes the following points stand out:

> The Derg and the EPRDF governments both promised improvements, change, and development when they came to power. Their message was, "we have come for you." They created a "we" and a "them," where "them," to start with, were those that ruled before them, and the "we" referred to the new government and all Ethiopians who had not been members of the Imperial rulers or the Derg's socialist party or elected to official positions. Both governments were, to start with, open and flexible, inviting people to talk of their grievances, especially those they had about the previous government. Slowly, however, the initial flexibility and openness towards the population changed and the approach became more rigid. Control measures increased and cadres were placed ever deeper into the peasant community, allowing them to hear and

see more intimately what individual peasants felt about the government. The language in use also changed and people were asked to state whether they were for or against the government. To be "for" the government also implied to be "for" development. Government officials' arrogance towards individual peasants, often implicit in their behaviour, became more and more explicit, and was expressed in a growth of intimidations, threats, imprisonments as well as bribery and misappropriation of funds. There were quick reprisals for what government officials considered criticism of their acts or ideology. All these actions together promoted a sense of insecurity. Those, who initially had been curious and eager to get to know the new government, started to pull back from official encounters and refrained from initiatives. Keeping away from officials and public meetings, they still, however, closely followed all that took place.

Taking a closer look at the learning process, focusing on *how* the peasants learned, the following mechanisms stand out:

First of all, peasants learned about the government through their personal encounters with both politicians and civil servants. Ashena peasants also made observations during these encounters and at official meetings, looking at how officials treated each other and individual peasants, listening to what was said and later, taking note of what was done. This taught them how to show respect in both words and bodily postures. They also studied the proclamations and compared these with actual practice. Their individual experiences and observations were later exchanged in the peasant community, often at small gatherings, when they were presented as stories or jokes about themselves, illustrating how foolish or naïve they had been; or about individual officials, illustrating their arrogance, cruelty and stupidity, but also holding up those officials that were considered decent. As a result, a common understanding, a shared knowledge or cultural schema developed, essentially emphasizing that government officials were a separate category of people, distinct from the peasants. They wanted to order peasants about, use and misappropriate their products while expecting deference. Still, there was hope among the peasants that one day a good government might come to power. So they attentively observed and noted all that was said and done.

Children Learning to Become Good and Respectable Citizens

The next case[552] is based on fieldwork in a poor area in Addis Ababa conducted from January 2000 to January 2001, with some brief subsequent visits, the last of which took place in 2005. Fieldwork consisted of sitting in the classroom of a grade four, later grade five class, together with about 100 students aged 9-15. In class, I followed the teaching process, but I also made individual and group interviews, asked students to write essays on topics of interest to me and enrolled some 20 students to write diaries for two weeks.

The major question behind my research with the children, came from my experiences in Ashena, as well as from my personal observations of relations between government officials and people since the late 60s, and can be expressed through the question "why do hierarchical modes of government have such durable forms?" or, "why do government officials continue to act in such authoritarian, arrogant and controlling ways towards citizens despite radical regime change?"

To answer this question I had decided to focus on cultural cognition among children. I wanted to see what they learned and how, through observations of their everyday life experiences. The underlying question made me pay special attention to what the children learned about subordination, and how they were supposed to exercise it. But I was also interested to learn about how they understood the logic behind it, namely why act hierarchically? In the following I shall present some of the most relevant findings.

The geographical and social arenas where the children spent most of their time were in their homes, in the school, in the religious, Christian or Muslim, institution they attended, and in the streets they used to commute between these places. Thus it was the local, person-to-person context which was most important to them and which had the greatest impact on their lives. In the home they met with immediate family as well as relatives and neighbours, in the school it was with other students, teachers and administrative personnel and in the mosque or church it was the priest or teacher as well as co-religionists. The streets were covered with people of all ages but most came from a similar economic background, meaning that they were very poor.

From observations and talks with the children I soon understood they were very active in their learning process. Social relations, cultural understandings and economic aspects of life, were all tested, evaluated and adapted to. They tested pens and exercise books to find out which combined an acceptable price, a good quality and would last them long. They tested their behaviour in interactions with siblings, parents, teachers, co-students, girls as well as boys, to see what the response would be and how they would be treated in turn. They tested speech, dress and body behaviour to see what the reactions would be.

Children's major points of self-referral were to the different collectives, family, friends, religion and Ethiopian citizens, of which they felt they were an integral part. All these collectives, apart from friends, were, according to the children, hierarchical. They did not see hierarchy as something negative, though. All these hierarchical collectives gave the children support, love and encouragement. There was also economic redistribution within the collectives especially in the extended family. Key concepts used by the children when they talked of parents, neighbours or teachers were control, respect and obedience. The concept of control was used in a positive sense, implying that concerned adults cared for and worried about the children and saw to it that they would not be lost. The children responded with showing these adults both respect and obedience.

Important criteria defining the hierarchical relations were age, gender, social status and physical strength. Age indicated older sisters or brothers could neither be praised nor punished by their younger siblings nor could anyone act as a mediator to children above her or him in age. Gender relations showed women and girls were in general subordinate to men. An exception could occur if the economic background or social status of a woman was higher than that of a man. In this way the economy could also have an impact on the social relations. Despite being very strict, the hierarchy also had an built-in flexibility which made it possible for those with low rank to reach the top, if *Edel* (luck and opportunity)[553] or Donna *Fortuna* [554] was with them. Ethiopian history and daily incidents show people from a poor background sometimes really do reach the top. The way it is explained is that luck, *edel*, was with them. In my study, even children with very poor exam results sincerely believed they could reach a top position in the country, that is, if only their luck or chance was with them. Similarly, most children believed it would not be good to abort a child, since "who knows how far that child will reach," "he can become anything, even a doctor who can treat people to health." According to this understanding *edel,* or a kind of "undeserved reward"[555] can befall an individual, but the change or luck that it brings will always take place within the framework of the dominant cultural schema. *Edel* will thus not cause structural change or contest the hierarchy in and of itself. On the contrary, believing in *edel* implies that you accept the hierarchy and act within its framework.

The major explicit means through which children were taught were through various kinds of rewards and punishment. Rewards could be gifts of clothes, of food or school materials but the most common reward in this poor neighbourhood was to praise or give a blessing to well-behaving and obedient children. Punishments, in turn, mostly consisted of various kinds of beatings handed out by fathers, older brothers and more seldom by mothers or sisters. Teachers could also see to it that a disturbing child would be sent out of school. The worst form of punishment feared by everybody was to be cursed, because a curse would never go away. Still, all rewards as well as punishments were distributed hierarchically. No one in a lower position could bestow either rewards or punishments on somebody who was older, stronger or of a superior status than her-, himself.

In school children learned through memorization. They learned to attach the greatest importance to the written word, words which their teacher had taught them and which they should be able to reproduce for examinations. Knowledge was in this sense considered as bounded, stable and unchangeable and teachers tried to communicate the proper amount of knowledge with the right degree of complication so that children would be able to take it all in. Children were thus not encouraged to question the information they were taught; on the contrary initiative and inquiry were discouraged.[556] In class, students were expected to be attentive and to listen to their teachers. The latter were the ones who acted, lecturing, writing on the blackboard, and explaining, while the students in class were expected to absorb what their teachers said. In this way teachers controlled students, seeing to it that they reproduced the correct written words for the exams; and supervisors controlled teachers, checking their lesson plans and reports about what had been done in class. Control was, accordingly, a key concept in all these relations. When students or teachers failed there were different kinds of punishments to which they were exposed and when they were successful there were a number of rewards, which were granted to them.

The children also learned about the importance of gender in all the arenas to which they had access. A child's gender had great implications for how she or he could act, what was expected of her or him and what she or he could expect in turn. The way girls and boys could use space thus differed widely. While girls stayed at home to assist their mothers or be responsible for cooking, cleaning, washing clothes or to run errands, boys spent much time outside the home, in the streets talking or playing ball, or with friends. Boys were, somehow, expected to be in the streets, even if it was not thought to be good for them, while girls more used the streets to go from one place to the other. In school, girls stayed inside the classroom or close to the building while boys used the whole compound to play. Public places became more accessible to boys than to girls; there boys learned how to act and interact with known and unknown others. Boys also used time more freely and could come home late while girls were expected to be home before dark.

Although both boys and girls were expected to show respect and obedience to their elders, more respect and obedience was expected from girls. Girls and boys also learned what men did, or what was considered as male work, had a higher status than female work. A girl could be good at cooking or taking care of a house, better than many other girls, but when compared with boys' work it was of little value. Both girls and boys learned man was the norm, and that men and boys continuously derived benefits from their gender even though the children did not seem to be intellectually conscious of it or and did not express it in those terms.[557]

Women and girls were the ones most manifestly involved in the gender teaching process while men and boys were much less engaged. Through various kinds of exhortations and even insults, girls could be told by older women or friends not to misbehave, or to leave the street and go home to work, thereby seeing to it that girls adapted to prevailing norms, and implicitly to their subordinate status. At the same time, these women and girls could indulge and even commend boys, brothers or friends, for behaving in a masculine way, such as to stay out late or play football in the street which was considered dangerous. It sometimes happened that boys policed male norms, especially when a friend or classmate started playing with much younger children or individually with girls. Mostly, however, they did not involve themselves, safeguarding gender norms, and few boys questioned their superior position.

In these ways children were taught to manage and master the different modes of communication of their society, especially those which were considered proper for them in view of their age, gender, social status and size. They learned that most relations, apart from those between friends, were hierarchical, but also that this hierarchy was rather complex. The collective in which the hierarchy was most strongly expressed, namely the household or extended family, also gave them protection, love and care. It provided reciprocity and economic redistribution. And, as previously mentioned, although hierarchies should be strictly observed, this did not mean they lacked flexibility, or that even a poor person could not gain influence and reach a powerful position. According to the hierarchical system you could become anything, so long as your *edel* was with you.

Children thus learned was what their elders considered important and relevant, what was considered acceptable behaviour, necessary to know to be able to live in peace with the community and, not least, which would earn both children and their parents respect. Children thus learned to re-enact what the people around them, especially those close to them, like parents, grandparents and siblings, did. They were not copies of those who surrounded them but it was often possible to recognize the parents in the bodily comportment and choice of words of the children. Children's acts and thinking in this way tended to promote continuity rather than change. This process is closely related to how we learn as human beings. As discussed by Strauss and Quinn, we take in new information through learned and innate structures and sort new information according to previous knowledge and categories; information processing thus in itself tends to emphasize what is already established in our minds and is part of our ways of thinking and acting.[558]

Cultural Schemas and Patron-Client Relations

What children learned and re-enacted in the Birabiro school in Addis can be seen as a cultural schema, one which had many similarities with the schema we saw in Ashena and which has guided people-state relations for, at least, the last 150 years. A cursory overview of what has happened in Ethiopian history in five fields, politics and administration, police and army, economy, education and ideology, shows the major trend over these years has been for those governing the country to establish a strong state so they could both control the administration and the people whom they governed. Through changes in politics and administration, in the organization of the police and the army and with reference to various ideologies (religious, socialist, democratic) power holders have succeeded in steadily increasing their patriarchal control of the people. At the same time, there have been very little investment in the economy or in the educational system, areas which could have promoted alternative ways of both thinking and living.[559]

The increased control state power holders have exercised over people was illustrated at the local level by the Ashena peasants' experiences with the state under three different regimes. In other contexts[560] such relations have been described as patron-client relations. In Ethiopia, patrons have usually come to occupy their position as a result of various criteria like having economic assets, being men, or referring to themselves as the elect of God. [561] The decisive factor in Ethiopian history has, however, been that patrons have been in command of a military establishment. Most have risen to power through establishing links with other strong men, whom they have tried to make into their followers and clients, and they have stayed in power through the elimination of competition and by having close relations with ,as well as good control of, their clients. Clients in turn were people who obtained land, jobs, salaries or other economic advantages from their patrons. For these gifts they were expected to show their patrons obedience, deference and respect. Above all, however, they were expected to show their patrons loyalty. Patrons expected such loyalty from their clients and were for this prepared to protect them, show them benevolence, and give them gifts. Patrons could also dismiss their clients when they no longer were of use or loyal to them, while clients could criticize their patrons, especially indirectly. Still, the *shum shir*, the right to appoint and dismiss people, was the prerogative of the patron.

The strength of the patron-client relationship in Ethiopian history was that everybody knew the rules for how to behave. Because of this, all parties to a relationship could read and interpret each other's words, acts and behaviour. This shared knowledge of the system promoted a sense of security among the participants. But the system was not stable. The reason for this, as I will argue, is there was also an inherent weakness in the patron-client relationship, a weakness that promoted instability and created insecurity among the power holders.

If we look at Ethiopia's past, we can see there has never been a peaceful change of government, instead all transfers of power have been carried out with the use of arms. Those who have come to power have done so by trying their luck, *edel*, but, more than that, they have seen to it that they have had the help of loyal clients and supporters and, they have also secured their own access to arms. From the perspective of previous power holders, this was disloyalty, because it was their own clients, whom they had expected to be loyal, who rose up against them, as their enemies. These historical experiences have taught those in top positions, and those aspiring to such positions, they can never be sure of keeping power because there may always be someone who wants to try his luck and gain the supremacy himself. This knowledge, that hierarchical relations are flexible and subordinates cannot be trusted, is shared by all Ethiopian potential and existing power holders. A key consequence, resulting from this knowledge, which as far as I know has not been discussed in the literature, is rulers feel they incessantly have to strengthen their hold on both state apparatus and people. The last 150 years of Ethiopian history is a rich illustration of how governments have invested in the administration, in the court system, in prisons, police and army, and leaders have used any means, including terror, torture and killings, to silence people and make them obedient, all in order for leaders to stay in power. A major and devastating consequence of all these costly investments in the control system has been that comparatively very few resources have been left to develop key areas like education, technology and the economy, areas which could have promoted a better standard of living for the people.

Mechanisms and Processes Promoting Continuity

What do these examples of peasants' and children's learning processes tell us about how continuity is promoted? If we look at both how children and peasants learned as individuals, it is obvious they all were very observant of their surroundings. They looked at and analysed what happened during interactions and negotiations both when they themselves were involved and when they were merely observers. They took in words and sentences used in conversations or pronouncements, watched bodily and facial expressions, gestures, postures and physical acts. They studied how emotions of support, encouragement and love as well as disdain, dislike and hate were expressed, and for what reasons. Even though they all did this individually, and each person's knowledge was unique, many experiences were shared and became part of a common cultural schema. This was also a result of their interactions and negotiations with each other, the way they recounted their experiences and, not least, because they shared and discussed events that had triggered various feelings and insights. Although the children in Addis mainly got their impressions from people in their vicinity, they also had access to radio, TV and, through the school, to books and papers. The various influences combined to make those involved aware of their community's cultural schema. They knew what they were expected to do and how, even if they did not necessarily subscribe to all of it themselves.

What they all learned was that hierarchical relations predominated in society. This implied that you should show respect and obedience to those in a super ordinate position, and control, follow-up and support to those in a subordinate position. Control was the result both of caring for and supporting your subordinates and of the need to know about their whereabouts and activities so that they would not stray away from you. These hierarchical relations were characterized by both rights and obligations and were usually exercised within various collectives. Children and peasants also learned that hierarchies were strictly upheld, so much so that those who questioned them, would be punished. Yet there was flexibility in the hierarchy. Things might change if you gathered your resources and/or supporters and if luck (*edel*) was with you. Then you might even reach the apex of the hierarchy yourself.

Children and peasants also learned knowledge, information or the official doctrine was not to be questioned. What higher-ups stated, those below them should accept. They were not expected to argue against what they had been told. Criticism was not understood as something positive, something that could bring knowledge or society forward. Rather it was equalled with disobedience and lack of respect. Continuity was thus emphasized, both mentally and physically, and peasants and children learned that to initiate change was dangerous and mostly met with swift and harsh reprisals. Clegg, professor of Management, studying, among other things, how power works in organizations, refers to similar experiences with regard to continuity and change in organizations.[562] Clegg states organizations tend to obtain and perpetuate their patterned system of rules, thus promoting continuity, through many and various means. One such mechanism is control, especially disciplinary control, which is often exercised in the form of surveillance. Another means he mentions is repetition, since each repetition makes the routines more established and consequently makes it more difficult to question the acts and thoughts surrounding the required acts. Clegg also identifies time as an aspect which facilitates institutional isomorphism which is effectuated through what is called, coercive, mimetic and/or normative pressure.[563] All these mechanisms together make it difficult to introduce change into an organization. A further reason why radical change is so rare is, according to Clegg, what he refers to as Mann's theory of "organizational outflanking."[564] According to this theory, subordinates in any organization usually lack collective organizations to contest existing procedures. The lack could be due to ignorance of how organizations function, lack of a strategy, or not enough knowledge of how to get or change an agenda or of how to build alliances.[565] In the final analysis, change according to Clegg [566] seems very much to be a question of power.

Preconditions for Change

Still, all is not a question of continuity even if cultural continuity is a more frequent result of human interaction than change. Change happens and individuals, all with their own personalities, perpetually adapt and change as a result of their experiences. More radical change, of a cultural schema or of a traditional social institution, seems to be more difficult to bring about than individual change, however.

In his discussion on change, Clegg[567] argues change will only be successful if important agencies that dispute old discourses are able to have an impact on key arenas in their respective organizations. Clegg depicts the functioning of organizations, like the establishment and implementation of rules, regulations, orders and hierarchies, as taking place within 'circuits of power' where the traffic follows pre-established routes. Along these routes there are what Clegg calls 'nodal points,' something like key arenas, positions or places with people who do what is expected of them. As links in a chain, they follow and redistribute rules and orders they have received to their respective departments and further the chain thereby reconfirming and validating the system. It is only when some such agent or agency succeeds in establishing new nodal points, or in changing the order or content of those which exist, that the whole organization may change and take on new practices, discourses or routines. To understand change we must therefore study how such 'nodal points' function. We must learn to identify them, together with the practices and knowledge that exist within them, and distinguish what is taken for granted, as well as recognize what may already be contested. Contradictions between different discourses at such 'nodal points' thus seem to be the key to change.

A brief review of some anthropological studies about change similarly indicates the importance of nodal points, together with some other key factors necessary for large scale change to be possible. The first of these factors appears to be access to new critical and/or attractive information or rewards for an established discourse or cultural schema to be identified, opened up and critically reviewed. The new information must either contradict or, at least, pose an alternative to the old knowledge or the already established practices. An example from Papua New Guinea and another from the USA[568] illustrate it was new, critical information that made it possible for people to see previously established truths in a new perspective and opt for an alternative.

Another case from the Gamo Highlands in Ethiopia[569] indicates new information was not enough for change to take place. A hierarchical decision-making system made it difficult for people at the bottom of a hierarchy to initiate change despite access to new information, while it was much easier to do so within an egalitarian system because there were fewer 'nodal points' to pass. On the other hand, a hierarchical system may facilitate change which is introduced from the top. Still, there is always the possibility that people will not accept the change but resist it in different ways.

The case from the USA also suggests new information was not enough for change to take place. What was necessary was also the right to contest the discourse of the U.S. government and to do so openly. Accessibility to media and an 'open' society were preconditions for a struggle against the government discourse. Even that was not enough, however. What was more important was, to even question the hegemonic government discourse, a greater number of influential and respected people coming from various walks of life, needed to provide an alternative discourse strong enough to replace that of the government.

Another case from Britain[570] illustrates that even if all the above-mentioned preconditions are in place it is still possible for gate-keepers, like government officials, to prevent change from taking place, especially since their position gives them special access to media, the political apparatus, influential economic institutions or the police and military.

To summarize about cultural schema or system change, it appears even when there is access to alternative, attractive and manageable information, when there is a system which, even if hierarchical, allows for discussion and spread of information, and when there are secure and predictable rules of the game, an 'open' society, these circumstances can only be seen as preconditions which make change possible. They do not imply cultural schema or system change follows, as the case with the strong British gate-keepers illustrates.

Counter Discourses in the Ethiopian Context – Can they Prevail over the Power of Continuity?

To broaden the discussion about Ethiopia and cultural schema change I want to present two counter discourses, one from the children, which took place in the year 2000, and one from the peasants which took place in the year 2005, but which I learned about in the spring of 2006. I shall use these as question marks, wondering whether they are indications of schema change or if they rather should be seen as individual adaptations and a reproduction of the prevailing cultural schema.

Children in the Birabiro School in Addis Ababa

The first case comes from my diary:[571]

> It is the fifth period and I sit on my chair at the back feeling tired and hungry. Now we only have mathematics and then lunch. The students are talking to each other, moving around the desks. Slowly the noise increases and the monitors start moving forward. In comes the mathematics teacher. He says something in a low voice that I cannot hear. The monitors are at work with their sticks and many children sit down. The teacher also sits.

> Then there is commotion all over the class. Petros, a young boy of 12, first begs then pushes his female neighbours of 15 to let him pass with his exercise book. Breasts and stomachs are in the way and he jumps on top of the desk to be able to get out. 11-year old Etalem, sitting by the wall inside of big Ermias and three young girls, respectfully asks him to let her pass, and when he won't,

she also jumps on top of the desk and bypasses them all. She wears trousers under the school uniform skirt. Even Adanech, my goodness, she is 16, on the plump side, with big breasts and long hair, walks on the desk when her friends do not move out of the way quickly enough. All their movements are hurried and I only understand why when I see the queue forming up beside the seated math teacher. He is going to correct their exercise books and since he will not be able to do all during this period, each child tries to see to it that at least hers or his is corrected, and that they get their marks.

The students talk a lot to each other, a few move around, but the latter are told to go back to their places by the monitors. Many girls and boys jump over their friends also when returning to their seats. Others squeeze themselves in past breasts and stomachs. Bodies do not seem to matter just now, other than as possible obstacles to free passage.

What happened in class when the maths teacher entered? Here is my interpretation:

Although I could not hear what the teacher said, the children were evidently quickly aware of the situation and prepared their books to come forward. Petros and Etalem did what they had been taught to do, they kindly asked their older neighbours to let them pass. When the latter did not react in the expected way, polite behaviour says young children should wait, because their neighbours were older and should be respected. Etalem and Petros were in too much of a hurry for this, however. I could see a very brief hesitancy on their part and then they were off, onto the bench.

With Adanech, I was a bit shocked myself. Her behaviour was just not the way a mature young girl acts. When a young Ethiopian girl sits, her knees should be kept together and her arms held close to the body. She should not make any large gestures with her hands, arms or other parts of the body. And when a girl of this age walks, her eyes should be on the floor. She should not take up any space or be conspicuous. Preferably, she should melt into the background and become invisible. This embodiment of what it is to be a girl or young woman is part of what most Ethiopian girls, irrespective of ethnic background learn through practice, interactions, observations and comments since birth.[572] Then, to see somebody like Adanech, forget all she has learnt about bodily behaviour, jump on to the table and walk on it to reach the teacher, that really was astounding.

During the maths period, the girls and boys thus behaved against all norms that they had been taught as proper. The context in which they did this was specific, namely the gain or loss of necessary marks. These marks were so important to them that after an initial, very brief moment of hesitation, they went for them even when it required unacceptable behaviour.

Although this behaviour was never repeated, the children's reaction to the situation shows they were prepared to adapt and behave in new ways when the rewards were attractive enough. In this way, the children indirectly came to act contrary to a pattern that was deeply embedded in their norms, values, speech and behaviour.[573] The question is, can we talk of system change or at least the beginning of it here?

Peasants in Ashena in Gojjam

The case from Ashena comes from a visit I made in March 2006, when I went to see my friends in the Peasant Association and the 2005 elections came up. Very briefly, these elections can be summarized under the following points:

To start with, the EPRDF for the first time during its rule, let go of its control over the election process.[574] All parties, including the opposition, were allowed to present their ideas, programmes as well as their criticism of what the others had done or were promising to do during the next term. Why the EPRDF government relinquished its control over the population for the 2005 elections is difficult to know. Probably several factors contributed to this decision, amongst which could have been the conviction that the peasant population really supported them, there was no viable alternative, and that there was pressure from Western countries to allow the opposition to speak out in public.

In hindsight it appears both the urban and the rural population were electrified by the debates, especially the fact that representatives of the government were challenged by the opposition. Listening attentively to the debates, it seems as if people often found the opposition had better arguments than the government.

Thirdly, the government invited several foreign observers, among which many from the E.U., the Carter Institute and the African Union, to observe the elections. Both peasants and townspeople expressed a belief that the Western observers were going to act as guarantors of the elections and they, for the first time, would really be able to choose between the parties. In various ways, people demonstrated both physically and mentally that they were prepared for change.

It is difficult to know what the actual results of the elections were. All over the country people began to express discontent when it was stated that the government had won the elections, even before the poll results were available. Public demonstrations were then prohibited and of those who persisted in carrying them out, large numbers were imprisoned and not so few were killed or injured. Then, in November 2005, most of the opposition leadership was imprisoned when they refused to take their seats in parliament. Their refusal was bound up with a number of demands they had presented to the government. Since then, pupils have demonstrated in schools, and they, and individual citizens accused of being part of the opposition, have been harassed by the Federal Police.

When I went to the Peasant Association in Ashena in March 2006 I first visited Ayehu, the eldest of six brothers whom I have known closely for the past 28 years. Ayehu was now a 79 year-old man who had recently suffered from stroke. After the first formal greetings, Ayehu said:

> Ayehu: Eva, you white people, what kind of people are you?
>
> Eva: What do you mean, what have we done now?
>
> Ayehu: Well, what are you doing now? We used to have our own way of changing government (*yemengist shigigir*) but then you white people came and said your democracy was much better. So we listened to you and said to ourselves we will try this democracy. Then we went to vote for the people we believed in.

Eva: OK, good, so what then?

Ayehu: Well we did what you told us to but now, when the people we voted for are in prison, where are you now?

I must admit I had no good answer to Ayehu's question and that he made an important point.

The next day I visited his oldest son, Workneh, who explained to me what had happened during the pre-election.

Workneh: When they started the political discussions on radio, all peasants here got hold of a radio and listened. We listened to what EPRDF said and we listened to what the opposition said. Sometimes we were working, being in the middle of the ploughing season, but we stopped ploughing to be able to listen to what they said, because we were interested in the way they talked and argued. Then we discussed among ourselves what they had said and which groups had solutions to the problems we peasants are facing. And most of us agreed we wanted the opposition. Actually, here in Ashena 880 persons voted for the opposition and only 198 persons voted for the government. And it was the same all over Gojjam. Still, nothing has happened, there is no change. They were smart though, the government, he said and laughed. They took away our arms first. Otherwise we would have fought for the people we voted for.

While Workneh talked he mentioned the names and arguments of various representatives of the opposition, showing he was well aware of who they were and the ideas they stood for. Even the name of Ana Gomes, the EU representative who had criticized the government for unfair election procedures, was mentioned, as the only white person who had supported the results of the election. The worst of all, according to Workneh and others, who later commented on the elections, were the Americans. They were the real enemies of the choices made by the Ethiopian people and were only interested in supporting Meles.

What I heard during my visit to my friends in Ashena came as quite a surprise to me. I knew several of them had a radio but I also knew they had stopped buying the necessary batteries since listening to the news or programmes controlled by the government did not appeal to them. Thus, I had not expected them to follow the discussions on the radio so closely, to take it all in, know the names and arguments of various individuals and even be aware of Ana Gomes's critical comments about the elections. But how can we interpret what had happened? Does it mean that the 2005 elections, even though they led to the imprisonment of the opposition, have resulted in a change in the ways in which people think, reason and act politically? On the one hand, I think the elections have convinced people their political participation is possible and also that it might have an impact on how the country could be governed. On the other, several of my friends in Ashena told me, again, they had become silent, reluctant to speak out in meetings or with people they did not know. Power relations and control over the military apparatus had, again, as mentioned above, given those gate-keepers in government positions the possibility to prevent change. Still, the experiences and impact of the 2005 elections might be a first step towards prevailing over the power of continuity, because change also emerges from within this continuity. The children's behavioural change was not a result of their own reflections. Still, the visualized benefit evidently made them forget what, under other circumstances, could be seen as deeply embedded behaviour. In this respect the case corresponds to one of the preconditions for change mentioned above, according to which a reward could challenge old behaviour. With regard to the peasants in Ashena, the number of votes for the opposition illustrates a majority wanted a change of government. This might also be interpreted as an initiation of change, a challenge to the prevailing hierarchy of those which are at the top today. It may, in the long run, also be a challenge to the whole hierarchical system of patron-client relations in itself. However, only time will be able to tell us what will happen.

Notes

Introduction
[1] Michael H. Hart, *The 100: A Ranking of the Most Influential Persons in History*, Hart Publishing Company: New York City (1978), 105-109:
[2] I would like to thank Gerardo Mosquera for his comments on a draft of this paper.

Chapter 1

[1] This study is based on the following untested hypothesis: there is a causal link between the use of local/indigenous language as a medium of instruction and the overall societal development (economic, social, political and cultural) of a country/state.
[2] The section on the educational policies of the various regimes is extracted from my *Education in Ethiopia: from crisis to the brink of collapse*, (Uppsala: Nordic Africa Institute, 2006): 1-60
[3] Mulugeta Wodajo, "Secondary education and manpower requirements of the Second Five Year Plan," in *Educational Journal of the University College Education Students Association*, Bulletin no,11, Addis Ababa,(1963/4), [I was one of those 8000 students enrolled in grade 8.
[4] Negash, *Rethinking Education*, P. 100
[5] Tekeste Negash, *The Crisis of Ethiopian Education: Implications for nation-building*, Uppsala Reports on Education, 29, Uppsala: Uppsala University, Department of Education (1990):20
[6] The actual sate of Ethiopian education sector during the Socialist-communist epoch of Ethiopian current history is narrated in a small study I published in 1990. 20
[7] Negash, *the Crisis of Ethiopian Education...* 18
[8] Ibid.
[9] International Labour Organization, 1986, *Youth Employment Programmes in Africa, A comparative sub-regional Study: The case of Ethiopia,(Addis Ababa* 1986): 21.
[10] Tekeste Negash, *Rethinking Ethiopian Education*, (Uppsala: Nordic Africa Institute, 1996): 100
[11] Negash, (1990): 18-20.
[12] Ibid.
[13] Ibid, 72-83.
[14] Ibid.
[15] Ibid
[16] Transitional Government of Ethiopia, *Education and Training Policy*, Addis Ababa, (1994), 10
[17] United Nations Millennium Development Goals, 2000: http://www.un.org/millenniumgoals/
[18] World Bank, "Education in Ethiopia: Strengthening the Foundation for Sustainable Progress, AFTH 3," *Human Development Department, Africa Region,* (2004):107-10.
[19] Ibid.
[20] Ibid,51.
[21] Ibid,106.
[22] Ibid,105.
[23] Allowing or encouraging the establishment and proliferation of private schools is bound to affect the aim of education as either a public or an essentially private good.
[24] World Bank, Education in Ethiopia, (2004): 105
[25] They were tested in Reading, English, Mathematics and Environmental Sciences. Ibid, 27
[26] Ibid:147, The 33 percent average refers to the average of the percentage correct answers for eight subjects, This means for some subjects, such as English, the score might have been much lower.
[27] It is difficult to establish a cause and effect relationship between high unemployment and political stability of a regime, There are a number of studies showing the role of University and secondary school students in the downfall of the imperial system. I argued in an earlier study (Negash, 1990) that an educational system that produces unemployable youth could either lead to rebellion or to the increasing growth of authoritarian rule, But the argument was not empirically substantiated.
[28] Ibid,54.
[29] There were several but brief power cuts in Addis Ababa during my visit at Menelik Secondary School on October 28 and 29, 2004. Mekelle and the whole of Tigray and northern Wallo had a three day power cut in early November of 2004.
[30] Both teachers and students told me about this division of labor. I asked how and where the balance of two kinds of inputs (two thirds for students) and one third input (one third for teachers) was identified but did not get answers.

[31] UN Millennium Development Goals, (2000): http://www.un.org/millenniumgoals/

[32] Messay Kebede, *Survival and Modernization: Ethiopia's enigmatic present, A Philosophical Discourse,* (Lawrenceville, NJ: Red Sea Press, 1999); Maimire Mennesemay, "Towards a critical Ethiopian theory of Education," in Messay Kebede, Paulos Milkias and Eva Poluha (eds,) *Education, Politics and Social Change in Ethiopia* (Los Angeles, CA: Tsehai Publishers, 2009): 67-97.

[33] Maimire Mennasemay Ibid: 6

[34] Ibid: 2008.

[35] Negash, (1990).

[36] Alamin Mazrui, "The World Bank, the language question and the future of African education," in Harris, R, and B, Rampton (eds), *The Language, Ethnicity and Race Reader,* (London: Routledge, 2003):94.

[37] Negash, (1996), 33-4.

[38] Messay Kebede, (1999):389.

[39] Bahru, Zewde, Pioneers of Change in Ethiopia: the reformist Intellectuals of the early 20th century, (Oxford: James Currey, 2002), 33

[40] Messay Kebede, (1999), 276-7.

[41] I fully concur with Messay Kebede's insightful comments on the role of revolutions on social changes which says: "Social change has resulted in greater adaptability every time it has succeeded in salvaging and enhancing the inner characters of the societies it has affected, The theory according to which class struggle is the mid-wife of a better society has never been verified, Instead, societies which were prudent enough to avoid revolutions by promoting evolutionary changes have best succeeded, while those torn by revolutionary upheavals were either swept away or prevented from making any further progress by their own internal contradictions" Messay Kebede (1999):168.

[42] Ibid, 292.

[43] Ibid, 363.

[44] Ibid, 360. I do not share Messay Kebede's pessimism. Certainly Ethiopia runs the danger of being marginalised, and one can even argue it is already a highly marginalised part of the world, But this process of marginalization has a great deal to do with the geometric rate of growth of the Western world enhanced by the rapid growth of information and computation technology. Marginalization may make the life of Ethiopians hard as well as short (in terms of stagnant or even decline of life expectancy and other health indicators), but would not necessarily lead to disintegration of the Ethiopian society. Ethiopian religiosity in general and the Orthodox Church in particular – the main pillar of nationalism - would, I believe, continue to play a unifying role. If the revival of the Christian faith among the youth is something to go bye, then one can say that the values the Orthodox Church embodies have functioned and would continue to function as bulwark against secular/modern state ideologies that tended to deny the citizen any meaningful role. But survival and modernization are not synonymous concepts.

[45] Shiferaw Beqele, "Review of Education in Ethiopia: From Crisis to the Brink of Collapse," in *Forum for Social Studies,* Bulletin, vol. 3&4: no. 2, (2006). The discussion paper under review is: *Education in Ethiopia: From the Crisis to the brink of Collapse,* (Uppsala: Nordic Africa Institute, 2006), 20

[46] Negash, (1996): 20-50.

Chapter 2

[47] Bahru Zewde, "The Intellectual and the State in Twentieth Century Ethiopia," *New Trends in Ethiopian Studies: Papers of the 12th International Conference of Ethiopian Studies,* vol. 1 (N.J.: The Red Sear Press, Inc., 1994), 490.

[48] Sylvia Pankhurst, *Ethiopia: A Cultural History* (Woodford Green: Lalibela House, 1955), 232.

[49] Ibid., 234.

[50] Paulos Milkias, "Traditional Institutions and Traditional Elites: The Role of Education in the Ethiopian Body-Politic," *African Studies Review,* 19: 3 (December 1976), 81.

[51] Ibid.

[52] Pankhurst, *Ethiopia: A Cultural History,* 237.

[53] Paulos, "Traditional Institutions and Traditional Elites: The Role of Education in the Ethiopian Body-Politic," 81.

[54] Ibid.

[55] Ibid., 82.

[56] Pankhurst, *Ethiopia: A Cultural History,* 245.

[57] Royal Chronicle of Abyssinia, *The Glorious Victory of Amda Tsiyon, King of Ethiopia,* trans. and ed. G. W. B. Huntingford (Oxford: Clarendon Press, 1965), 59.

[58] Mulatu Wubneh and Yohannes Abate, *Ethiopia: Transition and Development in the Horn of Africa* (Boulder, Colorado: Westview Press, 1988), 1.

[59] An objection can be raised according to which the Semitic element is so heavily present in the *Kebra Nagast* that it is difficult to consider it as Ethiopia's national epic. I answer that the Ethiopian version of the *Kebra Nagast* specifically refrains from assigning a Semitic or Sabaean origin to Queen Saba. Moreover, the connection it establishes between the Ethiopian ruling elite and Judaism is cultural rather than racial. For more discussion, see Messay Kebede, "Eurocentrism and Ethiopian Historiography: Deconstructing Semitization," *International Journal of Ethiopian Studies* (Hollywood: CA) 1=1 (Fall, 2003), 1-19.

[60] Teshome G. Wagaw, *Education in Ethiopia: Prospect and Retrospect* (Ann Arbor: The University of Michigan Press, 1979), 10-11.

[61] Addis Alemayehu, *Ye Timirtna Yetemaribet Tirgum* (*The Meaning of Education and School*), (Addis Ababa: Artistic Press, 1956), 107 (my translation).

[62] Ibid., 101 (my translation).

[63] Alaqa Embaqom Kalewold, *Traditional Ethiopian Church Education*, trans. Mengistu Lemma (New York: Teachers College Press, 1970), vi.

[64] Mulugeta Wodajo, "Postwar Reform in Ethiopian Education," *Comparative Education Review*, 2: 3 (February 1959), 25.

[65] Ibid.

[66] Ibid., 26.

[67] Teshome, *Education in Ethiopia*, 12.

[68] Ibid., viii.

[69] Ibid., 17.

[70] Ibid., 21.

[71] Addis, *The Meaning of Education and School*, 108 (my translation).

[72] Teshome, *Education in Ethiopia*, 48.

[73] Ibid., 183.

[74] Randi Rønning Balsvik, *Haile Selassie's Students: Rise of Social and Political Consciousness* (PHD Thesis: University of Tromsø, Norway, 1979), 6-7.

[75] Ibid., 15.

[76] Ibid., 26.

[77] Ibid.

[78] Mulugeta, "Postwar Reform in Ethiopian Education," 27.

[79] Balsvik, *Haile Selassie's Students*, 4.

[80] Ibid., 23.

[81] Ibid., 16.

[82] Teshome, *Education in Ethiopia*, 186.

[83] Forrest D. Colburn, *The Vogue of Revolution in Poor Countries* (Princeton, N.J.: Princeton University Press, 1994), 21.

[84] Ali A. Mazrui, *Political Values and the Educated Class in Africa* (Berkeley: University of California Press, 1978), 203.

[85] Anne Cassiers et Jean-Michel Bessette, *Mémoires Ethiopiennes* (Paris: L'Harmattan, 2001), 333 (my translation).

[86] Paulos, "The Political Spectrum of Western Education in Ethiopia," *Journal of African Studies*, 9: 1 (1982), 25.

[87] Teshome, *Education in Ethiopia*, 123.

[88] Balsvik, *Haile Selassie's Students*, 61-62.

[89] Haile Selassie, *Selected Speeches of his Imperial Majesty Haile Selassie First 1918 to 1976* (Addis Ababa: Artistic Printers Ltd, 1967), 19-20.

[90] Ibid, 20-21.

[91] Ibid, 25.

[92] Tekeste Negash, *Rethinking Education in Ethiopia* (Uppsala: Nordiska Afrikainstitutet, 1996), pg. 37.

[93] Ibid, 37.

[94] Kostas Loukeris, "Church and Attempted Modernization in Ethiopia," *Ethiopia in Broader Perspective: Papers of 13th International Conference of Ethiopian studies*, eds. Fukui K. E. Kurimoto and M. Shingeta, Vol. II, (Kyoto: Shokado Book Sellers, 1997), 217.

[95] Germa Amare, Abraham Demoz, and Aba Gabre Egziabher Degou, "Education Sector Review: Educational Objectives," Draft Paper, (1971), 14.

[96] Addis Hiwet, "A Certain Political Vocation: Reflections on the Ethiopian Intelligentsia," *The Ethiopian Revolution and its Impact on the Politics on the Horn of Africa, Proceedings: 2nd International Conference on the Horn of Africa* (New York: New School for Social Research, 1987), 45.

[97] Kaigo Tokiomi, *Japanese Education: Its Past and Present* (Tokyo: Kokusai Bunka Shinkokai, 1968), 53.

[98] Hugh Ll. Keenleyside and A. F. Thomas, *History of Japanese Education and Present Educational System* (Tokyo: The Hokuseido Press, 1937), 98.

[99] Tokiomi, *Japanese Education: Its Past and Present*, 54.

[100] Mazrui, *Political Values and the Educated Class in Africa*, 32-33.

[101] Tekeste, *The Crisis of Ethiopian Education: Some Implications for Nation-Building* (Uppsala, Sweden: Uppsala University, 1990), 76.

[102] Daniel R. Brower, "A Sociological Analysis: Fathers and Sons in Tsarist Russia," *The Youth Revolution: The Conflict of Generations in Modern History*, ed. Anthony Ester (Lexington: D. C. Heath and Company, 1974), 81.

Chapter 3

[103] Paulos Milkias is Professor of Humanities and Political Science at Marianopolis College/Concordia University in Montreal, Canada. This is a paper presented to a conference entitled "Education and Social Change in Ethiopia" which was held at the University of Dayton [Ohio] on May 14, 2006. The essay is based on his book, entitled, *Haile Selassie, Western Education and Political Revolution in Ethiopia*, Youngstown, New York: Cambria Press, 2006

[104] Czeslaw Jesman, *The Ethiopian Paradox* (London: Oxford University Press for the Institute of Race Relations, 1963): 1-5.

[105] See Blair Thomson, *Ethiopia: The Country that Cut off Its Head* (London: Robson Books, 1975).

[106] See, for example, Joseph Tubiana, "The Linguistic Approach to Self Determination" in I.M. Lewis, (Editor) *Nationalism and Self Determination in the Horn of Africa*, (London: Ithaca Press, 1983): 23-30; T.W. Baxter, "Ethiopia's Unacknowledged Problem: The Oromo, "*African Affairs* the Royal African Society, Vol. 77, No. 308' (July, 1978): 283-296; and D. Gabrakidan, "YeTigray Hizb Enna Ye-[Showa Amhara] timkhitegnoch Séra Ke-tnant Eske-Zaré." [Addis Ababa (1988) [On the generation-long conspiracies of the [Shoa Amhara] chauvinists against the people of Tigray.]: 1-30.

[107] For an analysis that emphasizes the movement of nationalities, see Bereket Habte Selassie, *Conflict and Intervention in the Horn of Africa* (New York: Monthly Review Press, 1980): 74-96.

[108] Vildredo Pareto, *The Rise and Fall of the Elites; An Application of Theoretical Sociology* (Totowa, N. J.: Bedminster Press, 1968) Walt Whitman Rostow, *Politics and the Stages of Growth* (Cambridge: Cambridge University Press, 1971); Neil Smelser and Seymour: Lipset *Social Structure and Mobility in Economic Development* (Chicago: Aidine Publishing Company, 1966).

[109] B.N. Ghosh, *Dependency Theory Revisited, (*London: Aldershot, 2001).

[110] Lawrence Stone, "Theories of Revolution," *World Politics,* Vol. X, No. 2, (Jan. 1966): 159–176; Isaac Krammick, "Reflections on Revolution-Definition and Explanation in Recent Scholarship," *History and Theory,* Vol. XI, No. 1 (1972): 26–63; Perez Zagorin, "Theories of Revolution in Contemporary Historiography," *Political Science Quarterly,* Vol. 88, No. 1(March 1973): 23–52; Details of these categorizations are found in Jack A. Goldstone, "Theories of Revolution: The Third Generation," World Politics, Vol. XXXN, No. 3 (April 1980): 425–453 and James Geschwender, "Explorations in the Theory of Social Movements and Revolution," Social Forces, Vol. XLVII (December, 1968): 127–135.

[111] Charles Ellwood, "A Psychological Theory of Revolutions," *American Journal of Sociology,* Vol. XI, No. 1 (July 1905): 49–59; Gustave LeBon, *The Psychology of Revolutions* (New York: Ernest Benn, 1913); Purim Sorokin, *The Sociology of Revolution* (Philadelphia: Lippincott, 1925); Lyford Edwards, *The Natural History of Revolution* (Chicago: University of Chicago Press, 1927); Emil Lederer, "On Revolutions," *Social Research,* Vol. VI, No. 1 (February 1936): 118; George S. Pettee, *The Process of Revolution* (New York: Harper, 1938); Crane Brinton, *The Anatomy of Revolution* (Englewood Cliffs, N. J.: Prentice Hall, 1938).

[112] James Davies, "Toward a Theory of Revolution," *American Sociological Review,* Vol. xxvii, No. 1 (Feb. 1962): 5–19; Ted Robert Gurr, *Why Men Rebel* (Princeton: Princeton University Press, 1970); Ivo K. Feierabend, Rosalind L. Feierabend and Ted Robert Gurr, eds., *Anger, Violence and Politics; Theories and Research* (Englewood Cliffs, N. J.: Prentice Hall, 1972); Ivo K. Feierabend, Rosalind Feierabend, and Betty Nesvold, "Social Change and Political Violence: Cross National Patterns," in Hugh D. Graham and Ted Gurr, eds., *Violence in America.* (New York: Signet, 1969); David Schwartz, "Political Alienation: The Psychology of Revolutions' First Stage," in Feierabend, Feierabend and Gurr, *Anger, Violence and Politics:* 58–66.

[113] Neil Smelser, *Theory of Collective Behaviour* (New York: Free Press, 1963); Charles Johnson, *Revolutionary Change.* (Boston: Little Brown, 1966); Edward Tiryakian, "A Model of Social Change in Its Lead Indicators," in Samuel Z. Klausner, ed., *The Study of Total Societies* (New York: Anchor Books, 1967); Mark Hart, *The*

Dynamics of Revolution (Stockholm: Toto Beckman, 1971); Bob Jessop, *Social Order, Reformed Revolution* (New York: Macmillan, 1973); Mark Hagopian, *The Phenomenon of Revolution* (New York: Dodd, Mead, 1974).

[114] Peter Amman, "Revolution: A Redefinition," *Political Science Quarterly* Vol. 77, No. 1 (March 1962): 36–53; Samuel Huntington, *Political Order in Changing Societies* (New Haven: Yale University Press, 1968); Arthur Stinchcombe, "Stratification Among Organizations and the Sociology of Revolution," in James March, ed., *Handbook of Organizations* (Chicago: Rand McNally, 1965): 169–180; Charles Tilly, "Revolutions and Collective Violence," in Fred Greenstein and Nelson Polsby, (eds.), *Handbook of Political Science,* Vol. III (Reading, Mass.: Addison-Wesley, 1975): 483–555; Charles Tilly, *From Mobilization to Revolution* (Reading, Mass.:Addison-Wesley, 1978).

[115] S. N. Eisenstadt, "Sociological Theory and an Analysis of the Dynamics of Civilizations and of Revolutions," *Daedalus,* Vol. 106, No. 1 (Fall, 1977): 59–78.

[116]. Harry Eckstein, "The Etiology of Internal War," *History and Theory,* Vol. IV, No. 2 (1965): 133–165

[117] Ibid., 86.

[118] Theda Skocpol "Explaining Revolutions: In Quest of a Social Structural Approach," in Lewis Coser and Otto N. Larson, eds., *The Uses of Controversy in Sociology* (New York: Free Press, 1976): 155-75; Theda Skocpol, *States and Social Revolution: A Comparative Analysis of France, Russia and China* (Cambridge: Cambridge University Press, 1979).

[119] Kay Ellen Trimberger, Revolution. from Above: *Military Bureaucrats and Development in Japan,* Turkey. Egypt and Peru (New Brunswick, N. J.: Transaction Books, 1978).

[120]. Sigmund Neumann, "The International Civil War," *World Politics,* Vol. XXII, No. 1 (April, 1949): 333–350; Barrington Moore, *Social Origins of Dictatorship and Democracy* (Boston: Beacon Press, 1966); Eric Wolfe, "Peasant Wars of the Twentieth Century," in Norman Miller and Roderick Aya, eds., *National Liberation: Revolution in the Third World* (New York: Free Press, 1971); George A. Kelly and Linda B. Miller, "Internal War and International Systems: Perspectives on Method," in George A. Kelly and Clifford Brown, *Struggles in the State: Sources and Patterns of World Revolution* (New York: Wiley, 1970): 223–260;James Rosenau, "International War and International Systems," in Kelly and Brown, *Struggles in the State,* 196–222; Jeffrey M. Paige, *Agrarian Revolution: Social Movements and Export Agriculture in the Developing World* (New York: Free Press 1975).

[121] James N. Rosenau, ed., *Linkage Politics: Essays on the Convergences of National and International Systems* (New York: Free Press, 1969).

[122] Katherine Chorley, *Armies and the Art of Revolution* (London: Faber and Faber, 1943); David Russell, *Rebellion, Revolution and Armed Forces: A Comparative Study of Fifteen Countries with Special Emphasis on Cuba and South Africa* (New York: Academic Press, 1974).

[123]. Moore, *Social Origins of Dictatorship and Democracy* ; Wolfe, "Peasant Wars of the Twentieth Century," in Miller and Aya, eds., *National Liberation*; H.H. Landsberger, ed., *Rural Protest: Peasant Movements and Social Change* (New York: Barnes and Noble, 1973); Joel Migdal, *Peasants, Politics and Revolution: Pressures Toward Political and Social Change in the Third World* (Princeton: Princeton University Press, 1974); Paige, Agrarian Revolution: Social Movements and Export Agriculture in the Developing World; Roy L. Prosterman, "A Simplified Predictive Index of Rural Instability," Comparative Politics, Vol. 8, No. 3, Special Issue on Peasants and Revolution (Apr., 1976): 339–353; Juan Linz, Patterns of Land Tenure, Division of Labour and Voting Behaviour in Europe, *Comparative Politics,* Vol. ill, No. 3 (April, 1976).

[124] Skocpol, "Explaining Revolutions: In Quest of Social Structural Approach," in the *Uses of Controversy in Sociology,* (Ed.)Lewis Coserand Otto N. Larson, (New York: The Free Press, 1976).

[125] Eisenstadt, "Sociological Theory and an Analysis of the Dynamics of Civilizations and of Revolutions" *Daedalus,* 106, 1, (Fall, 1977): 59–78.

[126] Skocpol, "Explaining Revolutions: In Quest of Social Structural Approach."

[127] Alexi de Tocqueville, *The Old Regime and The French Revolution* (New York: Harper and Bros, 1856): 214.

[128]. Lyford: Edwards "The Natural History of Revolution," Review author:Crane Brinton, *Political Science Quarterly,* Vol. 44, No. 2 (June, 1929): 302–303.

[129] Karl Marx and Frederick Engels, *"Wage, Labour and Capital,"* Selected Works, Vol. I (Moscow: Foreign Languages Publishing House, 1955): 94.

[130] Edwards, *The Natural History of Revolutions* ; Brinton, *The Anatomy of Revolution.*.

[131] James Davies, "Toward a Theory of Revolution," *American Sociological Review,* Vol. XXVII, No. 1 (February 1962): 6.

[132] Brinton, *The Anatomy of Revolution.*

[133] C. Marriam, *Civic Education in the United states,* Report of the Commission on the Social studies, American Historical Association, Part 6 (New York: Scribner, 1934); B. Pierce, *Citizens' Organizations and the Civic Training of Youth,* Report on the Commission on the Social studies, American Historical Association, Part 3 (New York: Scribner, 1933).

[134] Inkles and Daniel J. Levinson, "National Character: The study of modal personality and socio-cultural systems," Vol. 2 in Gardner Lindsey, ed., *Handbook of Social Psychology* (Cambridge, Mass: Addison Wesley, 1954): 977–1020.

[135] H. Hyman, Political Socialization: A Study in the Psychology of Political Behaviour (Glencoe, ill.: Free Press, 1959); D. Easton and Robert D. Hess, "The Child's Political World," *Midwest Journal of Political Science,* Vol. 6, No. 3, (1962): 202–216.

[136] H. Lasswell, *Politics: Who Gets What, When, How* (Cleveland: World Publishing Co., 1958).

[137] Michéle Barrett, The Politics of Truth: From Marx to Foucault (Cambridge: Polity Press 1991): 6.

[138] Durham, M., Kellner, D. (Eds.), *Media and cultural studies: Keywords* (Malden, MA: Blackwell Publishers, 2001): 6.

[139] 32. Antonio Gramsci, *Selections from the Prison Notebooks* (Lawrence and Wishart, 1971): 31.

[140] Althusser, Louis, "Ideology and Ideological State Apparatuses" *Contemporary Critical Theory,* (Ed.) Dan Latimer (San Diego: Harcourt, 1989): 61–102.

[141] E. Reimer, School Is Dead (New York: Penguin, 1971); N. Postman and C. Weinberger, Teaching as a Subversive Activity (New York: Penguin, 1971); I. Lister, (ed), *De-schooling: A Reader* (Cambridge: Cambridge University Press, 1974); Ivan Illich, *After De-schooling What?* (New York: Macmillan, 1973); Ivan Illich, *De-schooling Society* (New York: Penguin, 1973).

[142] Paolo Friere, Education for Critical Consciousness (New York: Seabury Press, 1973); Paolo Friere, Pedagogy of the Oppressed (New York: Herdes and Herdes, 1970); Friere has criticized many of his previous assumptions after the partial failure of his method; see Friere recent book on Guinea Bissau, *Lettres à la Guinee-Bissau sur l'alphabetization: Une experience ... de realization* (Paris: F. Maspero, 1978).

[143] See Karl Marx, *Economic and Philosophical Manuscripts of 1844* (trans). M. Milligan (Moscow: Progress Publishers, 1959): 21.

[144] Government of Ethiopia, Ministry of Education and Fine Arts, Bureau of Educational Research and Statistics, *Government, Mission, Private…:*16

[145] "Awaj" entitled: "Those who insult the Worker Should Desist from doing so on My Orders," Mahtama Selassie Wolde Mesqel, *Zikre Neger* [Amharic], (Addis Ababa: Berhanenna Selam, 1959): 421–422.

[146] Henry de Monfried, Vers les terres hostiles de l'Ethiopie (Paris: Bernard Franet, 1933): 229-30.

[147] 39. Paulos Milkias, "Traditional Institutions and Traditional Elites: the Role of Education in the Ethiopian Body Politic," *African Studies Review,* 19, 3, (December 1976).

[148] UNESCO, *International Yearbook of Education* (Geneva, 1963–1974); *Statistical Abstracts* (Paris: United Nations Publications, (1962–1972); Aklilu Habte, "Higher Education in Ethiopia" (Addis Ababa, 1973).

[149] UNESCO E.D./181/1961, *International Yearbook of Education* (Geneva, 1950–1962); *Statistical Yearbook* (Paris: United Nations Publications, 1963–1985).

[150] 42. UNESCO-ECA. "Final Report. /181/1961," *International Yearbook of Education* (Geneva, 1950–1962), *Statistical Yearbook* (Paris: United Nations Publications, 1963–1977).

[151] Ethiopian Students and Teachers. "Atawolawul Wotte" [Do Not Hesitate, Soldier] (Addis Ababa: Yekatit 21, 1966 [March 2, 1974]).

[152]. "Ye-Etiopia Hezb" [To the People of Ethiopia], Political tract distributed in Addis Ababa (March 4, 1974).

[153] UNESCO-ECA. Final Reports, (/181/1961) *International Yearbook of Education* (Geneva, 1950–1962), *Statistical Yearbook* (Paris: United Nations Publications, 1963–1977).

[154] Richard Greenfield, *Ethiopia: a New Political History* (London: Pall Mall Publishers, 1965).

[155] Paulos Milkias, "The Political Spectrum of Western Education in Ethiopia," *Journal of African Studies,* 9, 1, (Spring 1982).

[156] The political machinations involved in the Crown Council have been described by Haile Selassie's closest American adviser, John Spencer. See, John Spencer, *Ethiopia at Bay: Personal Account of the Haile Selassie Years* (Algonac, Michigan: Reference Publications, 1984): 257.

[157] Ministry of Education and Fine Arts, "Report of the Education Sector Review" (Addis Ababa, August 1972).

[158] UNESCO-ECA "Final Report. /181/1961" *International Yearbook of Education* (Geneva, 1950–1962), *Statistical Yearbook.* (Paris: United Nations Publications, 1963–1977).

[159] Aklilu Habte, "Higher Education.." Op.Cit.

[160] Fred Halliday and Maxine Molyneux, *The Ethiopian Revolution* (London: Verso, 1981): 64–95.

[161]. Ibid. 81–82.

[162] Patrick Gilkes, *The Dying Lion: Feudalism and Modernization in Ethiopia* (New York: St. Martins Press, 1975): 70–71, 101–136.

[163] Paulos Milkias, "Political Linkage," Ph.D. Dissertation, McGill University, Montreal, Canada (1982): 439.

[164] See "the National Democratic Revolution Programme of the World Wide Union of Ethiopian Students, (1973).

[165] A detailed treatise on the subject which was developed by die author was lint presented to the Canadian Political Science Association in June, 1980. See Paulos Milkias, "Political Linkage: The Relationship between Modern Education and the Fall of Haile Selassie' s Feudal Regime, "paper presented to the Canadian Political Science Association at the Annual Meeting of the Learned Societies of Canada, held at the University of Quebec in Montreal, (June 3, 1980).

[166] Ibid.

[167] This idea was discussed by the author in some detail in Seleda. See Seleda Ethiopia, (July/August 2002).

Chapter 4

[168] James C. N. Paul & Christopher Clapham. S. *Ethiopian Constitutional Development: A Source Book.* Addis Ababa Haile Selassie I University; Faculty of Law Volume1; (1972*):283.

[169] Ibid: 292-3.

[170] Mahtama Selassie Wolde Maskal (English translation quoted from Paul and Clapham, *Ibid.:* 287.

[171] Mahtama Selassie Wolde Maskal (English translation quoted in *Ibid.:* 287.

[172] This is not to deny the fact that the Ethiopian Students Union in North America (ESUNA) and the Union of Ethiopian Students in Europe (UESE) did pass their respective resolutions calling for the replacement of the monarchy by a democratically instituted government.

[173] It was while he was yet a regent that Haile Selassie showed his keen appreciation of the need for a robust educational movement. Teshome G. Wagaw, *Education In Ethiopia: Prospect and Retrospect (*Ann Arbor; University of Michigan Press; 1979): 35; Margery Perham, *the Government of Ethiopia, (*Evanston: North-Western University Press 1969): 246.

[174] *Ibid.:* 41. See also: 36.

[175] Perham, Op. Cit: 249-50.

[176] Wagaw, *Op. Cit:* 55.

[177] The British were able to gain a considerable political clout in the affairs of the government of Haile Selassie in the early years of the 1940s owing to their military intervention that helped to bring about the expulsion from Ethiopia of the invading army of Fascist Italy.

[178] Perham, *Op. Cit.:* 255.

[179] Delta Asayehegn, *Socio-economic and Educational Reforms in Ethiopia 1942-1974: Correspondence and Contradiction (* Paris; International Institute of Educational Planning United Nations Educational Scientific and Cultural Organization; 1979): 42.

[180] Asayehegn, *Ibid.:* 42.

[181] Concerning this state of affair, an Ethiopian student of the time is said to have remarked: "A secondary school curriculum which duplicates the secondary curriculum of conservative academic schools in English speaking countries is not appropriate for us in Ethiopia." Wagaw, *Op. Cit.:* 71.

[182] For additional information, see Wagaw *Ibid.:* 64; *See also* Asayehegn, *Op. Cit:* 46.

[183] For details regarding the activities of the Point IV Programme in Ethiopia, see Asayehegn, *Ibid.:* 44-47; See also Wagaw, *Ibid.:* 141-42.

[184] Wagaw, *Ibid.:* 142.

[185] Asayehegn, *Op. Cit:* 46.

[186] Wagaw, *Op. Cit:* 142.

[187] Asayehegn, *Op. Cit:* 44.

[188] Ibid.: *44.*

[189] Ibid.: 48.

[190] Ibid.: 49.

[191] Wagaw, *Op. Cit:* 171-2.

[192] Ibid.

[193] Peace Corps volunteers served in Ethiopia from 1962 until 1976, and then from 1995 until 1999. Details are available on the web at: www.ethiopiaeritrearpcvs.org/pages/rpcvs/vols.html

[194] Wagaw, *Op. Cit:* 130.

[195] *Ibid.:* 163-64.

[196] *Ibid.:* 164.

[197] As late as 1972-3, reliance was placed on recruitment of Peace Corps and other volunteer teachers from America and Europe as well as on foreign teachers on contract, most of them from India. See *Ibid.:* 173.

[198] Perham, *Op. Cit:* 258.
[199] Wagaw, Op. Cit: 143.
[200] *Ibid.*: 146.
[201] *Ibid.*: 146.
[202] For further information on the recommendations of the Committee on the Education Sector Review, See *Ibid.*: 186
[203] The Government of Haile Selassie seemed to have had the rather naïve view that the Amharic and Geez lessons were sufficient to introduce the students to the tradition of the Ethiopian society.
[204] For striking accounts of travelers on the subject, see Paul and Clapham, *Op. Cit:* 292.
[205] For a discourse on how the Amharic Language has attained the position of a Lingua Franca in Ethiopia, see Beqele Haile-Selassie, Ethiopia, "A Precarious Ethno-federal Constitutional Order" (PhD Diss., University of Wisconsin Law School, Madison, 2002), 263-70.
[206] Tewodros attempted to stimulate private initiative and enterprise under the slogan: "turn the swords and the spears into ploughs!" Wagaw, *Op. Cit:* 4.
[207] *The Bible*, Genesis 3:19.
[208] Paul and Clapham, *Op. Cit:* 308.
[209] The Kebra Nagast provides valuable insights on the mythical foundations of the Ethiopian state and the paramount importance of myths for the identity and unity of a nation.
[210] An elabourate historical survey of this epoch is available in the work of Mordechai Abir, *Ethiopia: The Era of the Princes: The Challenge of Islam and Reunification of the Christian Empire, 1769-185). (New* York: Praeger; 1968).
[211] Paul and Clapham, *Op. Cit:* 326.
[212] See article 1 of the Establishment of the Board of Education and Fine Arts, Order 1947.
[213] Scarcely anyone, let alone the students imagined that the liquidation of the monarchy would soon be followed by an agonizing period of a gory fratricidal feud that wiped out tens of thousands of Ethiopians, mostly young men and women.
[214] For an extensive discourse on the subject, see Beqele Haile-Selassie, *Op. Cit.*
[215] Beqele Haile-Selassie, *Ibid.*: 220.

Chapter 5

[216] Bahru Zewde, *Pioneers of Change in Ethiopia: The Reformist Intellectuals of the Early Twentieth Century.* (Addis Abeba: Addis Abeba University Pres, 2002), 23.
[217] Sylvia Pankhurst, *Ethiopia: A Cultural History.* (Essex: Lalibela House, 3 Charteris Road, Woodford Green, 1955), 537.
[218] Ibid. 536.
[219] Bahru Zewde, *Pioneers of Change in Ethiopia*, 51.
[220] *Ibid.* 100.This is a view that is surprising in its prescience in that, a century after Tekle Hawaryat's musings, some commentators on Africa seriously propose recolonization as a solution to Africa's problems. William Pfaff, "A new colonialism? Europe must go back into Africa", *Foreign Affairs* 74, no.1 (1995): 2-7.
[221] Ibid. 209.
[222] Ibid.140, 142, 146.
[223] Ibid. 141.
[224] Ibid.138.
[225] Ibid. 144
[226] UNDP, *Human Development Report 2005* (UN Plaza, New York, New York, UNDP, USA), 261.
[227] The World Bank, *Education in Ethiopia: Strengthening the Foundation for Sustainable Progress.* (Washington, D.C. 20433, U.S.A. 2005), xxiii.
[228] Ibid. 47, xxviii.
[229] Ibid. xxix, 124, 184.
[230] Ibid. 124.
[231] Fra von Massow, "International development targets, poverty, and gender in Ethiopia". *Gender and Development* 8, no. 1 (2000): 46.
[232] The World Bank, *Higher Education Development for Ethiopia: Pursuing the Vision.* (Washington, D.C. 20433, U.S.A.2003), 6.
[233] Ibid. x.
[234] The World Bank, *Education in Ethiopia,* 130; Fra von Massow, "International development targets", 47.

[235] Pauline Rose and Samer Al-Samarrai. "Household Constraints on Schooling by Gender: Empirical Evidence from Ethiopia". *Comparative Education Review* 45, no. 1 (2001): 40

[236] The World Bank, *Higher Education Development for Ethiopia...*, x.

[237] Ibid.

[238] James L. Hoot, Judit Szente, and Belete Mebratu, "Early Education in Ethiopia:Progress and Prospects." *Early Childhood Educational Journal* 32, no.1 (2004): 6; Philip Verwimp, "Measuring the Quality of Education at Two Levels: A Case Study of Primary Schools in Rural Ethiopia" *International Review of Education* 45, no.2 (1999): 167-196; Abebayehu Aemero Tekleselassie. "The Deprofessionalization of School Principalship: Implications for Reforming School Leadership in Ethiopia." *International Studies in Educational Administration* 30, no.3 (2002): 57-64.

[239] The World Bank, *Higher Education Development for Ethiopia*, 17.

[240] David H Shinn, "Reversing the Brain Drain In Ethiopia", (Paper delivered to the Ethiopian North American Health Professionals Association, The George Washington University, Alexandria, Virginia, November 23, 2002).

[241] The World Bank, *Education in Ethiopia*, 197.

[242] Central Statistical Authority, *Ethiopia Child Labour Survey Report. Federal Democratic Republic Of Ethiopia,* 2001. http://www-ilo-irror.cornell.edu/public/english/region/afpro/ addisababa/publ.pdf. Accessed December 19, 2005.

[243] The World Bank, *Education in Ethiopia,* 19-20, 42, 100-194.

[244] The World Bank, *Higher Education Development for Ethiopia,* vi-xvi, 43-50; The World Bank, *Education in Ethiopia...*, xxix, xxxi.

[245] Tekeste Negash. *Rethinking Education in Ethiopia.* (Uppsala: Nordiska, Africainstitute,1996), 11.

[246] Tekeste Negash. *The Crisis of Ethiopian Education: Some Implications for Nation Building* (Uppsala: Uppsala University, Uppsala Reports on Education no.29, 1990), 64-69.

[247] Tekeste Negash. *Rethinking Education in Ethiopia,* 6.

[248] Elleni Tedla, *Sankofa: African Thought and Education.* (New York: Peter Lang. 1995).

[249] Ibid. 149-164.

[250] Donald N Levine, *Wax and Gold: Tradition and Innovation in Ethiopian Culture.* (Chicago: Chicago University Press, 1972), 11,13.

[251] Ibid. 13.

[252] David Bridges, Amare Asgedom and Setargew Kenaw, "From 'deep knowledge' to 'the light of reason': source for philosophy of education in Ethiopia", *Comparative Education* 40, no.4 (2004): 538.

[253] David Bridges, Amare Asgedom and Setargew Kenaw, "From 'deep knowledge' to 'the light of reason", 540-542

[254] John Binns, "Theological Education in the Ethiopian Orthodox Church", *The Journal of Adult Theological Education* 2, no.2 (2005): 110-111.

[255] I use the term culture in a generic sense to refer to the ensemble of the cultures of Ethiopia.

[256] Reidulf Molvaer, *Tradition and Change in Ethiopia: Social and Cultural Life as* Reflected in Amharic Fictional Literature (Leiden: E.J. Brill, 1980), 170-207.

[257] This requires a historical analysis of the social formations that characterized Ethiopia for centuries. Since this is not the objective of this paper, I will hardly touch on this aspect.

[258] See also the discussion on the *Daqiqa Estefanos* below.

[259] Richard Pankhurst, *A Social History of Ethiopia* (Trenton, NJ.: Red Sea Press,1992), 126.

[260] Auguste Comte, *The Essential Comte,* ed. S.Andreiski (New York: Barnes and Noble), 199.

[261] Eric Wolf, *Europe and the People without History* (Berkeley: University of California Press, 1982).

[262] Gerard LeClerc, *Anthropologie et Colonialisme: Essai sur l'Histoire de l'Africanisme.* (Paris: Fayard, 1972).

[263] Ernst Cassirer, *An Essay on Man: An Introduction to a Philosophy of Human Culture* (New Haven CT: 1944), 228.

[264] Donald D Levine's oft cited work, *Wax and Gold,* is a good example of this. Ibid.

[265] John Binns, "Theological Education in the Ethiopian Orthodox Church", 110.

[266] Quoted in John Binns, ibid.111.

[267] Donald Levine, *Wax and Gold,* 242-252.

[268] Ibid. 266-267.

[269] I have tried to give a preliminary sketch of the concept of surplus-history elsewhere. I explore it here from a different perspective. Maimire Mennasemay, "Ethiopian Political Theory, Democracy, and Surplus-History" *International Journal of Ethiopian Studies* 2, no. 1&2 (2005-2006): 1-32.

[270] Charles Taylor, *Philosophy and the Social Sciences: Philosophical Papers,* vol. 2. (Cambridge: Cambridge University Press, 1988), 28.

[271] Hans-Georg Gadamer, *Truth and Method* (New York: The Seabury Press, 1975), 58-73, 252-253, 313-325; Charles Taylor, *Philosophy and the Social Sciences*,15-57.

[272] As how the Adwa victory may be seen as an unfinished work, see Maimire Mennasemay. "Ethiopian History and Critical Theory: The Case of Adwa", eds, Paulos Milkias and Getachew Metaferia, *The Battle of Adwa*. (New York, Agora, 2005).

[273] Alain Badiou, *L'Être et L'Événement* (Paris: Seuil, 1988) 201-212, 223 233.

[274] Ernst Bloch, *The Principle of Hope*, vol.I, translated by Neville Plaice, Stephen Plaice and Paul Knight (Cambridge, Massachusetts: The MIT Press, 1986), 115.

[275] Ibid. vol.I, 116.

[276] Ibid. vol.I, 115-47, 9; vol III: 1354-1376.

[277] Ibid. vol. III: 1355.

[278] Michel De Certeau, *The Practice of Everyday Life*. (Berkeley: University of California Press, 1984).

[279] James C. Scott, *Weapons of the Weak: Everyday forms of Peasant Resistance* (New Haven: Yale University Press, 1985).

[280] Karl Marx, *Early Writings* (New York: Vintage Books, 1975), 209.

[281] David Levine, *Wax and Gold...*, 250.

[282] Sven Rubenson, *The Survival of Ethiopian Independence*. (London: Heinemann, 1976), 1.

[283] See discussion below on *Daqiqa Estefanos* on the critiques of *dabtara*.

[284] Richard Pankhurst, *A Social History of Ethiopia*, 359.

[285] Donald Levine, *Wax and Gold*, 310.

[286] Getatchew Haile, *Daqiqa Estefanos: BeHeg Amlak*. (Minnesota: Avon, 2004).

[287] Ibid. 46-48, 95, 110-111, 140-161, 156-167, 170-181, 194, 197, 201, 204. All translations from Amharic into English are mine.

[288] Ibid. 84

[289] Ibid. 102-103, 109, 120.

[290] 93, 108-109, 112, 128-129, 134-138, 170-171.

[291] Ibid. 70, 86-88, 92-93, 96, 102, 109.

[292] Ibid. 127, 132-135, 198-199, 249.

[293] Ibid. 276.

[294] Ibid. 32-33, 127, 170, 298-300.

[295] Ibid. 103, fn 153.

[296] Ibid: 93, 108-109, 112, 128-129, 134-138, 140, 170-171, 261-264.

[297] Ibid. 58.

[298] Ibid. 298.

[299] Ibid. 301-304.

[300] Ibid. 305.

[301] Ernst Bloch,. "Non-synchronism and Dialectcs", *New German Critique* 11 (1977): 22-38.

[302] Getatchew Haile, *Daqiqa Estefanos*, 258-265, 271-276.

[303] *Tezeta*. Ethiopiques Collection # 10, Paris, Non-dated.

[304] Ernst Bloch, *The Principle of Hope*, vol. I: 127-164, 195-223, 235-241.

[305] Ibid. 144-146.

[306] Ibid. 164.

[307] Ibid. 75, 127, 131, 196-199.

[308] Ibid. vol. III: 1380; vol. I: 199; vol. III: 1372.

[309] I use *zefen* and *iskesta* as generic terms to refer to the songs and dances of the various regions of Ethiopia, from Wallo to Wellega, from Gondar to the Ogaden.

[310] For a discussion of the social dimensions of popular music, see Jacques Attali, *Noise: The Political Economy of Music* (Minneapolis: University of Minnesota Press, 1985), 9-13.

[311] Ernst B;och, op cit. vol. III: 1063.

[312] Adugnaw Worqu's poetic version of *tezeta* is a profound meditation on the temporal depth, the intensity of experience, and the anticipatory force of *tezeta*. Adugnaw Worqu, *YeMeskel Wëf*. (Angwin. CA. Shinfa Press.1984), 146-147.

[313] Ayele Bekerie. *Ethiopic: An African Writing System: Its History and Principles* (Lawrenceville, NJ: Red Sea Press,. 1997), 126.

[314] Every singer adapts *tezeta* to the memory of interrupted happiness he or she refers to—be it an individual's loss of what he or she loves, a community's feeling of having been torn away from their land, or the feeling that one's homeland has become one's perdition. From Mahmoud's *Tezeta* to Teddy Afro's *"Yasteseriyal"* version, one finds the haunting memory of a lost love eating away at one's soul, but out of which is born a militant desire to cling, in the lyrics of Mahmoud, to the "wings" of the "bird" so that one "will live" and fly

into the future and redemption. One finds in all versions of *tezeta* this motif of an interrupted past happiness that makes the present unbearable and yet makes it the trampoline for a redemptive future where unhappiness and its causes are overcome. Alemayehu Eshete mourns, "He who has nothing is already dead" and yet, he sings that as long as we reclaim the future, we always have something, making the *tezeta* a militant memory of a possible future and a driving force for overcoming the decay of the present. Menelik Wesnatchew laments his "impossible desire", then "contemplates" it as a "vision" that appears as a "*tezeta*" that "calls out" to him to dream forward to a different future. In Getatchew Kassa's version, *tezeta* is an interrupted happiness that "haunts my spirit constantly" and throbs as an anticipatory consciousness that makes him want that which the present cannot give him; his *tezeta* is a forward pull that refuses to accept the putrefaction of the present. Out of *tezeta* gushes forth an intense desire to undertake a new journey whose path we do not know in advance but which prefigures a future that resurrects out of the present darkness the bright sun of our aborted hopes beckoning from the future. There are also poetic versions of *tezeta*. Adugnaw Worqu's version captures, in its purity and simplicity, the temporal complexity, experiential density, and the emotional intensity that characterizes *tezeta*. To grasp the memory of lost happiness and the anticipatory consciousness of emancipation that emanate from Adugnaw's *Tezeta*, one must see with unblinkered eyes the shameful conditions of our present existence as Ethiopians. We are one of the poorest, sickest, and oppressed members of the human species, dependent, for even the basic necessities of life, on the charities of a world that has made Ethiopia a metaphor for hunger and begging. Adugnaw completely ignores these conditions in his *Tezeta*, not because he is oblivious to them, but to express his total and radical rejection of the putrefied present. He rhapsodizes on an Ethiopia that is hauntingly beautiful, bountiful and generous. In his *Tezeta*, plants and animals, the sky and the earth, the sun and the flowers, are interlaced in joy and are inhabited with beauty, truth and justice. And when an Ethiopian makes an appearance, it is as a happy peasant. Thus, Adugnaw tellingly chooses the peasant, the ultimate symbol of the suffering body of destitute Ethiopia, to symbolize the joy that is "Not-Yet". Out of the poem emerges the sadness of being exiles in our own land—a home of grinding poverty, pandemics and tyranny, made even more unbearable by the beauty of a land we have inherited from our ancestors but have transformed into a vale of tears and skeletons. And yet, the poem exudes the refusal to give up the hope of a better Ethiopia and gushes with the joy to come.

[315] Immanuel Kant, *On Education* (Boston: D.C.Heath, 1900), 14.

[316] A current example of historical-cultural amnesia that has plunged Ethiopia into a dangerous political crisis is the claim espoused by the current Prime Minister, Meles Zenawi, and the ethnic ruling elite that Ethiopia is a creation of the colonial scramble of the 19th century and is a "prison-house of nations Meles Zenawi, *YeErtra Hezb Tegel: Keyet Wedet Gimgema*, (1979), translated into Amharic from Tigrigna and with a preface by Abraham Yayeh (Washington, 2000).

[317] Tekeste Negash, *Rethinking Education*, 7.

[318] Alfred Fouillée, *Les Etudes Classiques et la Démocratie* (Paris: A.Collin, 1898). My thanks to Geneviève Marcoul for drawing my attention to this work.

[319] John Dewey, *Democracy and Education* (Carbondale: Southern Illinois University Press, 1985).

[320] This familiarization with the educated hope of the West to the detriment of educated *tezeta* is extended and deepened by the increasing presence of Western popular culture in urban Ethiopia. One of its curious effects in urban Ethiopia is the practice of giving children American forenames in certain Ethiopian families.

[321] Messay Kebede. *Survival and Modernization: Ethiopia's Enigmatic Present Philosophical Discourse* (Lawrenceville, NJ.: The Red Sea Press, 1999), 352.

[322] Bahru Zewde, *Pioneers of Change in Ethiopia*, 102.

[323] Ernst Bloch, *The Principle of Hope*, vol. III: 1375.

[324] That the truth of a practice is revealed in its pathologies is a demystifying approach. For Marx, the truth of capitalism is revealed in its economic crises; for Freud, the truth of psychic life is revealed in its psychopathologies; and according to Horkheimer and Adorno, the truth of instrumental reason is revealed in totalitarianism. Sigmund Freud, *The Psychopathology of Everyday Life* (Harmondsworth: Penguin 2003); Max Horkheimer and Theodor W. Adorno, *Dialectic of Enlightenment* (New York: Seabury Press, 1972).

[325] Amartya Sen, *Development As Freedom* (New York: Anchor Press, 2000), 242.

[326] Ellwood P. Cubberley, *The History Of Education: Educational Practice and Progress Considered as a Phase of the Development and Spread of Western Civilization* (Stanford: Stanford University Press, 1920).

[327] I speak of the West, because Ethiopia has mainly borrowed her "modern" educational system and knowledge from Europe and the United States.

[328] I use development and modernization as equivalent terms, which they are from the perspective of educated *tezeta*.

[329] Alain Badiou, *L'Être et L'Événement*, 361-377.

[330] Donald Levine, *Wax and Gold*, 241-244

[331] Maimire Mennasemay. "Ethiopian History and Critical Theory: The Case of Adwa".

[332] UNESCO, *Education in a multilingual world*, 2003, (http://unesdoc.unesco.org/images /0012/001297/

129728e.pdf. Accessed December 19, 2005), 15.
[333] Ernst Bloch, *The Principle of Hope,* vol. III: 1374.

Chapter 6

[334] For further see, Karla Poewe (ed.), *Charismatic Christianity as a Global Culture* (Columbia: University of South Carolina Press, 1994); David Martin, *Forbidden Revolution: in Latin American and Catholicism in Eastern Europe* (London: SPCK, 1996); Corten Marshall-Ftatani (ed.), *Between Babel and Pentecost: Transnational Pentecostalism in Africa and Latin America* (Bloomington: Indiana University Press, 2004).

[335] Many informants agree that they do not recall the term *Pente* being used at any time and at any where to any religious group prior to the Dabra Zeit incident. Doctor Tilahun Adera, one of the Pentecostal students active in Haile Selassie University in 1966 recalls that students, opposed to their movement, continued to refer to them as followers of *tsere Maiaym*, anti-Mary. Informant: Tilahun Adera

[336] *"Be-Dabra Zeit ketema lijochena Wallagoch tegachu,"* *Addis Zemen*, Vol. 27, No. 826, September 19, 1967, p. 1. According to the report, the "unknown religion started a year before the incident by three young men and enlisted more than 200 people in the town alone. Their sudden rise and increase in membership coupled with rumors of "vulgar" practices, including promiscuous sex under the disguise of night prayers, set the context for the attack. According to *Addis Zemen*, more than 6,000 people were involved in the assault. Informants: Melese, Debebe and Asseffa.

[337] It is very hard to come up with a uniform definition of the Pentecostals. W.J. Hollenweger, a noted scholar in the field defined Pentecostals: "all groups who profess at least two religious crisis experience (1. baptism or rebirth; 2 baptism of the Spirit), the second being subsequent and different from the first one, and the second, usually, but not always, being associated with speaking in tongue" W.J. Hollenweger, *The Pentecostals*, (Minneapolis: Augsburg, 1972), p. xix. Ethiopian Pentecostal are in agreement that the term refers to those Christians who express the power and presence of the Holy Spirit and the gifts of the spirit directed towards effectively witnessing that Jesus Christ is Lord and Savior. Most Pentecostals embrace the view that the baptism of the Holy Spirit comes subsequent to conversion. Though there is no unanimity, speaking in tongues is considered to be the chief indication of the in-filling of the Spirit and a mark of being a true Christian. In addition to the baptism of the Holy Spirit, Pentecostals believe that nine Biblical gifts of the Spirit, "the word of wisdom, the word of knowledge, the gift of faith, the gifts of healing, the gift of miracles, the gift of prophesy, the gifts of discerning spirits, the gifts of tongues and the gifts of interpretation of tongues are available today" to those Christians who earnestly seek them. David E. Harrell, *All Thing Are Possible* (Bloomington: Indiana University Press, 1975), pp. 11-12.

[338] Marie S. Rice, *Sister Bertha Sister Ruth* (Nashville: Jonathan Publishers of Nashville, 1984), pp. 112-113; 118-194.

[339] The American Grade School and Mission had three levels: lower (beginners), intermediary and higher. Just a month after it's opening the missionary report that there were about 90 students enrolled, a high figure for its time. Rice, pp. 112-118.

[340] The Ethiopian Mission of BCMS began in 1934 when Messrs. Colin Mackenzie and Stanley Metters established a station at Asebe Teferi with the encouragement of Dr. Martin, (*Hakim* Workeneh). Later parties of recruits led by Mr. Mrs. A. Buxton settled in Addis Ababa and set up a Bible school for young Orthodox Christians. Their activities resulted in the creation of an association whose members were known as *Serawit Kirstos*, Army of Jesus. We know very little about the religious legacy of this group. Norman Grubb, *Alfred Buxton of Abyssinia and Congo* (London: Luther Worth Press, 1942), pp. 114-123; Informant: Tuji Jimma, a former member of *Serawita Krestos.*

[341] Originally a priest from Gojjam, *Qes* Badma Yalew, played a key role in the creation of the Makana Yesus church, a name that was proposed by him. He also made pioneering efforts to form a united Evangelical church in Ethiopia. Gustav Aren, *Envoys of the Gospel in Ethiopia*, (Stockholm: EFS forlaget, 1999), pp. 94-97 See also his obituary *Addis Zemen*, Miazia 7, 1965/ 1973.

[342] Elen French, "Revival in Ethiopia," *Elim Pentecostal Herald* vii, 51 (June 1937), p,7.

[343] The missionaries report that the young Ethiopians told them that most of their people spent much of their times in prayer and piety without experiencing radical spiritual changes. Berth Dommermuth points out that she spoke to Worqu and his friends about the power of God and the baptism of the of the Holy Spirit and notes that their hearts were stirred since she saw them wiping their tears. Rice, p. 133. It is not clear from the statement whether or not the young Ethiopians spoke in tongue. Dommermuth reports that it was following this conversation with Worqu and his friends that many young Ethiopians began to come to their place. See also, the report of Ellen French *Elim Pentecostal Herald,* vii, 61 (1938), p. 10.

[344] Rice, p. 191. It is interesting to note that the missionary used both the word "bury" and "resurrection"

in the metaphoric and spiritual sense. They were expecting the fruits of their labour at a distant future. Though the Pentecostal missionaries visited Ethiopia in June 1969, they do not mention any thing about the sprouting movement, which suggests that they were unaware of its existence. Instead of referring to the Ethiopian Pentecostals, who at the time of their visit, were active in Addis Ababa, they mention about the how communism had already attracted young men and point out to its danger. Rice p. 242

[345] Rice, p. 239.

[346] Informants: Pastor Yohannes Ijigu, Carlten Spencer, former President of the Elim Bible Institute. The group, however, could be characterized as proto-Pentecostals.

[347] *The Ethiopian Herald*, No. 25, vol. 10, December 13,1952.For a fuller report and more detailed account, see, Jane Collins, *Miracles and Missions and World Wide Evangelism* (Dallas: Jane Collins Daoud, 1953), pp.78-106.

[348] A term used in the religious parlance of the evangelical/charismatic world to describe religious public gatherings essentially for outreach purposes. Another equivalent word that has entered into a popular usage is "conference."

[349] It is also reported that the prayer session led to intimate relations with the Emperor and the missionary. The Emperor promised the missionary that he would be welcome to start missionary work in Ethiopia. Seleshi Kebede, "The History of Genet Church", Makana Yesus Seminary, 1990, p.2; Beqele Wolde Kidan, *Revival: Etiopia ena Yemechereshaw Revival* (Addis Ababa: Mulu Wangiel, 2001/2), p.131. The Emperor had several contacts with church leaders and leading evangelical figures who prayed for him and assured him of that the day would come when he would be restored to his country and to his throne. His exile period significantly shaped his attitude toward missions in general. For further, see, Doris M. Rouse, *The Intercession of Rees Howells* (Cambridge: Luterwoth Press, 1983), pp. 22-23.

[350] Karl Ramstrand, the first missionary from the SPM, reported that he came to Ethiopia after encountering a vision, while he was in Liberia as a missionary, in which he saw a powerful light originating from Liberia stretching across the map of Ethiopia. He interpreted the vision to be a new call from God to serve the nation of Ethiopia as a missionary. Beqele, 67; Heywat Berhan: *"Ye Awasa Heywat Berhan Beta Kristian 40 gna amet mesereta be 'al,"* Awasa, 2000, p. 3.

[351] The activity of the Finnish Mission gave rise to the formation of *Sefere Genet* church in 1971 under its first Ethiopian pastor, Hiruy Tsige, and the Swedish Philadelphia mission gave birth to *Ye Heywat Berhan* church, established as an independent local church in 1975. *YeHeywat Berhan Metshet*, p.11.

[352] The issue of conversion has been purposely avoided in the discussion. The religious experience those who embraced Pentecostalism from the Orthodox background, needs a serious theological reflection. Perhaps, the term "adhesion" as developed by Nock might serve a better purpose.

[353] Informants: Asseffa and Zeleke.

[354] Informants: Dr. Negussie Tefera, Girma Tessemma, Asseffa Alemu, Reverend Zeleke Alemu, and others. See also Mulu Wangiel, *"Ye Mulu Wangiel Amagnoch Bete Kristian, 25 gna Beal,1959-1984,"* 1991, p. 30.

[355] According to Desta Wedajo, there were a few Christians in the Institute, such as Nega Ayele (who later became a professor of political science in the national university and lost his life during the Revolution), Abdi Yusuf and Desta himself, who visited the Swedish Lutheran church in Harar, but whose presence, as a religious group was not visibly felt in the campus. Informant: Desta Wedajo.

[356] Among the literatures that have influenced the young in the 60's were materials written by T. L. Osborn, a radical Pentecostal minister from US. His books and magazines include: *Healing the Sick, Healing in His Wing, The Purpose of Pentecost, The book of Acts,* and *Faith Digest.* T. L. Osborn formed the Association for Native Evangelism (1953) to train local evangelists to serve as missionaries and used his networks to distribute extensive Pentecostal literature in several countries in Africa. He had been organizing major revivalist crusades gathering huge crowds in Kenya since 1957. Oral Robert's book, *Abundant Life* was also circulating in small numbers. There were also some periodical items like, The Herald of His Coming, Voice of Healing, World Harvest and Decision in circulation, albeit in limited numbers and localities. Informants: Asseffa, Zeleke, Solomon Kebede, Bedru Hussein, Girma Tessemma and Ferne and Campbell Miller.

[357] *Haymanote Abew* is an association of young Ethiopian Christians from the Orthodox Church, which was created in 1958, mainly by university students of Addis Ababa. It was both a religious and social organization whose principal objectives seem to introduce reform from within. The association also received strong support and inspirations from members of the royal family and high-ranking officials, such as Akale Work Habtewold, who saw the need for the Orthodox Church to undergo some changes if it should desire to accommodate the challenge of modernity, particularly as it effected the youth. The *Haymanote Abew* groups were very hostile towards foreign missionaries in general and were very critical of the Pentecostal movement. Informants: Tenagne Lemma, Dr. Alem Bazezew, Solomon Kebede.

[358] Informants: Solomon Kebede; Mulugeta and Girma Tessemma.

[359] Among them were: Solomon Kebede, Girma Tessemma, Tilahun Yilma, Mulugeta Zewde, etc.

[360] Melese Wegu (later, Dr.), now Director Ethiopian Outreach Ministry based in York, Pennsylvania, and

Kebede Wolde Mariam (later, Dr.), now residing in US, played conspicuous role in rallying the youth for the creation of an independent Pentecostal church in Ethiopia in the 60's.

[361] Informant: Paul Johansson. Paul Johansson, ex- President of the Elim Bible Institute, was the founder of the All Nation Gospel Church in Kenya was intimately connected with the East African Revival movement which gave rise to a number of Pentecostal churches and organizations such as Pentecostal Evangelical Fellowship of Africa (PEFA) established in 1963. Omahe Chacha's participation in one of the Pentecostal conferences in Awasa is reported in Elim's *Missionary News Report of 1965.* The report states, "The ministry of Chacha Omahe, a Kenyan overseer in training course in Southern Ethiopia, was a great blessing. Two hundred Ethiopian brethren attended!" *Missionary News Report,* Elim Bible Institute, February 9, 1965, p. 1.

[362] Informants point out that he was one of the key players in the spread of Pentecostalism in Ethiopia. For one thing, Ethiopians easily identified with him as a black evangelist. Second, he preached in simple, yet bold terms followed by some dramatic occurrence adding new vitality to their religious convictions. His being a short-term visitor, unlike those Pentecostal missionaries stationed in Ethiopia, might have lent him the leeway to conduct his preaching and boldly exercise his spiritual gifts the way he wanted. Omaha died in 1991 after a long life of active service as a pastor of a church in Kenya. Informants: Beqele W/ Kidan, Solomon Kebede, Asseffa, and Dr. Melese Wegu,, Gaati Chacha Maluki. Omaha died in 1991 after a long life of active service as a pastor of a church in Kenya.

[363] Informant: Kebede Wolde Mariam.

[364] Informant: Kebede Wolde Mariam. Kebede commented, "We grew quickly, we knew more than they expected, we became better than the women and we wanted to go beyond."

[365] Those Ethiopians, who chose to stay with the Finnish mission group later found a local church under the name *Sefere Genet,* the "land of the paradise." Because of its location, the church attracted mostly poor people and later merchants from the Gurage ethnic community. Informants: Pastor Heruye and Pastor Seleshi.

[366] Informants: Girma, Bedru Hussein, Solomon Lulu, and Beqele; Yoseph Kidane Wolde, "The History of the Pentecostal Movement in Addis Ababa," Department of History, AAU, 1976, p. 17. According to Tilahun, some of the EUS returnees like Berhane Abraha, already had the experience of the Baptism of the Holy Spirit at the Awasa Conference1965. Tilahun. *Bete Kristianen Eseralehu...,*p. 94.

[367] For the latter view, see, Yeshitla Mengistu, "History of the Meserete Krestos Church," Addis Ababa, Makana Yesus Seminary, 1984, p.16.

[368] Beqele Wolde Kidan, *Rivaival,* p. 90.

[369] Informants: Girma Demissie, Philipos Kemere and Solomon Kebede.

[370] Chapel was the term the young Ethiopians used to refer to their worship centre or prayer house. According to informants, they could not use the term *Bete Kristian,* which means church, since it is reserved for the national Ethiopian Orthodox Church. The church in the traditional sense, must have the *tabot (* a wooden representation of the Ark of the Covenant) and *kahen,* an ordained priest. The young Pentecostals established chapels wherever they went, regardless of the size of the congregation, and used them as launching pads for evangelizing.

[371] Informants: Girma Tessemma, Solomon Kebede and Bedru Hussein.

[372] Informants: Bedru, Solomon Kebede, Solomon Lulu and others.

[373] Informants: Evelin Brant Thompson and Dr. Howard Brant.

[374] According to an American missionary who was in charge of the centre in the early 60's, the radical students not only disrupted programs but also were engaged in verbal attacks and character assassinations. The missionary was sarcastically called "General Manzke" of the CIA, and Christian students associated with the centre were labeled as disciples of "General Manzke." The opposition they faced from the radical students and some clergies from the Orthodox Church compelled the missionary to look for another site. According to Manzke, Prince Sophia Desta allowed one of her places near *Afincho-Ber* to be temporarily used as the new youth centre. Informants: Albert and Marian/ Manzke.

[375] Among those taking part in these informal meetings were: Tessemma Jembere, Kebede, Tessemma, Zeleke, Philipos, Fantahun, Asseffa, Melese and others. Informants: Asseffa, Zeleke, Bete and others

[376] Though not articulated in the form of a slogan, the idea of "the Gospel for Ethiopia by Ethiopians" had already existed in its crude form among the pioneers of the Harari Pentecostals. Informants: Zeleke and Asseffa.

[377] Though not the first of its kind, the Awasa Conference was the biggest in terms of the size of participants it had attracted and the length of time it lasted, which all in all, took more than two weeks. *Heywat Berhan,* p.9.

[378] Among the speakers of the Awasa Conference were: Omaha Chacha, Mattson Bosze Joseph, the American evangelist, and Rev. Karl Ramstrand, the Swedish Pentecostal Missionary based in Awasa.

[379] Informant: Solomon Lulu.

[380]An overwhelming number of my informants intimated to me that they came to embrace their faith by this simple method. Cultural elements, as reflected through bonds of friendship and other social ties and networks,

constitute ingredients through which the witnessing activities were vehicled. Witnessing, for the most part, was a deliberate act involving multi-faceted activities, such as praying, visiting, dialoguing, distributing tracts and sharing salvic-oriented verses from the Bible. Informants: Asseffa, Abera Tilahun, Seifu Kebede, Zeleqa, Evangelist Abere Darge, Evangelist Tadesse Feisa, and others.

[381] Later, the name changed to EvaSU, Evangelical Student Union. See, *Hebron*, 1, 1 (1993), pp.11-14.

[382] According to Hege, the list of those joining the Pentecostal movement include; Bedru Hussein, a student from a Muslim background, Teka Gabru, Girma Tessemma, a distinction student who later became one of the finest soil experts of the nation, Asnake Erque, Tilahun Adera, currently a professor in Pharmacy (US), Tekeste Teklu, a former university professor in US now a prominent church leader in the Diaspora and a key figure in promoting EvaSU's mission during the Revolution, Chaltu Geffawossen(now deceased), wife of Goshu Wolde, a former ministers of the *Derg*, Tenagne Lemma, currently Country Director of World Vision/ Int. Ethiopia, Yenagu Dessie, and Tiruworq Mesfin, now assistant pastor of an Ethiopian church in California. Hege. p. 151. Informants: Tekeste Teklu, Pastor Tiruworq Mesfin, Solomon Lulu, and others.

[383] The tension between the Pentecostals and radical elements of HSIU students, definitely requires a separate study. At that moment of their history, the Pentecostal students, small as they were, keenly understood the danger of Marxism, perhaps more than any group in the university or even outside of it, and combated it on all fronts, be it in dormitory discussions, public meetings, EUS service stations. Solomon Lulu, now chairman of Ethiopian Christian Business Men's Association, and a key person behind the creation of the fellowship, recalls that they were at loggerheads with the "small but pernicious" group called the Crocodile. It is reported that this articulate Christian groups conducted a highly organized campaign to foil the plan of the Crocodiles and other student radicals who were working hard to make the late student leader Tilahun Gizaw, the President of USUAA. The Pentecostals were deeply offended by the radicals' open censure of God. According to Randi Balsvik, most of the candidates during the student election of 1971 vigorously attacked the church, but the statements which received the most spontaneous and loud applause was: "we, the students teach the Ethiopian mass that there is no God." R. Rønning Balsvik, *Haile Selassie's Students* (East Lansing: 1985).p. 240. The Pentecostal students collabourated with those who campaigned for the election of Makonnen Bishaw, a relatively more liberal candidate, who at the end of the day won the contest. Informants: Makonnen Bishaw and Solomon Lulu.

[384] From the point of view of the Pentecostals, the student radicals were not only anti-God, but also of low moral standards, who could not be emulated as examples and models of change. Balsvik, p.242; Informants: Ayalew, Solomon Kebede and Solomon Lulu.

[385] Informant: Solomon Lulu

[386] The original seven members of the leadership team were: Asseffa Zeleke(Dr. Rev, pastor of an Ethiopian evangelical church in Kansa), Bete (Dr. a former Director of International Bible Society in Africa, based in Kenya and founder of the Assembly of God Church in Ethiopia), Philipos Kemere (Dr. now residing in Washington), Kebede W/ Mariam(Dr. now residing in US), Zeleke Alemu (now Rev. serving as a pastor in Maryland), Melsese Wegu(Dr. founder of the Ethiopian Outreach Ministry based in US), Fantahun Gabre (deceased).

[387] According to Engelsviken, the name finally adopted was "Old Time Full Gospel Believers, Association," which is strongly indicative of a restorationist tendency. T. Engelsviken, "Mulu Wengiel; A Documentary Report," 1975, pp. 45-45. Ethiopian Christians of this time opted out for indigenous names, such as the *Qala Heywat, Masarata Krestos, Mesgana, Berhana Heywat*, etc., unlike the Christians of the present generation, for whom exotic names(the Crusaders, the Winners chapel, Victory Chapel, etc) make strong appeal.

[388] Informants: Ashenafi Zemat, Bete, Melese, and others.

[389] Haile Michael was not only the first evangelist but also a man who later on played a key leadership role in the Mulu Wangiel Church. He later completed his Ph. D. from Fuller Theological Seminary and became an itinerant preacher having his base in the US serving the Ethiopian nationals and the Diasporic communities. He passed away while conducting his ministry in the southwestern part of Ethiopia a few years ago.

[390] Informants: Kebede and Bete.

[391] The history of the expansion of the Pentecostal movement out side the vicinity of the capital and the role of the young Ethiopians who were involved in the process needs to be documented chapter by chapter. To mention, but few: Endalkachew and Itefa, now Rev. and the current General Secretary of the EECMY, influential in the area of Illubabor; Tsadiqu, a Muslim convert, active in the former province of Bale; Merid Lemma, a man who spent a number of years in Gojjam and Wellega together with evangelist Tadesse Nagawo and Mekuria Mulugeta; Pastor Tekle Medhin, active in the area of Harar, Dire-Dawa and Jijjiga area; Pastor Taye Takele, active in the area of Arsi; Pastor Tehsome Worqu and Belete, in the area of Wolaita; Dr. Bete and Sewhit, in the former province of Eritrea, etc.

[392] Informants: Asseffa, Melese, Ashenafi, Ferne Miller and Eearlin Scottman.

[393] On the concept of "geographical peel off" see, Luther P. Gerlach, *People, Power, Change: Movements of Social Transformation* (New York: The Bobbs-Merrill Company, 1970), p. 46.

[394] A report submitted to the Makana Yesus Church by one of the Swedish missionaries states that the ties of the Ethiopian Pentecostals with foreign missionaries was extremely loose and that the movement had basically remained indigenous with Ethiopian leaders and without financial support from outside. T. Eengelsviken, "Report on the Pentecostal Movement in Ethiopia and its Relations to Evangelical Church of Makana Yesus" (MY Seminary library) 1972, p. 2. This has also been supported by several mission reports.

[395] Informants: Asseged, Tesfahun Agidew Tesfa Lidet, and Zelalem.

[396] Addisu Legges who now lives and works in Los Angeles, California, is still continuing his service among the Diaspora. Legesse Watero, one of the few Astrophysicist the country is still singing and composing songs. Tesfaye Gabisso suffered 7 years of imprisonment during the military regime because of his refusal to deny his faith. Tamrat Haile, a singer who composed and sang many encouraging and comforting songs (as well as songs of social and political nature) through out the duration of the Revolution is now a pastor of a church in California.

[397] In fact, according to Addisu, who now resides in the US, the Emperor was so fascinated by the songs he heard aired through Voice of the Gospel that he wanted to know more about the singer. Addisu was called by the Emperor and held brief, as he described, "intense conversations." The Emperor offered him a scholarship in appreciation of his talent so that it could be used for the advancement of modern music in Ethiopia. Addisu faced some bureaucratic hurdles in the formality procedures, and could not make use of the opportunity offered Informant: Addisu Worqu.

[398] In this section, I will use the term persecution in its ordinary sense to refer to the act of harassment people experience because of their different religious convictions. Harassment could take the form of public or verbal condemnation, ostracizing or exclusion, physical attacks and obstructions of public worship and banning including imprisonment of participants. Pentecostals experienced them with more severity because of the radical commitment to expand and the strong influence they exerted upon young adherents of the established church.

[399] "BeDabra Zeit Ketema Lijochina Welajoch Tegachu," *Addis Zemen,* vol. 27, No. 826, 20-09-67, p. 1; *Ethiopian Herald,* 13-01-73, p. 2.

[400] *Logo Journal,* p.15.

[401] Informant: Philipos Kemere.

[402] Informant: Kebede Wolde Mariam

[403] See, "Persecution in Ethiopia," *Target,* 2,25 (1972), p. 12; "Persecution in Ethiopia and Malawi," *Newsweek,* January 15, 1973; *The Ethiopian Herald* published material in defence of the action of the police raid and subsequent imprisonment *The Ethiopian Herald,* September 1, 1972, p. 1. By providing pictures of some of the imprisoned Pentecostals, *Logos Journal,* also reported on the existence of severe persecution in Ethiopia and appealed to the international communities for interventions. See, "Persecution in Ethiopia," *Logos Journal,* May-June, 1973, pp. 12-16. What might have triggered the persecution is the rapid expansion of the movement. A movement that started from a scratch in the early 1960's garnered followers to the tune of 4,000 by 1967, rising to 50, 000 at the commencement of the persecution. *Logos,* p.12; Nona Freeman, *Unseen Hands. The Story's of Revival in Ethiopia* (Hazle: World Aflame Press, 1988), p. 42; Balsvik observes that the Pentecostals claimed 15, 000 in the towns by 1972 without being specific about the towns she was alluding to. The figure for 1972, according to Engelsviken, is any where between 20, 000 to 50, 000. By the year 1986, the number of the Pentecostals, at least, members of the *Mulu Wangiel* was estimated to be 100, 000 which by 1993 rose to 150,000. Haile Wolde Michael, "A Comparative Study of Leadership Development Methods with Reference to the Ethiopian Full Gospel Church," Ph. D. dissertation, Fuller Theological Seminary, 1993 p.201.

[404] This was a direct conflagration of article 40 of the existing constitution, which clearly stipulates: "Ethiopian subjects shall have right in accordance with conditions prescribed by law to assemble peacefully and without arms." Perhaps the context used for arresting this group was a memorandum released by Major Derese Dubale and Akale Work Habte Wold on November 03,1967 following the Dabra Zeit incident. The document that was passed to the provincial governors stated that founders of the Pentecostal movement had been notified that they could not conduct meeting under the guise of holding prayers. Girma Zewde, *Etiopis* (Addis Ababa: Negde Matemia Derigit, 1985), p.137, 138;Yoseph, p.24. *Etiopis,* also contains the full text of a letter that was released in October 7, 1971 by Solomon Kedir which banned the *Mulu Wangiel* church for good. Girma Zewde, *Etiopis,* pp. 138-142.

[405] Yoseph, sets the estimate at 165: Yoseph, p. 48; The figure reported by the official newspaper, *Addis Zemen* is 480; *Addis Zemen,* September 1, 1972.

[406] The comment on the Pentecostal movement in Ethiopia appeared in the international version of *Newsweek* magazine under, "Persecuting the Sect" on January 15,1973.

[407] *The Ethiopian Herald,* "Newsweek Report Unfounded," vol. XXIX, no. 630, 01-21-73, p.2.

[408] Ibid.

[409] Messay, p. 255. In essence, what Messay is saying is that the Orthodox Church did not learn much from all these encounters. I think recent developments indicate that the church is making a major improvement because of the challenge of the Pentecostal movement.

[410] Haile Selassie I, *My Life and Ethiopia's Progress, 1892-1937:* translated and annotated by Edward Ullendorff (London: 1976), p. 3; 69.

[411] Harold Marcus, *Haile Selassie I: The Formative Years, 1892-1936* (Berkeley: University of California Press, 1987), p.57.

[412] This does not mean that the Emperor had not made some gestures to bring the National Church aboard but, in general, it appears that Haile Selassie moved away from the Church and opted to use other institutional channels he had created like, the Ministry of Education to advance modern education. For further see, Abebe Fiseha, "Education and the Formation of the Modern Ethiopian State, 1896-1974,"Ph. D. dissertation, University of Illinois, 2000, pp.154-167.

[413] This was the view of a prominent Historian Dr. Berhanu Abebe. Informant: Berhanu Abebe.

[414] Simon D. Messing, "Changing Ethiopia," *The Middle East Journal,* 9,.4(1955), p.429. The process must have started earlier but it was ever intensified since the 60's and by the 70's for most educated Ethiopian religious dietary restrictions lost any serious meaning.

[415] Teshome, p. 156. According to Tehsome, "this rejection was then extended to include values, ideas, and beliefs of most authorities, including those in high positions in traditional religious and political situation." Teshome, p. 156.

[416] Balsvik, pp. 240-241.

[417] Ibid.

[418] Rickard, p. 56.

[419] Paulos, Milkias, "Traditional Institution and Traditional Elite," *African Studies Review,* XXI, 3 (December, 19760), p. 87.

[420] Rickard picks and further develops the concept based on its first application by Donald Levine in his ground-breaking book of *Wax and Gold* (Tsehai, 2007). See Richard, pp. 22-32.

[421] Indrias Getachew, *Beyond the Throne: The Enduring Legacy of Emperor Haile Selassie* (Addis Ababa: Shama Books, 2001), p.134.

[422] John Markakis, *Ethiopia: Anatomy of a Traditional Polity (*Addis Ababa: Oxford University Press, 1974), p. 359. John Markakis, who is critical of Haile Selassie's regime, contends that the Emperor's modernization Programme did not focus on increasing the production of social values through the process of resource mobilization and massive investment and planned economic growth. Markakis, p. 335; For a similar view, see, Rickard, p. 48.

[423] Charles McClellan, *State Transformation and National Integration*(East Lansing: Michigan State University 1988), p.p. 4-5

[424] Messay, pp. 301-302.

[425] Harold Marcus, Foreword section of Indrias' *Beyond the Throne,* p.8

[426] Indrias Getachew, p. 149.

[427] According to Teshome Wagaw, at the inception of the national university, the public expressed concern and apprehension as to the manner of the creation and organization of the university and how it could effectively address Ethiopia's economic and cultural situation and herald national renewal and development. Teshome G. Wagaw, *The Development of Higher Education and Social Change: an Ethiopian Experience(* East Lansing: Michigan State University Press, 1990), p. 153.

[428] For more see, Mulugeta Wodajo, "Postwar Reform in Ethiopian Education." *Comparative* Education Review, 2, 3 (1959), pp. 24-27.

[429] Daniel Lemma, "Development of A Student Personal Programme for Ethiopia's National University to meet the Needs of Ethiopia's Youth, "Ph. D. Dissertation, Michigan State University,1976. Abstract section unpaged and introductory remarks, pp.8-22.

[430] Rickard, p. 40. Rickard further notes that the youth in the 60's live in a torn world, their identities made up of inconsistent beliefs and attitudes. Concerning the impact of education on the formation of negative attitudes see, Nagawo Beyene, "The Impact of University Education on the Formation of Political Attitudes: Sources of Negative Political attitudes of Ethiopian Students" Ph. D. dissertation, Stanford University, 1977.

[431] Teshome, pp.203-221

[432] John Summerskill, *Haile Selassie I University: A Blue Print for Development (*Addis Ababa: Haile Selassie I University, 1970), p. 110. Balsvik, pp. 44-45.

[433] Daniel, Abstract section (unpaged); Informants: Ayalew, Daniel, Wubshet, and Seyum Gabre Egziabher.

[434] Informants: Daniel Lemma, Muleta, Negussie, and Desta Wedajo. See also Teshome Wagaw. pp. 209-221; Balsvik, pp. 138-140; Asres, pp. 78-80

[435] Donald Levine, "Understanding Ethiopia Today: Some Observation of a Sociologist," A paper presented at the 2nd Annual Convention of Ethiopian Student Association of North America, Washington D.C, September 9,1961, p. 8.

[436] Among such people are distinguished scholars, university professors in Ethiopia and abroad. Some of them discontinued their education from the university and served as preachers of the Gospel and completed their university education at a later time. Some have gone into the monasteries of Dabra Libanos for a while and returned to start normal life. Informants: Daniel Lemma, Temesgien Gobana, Desta, Million Belete, Bete, and others.

[437] For more on the theme of alienation concerning the youth in Ethiopia, see, Desta Asayehegne, "Student Alienation: A Study of High School Students in Ethiopia," Ph. D. dissertation, Stanford University, 1977.

[438] Haile, "A Comparative Study of Leadership." p. 177. According to Haile, the Bible became the most important book to be read daily, it was read discussed, studiously studied individually and corporately.

[439] A statement that was released by some members of the clergy in 1974 under the heading, *Yeteresa Mastawesha*, expresses lamentation at the fact that the youth is hearing the Bible from foreign agents who have crossed the see (*"kebaher mado"*) and accused the national Church for failing to meet her call. It caricatures the Church's radio Programme as *"Yesebeka teyater"* (a theater of rhetoric), and the role of the Patriarch as some one who appears (in the media) twice in a year just to give *Burake* (blessings with the Cross). See, *Ye Tarik Mastawesha*, File number 2396/0116, 1966, Institute of Ethiopian Studies, Amharic document section.

[440] Markakis makes a very interesting remark about the rise of student radicalism in the university. He notes that, "the social and political awakening of the Ethiopian students has been a spontaneous, self-accomplished process achieved in a situation of great isolation." Markakis, p.358. It is interesting to notice the striking parallel in the manner in which the Pentecostal movement also arose in Ethiopia.

[441] Ibid. p. 359;.Balsvik, pp.93-100. For a recent analysis of the coup of 1960 see, Harold Marcus, "1960, the year the Sky Began Falling on Haile Selassie," *Journal of Northeast African Studies,* New Series, 6, 3 (1999), pp. 11-25.

[442] Asres Alem, "History of the Ethiopian Student Movement (In Ethiopia and North America: Its Impact on Internal Social Changes," Ph. D. Dissertation, University of Maryland, 1990,, pp. 74-75.

[443] Ethiopian Pentecostals, for the most part, did not demonstrate active interest in politics. They generally adopted a pacifist rather than an activist line. Though Pentecostalism has succeeded in embracing fine intellectuals of the country (from the filed of social as well natural sciences, including many university professors at home and abroad), political voice is conspicuously absent from their discourse. This is unlike many countries in Africa, Ghana, for instance, which has produced Pentecostals like Mensa Anamuah Otabil, whose political articulation approached an African version of liberation theology. See, Emmanuel Kingsley Larbi, *Pentecostalism: The Eddies of the Ghanaian Christianity* (Accra:SAPC Series, 2001), pp. 235-366. In my field research, I noticed that the newer generation of Ethiopian Pentecostals are showing an unusual interest in social and political activism.

[444] Informant: Legesse Watero.

[445] Paul Gifford, *African Christianity: Its Public Role* (Bloomington: Indiana University Press, 1998), p. 329.

[446] This is an opinion strongly expressed by Wubshet a prominent church leader and a man of extensive public service in the Ethiopian government and a student of HS I University in the early 60's, and Captain Aylele, also a man of distinguished government service who had been in charge of the Imperial Naval Academy. Informants: Wubshet and Captain Ayele Zewde.

[447] In many higher learning institutions the *Haymanote Abew* Christian groups and those identifying either with Pentecostals or the evangelicals, represented two poles competing to win the attention of the fellow students. The tensions resulting from this keen competition, often led to acrimonious relations characterized by bickering, blackmailing and character assassinations. The Pentecostals viewed members of the *Haimanote Abew* group as conservatives, while the *Haymanote Abew* saw the former as stooges of foreign missions. Informants: Melaku Makonnen, Captain Yohannes, Solomon Kebede.

[448] The Pentecostal movement in Ethiopian can also be viewed as a restorationist movement. The appellation *Tintawi,* is strongly indicative of the youth's desire to restore an idealized past as was exemplified by the communities of Christians as describes in the Book of Acts.

[449] It has to be emphasized that the Pentecostal movement arose out of encounter-situations resulting from a congruence of several happenings: the increasing presence of foreign communities, be it missionaries, the peace corpse, or other foreign agencies bringing new ideas.

[450] The main recipients of the evangelical Christian faith had mainly been the Oromo people of south-western Ethiopia and the diverse ethno-linguistic communities of the south. Many Evangelical Christians agree that it was the Pentecostals, who either as volunteers (government employees working in line ministries, school

teachers, etc) or as local missionaries, spread the evangelical faith to many parts of Ethiopia, thus turning it into a potent national faith embraced by millions of followers from varied groups in Ethiopia.

[451] Concepts like, "Pentecostalization" and "Charizmatization" are beginning to appear in some theological circles. The term "Charismatic Renewal," is a more fitting to describe the spread of the new spiritual waves in established churches that are not Pentecostal doctrinally. According to Peter Hocken, a Roman Catholic Scholar, Charismatic Renewal refers to the "occurrence of distinctively Pentecostal blessing and phenomena, baptism in the Holy Spirit with the spiritual gifts… outside the denominational and /or confessional Pentecostal framework." Peter Hockman, "Charismatic Movement," in Stanley Burges, *Dictionary of Pentecostal and Charismatic Movement* (Grand Rapids: Zondervan, 1988), p. 130.

[452] For further see, Tibebe Eshete, "Marxism and Religion: the paradox of church growth in Ethiopia," A paper presented at Calvin College as part of the Lecture Series of the Negel Institute for World Christianity, October 29, 2008.

Chapter 7

[453] An earlier version of this paper was published under the title "Enduring Issues in State Society Relation in Ethiopia: A Case Study of WoGaGoDa Conflict in Wolaita, Southern Ethiopia," *The International Journal of Ethiopian Studies*, Volume 2, Number 1&2 (2005): 141-159. This version is substantially revised and updated.

[454] WoGaGoDa comes from the first phonemes (sounds) of Wolaita, Gamo, Gofa and Dawro which are closely related Omotic speaking ethnic groups. Other than being an acronym, the term might also mean in different dialects of Ometo either 'big lord' or 'lord of the traditions' depending on how one pronounces it.

[455] The Population of Wolaita was reported to be 1,268,445 in 1994 (CSA, 1998). The Wolaita Zone Finance and Economic Development Main Department claims that "According to the other sources (Polio House to House campaign, NGO survey etc) the population [of Wolaita] is estimated to be well above 2 million" (2003:17). Given the fact that a great deal hangs on numbers these days, population figures remain controversial in this country. For more details on Wolaita see Data Dea, 'Civil Society and Religious Difference: Note on Gutara Institution in Walaita, Southern Ethiopia,' in Brigitta Benzing,ed. *Civil Society in Ethiopia: Reflections on Realities and Perspectives of Hope.* (Frankfurt am Main: Verlag für Interkulturelle Kommunikation, 2005b).

[456] During the climax of Wolaita resistance against WoGaGoDa in 1999/2000, I was doing fieldwork among the neighbouring Dawro (one of the constitutive units of WoGaGoDa) for my doctoral dissertation in Social anthropology at the University of Bergen, Norway. Besides myself coming from Wolaita, I had many reasons to follow as closely as possible what unfolded around WoGaGoDa. Among other things, it was clear that either success or failure of WoGaGoDa would have wider implications.

[457] I acknowledge with gratitude that my field research of 2004 and 2005 was funded the Max Planck Institute for Social Anthropology, Halle/Saale, Germany.

[458] http://www.csa.gov.et/text_files/national%20statistics%202007/Population.pdf. Accessed on March 7, 2008.

[459] However, to call each of them a distinct "ethnic group" in conventional sense of the term is highly problematic (see Data, 2005).

[460] Dan Sperber, "Paradoxes of Seniority among the Dorze," in H.Marcus, ed., *Proceeding of the First United States Conference on Ethiopian Studies* (Michigan, Michigan State University, 1973; Wagner Lange, *History of the Southern Gonga, South-western Ethiopia* (Wiesbaden: Steiner, 1982); Remo Chiatti, *The Politics of Divine Kingship in Wolaita* (Pennsylvania: University of Pennsylvania, 1989); Asmorom Legesse, *Gada: Three Approaches to the Study of African Society* (New York: The Free Press, 1973); Herbert Lewis, *Jimma Abba Jifar: An Oromo Monarchy: Ethiopia, 1830-1932* (N.J.: The Red Sea Press, 2001).

[461] M. Staahl, *Ethiopia: Political Contradictions in Agricultural Development* (Stockholm: Raben & Sjogren, 1974) P.43.

[462] Daniel Gamachu, "A Nation in Perpetual Transition: The Politics of Changes in Administrative Divisions and Subdivisions in Ethiopia," in H.G. Marcus, ed., *New Trends in Ethiopian Studies: Paper of the 12th International Conference of Ethiopian Studies*, Vol. II (NJ.: The Red Sea Press. 1994).

[463] Ibid.

[464] Haileyesus Engdashet, Tifhit Lemma and Aster Tadesse, *Ye Sement Ometo Quanquawoch/ Kebelegnawoch Yemegiabat Derja Tinat* (In Amharic) (Addis Ababa: Ethiopian Languages Academy, Linguistic Research Team. 1980 E.C (1988 G.C).

[465] See Data Dea, *The Challenges of Integrative Power: Hierarchy and Political Change in Dawro, Southwestern Ethiopia* (Ph.D Diss, University of Bergen, 2003).

[466] Donald Donham, "Introduction," in W.James, et al, eds., *Remapping Ethiopia: Socialism and After* (Athens: Ohio University Press; Addis Ababa: Addis Ababa University Press; Oxford: James Currey, 2002) p. 154; emphasis added.

[467] See David Turton, 'The Politician, the Priest, and the Anthropologist: Living Beyond Conflict in South-western Ethiopia," *Ethnos* 68, no. 1 (2003); Donald Donham, *Marxist Modern: An Ethnographic History of Revolution in Ethiopia* (Oxford: James Currey, 1999); Data Dea, 2003).

[468] Daniel Gamachu, 1994:84.

[469] Fiseha Asseffa, "Theory versus Practice in the Implementation of Ethiopia's Ethnic Federalism," in David Turton, Ed., *Ethnic Federalism: The Ethiopian Experience in Comparative Perspective (Oxford: James Currey, 2006)*; Dereje Feyissa, "The Experience of Gambella Regional State" in David Turton, ed., *Ethnic Federalism: The Ethiopian Experience in Comparative Perspective (Oxford: James Currey, 2006)*; Sarah Vaughan & Kjetil Tronvoll, *The Culture of Power in Contemporary Ethiopian Political Life* (Stockhom: Swedish International Development Co-operation Agency, Sidastudies no.10, 2003); Sigfred Pausewang, K.Tronvoll and L.Aalen, eds., *Ethiopia Since the DERG: A Decade of Democratic Pretension and Performance* (London; New York: Zed Books, 2002); Merera Gudina, *Ethiopia: Competing Ethnic Nationalisms and the Quest for Democracy, 1960-2000* (Ph. D Diss, Institute of Social Studies (ISS), The Hague, 2002); Aklilu, *Ethiopia: The Challenges of Federalism Based on Ethnic Restructuring. A Case Study of the Sidama and Wolayta Ethnic Groups in the Southern Nations, Nationalities and Peoples Regional State* (A research report submitted to the Robert S. McNamara, 1997).

[470] See *The Constitution of the Federal Democratic Republic of Ethiopia,* article 39 p. 96 (1995). The same rights are also reiterated in *The Revised Constitution, 2001 of The Southern Nations, Nationalities and Peoples' Regional State*, article 39, p. 96.

[471] Sarah Vuaghan, *Ethnicity and Power in Ethiopia* (Ph.D Diss., University of Edinburgh. 2003).

[472] Some estimate that some 49 million birr (around 6 million USD) was spend on the preparation and publication of the WoGaGoDa books.

[473] Addis Zemen (Amharic daily news paper), Tikimit 30, 1992 E.C.

[474] Wolaita elders' letter to the Prime Minster's office dated 10/04/1992 E.C.

[475] One of the Wolaita elder representatives, in his letter to the Prime Minister's office, regrets that the current Ethiopian state, like the imperial state of Haile Selassie, still looks at these parts of our country as prisons for "criminals" instead of looking at them as places that deserve development and state attention. He mentions that the Tigrayan rebel Belatta Hailemariam, who was involved in the Tigrayan protest of 1943 was sent to Gamo-Gofa as punishment (Abraham Tanga, letter to the Prime Minister, dated 4/5/92 E.C (13/0112000).

[476] The VOA, Radio Deutsche Welle, BBC all reported on the WoGaGoDa conflict. The international media attention was critically sought and instrumental in attracting attention to what was going on as well as boosting the moral of the resistance. At the peak of WoGaGoDa resistance, an 'Eritrean' who owns a music shop in Soddo played recorded Deutsche Welle reporting on the WoGaGoDa conflict. The ruling party's cadres used this as evidence that this movement was connected to Shaibia/Eritrean government (which was war with Ethiopia at the time) and imprisoned the music shop owner.

[477] Note that this was the time when questions related to language and/or administrative status were being raised in a few other places as well.

[478] Ensete, Tuesday, Nov. 23, 1999.

[479] Haileyesus Seba, *A Study of Social Change in Wolaita, Southern Ethiopia* (MA Thesis, Addis Ababa University, 1996); Remo Chiatti, 1982).

[480] For more details on this see Alula Pankhusrt & Dena Freeman, eds., *Peripheral People: The Excluded Minorities of Ethiopia* (London: Husrt & Co. 2003); Gunnar Haaland, Randi Haaland & Data Dea, Haaland, R., Haaland, G. and Data Dea, "Furnace and Pot: Why the Iron Smelter Is a Big Pot Maker: a Case Study from Southwestern Ethiopia," *Azania XXXIX* (2004a):143-165; Gunnar Haaland, Randi Haaland and Data Dea, "Smelting Iron: Caste and Its Symbolism in South-western Ethiopia," in T. Insoll, ed., *Belief in the Past: The Proceeding of the 2002 Manchester Conference on Archaeology and Religion* (BAR International Series, 2004b).

[481] In passing it could be noted that both clanship and "caste" (social stratification) do continue to play some role in politics throughout contemporary southern Ethiopian.

[482] Sarah Vaughan, 2003.

[483] *Ibid.*: 128.

[484] *Ibid.*: 129.

[485] *Ibid.*: 27.

[486] Interview with Ato Abraham Tanga, June 2004.

[487] Cf. Sarah Vaughan and Kjetil Trovoll, 2003.

[488] Jon Abbink, "New Configurations of Ethiopian Ethnicity: The Challenge of the South," *Northeast African Studies*, Vol. 5, No.1 (1998): 75-76.

Chapter 8

[489] I want to thank all the participants in the Workshop on Education and Social Change in Contemporary Ethiopia, held at the University of Dayton, Dayton, Ohio, 12-13 May, 2006 for inspiration as well as for their comments on an earlier draft of this paper. Special thanks to colleagues Tekeste Negash and Eva Poluha, both at Högskolan Dalarna, Falun, Sweden, for their support, critique, many good talks and many good times.

[490] This dynamic has been explored by, for instance, Annika Rabo, Change on the Euphrates: Villagers, Townsmen and Employees in Northern Syria, (Stockholm: Stockholm Studies in Social Anthropology. 1986); Eva Poluha. Central Planning and Local Reality. The Case of a Producers Co-operative in Ethiopia, (Stockholm: Stockholm Studies in Social Anthropology, 1989); Sandra Wallman, (Ed,) Dalarna, Perceptions of Development, (Cambridge: Cambridge University Press, 1977).

[491] Judith Narrowe, "All you have to do is teach me", Reflections on Women, Education and Training in the Dodota Water Supply Project in Arsi, Ethiopia, (Stockholm: Stockholm University, Development Studies Unit, 1989).

[492] Judith Narrowe, "Putting Women in the Map". *Problems, Progress and the Next Phase of the Women in Adult Education Pilot Project,* (Stockholm/Addis Ababa: Sida, 1990)

[493] Narrowe, Judith. 2006. "It's a question of Boundaries": Discourses of gender and modernity at an Ethiopian teacher's college", (Paper presented to the Proceedings of the 15th International Conference of Ethiopian Studies, Hamburg: University of Hamburg, 2006).

[494] Affirmative action was established in the United States by an executive order number 11246, signed by President Lyndon Johnson in 1965. It was an official extension of the Civil Rights Act of 1964 which "permitted courts to order 'such affirmative action as may be appropriate' to end discrimination and to re-establish restitution in cases where de jure or de facto discrimination has been found," See Richard Tomasson, Faye Crosby, Sharon Herzbrger, *Affirmative Action. The Pros and cons of Policy and Practice*, (New York: Rowman and Littlefield. 2002): 12.

[495] Rod Hague, Martin Harrop and Shaun Breslin, (Eds.) *Comparative Government and Politics: an Introduction,* (London: Macmillan.Hague et al 1998,): 255-56.

[496] In doing so, I view policy as something more than a 'framework for action' and am concerned rather with policy as expressed in concrete directives and practiced in the context of formal, government-supported programs.

[497] Cris Shore and Sue Wright, "Policy: a New Field of Anthropology" in Shore, Cris and Wright, Sue, (Eds.). *The Anthropology of Policy: Critical Perspectives on Governance and Power,* (London: Routledge 1997): 3

[498] Ibid. 5

[499] I would agree with Okongwu and Mencher who have maintained that "…ideology and policy are critically linked," See Anne Francis Okongwu, and Joan P. Mencher, "The Anthropology of Public Policy, Shifting Terrains," in *Annual Review of Anthropology* 29, 2000:110. They argue that policies reflect and inculcate a range of ideas and ideals and thereby affect people's beliefs as well as their actions and activities. Some of the women's comments I quote farther on in this paper substantiate this view.

[500] Escobar has argued that the very concept of development in effect creates countries which need it, specifically, the 'Third World'. See Arturo Escobar, *Encountering Development. The Making and Unmaking of the Third World,* (Princeton, N.J.: Princeton University Press, 1995).

[501] Katy Gardner, and David Lewis, *Anthropology, Development and the Challenge of Post-Modernism,* (London: Polity Press, 1996.) 2.

[502] R.D. Grillo, and R.L. Stirrat, (Eds,): *Discourses of Development: Anthropological Perspectives,* (Oxford: Berg 1997): 117.

[503] Some of the review presented here is based on Shahra Razavi, "Fitting Gender into Development Institutions," World Development 25, 7, (1997): 1111-1125. He offers a rather comprehensive analysis of the relationship between gender-related development discourses and the institutions which devise and implement mainstream development policies. Razavi emphasizes throughout his article that individuals or movements which propagate gender policies in the development aid context must consider the concerns (culture?): of these macro institutions and, to be heard and taken seriously, must find a strategy and a 'language' to match these institutions' at base essentially financial concerns. See also Naila Kabeer, "Resources, Agency, Achievements: Reflections on the Measurement of Women's Empowerment" in Discussing Women's Empowerment – Theory and Practice, (Stockholm: Sida Studies no.3, (2002): 17.

[504] Shhra Razavi, "Fitting Gender into Development Institutions," World Development, 25.

[505] The Women in Development-type programs (WID): were soon replaced with the much broader and more relevant Gender and Development (GAD): programs, and the focus changed from a concern with women and women-oriented projects to a concern with gender, that is, culturally constituted categories of 'men' and 'women' and the peculiarity of their relationships. See Carolyn Moser, *Gender Planning and Development. Theory, Practice and Training,* (London: Routledge. 1993).

[506] Several articles in the Ethiopian Constitution might be an example of this. See below, note 25.

[507] See Naila Kabeer, "Resources, Agency, Achievements: Reflections on the Measurement of Women's Empowerment" in Discussing Women's Empowerment – Theory and Practice, (Stockholm: Sida Studies no.3, (2002): 17

[508] Ibid.

[509] Recent research on affirmative action in East and South Africa reveals a highly critical view of the policy by university students. For a critique of affirmative action policies in the East African context, see for example Elizabeth Kharono, "Review of Affirmative Action in Uganda," (*Kampala: Uganda Women's Network* [UWONET], July, 2003); Josephine Ahikire, "Women, Public Politics and Organization, Potentialities of Affirmative Action in Uganda," *Economic and Political Weekly.* Volume 29, 44, (1994): 77-83; Tamale 1999. I am aware that the view presented here differs in kind from the views offered in these studies.

[510] REWA's rhetoric notwithstanding, Helen Pankhurst points out very clearly that the socialist regime was concerned with production and workers and party objectives, and not specifically with women's lives. She writes: "…after 'liberation', life resumed as before; gender inequalities unchallenged," Helen Pankhurst, *Gender Development and Identity, An Ethiopian Study,* (London: Zed Press, 1992:4).

[511] More formally: "The National Policy on Women (Women's Policy): formulated in 1993, aimed to create appropriate structures within government offices and institutions to establish equitable and gender-sensitive public policies. The Government of Ethiopia in 1995, under its new constitution, renewed its commitment towards this policy," *Implementing the Ethiopian Policy for Women: Institutional and Regulatory Issues,* 1998, (The Women's Affairs Office, Federal Democratic Republic of Ethiopia, The World Bank).

[512] Article 25 reads" All persons are equal before the law and are entitled without any discrimination to the equal protection of the law. In this respect, the law shall guarantee to all persons equal and effective protection with out discrimination on grounds of race, nation, nationality, or other social origin, color, sex, language, religion, political or other opinion, property birth or other status," Article 36 specifically mentions that affirmative action policies are to be instituted in order to redress the wrongs often upheld by tradition.

[513] A recent ethnographic study by Emire Guday of early marriage in Gojjam shows quite conclusively that early marriage is still widely practiced and locally approved in the region. See Emire Guday, *Early Marriage and Its Effect on Girls Education in Rural Ethiopia: The Case of Mecha woreda in Weat Gojjam, North-Western Ethiopia,* (PhD diss. Georg-August University of Göttingen, Germany, Website, 2005): http://webdoc.sub.gwdg.de/diss/emirie/index.htm. Still, the trend might be changing. See Tamene Ayele, *Growing up in' Town and in the Countryside,* (Addis Ababa: Save the Children Sweden): 2006. has found that teachers in the area do report girls involved in early marriage to the public authorities.

[514] In an ethnographically rich article, Original Wolde Giorgis has examined the legal rights of women in today's Ethiopian and explores specific cases where these rights are or are not respected. See Original Wolde Giorgis, "Democratization and Gender" in Bahru Zewde and Siegfried Pausewang (Eds.). *Ethiopia. the Challenge from Below,* (Uppsala: Nordiska Afrika Institutet. 2002).

[515] Zewde, Bahru, 2002:12. Introduction. In Zewde, Bahru and Pausewang, SigfriEd. *Ethiopia. The Challenge of Democracy from Below.* Uppsala: The Nordic Africa Institute.

[516] Tsehai Berhane-Salassie, "Ethiopian Rural Women and the State," in Mikell, Gwendolyn (Ed.): *African Feminist: The Politics of Survival in Sub-Saharan Africa, (Philadelphia,* PA.; University of Pennsylvania Press. Berhane-Selassie, 1997.)

[517] Ibid: 187

[518] Vijayendra Rao and Michael. Walton, (Eds.): *Culture and Public Action,* (Stanford, CA. Stanford University Press): 2004.have labelled these types of beliefs as '*constraining preferences*' (2004): 15.

[519] These views resonate with particular clarity in the recent work by Messy Kebede, Surviv*al and Modernization, Ethiopia's Enigmatic Present: A Philosophical Discourse,* (Lawrenceville, New Jersey: The Red Sea Press, 1999): and Tekeste Negash, *Education in Ethiopia: From Crisis to Brink of Collapse,* (Uppsala: Nordiska Afrika Institutet, 2006).who have argued that the failure of modernization in Ethiopia relates to and is a result of the lack of concern with and respect for Ethiopian traditional values. See, as well, D. Bridges, and B. Ridley "Tradition and modernity: educational development and teacher training in Ethiopia", in Bridges, D. and Marew Zewdie (Eds,): *Secondary Teacher Education in Ethiopia,* (The British Council, Addis Ababa in association with Addis Ababa University and the University of East Anglia, Norwich, 2000). for the importance of including traditional values and practices in educational contexts.

[520] For a more specific view of the position of women in Ethiopian political life, see Marta Camilla Wright, "'Women are not Corrupt': The Elections in Addis Ababa in a Gender Perspective" in: 46.62.

[521] Ibid.

[522] Ibid: 187.

[523] Ibid: 72.

[524] See for example Belachew Mekuria, *Gender Inequalities and the Need for Affirmative Actions in Ethiopia: A Work in Progress,* (Stockholm: Swedish Royal Institute of Technology, 2004):12. Belachew states quite clearly that "The lack of or differentiated access to education accounts as the prime cause for most of the inequalities that have surfaced today."

[525] Narrowe, Judith," All you have to do is teach me" Reflections on Women, Education and Training in the Dodota Water Supply Project in Arsi, Ethiopia, (Stockholm: Stockholm University, Development Studies Unit, 1989).

[526] Many of the women in the area were well acquainted with Sida and Sweden due to the fact that the Swedish International Development Agency (Sida): had for many years co-operated with Ethiopian researchers and practitioners in CADU (previously ARDU): a prominent agricultural research institute based in nearby Assela. The Swedish Agency was also very visible in conjunction with the construction of hundreds of elementary school buildings in Ethiopia. I was thus not surprised to hear one elderly woman laud Sweden: "Sweden, Sweden, Sweden," she said, "whatever we do, you love us! I think of you and thank you every time I turn on the water tap."

[527] Unlike Agar, I regarded myself more specifically as a boarder: I lived temporarily with my hosts, was dependent upon them and eager to learn how to behave, but was quite aware, as are boarders, that at one point, I would leave. See Agar, Michael. *The Professional Stranger. An Informal Introduction to Ethnography* (London: Academic Press 1980.)

[528] One more comment about method. Fabian has identified a difference between 'informative ethnography' and 'performative ethnography'. In 'informative ethnography', the researcher maintains control; he/she asks the questions, determines what counts as information and draws conclusions. 'Performative ethnography' is quite different and refers to a situation where the"ethnographer's role...is no longer that of a questioner; he or she is but a provider of occasions, a catalyst in the weakest sense, a producer...in the strongest". See Fabian, Johannes. *Power and Performance: Ethnographic Explorations through Proverbial Wisdom and Theater in Shaba, Zaire,* (Madison, WI.: University of Wisconsin Press, 1990:7). While I undoubtedly provided the occasion for discussion and contemplation in each of these studies and was clearly a catalyst, I also 'entered the occasions' and was very much a producer and contributor to the dialogue.

[529] Helen Pankhurst doubts that living together in villages was seen as totally positive. Because people now lived rather close to each other, social control increased as did competition between the households. See Pankhurst, Helen. *Gender, Development and Identity. An Ethiopian Study*, (London: Zed 1992).

[530] Eva Poluha, "A Study in two Ethiopian woredas on the economic activities of peasant women and their role in rural development" Sida, mimeo, (1980).

[531] Olsson, Bror, Judith Narrowe, Negatu Asfaw, Tefera Eneye, Negussie Amsalu, *Water Supply System in Dodota, Ethiopia,* Sida Evaluation (Stockholm: Sida, Department for Natural Resources and the Environment): 1996): 23.

[532] These comments were made by W/O Tedebab, now 75 years old, who told me she was referring to her participation in the nation-wide literacy Programme which had been completed in the mid-1980s.

[533] Poluha, Eva, Engstrand Göran, Idemalm, Annika, Johan Melkert, Narrowe, Judith. 1990. *Concern and Responsibility. An Evaluation of the Dodota Water Supply Project in Ethiopia.* Stockholm: Sida Evaluation Report 1990/1.

[534] Judith Narrowe, "Putting Women in the Map."

[535] Ibid. 11

[536] At this writing (Fall 2005): the workshops do not include male students. I have heard that this will soon be rectified due to the fact that many male and female students find this unacceptable.

[537] Rao Vijayendra and Michael Walton, (Eds.): *Culture and Public Action*, (Stanford, CA. Stanford University Press): 2004): 15). They have labelled these types of beliefs as '*constraining preferences*'.

[538] Ibid.

Chapter 9

[539] Poluha, Eva, "Learning Political Behaviour: Peasant-State Relations in Ethiopia", In Poluha, E, and M, Rosendahl, (eds), *Contesting 'Good' Governance, Cross-cultural Perspectives on Representation,*

Accountability and Public Space, (London: Routledge Curzon, 2002 a); Poluha, Eva, "Beyond the Silence of Women in Ethiopian Politics", In (eds) Cowen, M, and L, Laakso, *Multi-party Elections in Africa*, (Oxford: James Currey; E. 2002 b); Poluha, *The Power of Continuity: Ethiopia through the eyes of its children*, (Uppsala: Nordiska Afrikainstitutet, 2004).

[540] Strauss, C, and N, Quinn, *A Cognitive Theory of Cultural Meaning*, (Cambridge: Cambridge University Press, 1997).

[541] Allan Hoben, *The role of ambilineal descent groups in Gojjam Amhara social organization*. Unpublished Ph.D. dissertation. (University of California at Berkeley; (1963); Allan Hoben, Social Stratification in traditional Amhara society. In *Social Stratification in Africa*. A. Tuden and L. Plotnicov, eds. (New York: The True Press, 1970); Weissleder *The Political Ecology of Amhara Domination*. Unpublished Ph.D. dissertation. (The University of Chicago.1965); Donald Levine, *Wax and Gold. Tradition and Innovation in Ethiopian Culture*. (Chicago: The University of Chicago Press, 1972 - Tsehai Publishers, 2007; Reminick, R,A, *The Manze Amhara of Ethiopia: A Study of Authority, Masculinity and Sociality*, Unpublished Ph.D. dissertation, (The University of Chicago,1973); Reminick, R,A, "The Structure and Functions of Religious Belief among the Amhara of Ethiopia," In *Proceedings of the First United States Conference on Ethiopian Studies*, H, Marcus, ed, (East Lansing: African Studies Centre, Michigan State University, 1975); Messay Kebede, *Survival and Modernization: Ethiopia's Enigmatic Present: A Philosophical Discourse*, (Lawrenceville: The Red Sea Press 1999).

[542] L, Abu Lugod, "Writing Against Culture," In (ed) Fox, R, *Recapturing Anthropology*, (Santa Fe: School of American Research Press 1991); U. Wikan, Beyond the Words: The Power of Resonance", *American Ethnologist*, (1992): 460-482; T, Ingold, The Art of Translation in a Continuous World, In (ed) G, Pálsson *Beyond Boundaries: Understanding, Translation and Anthropological Discourse*, (London: Bergh,1993).

[543] Ulf, Hannerz, "When Culture is Everywhere, Reflections on a Favourite Concept," *Ethnos*, Vol. 58, (1993):1-2;109.

[544] D'Andrade, Roy, "The cultural part of cognition," *Cognitive Science 5:179-195,1981; D'Andrade, Roy, The development of cognitive anthropology*, (Cambridge: Cambridge University Press 1999); Dorothy Holland, and Naomi Quinn, *Cultural models in language and thought*, (Cambridge: Cambridge University Press, 1987); Strauss, C, and N, Quinn, *A Cognitive Theory of Cultural Meaning*, (Cambridge: Cambridge University Press, 1997).

[545] P. Bourdieu, *The Logic of Practice*, (Cambridge: Polity Press, 1992).

[546] Strauss, C, and N, Quinn, *A Cognitive Theory of Cultural Meaning*, (Cambridge: Cambridge University Press 1997).

[547] Ibid: 6

[548] Ibid

[549] Ibid

[550] Ibid: 122-134

[551] Poluha, Eva, "Learning Political Behaviour: Peasant-State Relations in Ethiopia", In Poluha, E, and M, Rosendahl, (eds), *Contesting 'Good' Governance, Cross-cultural Perspectives on Representation, Accountability and Public Space*, (London: Routledge Curzon, 2002

[552] Poluha, E, *The Power of Continuity: Ethiopia through the eyes of its children*, (Uppsala: Nordiska Afrikainstitutet, 2004).

[553] For an elabourate discussion of *edel*, see Messay Kebede 1999.

[554] Goddess of chance or lot in Roman religion often holding a cornucopia, to indicate abundance, a rudder, to control destinies and standing on a ball to indicate the uncertainty of fortune.

[555] An alternative translation suggested to me by Tekeste Negash

[556] The teaching process that I observed is thus totally different from that described in the chapter by Maimire Mennasemay in this volume. Maimire's fascinating description of critical learning and teaching among the 15th century monks in Daqiqa Estefanos also includes the monks' challenge to the hierarchical order.

[557] For an interesting discussion on this subject see Judith Narrowe's chapter in this volume on the use of affirmative action to recruit women to train as school teachers

[558] Strauss, C, and N, Quinn, *A Cognitive Theory of Cultural Meaning,*, (Cambridge: Cambridge University Press, 1997).

[559] Poluha, E, *The Power of Continuity: Ethiopia through the eyes of its children*, (Uppsala: Nordiska Afrikainstitutet, 2004).

[560] S. Silverman, "Patronage as myth," In *Patrons and Clients*, E, Gellner and J, Waterbury, eds, (London: Duckworth, 1977); J.C. Scott, *The Moral Economy of the Peasant: Rebellion and Subsistence in Southeast Asia*, (New Haven:Yale University Press, 1976); J,C Scott,, Patronage or Exploitation, In *Patrons and Clients*, E, Gellner and J, Waterbury, eds, (London: Duckworth, 1977).

[561] Weissleder *The Political Ecology of Amhara Domination*. Unpublished Ph.D. dissertation. (The University of Chicago.1965); John, Markakis, *Ethiopia, Anatomy of a Traditional Polity*, (Addis Ababa: Berhanenna

Selam Printing Press, 1975); J, Cohen, and P. Koehn, *Ethiopian Provincial and Municipal Government: Imperial Patterns and Postrevolutionary Changes*, (Lansing, MI: Michigan State University, African Studies Centre, 1980); Poluha, Eva. *Central Planning and Local Reality, The case of a producers' co-operative in Ethiopia*. Stockholm: Stockholm Studies in Social Anthropology, No 23, 1989); Poluha, E, *The Power of Continuity: Ethiopia through the eyes of its children*, Uppsala: Nordiska Afrikainstitutet, (2004).

[562] Stewart, R. Clegg, *Frameworks of Power*, (London: Sage Publications, 1989).

[563] Ibid

[564] Stewart, R. Clegg, *Frameworks of Power*, (London: Sage Publications, 1989); M. Mann, *The Sources of Social Power*, Vol 1: *A History of Power from the Beginning to A,D, 1760*, (Cambridge: Cambridge University Press, 1986).

[565] Ibid: 220

[566] Stewart, R. Clegg, *Frameworks of Power*,(London: Sage Publications, 1989); Barry Barnes, "Power," In (ed) R, Bellamy *Theories and Concepts of Politics*, (Manchester University Press, 1993): 197-219

[567] Ibid

[568] Don, Kulick, "'Coming up' in Gapun, Conceptions of Development and their Effect on Language in a Papua New Guinea Village", In (eds) Dahl, G, and A, Rabo *Kamp-Ap or Take-Off, Local Notions of Development*, Stockholm: Stockholm Studies in Social Anthropology, No 29, (1992); Hugh Gustersson, *Nuclear Rites, A weapons laboratory at the end of the cold war,* (Berkeley and Los Angeles: University of California Press, 1998)

[569] Deena Freeman, *Initiating Change in Highland Ethiopia, Causes and Consequences of Cultural Transformation*, (Cambridge: Cambridge University Press, 2002)

[570] Susan Wright, "The Politicization of Culture," *Anthropology Today*, Vol, 14, No 1: (1998a) 7-15;

[571] E. Poluha, *The Power of Continuity: Ethiopia through the eyes of its children*, (Uppsala: Nordiska Afrikainstitutet, 2004): 118-119

[572] P. Bourdieu, *Outline of a Theory of Practice*, (Cambridge: Cambridge University Press, 1977); Helle Rydström, *Embodying Morality, Girls' Socialization in a North Vietnamese Commune*, (Linköping: Linköping University Press, 1998); Poluha, Eva, "Learning Political Behaviour: Peasant-State Relations in Ethiopia", In Poluha, E, and M, Rosendahl, (eds), *Contesting 'Good' Governance, Cross-cultural Perspectives on Representation, Accountability and Public Space*, (London: Routledge Curzon, 2002 a).

[573] E. Poluha, *The Power of Continuity: Ethiopia through the eyes of its children*, (Uppsala: Nordiska Afrikainstitutet, 2004): 118-119

[574] H. Aspen, "The 1995 National and Regional Elections in Ethiopia: Local Perspectives," The University of Trondheim, *SMU, Working paper*, no 10, (1995); Donor Election Unit's Report *The Ethiopian Register*, (July, 1995):41-53; Siegfried Pausewang, *The 1994 Election and Democracy in Ethiopia*, Oslo: Norwegian Institute of Human Rights, Human Rights Report No, 4, (1994); Pausewang, S, K, Tronvoll and L, Aalen, (eds) *Ethiopia since the Derg, A Decade of Democratic Pretension and Performance*, (London: Zed Books, 2002); K. Tronvoll, O, Aadland, *The Process of Democratization in Ethiopia – An Expression of Popular Participation or Political Resistance?* (Oslo:Norwegian Institute of Human Rights, 1995); S. Vaughan, and K. Tronvoll, *Structures and relations of power in Ethiopia*, A report for Sida, (2002); Eva Poluha, "Conceptualizing Democracy: Elections in the Ethiopian Countryside," *Northeast African Studies*, Vol, 4, No 1, New Series, (1997): 39-70

Glossary of Terms

Abetuta: petition
Adirbays: amharic word for "careerists"
Asmat: magi, sorcery
Awaqi: proclamation
Beheg yaltefeqede sebseba: illegal meetings
Beta israel: ethiopian jews
Chat: a mild halicinogenic drug chewed by people in the horn of africa and arabia
Chewa: a polite person
Chewanet: being polite
Chewanet: politeness; being polite
Dabtara: church scholar
Daqiqa Estefanos [also known as Stephanites] were church scholars who appeared in the 15th century and sought separation of church and state and were opposed to veneration of the virgin mary, insisting on the exclusive worship of god the father
Defar: bold
Derg: the military junta that came to power in ethiopia after the overthrow of emperor haile selassie's government in 1974
Donna fortuna: goddess of chance or lot in roman religion often holding a cornucopia, to indicate abundance, a rudder, to control destinies and standing on a ball to indicate the uncertainty of fortune
Edel: luck, destiny
Encadrement: incorporation into structures of control
Eshi nege: literally "i will do it tomorrow" indicating procrastination
Eskesta: traditional amharic shoulder-based dancing
Eskesta: traditional amharic shoulder-based dancing
Ewnet: truth
Ewqet: knowledge
Fetno-derash: commando force
Fiteha-nagast: laws of the kings
Gubzenna: bravery
Haqegnennet: honesty
Heg: law
Kebra Nagast: glory of the kings
Ketab: amulet
Kiné Bet: school of poetry
Kiosk: small shop
Kitabs: magic scrolls
Kyôgaku taishi: japanese adopted principle of traditional confucian philosophy and ethics which they injected into the modern educational system
Liq: scholar [referring to a person who has successfully completed the three stages of advanced level church education.]
Mammar: to learn
Mehandis: engineer

Melkam astedadeg: good breeding
Metsahaf bet: schools of texts
Metsahafe-falasfa Tabiban: book of wise philosophers
Mirmera: enquiry
Mirmera: questioning and research
Moya: mastery of skills/skill
Mulu wangiel: total gospel
Nege: tomorrow
Nekiki: rubbing shoulders
Qegni: musical motif
Qené: poetry
Qube: latin script to write the oromo language
Rassen makber: self-respect
Rassen mawwared: demeaning oneself
Sam enna worq: wax and gold
Sam: wax
Sena ser'at: right conduct
Tarike-nagast: monarchic history
Tehetenna: humility
Temhirt: education
Tibeb: wisdom
Wolaita chima: influential elders in the wolaita cultural system
Woredas: districts
Worq: gold
Yaltaweke addis haymanot: uknown new religion
Yemengist shigigir: a period during a government change
Ye-mulu wangiel amagnoch andenet mahbar: pentacostal "total gospel: believers'
                       association
Yetemare sew: an educated person
Zamana masafint: era of the princes
Zamanawi-seletane: modernity
Zare: today
Zefen: songs
Zema Bet: school of music

Bibliography

Abadir, M., K. Chanyalew, et al. 2000. *Proceedings of the XIth Annual Conference of the Ethiopian Public Health Association: theme, community-based education training health professionals for the new Millennium, 16-18 November 2000, Jimma University, Jimma, Ethiopia.* Addis Ababa?, Ethiopian Public Health Association. 2000.

Abbink, J. "New Configurations of Ethiopian Ethnicity: The Challenge of the South." *Northeast African Studies.* Vol. 5, No.1. 1998.

Abdi, A. A., K. P. Puplampu, et al.. *African education and globalization: critical perspectives.* Lanham, Lexington Books.. 2006.

Abebayehu, Aemero Tekleselassie. "The Deprofessionalization of School Principalship: Implications for Reforming School Leadership in Ethiopia." *International Studies in Educational Administration.* Vol 30.no.3, 2002: 57-64.

Abebe Fiseha. "Education and the Formation of the Modern Ethiopian State, 1896-1974. Ph. D Dissertation, University of Illinois, 200.

Addis Ababa University. Bahir Dar Teachers' College. Research and Publications Committee. *Programme and abstracts of the Tenth Educational Seminar: Bahir Dar Teachers' College, Addis Ababa University, Bahir Dar, May 16, 1992.* Addis Ababa, The College Research and Publications Committee. 1992.

Addis Ababa University. Dept. of Community Health. and K. Derege Education advancing the public's health: training, research, and service in the Department of Community Health, 1991-98. Addis Ababa, 1998.

Addis Ababa University. Institute of Educational Research. *Proceedings of the National Workshop on Strengthening Educational Research.* Addis Ababa, Institute of Educational Research, Addis Ababa University. 1995.

Addis Alemayehu, *Feqer Eske Maqaber.* 8th Edition. Addis Abeba: Mega, 2000.

Addis Alemayehu. *Ye Timirtna Yetemaribet* Tirgum The Meaning of Education and School. Addis Ababa: Artistic Press, 1956.

Addis Hiwet. "A Certain Political Vocation: Reflections on the Ethiopian Intelligentsia." In T*he Ethiopian Revolution and its Impact on the Politics on the Horn of Africa: Proceedings of the 2nd International Conference on the Horn of Africa,* 41—64. New York: New School for Social Research, 1987.

Adugnaw Worqu, *YeMeskel Wëf.* Angwin. CA. Shinfa Press.1984.

Afework, Gabre Yesus. *Berhanenna Selam* Amharic. July 1929.

Afework, Gabre Yesus. *Guide de voyageur en Abyssinie.* Rome: Geuthner, 1908.

Affairs of the House Committee on Foreign Affairs, U.S. Congress. Washington, D.C. March 5, 1975.

Africa Contemporary Record. New York: Africana, 1974.

African Development Forum 2000: AIDS: the greatest leadership challenge: 3-7 December 2000, Addis Ababa, Ethiopia. Addis Ababa, Ethiopia, United Nations, Economic Commission for Africa. 2000.

Aklilu Abreham. "Ethiopia: The Challenges of Federalism Based on Ethnic Restructuring. A Case Study of the Sidama and Wolayta Ethnic Groups in the Southern Nations, Nationalities and Peoples Regional State." A research report submitted to the Robert S. McNamara. 1999.

Aklilu Habte "Brain Drain in the Elementary School: Why Teachers Leave the Profession." *Ethiopian Journal of Education* 1 June 1967: 27–39.

Aklilu Habte, Mengesha Gabre Hiwet, and Monika Kehoe. "Higher Education in Ethiopia." *Journal of Ethiopian Studies.* 1 January 1963: 3–7.

Aklilu Habte. "Higher Education in Ethiopia in the 1970s and Beyond." Unpublished material, Addis Ababa, 1973.

Alamin Mazrui, "The World Bank, the language question and the future of African education", in Harris, R, and B, Rampton eds, *The Language, Ethnicity and Race Reader,* London: Routledge, 2003:94.

Alemneh, T. *The Ethiopian higher education: creating space for reform.* Addis Ababa, Ethiopia, St. Mary's UC Printing Press.. 2007.

Altbach, P. G. and D. Teferra *Publishing in African languages: challenges and prospects.* Chestnut Hill, MA, Bellagio Pub. Network Research and Information Centre in association with the Boston College Centre for International Higher Education. 1999.

Amare, A. *Quality of primary education in Ethiopia: proceedings of the national conference held in Adama Ras Hotel, November 9-11, 2001.* Addis Ababa, Institute of Educational Research, Addis Ababa University. 2002.

Amare, A., D. Derebssa, et al. *Current issues in educational research in Ethiopia: proceedings of national conference held in Nazareth, March 10-11, 2000*. Addis Ababa, Institute of Educational Research, Addis Ababa University. 2000.

Amare, A., Ethiopia. YaTemhert ministér., et al. *Quality education in Ethiopia: visions for the 21st century: proceedings of national conference held in Awasa College of Teacher Education, 12-18 July 1998*. Addis Ababa, Institute of Educational Research, Addis Ababa University. 1998.

Amare, A., L. Wanna, et al, *Establishing National Pedagogical Centre for Higher Education in Ethiopia: proceedings of the national conference held at AAU, School of Graduate Studies, conference hall Amist Kilo, Addis Ababa, August 11-12, 2000*. Addis Ababa, Institute of Educational Research, Addis Ababa University. 2000.

Amare, A., W. Getahun, et al. *Database on Ethiopian educational research: 1974-1998*. Addis Ababa, Institute of Educational Research, Addis Ababa University. 2000.

Anbesu, B. *Educational opportunities and disparities in Ethiopia*. Addis Ababa, Ethiopia, Institute for Curriculum Development and Research, Ministry of Education. 1992.

Archer, George D., and Paulos Milkias. "The Second Scramble for Africa. *"Horn of Africa Journal*. 11 1979: 55–66.

Aren, Gustav. *Envoys of the Gospel in Ethiopia*. Stockholm: EFS, forlaget, 1999.

Aseffa Beqele. "The Educational Framework of Economic Development in Ethiopia." *Ethiopia Observer*. 11 1967: 49–58.

Asmorom Legesse. Gada: Three Approaches to the Study of African Society. New York: The Free Press. 1973.

Asmorom, Legesse. Gada: Three Approaches to the Study of African Society London: Collier-Macmillan, 1973.

Asres Alem. "History of the Ethiopian Student Movement In Ethiopia and North America: its Impact on Internal Social Changes." Ph. D. dissertation, University of Maryland, 1990.

Asseffa, H. Population policies and programmes. Addis Ababa, Ministry of Education, Institute for Curriculum Development and Research. 1994.

Asseffa, B. 1991. Female participation and performance in rural primary schools in Ethiopia: executive summary report. Addis Ababa, Institute for Curriculum Development and Research of Ministry of Education: UNICEF: SIDA.

Asseffa, B. *Female participation and performance in rural primary schools in Ethiopia: executive summary report*. Addis Ababa, Institute for Curriculum Development and Research of Ministry of Education: UNICEF SIDA. 1991.

Attali, Jacques. *Noise: The Political Economy of Music*. Minneapolis: University of Minnesota Press, 1985.

Ayalew Gabre Selassie. "Three Years' Experience in Education." *Ethiopia Observer. 8* 1 1964: 19–36.

Ayele Bekerie. Ethiopic*: An African Writing System: Its History and Principles*. Lawrenceville, NJ. 1997.

Badiou, Alain. *L'Être et L'Événement*. Paris: Seuil, 1988.

Bahru Zewde. "The Intellectual and the State in Twentieth Century Ethiopia." In *New Trends in Ethiopian Studies: Papers of the 12th International Conference of Ethiopian Studies*, vol. 1. Edited by Harold G. Marcus, 483—96. Lawrenceville, N.J.: The Red Sear Press, Inc., 1994.

Bahru Zewde. *Pioneers of Change in Ethiopia: The Reformist Intellectuals of the Early Twentieth Century*. Addis Abeba: Addis Abeba University Pres, 2002.

Bahru, Zewde, *Pioneers of Change in Ethiopia: the reformist Intellectuals of the early 20th century*, Oxford: James Currey, 2002.

Balsvik, Randi Rønning. "Haile Selassie's Students: Rise of Social and Political Consciousness." PhD diss., University of Tromsø, 1979.

Barnabas, Y. Emergence *and development of population and family life education*. Addis Ababa, Ministry of Education, Institute for Curriculum Development and Research. 1994.

Baxter, P. T. W. "Ethiopia's Unacknowledged Problem: The Oromo." *African Affairs: The Royal African Society.* 77 July 1978: 283–296.

Behailu Abebe and Data Dea. *"Dawro* on occupational minorities." In D. Freeman and Bekele Wolde Kidan. Rivaival: Etiopia ena Yemechereshaw Revival. Addis Ababa Mulu Wangiel 20001/2.

Belete, K. The attitude of teacher trainees toward gender issues in education: the case of Addis Ababa University. Addis Ababa, s.n.. 2000.

Benti, G. *Addis Ababa: migration and the making of a multiethnic metropolis,1941-1974*. Trenton, NJ, Red Sea Press. 2007.

Bereket Habte Selassie. *Conflict and Intervention in the Horn of Africa.*New York: Monthly Review Press, 1980.

Berhanu, D., B. Anbesu, et al. *Evaluative study of technical and vocational schools in Ethiopia*. Addis Ababa, Ethiopia, Insitute for Curriculum Development and Research, Ministry of Education. 1992.

Besemenawi Etiopia Yemigegnew Ye-Hulettegnaw Kifl e-Tor The Second Division from the Northern Front. Distributed in Addis Ababa March 4, 1974.

Binns, John. "Theological Education in the Ethiopian Orthodox Church". *The Journal of Adult Theological Education* 2.2, 2005: 103-113.

Blasvik, R. Rønning. *Haile Selassie's Students*. East Lansing: Michigan Sate University, 1985.

Bloch, Ernst. "Non-synchronism and Dialectcs", *New German Critique*, 11, Spring 1977: 22-38.

Bloch, Ernst. *The Principle of Hope*. 3 volumes. Translated by Neville Plaice, Stephen Plaice and Paul Knight. Cambridge, Massachusetts. The MIT Press, 1986.

Bridges, David, Amare Asgedom and Setargew Kenaw, "From 'deep knowledge' to 'the light of reason': source for philosophy of education in Ethiopia". *Comparative Education*, vol 40, no 4, November 2004: 531-544.

Britain. "Correspondence of the Foreign Office." 1943: J1284/78/16, J3051/78/16, J3051/78/1, J4121/4121/1.

Britain. "Correspondence of the Foreign Office." JI893/51/1. 1945: British Association for Applied Linguistics. Meeting 25th:: University of Southampton, G. M. Blue, et al. 1996. *Language and education: papers from the annual meeting of the British Association for Applied Linguistics held at the University of Southampton, September 1995*. Clevedon, England ; Philadelphia, British Association for Applied Linguistics in association with Multilingual Matters. 1995.

Brower, Daniel R. "A Sociological Analysis: Fathers and Sons in Tsarist Russia." In *The Youth Revolution: The Conflict of Generations in Modern History*. Edited by Anthony Ester, 62—81. Lexington: D. C. Heath and Company, 1974.

Calder, Grant H. "Business and Public Administration in Ethiopian Higher Edu cation." In University of Utah, "Survey of Higher Education in Ethiopia, 1959–1960." Sec. III. Addis Ababa, 1960.

Cassiers, Anne et Jean-Michel Bessette. *Mémoires Ethiopiennes*. Paris: L'Harmattan, 2001. Cassirer, Ernst, *An Essay on Man: An Introduction to a Philosophy of Human Culture*, New Haven CT: 1944.

Central Statistical Authority CSA. Statistical Abstract. Addis Ababa. 2004.

Chiatti, R. The Politics of Divine Kingship in Wolaita. Ph.D Dissertation in Anthropology, University of Pennsylvania, 1989.

Christian Relief & Development Association Ethiopia CRDA Workshop on Academic Education, Vocational Training, and Job Placement/Creation for the Orphans in the Present Changing Economy: November 12, 1992. Addis Ababa, Ethiopia, Christian Relief & Development Association. 1992.

Colburn, Forrest D. *The Vogue of Revolution in Poor Countries*. Princeton, N.J.: Princeton University Press, 1994.

Collins, Jane. Miracles and Missions and World Wide Evangelism. Dallas: Jane Collins Doud, 1953.

Dalin, P. How schools improve: an international report. London ; New York, Cassell. 1994.

Daniel Gamachu. "A Nation in Perpetual Transition: The Politics of Changes in Administrative Divisions and Subdivisions in Ethiopia." In H.G. Marcus ed., *New Trends in Ethiopian Studies: Paper of the 12th International Conference of Ethiopian Studies*. Vol. II. NJ.: The Red Sea Press. 1994.

Daniel Lemma. "Development of a Student Personal Programme for Ethiopia's National University to meet the needs of Ethiopia's Youth."Ph.D. dissertation, Michigan State University, 1976.

Data Dea. "Civil Society and Religious Difference: Note on Gutara Institution in Wolaita, Southern Ethiopia."' In Brigitta Benzing,ed. *Civil Society in Ethiopia: Reflections on Realities and Perspectives of Hope*. Frankfurt am Main: Verlag für Interkulturelle Kommunikation, 2005.

Data Dea. "Clans, Kingdoms and Cultural Diversity in Southern Ethiopia: the Case of Omotic Speakers." *Northeast African Studies* volume 7 number 3 2000: 163-188.

Data Dea. *The Challenges of Integrative Power: Hierarchy and Political Change in Dawro, Southwestern Ethiopia*. Ph.D thesis submitted to the Department of Social Anthropology, University of Bergen, Norway, 2003.

De Certeau, Michel, The Practice of Everyday Life. Berkley: University of California Press, 1984.

Derese, M., J. Wagner, et al. Factors affecting scholastic achievement of lower primary school pupils. Addis Ababa, Insitute of Curriculum Development and Educational Research Greenspan, M., A. Abt, et al. 1992. Journey to the Promised Land: the long home-coming of Ethiopian Jewry. United States, WZO Dept. of Information. 1991.

Derese, M., J. Wagner, et al. *Factors affecting scholastic achievement of lower primary school pupils*. Addis Ababa, Insitute of Curriculum Development and Educational Research. 1991.

Derese, M., J. Wagner, et al. *Factors affecting scholastic achievement of lower primary school pupils*. Addis Ababa, Insitute of Curriculum Development and Educational Research. 1991.

Desta Asayehegne. "Student Alienation: A Study of High School Students in Ethiopia." Ph. D. Dissertation, Stanford University, 1977.

Deutsche Stiftung für Internationale Entwicklung., M. Wesseler, et al. *On innovative teaching: experiences and insights from eastern and southern African universities.* Frankfurt, Verlag für Interkulturelle Kommunikation. 1992.

Dewey, John. *Democracy and Education,* Carbondale: Southern Illinois University Press, 1985.

Dodd, S. M. 1999. *O careless love: stories and a novella.* New York, William Morrow.

Donham, D. *Marxist Modern: An Ethnographic History of Revolution in Ethiopia.* Oxford: James Currey,1999.

Donham, Donald. "Introduction." In W. James. et.al eds., *Remapping Ethiopia: Socialism and After.* Athens: Ohio University Press; Addis Ababa: Addis Ababa University Press; Oxford: James Currey, 2002.

Eengelsviken, T. "Report on the Pentecostal Movement in Ethiopia and its Relations to the Evangelical Church of Makana Yesus." Makana Yesus Seminary, 1972.

Elleni Tedla. *Sankofa: African Thought and Education.* New York: Peter lang. 1995.

Teshome Wagaw. The Development of Higher Education and Social Change: an Ethiopian Experience East Lansing: Michigan State University Press, 1990.

Ethiopia. Aide memoire transmitted by Yilma Deressa, vice minister of finance of Ethiopia, to President Franklin D. Roosevelt, Washington, D.C. July 13, 1943.

Ethiopia. Central Statistical Authority. The 1994 population and housing census of Ethiopia: results for Amhara Region. Addis Ababa, The Authority. 1995.

Ethiopia. Central Statistical Authority.. The 1994 population and housing census of Ethiopia: results for Southern Nations, Nationalities, and Peoples' Region. Addis Ababa, The Authority. 1996.

Ethiopia. Central Statistical Office and Ministry of Commerce and Industry, *Survey of Manufacturing and Electricity Industry* 1965–1966, 1966–1967.

Ethiopia. Central Statistical Offi ce. *Statistical Abstracts.* Addis Ababa, 1954–1974.

Ethiopia. Election Commission. *Election Commission bulletin.* Addis Ababa, Ethiopia, Committee of Education & Propaganda of the Election Commission: v. 1992.

Ethiopia. Ministry of Education and Fine Arts, Bureau of Educational Research and Statistics. *Government, Mission, Private Community and Church Schools,* Addis Ababa, 1960.

Ethiopia. Ministry of Education and Fine Arts, Committee on the Operation of the Education System. "The Current State of Affairs: A Short Review." Addis Ababa, November 1966.

Ethiopia. Ministry of Education and Fine Arts, Planning Committee. "A Ten-Year Plan for trolled Expansion of Ethiopian Education." Ababa, 1955.

Ethiopia. Ministry of Education and Fine Arts. "Report of the Education Sector Review." Addis Ababa, August 1972.

Ethiopia. Ministry of Education and Fine Arts. "Report of the Education Sector Review." Addis Ababa, 1972.

Ethiopia. Ministry of Education and Fine Arts. "Report of the Technical Education Committee." Addis Ababa, 1951.

Ethiopia. Ministry of Education and Fine Arts. "Report on the Current operation of the Education System in Ethiopia." Addis Ababa, 1969.

Ethiopia. Ministry of Education and Fine Arts. "Secondary School Curriculum 1951 EC 1958."

Ethiopia. Ministry of Education and Fine Arts. "The Development of Pre-Service Teacher Education 1937–1963 1944–1971.

Ethiopia. Ministry of Education and Fine Arts. *A Proposed Plan for the Development of Education in Ethiopia.* Addis Ababa: Berhanenna Selam, 1961.

Ethiopia. Ministry of Education and Fine Arts. *Annual Report,* 1970–1971. Addis Ababa: Berhanenna Selam, 1973.

Ethiopia. Ministry of Education and Fine Arts. *Annual Report.* Addis Ababa: Berhanenna Selam, 1969.

Ethiopia. Ministry of Education and Fine Arts. *Yearbook* 1942–1943 1945–1951, G.C.. Addis Ababa: Berhanenna Selam, 1952.

Ethiopia. Ministry of Education Ye Hizb Ginignunet Agelglot Yetimhirt Zenna Educational newsletters. Addis Ababa, YaTemhert ministér, Ya*Hezb geneñunat *agelglot: v. 1995.

Ethiopia. Ministry of Education. *Indicators of the Ethiopian education system.* Addis Abeba, Ministry of Education.. 2001.

Ethiopia. Ministry of Education. *Indicators of the Ethiopian education system.* Addis Ababa, Ministry of Education. 2003.

Ethiopia. Ministry of Education. Ye Hizb Ginignunet Agelglot Yetimhirt Zenna Educational newsletters. Addis Ababa, v. 1994.

Ethiopia. Ministry of Education. Ye Hizb Ginignunet Agelglot Yetimhirt Zenna Educational newsletters. v. 1995.

Ethiopia. Ministry of Education. Ye Hizb Ginignunet Agelglot Yetimhirt Zenna Educational newsletters.: v. 2000.

Ethiopia. Ministry of Health. Health Education Centre: *National health communication strategy: Ethiopia, 2005-2014.* Addis Ababa, Health Education Centre.. 2004.

Ethiopia. Ministry of Information. "His Imperial Majesty Haile Selassie's Address to the United States Congress." May 26, 1954.

Ethiopia. Ministry of Information. *Ethiopia, the Official Handbook.* Nairobi: University Press of Africa, 1969.

Ethiopia. Ministry of Pen. "Public Safety and Welfare Order, 1964." *Negarit Gazeta.* April 7, 1969.

Ethiopia. Ministry of Pen. *Negarit Gazeta.* Proclamation No. 326 of 1966 1974.

Ethiopia. Planning Board. *Second Five-Year Development Plan.* Vol. 7. Addis Ababa, 1959.

Ethiopia. Provisional Military Administrative Council, Government Revolution Centre. *Revolutionary Ethiopia Fact Sheet.* Addis Ababa, January 1978: 10.

Ethiopia. Provisional Military Administrative Council, Zemecha Office.*Ye-1967–1968 Zemecha Atekalay Zegeba.* Unpublished document Addis Ababa, 1976.

Ethiopia. Provisional Military Administrative Council. "A Proclamation to Provide for the Public Ownership of Rural Lands." *Negarit Gazeta* April 29, 1975.

Ethiopia. Provisional Military Administrative Council. "Awaj" Proclamation.*Nagarit Gazeta.* No.1, 1967 1974.

Ethiopia. Provisional Military Administrative Council. "Etiopia Tiqdem," *The Origins and Future Directions of the Movement.* Addis Ababa, December 20, 1974.

Ethiopia. Provisional Military Administrative Council. "Urban Dwellers' Associations Consolidation and Municipalities Proclamation." *Negarit Gazeta,* No. 104, 1976.

Ethiopia. Provisional Military Administrative Council. *Abiyotawit Ethiopia.*Addis Ababa: Tahsas 15, 1969 December 7, 1977.

Ethiopia. Provisional Military Administrative Council. *Measures for Rural Transformation.* Addis Ababa: Artistic Printing Press, 1977.

Ethiopia. Provisional Military Administrative Council. *Negarit Gazeta.*Proclamation No. 1 of 1974 September 15, 1974.

Ethiopia. Provisional Military Administrative Council. *Years of Revolutionary Progress.* Addis Ababa: Ministry of Information and National Guidance, 1978.

Ethiopia. Provisional Military Administrative Council. *Yetigil Me'eraf* Chapter of Struggle. Addis Ababa: Artistic Printing Press, 1975.

Ethiopia. *The Revised Constitution.* Addis Ababa: Berhanenna Selam, 1955.*Ethiopian Herald.* April 29, 1973.

Ethiopia. Ye *Ethiopia Ye Shigigir Mengist Ataqalay Yetimhirtinna ye Siltana Polici* Provisional Ethiopian Government's General Educational and Training Policy Addis Ababa1994.

Ethiopian Human Rights Council. *27th Special Report Human Rights Violations in North Omo.* December 13, 1999.

Ethiopian Journal of Education. 3 June 1969.

Ethiopian Students and Teachers. "Atawolawul Wotté" Do Not Hesitate, Soldier. Addis Ababa: Yekatit 21, 1966 March 2, 1974.

Ethiopian Teachers Association. "From the Ethiopian Teachers Association." Addis Ababa: Yekatit 22, 1966 March 1, 1974.

Ethiopian Teachers Association. "Ke-Etiopia Universiti Memeheran Mahbar Yewetta Meglecha." Resolution of the Ethiopian University. Addis Ababa: Yekatit 26, 1966 March 6, 1974.

Ethiopian Teachers Association. "Petition to the Emperor". February 4, 1974.

Ethiopian Teachers Association. "The Education Sector Review." Unpublished material. Addis Ababa, 1974.

Ethiopian University Teachers Association. "Ke-Etiopia Ye-University Memheran Mahbar Yewetta Meglecha" Manifesto of Ethiopian University Teachers Association. Addis Ababa, April 23, 1973.

Federal Democratic Republic Of Ethiopia. *Central Statistical Authority. Ethiopia Child Labour Survey Report.,* 2001.

Forbes, Rosita, *Adventures From Red Sea to Blue Nile:* London: Cassell, 1925.

Foucault, Michel. *Power/Knowledge.* Trans. C.Gordon, New York: Pantheon. 1980.

Fouillée, Alfred. *Les Etudes Classiques et la Démocratie.* Paris: A.Collin, 1898.

Freeman, D. and Pankhurst, A. eds., *Peripheral People: The Excluded Minorities of Ethiopia.* Husrt & Co.: London, 2003.

Freire, Paulo. *Education for Critical Consciousness.* New York: Seabury Press, 1973.

Freud, Sigmund. *The Psychopathology of Everyday Life*. Harmondsworth: Penguin 2003.

Gadamer, Hans-Georg. *Truth and Method*. New York: The Seabury Press, 1975.

Gabre, W. K. Analysis of culture for planning curriculum: the case of songs produced in the three main languages of Ethiopia Amharic, Afan-Oromo and Tigrigna. Joensuu, University of Joensuu, Faculty of Education, Joensuu yliopisto,.: xii, 174 p.. 2002.

Gerlach, Luther P. *People, Power, Change: Movements of Social Transformations*. New York: The Bobbs-Merrill Company, 1970.

Germa Amare, Abraham Demoz, and Aba Gabre Egziabher Degou. "Education Sector Review: Educational Objectives." Interim draft paper, n. d.

Getahun, T. and A. Daniel *A look at the public education system in Ethiopia: an assessment of quality and financing issues based on a survey covering students, teachers, and parents*. Addis Ababa, EEA/Ethiopian Economic Policy Research Institute. 2004.

Getatchew Haile, *Daqiqa Estefanos: BeHeg Amlak*. Avon Minnesota, 2004.

Gifford, Paul. *African Christianity: Its Public Roles*. Bloomington: Indiana University Press, 1998.

Gillett, Margaret. "Symposium on Africa: Western Academic Role Concepts in Ethiopian University." *Comparative Education Review* 7 963: 149–151.

Girma, Amare. "Government Education in Ethiopia." *Ethiopia Observer* 1 1962: 335–342.

Greenfi eld, Richard. *Ethiopia: A New Political History*. London: Pall Mall, 1965.

Greenspan, M., A. Abt, et al. *Journey to the Promised Land: the long home-coming of Ethiopian Jewry*. United States, WZO Dept. of Information. 1992.

Greenspan, M., A. Abt, et al. *Journey to the Promised Land: the long home-coming of Ethiopian Jewry*. United States, WZO Dept. of Information. 1992.

Grubb, Norman. *Alfred Buxton of Abyssinia and Congo*. London: Luther worth Press, 1942.

Gupta, S., B. J. Clements, et al. *Helping countries develop: the role of fiscal policy*. Washington, D.C., International Monetary Fund. 2004.

Gutkind. Peter C. W., and Immanuel Wallerstein, eds. *The Political Economy of Contemporary Africa*. London: Sage, 1976.

Haaland, G, Haaland, R. and Data Dea. "Smelting Iron: Caste and Its Symbolism in South-western Ethiopia." In T. Insoll, ed., *Belief in the Past: The Proceeding of the 2002 Manchester Conference on Archaeology and Religion*. BAR International Series, 2004b.

Haaland, R., Haaland, G. and Data Dea.. "Furnace and Pot: Why the Iron Smelter Is a Big Pot Maker: a Case Study from Southwestern Ethiopia. *Azania XXXIX. 2004a:143-165*.

Haddis Alemayehu. *Feqer Eske Meqaber* Amharic. Addis Ababa: Berhanenna Selam, 1965.

Haile Selassie *Heywatenna Ye-Etiopia Ermeja*. Addis Ababa: Berhanenna Selam, 1972.

Haile Selassie University. "Programme of the Convocation Celebrating the Founding of Haile Selassie I University." Addis Ababa, 1961.

Haile Selassie. Selected Speeches of his Imperial Majesty Haile Selassie First 1918 to 1976. Addis Ababa, Ethiopia: Artistic Printers Ltd., 1967.

Haile Wolde Michael. "A Comparative Study of Leadership Development Methods with Reference to the Ethiopian Full Gospel Church." Ph. D dissertation, Fuller Theological Seminary, 1993.

Haile Wolde Michael. "The Problems of Admissions to the University through School Leaving Certificate Examinations." Unpublished material.May 1969.

Hailemariam, G. and Organization for Social Science Research in Eastern and Southern Africa. An investigation into the community-relevance of the Ethiopian senior secondary school formal education: the case of Illubabor Administrative Region. Addis Ababa. 1996.

Haileselassie, W., M. Emebet, et al. Moving beyond the classroom: expanding learning opportunities for marginalized populations in Ethiopia. Nairobi, Forum for African Women Educationalists. 2002.

Haileyesus Engdashet, Tifhit Lemma and Aster Tadesse. *Ye Sement Ometo Quanquawoch/ Kebelegnawoch Yemegiabat Derja Tinat* In Amharic. Ethiopian Languages Academy, Linguistic Reseach Team, 1980 E.C 1988 G.C.

Haileyesus Seba. *A Study of Social Change in Wolaita Research, Southern Ethiopia*. MA Thesis in Social Anthropology, Addis Ababa University, 1996.

Hansbury, William Leo. *Pillars in Ethiopian History* William Leo Hansbury African History Notebook. Vol. 1, edited by Joseph E. Harris. Washington,D.C.: Howard University Press, 1974.

Harrell, David E. *All Things are Possible*. Bloomington: Indiana University Press, 1975.

Hess, Robert L. *Ethiopia: The Modernization of Autocracy*. Ithaca, N.Y.: Cornell University Press, 1970.

Hiwet, Addis. *Ethiopia: From Autocracy to Revolution*. London: Review of African Political Economy, 1975.

Hoben, Allan. Land Tenure Among the Amhara of Ethiopias: The Dynamics of Cognitive Descent. Chicago: University of Chicago Press, 1973.

Hollenweger. W.J., *The Pentecostals.* Minneapolis, Augsburg, 1972.
Hoot, James L,. Judit Szente and Belete Mebratu, "Early Education in Ethiopia:Progress and Prospects." *Early Childhood Educational Journal.* Vol 32, no.1, August 2004: 3-8.
Horkheimer, Max and Theodor W. Adorno. *Dialectic of Enlightenment,* New York: Seabury Press, 1972.
Embaqom Kalewold Alaqa. *Traditional Ethiopian Church Education.* Translated by Mengistu Lemma. New York: Teachers College Press, 1970.
Indrias Getatchew. Beyoond the Throne: The Enduring Legacy of Emperor Haile Sellassie. Addis Ababa, Shama Books, 2001.
Institute of Curriculum Development and Research Ethiopia *Population education newsletter.* Addis Ababa, Ethiopia, Institute for Curriculum Development and Research, Ministry of Education: v. 1991.
Institute of Curriculum Development and Research Ethiopia *Population education newsletter.* Addis Ababa, Ethiopia, Institute for Curriculum Development and Research, Ministry of Education: v. 1991.
International Labour Organization, 1986, Youth Employment Programmes in Africa, A comparative sub-regional Study: The case of Ethiopia,Addis Ababa 1986:21.
International Yearbook of Education. Geneva, 1950–1962.
Ireland Aid Organization, Ye Ethiopia Akalagudatagnoch Mahbarat Federation Developing entrepreneurship among women with disabilities in Ethiopia: starting point: exploratory surveys in Addis Ababa and Tigray Region. Addis Ababa, 2005.
Iris, Brian. *Sun* London: October 29, 1973.
Kant, Immanuel. *On Education.* Boston: D.C.Heath, 1900.
Kebede Tessemma, Dajazmatch. *Yetarik Mastawesha.* Addis Ababa: Artistic Printing Press, 1969.
Kebede, M. 1994. *Migration and urbanization in Ethiopia.* Addis Ababa, Ministry of Education, Institute for Curriculum Development and Research.
Keenleyside, Hugh Ll. and A. F. Thomas. History of Japanese Education and Present Educational System. Tokyo: The Hokuseido Press, 1937.
Kinfe, A. A manpower development review: the financing of Ethiopian education: expansion under constraints and the role of aid. Addis Ababa, Ethiopia, Ethiopian International Institute for Peace and Development. 1997.
Kinfe, A. *The status of education in Region 1.* Addis Ababa, Ethiopia, Ethiopian International Institute for Peace and Development. 1997.
Kirschenbaum, V. *Goodbye Gutenberg: hello to a new generation of readers and writers.* New York, Global Renaissance Society. 2005.
Klein, P. S. Seeds *of hope: twelve years of early intervention in Africa.* Oslo, Norway, Unipub. 2001.
Lange, W. History of the Southern Gonga South-western Ethiopia. Wiesbaden: Steiner, 1982.
Larbi, Emmanuel Kingsley. Pentecostalism: The Eddies of Ghanaian Christianity. Accra: SAPC Series, 2001.
LeClerc, Gerard. Anthropologie et Colonialisme: Essai sur l'Histoire de l'Africanisme. Paris: Fayard, 1972
Legum, Colin. "The Night They Hanged Haile Selassie." *The Observer.* 15 London: September 1974.
Legum, Colin. *The Fall of Haile Selassie's Empire.* New York: Africana, 1975.
Letter from the War Office to the British Legation in Addis Ababa 1935: J4121/4121/I.
Levine, Donald N. *Wax and Gold: Tradition and Innovation in Ethiopian Culture.* Chicago University Press, 1972. (Los Angeles: Tsehai Publishers, 2007)
Levine, Donald. *Greater Ethiopia: Multi-ethnic Society.* Chicago: University of Chicago Press, 1974.
Levine, Donald. *Wax and Gold.* Chicago: University of Chicago Press, 1965.
Lewis, H.. *Jimma Abba Jifar: An Oromo Monarchy: Ethiopia, 1830-1932.* N.J, The Red Sea Press. 2001 1965.
Logos Journal, May-June, 1973
Loukeris, Kostas. "Church and Attempted Modernization in Ethiopia." In *Ethiopia in Broader Perspective: Papers of 13th International Conference of Ethiopian studies,* vol. 1. Edited by Katsuyoshi Fukui, Eisei Kurimoto, and Masayoshi. Shigeta, 206—18. Kyoto: Shokado Book Sellers, 1997.
Lulat, Y. G. M. A history of African higher education from antiquity to the present: a critical synthesis. Westport, Conn., Praeger Publishers. 2005.
Maimire Mennesemay. "Ethiopian Political Theory, Democracy, and Surplus-history" *International Journal of Ethiopian Studies,* Vol II No. 1 & 2, Summer/Fall 2005-2006.: 1-32
Maimire Mennesemay, "Towards a critical Ethiopian theory of Education", in Paulos Milkias and Messay Kebede, eds, *Education, Politics and Social Change in Ethiopia.* Los Angeles, Tsehai Publishers, 2009: 67-97.
Maimire Mennasemay. "Ethiopian History and Critical Theory: The Case of Adwa", in Paulos Milkias and Getachew Metaferia, eds. *The Battle of Adwa.* New York, Agora, 2005.
Marcus, Harold. *Haile Sellassie: The Formative Years 1892-1937.* Berkley, University of California Press, 1987.

Marew, Z., D. Bridges, et al. *Secondary teacher education in Ethiopia.* Addis Ababa. 2000.

Marin, David. *Forbidden Revolution in Latin America and Catholicism in Eastern Europe.* London: SPCK, 1966.

Markakis, John, and Nega Ayele. *Class and Revolution in Ethiopia.* London: Review of African Political Economy, 1978.

Markakis, John. *Ethiopia: Anatomy of a Traditional Polity.* Addis Ababa: Oxford University Press,, 1974.

Marx, Karl. *Early Writings.* New York: Vintage Books, 1975

Mazrui, Ali A. *Political Values and the Educated Class in Africa.* Berkeley: University of California Press, 1978.

Mbah, S. and I. E. Igariwey *African anarchism: the history of a movement.* Tucson, Ariz., See Sharp Press. 1997.

Mekasha, B. *The changes in health related behaviour of primary school pupils and their parents.* Addis Ababa, ICDR, Ministry of Education. 1993.

Merera Gudina. *Ethiopia: Competing Ethnic Nationalisms and the Quest for Democracy, 1960-2000.* Ph. D Thesis, Institute of Social Studies ISS, The Hague, 2002.

Mesfi n Wolde Mariam. "Twenty Years of Famine in Rural Ethiopia." Seminar paper. Addis Ababa, 1976.

Messay Kebede, "Eurocentrism and Ethiopian Historiography: Deconstructing Semitization," *International Journal of Ethiopian Studies* 1, no. 1 2003: 1-19.

Messay Kebede, "Eurocentrism and Ethiopian Historiography: Deconstructing Semitization," *International Journal of Ethiopian Studies* 1, no. 1 2003: 1-19.

Messay Kebede, *Survival and Modernization: Ethiopia's enigmatic present, A Philosophical Discourse,* Lawrenceville, NJ: Red Sea Press, 1999

Messay Kebede. Survival and Modernization: Ethiopia's Enigmatic Present. Lawrenceville, Red See Press, 1999.

Messay Kebede. Survival and Modernization: Ethiopia's Enigmatic Present: Philosophical Discourse. Larenceville, NJ.: The Red Sea Press, 1999

Messing, Simon D Changing Ethiopia." The Middle East Journal, 9. 4 1955

Mistahl, A. *Ethiopia: Political Contradiction in Agricultural Development.* Uppsala:Political Science Association in Uppsala, 1974.

Molvaer, Reidulf K. *Tradition and Change in Ethiopia: Social and Cultural Life as Reflected in Amharic Fictional Literature.* Leiden: E.J. Brill, 1980.

Mondoh, H. O. *The impact of pay-as-you-eat on university education in Kenya: a case study of Egerton University, Njoro.* Addis Ababa, Ethiopia, Organization for Social Science Research in Eastern and Southern Africa. 2002.

Mulatu Wubneh and Yohannes Abate. *Ethiopia: Transition and Development in the Horn of Africa.* Boulder, Co.: Westview Press, 1988.

Mulatu Wubneh and Yohannes Abate. *Ethiopia: Transition and Development in the Horn of Africa.* Boulder, Co.: Westview Press, 1988.

Mulinge, M. M. *The perceived nature and extent of gender discrimination in the teaching profession in Botswana.* Addis Ababa, Ethiopia, Organization for Social Science Research in Eastern and Southern Africa. 2002.

Mull, L. D., KURET Project., et al. *KURET, regional summary report: baseline study and situational analysis of child labour and education in HIV/AIDS affected communities in Kenya, Uganda, Rwanda, and Ethiopia.* Kampala, KURET Regional Office. 2005.

Mulugeta Wodajo, "Secondary education and manpower requirements of the Second Five Year Plan", in *Educational Journal of the University College Education Students Association,* Bulletin no,11, Addis Ababa,1963/4,

Mulugeta Wodajo. "Postwar Reform in Ethiopian Education." *Comparative Education Review* 2, no. 3 1959: 24—30.

Mulugeta Wodajo. "Postwar Reform in Ethiopian Education." *Comparative Education Review* 2, no. 3 1959: 24—30.

Mulugeta Wodajo. "The State of Educational Finance in Ethiopia." *Ethiopian Journal of Education.* 1 June 1967: 18–26.

Muthusami, I. J *Implementation of education projects: an Ethiopian experience.* Huntington,, W. Va., University Editions. 1993.

Negash, T. and Nordiska Afrikainstitutet. *Rethinking education in Ethiopia.* Uppsala Stockholm, Sweden, Nordiska Afrikainstitutet, 1996.

Negash, T. Education in Ethiopia: from crisis to the brink of collapse. Uppsala, Nordiska Afrikainstitutet. 2006.

Nagawo Beyene. "The Impact of University Education on the Formation of Political Attitude: Sources of Negative Political Attitudes of Ethiopian Youth."Ph. D. dissertation, Stanford University, 1977.

Nekatibeb, T. Media utilization and school improvement: a case study of primary education radio support programs in Ethiopia. Stockholm, Institute of International Education, Stockholm University, 1998.

O'Connor, Lillian. "Some Aspects of the Language Problem." *Ethiopia Observe* 2 May 1958: 143.

Ojoo, A., S. P. Wamahiu, et al. *Life skills education with a focus on HIV/AIDS: eastern and southern Africa region.* Nairobi, Kenya, UNICEF Eastern and Southern Africa Region. 2002.

Okurut, H. E. and Organization for Social Science Research in Eastern and Southern Africa. *Empowerment function of Vision Terudo's non-formal education programmes for rural women in Ngora County.* Addis Ababa?, s.n. 1998.

Organization for Social Science Research in Eastern and Southern Africa. 2006. Social science research report series. Addis Ababa, Ethiopia, Organization for Social Science Research in Eastern and Southern Africa.

Ottaway, Marina, and David Ottaway. *Ethiopia: Empire in Revolution.* London: Holmes and Meier, 1978.

Pankhurst, Richard. "The Great Ethiopian Famine of 1889–1892." *University College Review* Haile Selassie I University, 1 Spring 1961: 90–103.

Pankhurst, Richard. *A Social History of Ethiopia.* Trenton, NJ.: Red Sea Press,1992.

Pankhurst, Sylvia. "The University College of Addis Ababa." *Ethiopia Observer.*11 6 July 1958: 195–207, 210–213.

Pankhurst, Sylvia. *Ethiopia: A Cultural History.* Essex: Lalibela House, 1955.

Pankhurst, Sylvia. *Ethiopia: A Cultural History.* Essex: Lalibela House, 3 Charteris Road, Woodford Green, 1955.

Pankhurst, Sylvia. *Ethiopia: A Cultural History.* Essex: Lalibela House, 1955.

Pankhust, A. ed., Peripheral People: The Excluded Minorities of Ethiopia. Husrt & Co.: London, 2003.

Partnership for Higher Education in Africa. and United Nations. Economic Commission for Africa. *Securing the linchpin: ICT for teaching, learning and research: a workshop for African universities: 29 July-1 August 2002, United Nations International Conference Centre, Addis Ababa, Ethiopia.* New York, NY, Partnership for Higher Education in Africa. 2003.

Paulos Milkias. "The Political Spectrum of Western Education in Ethiopia," *Journal of African Studies* 9, no. 1 1982: 22—29.

Paulos Milkias. "Traditional Institutions and Traditional Elite. *African Studies Review,* XXI, 3 1976

Paulos Milkias. "Traditional Institutions and Traditional Elites: The Role of Education in the Ethiopian Body-Politic." *African Studies Review*19, no. 3 1976: 70—93.

Paulos, Milkias. Haile *Selassie, western education, and political revolution in Ethiopia.* Youngstown, N.Y., Cambria Press. 2006.

Paulos, Milkias. "Political Linkage: The Relationship between Modern Education and the Fall of Haile Selassie's Feudal Regime." Paper presented to the Canadian Political Science Association at the meeting of the Learned Societies of Canada, held at the University of Quebec in Montreal, June 3, 1980.

Paulos, Milkias. "The Political Spectrum of Western Education in Ethiopia." *Journal of African Studies.* 9 Spring 1982: 22–29.

Paulos, Milkias. "The Ethiopian Zemecha." Paper presented to the Canadian Society for the Study of Education, at the meeting of the Learned Societies of Canada, held at the University of Saskatchewan in Saskatoon, June 6,1979.

Paulos, Milkias.. "Education in Ethiopia." *World Education Encyclopedia.* New York: Facts on File Publication, 1985: 200–210.

Paulos, Milkias.. "The Political Economy of Education: Adult Literacy Campaign in Ethiopia." Paper presented to the International Council for Adult Education,Ontario Institute of Education, University of Toronto, January 1980.

Paulos, Milkias.. "Zemecha: Assessing the Political and Social Foundations of Mass Education in Ethiopia." *Studies in Comparative International Development.*15 Fall 1980: 54–69.

Pausewang, S., Kjetil Tronvoll and Lovise Aalen eds.. *Ethiopia Since the DERG: A Decade of Democratic Pretension and Performance.* London; New York: Zed Books, 2002.

Poewe Karla, ed. *Charismatic Christianity as a Global Culture.* Columbia: University of South Carolina Press, 1994.

Political Life." *Sidastudies,* No. 10. 2003.

Poluha, E. and Nordiska Afrikainstitutet *The power of continuity: Ethiopia through the eyes of its children.* Uppsala, Sweden, Nordiska Afrikainstitutet.. 2004.

Price, Kingsley. *Education and Philosophical Thought,* Boston: Allyn and Bacon. 1962

Rice, Marie S. *Sister Bertha Sister Ruth.* Nashville: Jonathan Publishers of Nashville, 1984.

Rose, Pauline and Samer Al-Samarrai. "Household Constraints on Schooling by Gender: Empirical Evidence from Ethiopia". *Comparative Education Review,* Vol. 45, no 1. 2001: 36-63

Rouse, Doris. *The Intercession of Rees Howells.* Cambridge: Luther worth Press, 1983.

Royal Chronicle of Abyssinia. *The Glorious Victory of Amda Seyon, King of Ethiopia.* Translated and edited by G. W. B. Huntingford. Oxford: Clarendon Press, 1965.

Rubenson, Sven. The Survival of Ethiopian Independence. London: Heinemann and Addis Ababa: Addis Ababa University Press, 1978.

Sambo, W. A. L. The impact of civil wars on basic education in the Great Lakes Region: a case study of Tanzania. Addis Ababa, Ethiopia, Organization for Social Science Research in Eastern and Southern Africa. 2003.

Schwab, Peter. Haile Selassie I: Ethiopia's Lion of Judah. Chicago: Nelson Hall, 1979.

Scott, James.C. *Weapons of the Weak: Everyday forms of Peasant Resistance.* New Haven: Yale University Press, 1985.

Seleshi Kebede. "The History of Genet Church." Senior essay, Makana Yesus Seminary, 1990.

Shiferaw Bekele, "Review of Education in Ethiopia: From Crisis to the Brink of Collapse", in *Forum for Social Studies*, Bulletin, vol,3&4: no,2, 2006.

Shinn, David H. "Reversing the Brain Drain In Ethiopia", Delivered to the Ethiopian North American Health Professionals Association, The George Washington University, Alexandria, Virginia, November 23, 2002.

Sikainga, A. A. and O. *Alidou Postconflict reconstruction in Africa.* Trenton NJ, Africa World Press. 2006.

Silva, P. and World Bank. Environmental factors and children's malnutrition in Ethiopia. Washington, D.C., World Bank. 2005.

Sperber, D. "Paradoxes of Seniority among the Dorze," In H.Marcus ed., *Proceeding of the First United States Conference on Ethiopian Studies*, African Studies Centre, Michigan State University. 1973.

Staahl, M.. Ethiopia: Political Contradictions in Agricultural Development. Stockholm, Raben & Sjogren, 1974.

Summerskill, John. Haile Sellassie I University A Blue Print for Development. Addis Ababa: Haile Sellassie I University, 1970.

Tadesse Tamrat. *Church and State in Ethiopia 1270-1527.* Oxford: Oxford University Press, 1972

Tadesse, Tamrat. *Church and State in Ethiopia.* Oxford: Clarendon Press, 1972.

Tayback, M. Prince. "Infant Mortality and Fertility in Five Towns of Ethiopia." *Ethiopian Medical Journal.* 41 965: 11–17.

Taylor, Charles. *Philosophy and the Social Sciences: Philosophical Papers* 2. Cambridge: Cambridge University Press, 1988.

Tegegn Yetesha Work. Editorial. *Ethiopian Herald.,* April 20, 1966.

Tekeste Negash, *Rethinking Ethiopian Education,* Uppsala: Nordic Africa Institute, 1996.

Tekeste Negash. *The Crisis of Ethiopian Education: Implications for nation-building*, Uppsala Reports on Education, 29, Uppsala: Uppsala University, Department of Education 1990

Tekeste Negash. Rethinking Education in Ethiopia. Uppsala: Nordiska Afrikainstitutet, 1996.

Tekeste Negash. Education in Ethiopia: From Crisis to Brink of Collapse, 2006.

Tekeste Negash. *Rethinking Education in Ethiopia.* Uppsala: Nordiska Africainstitute,1996

Tekeste Negash.*The Crisis of Ethiopian Education: Some Implications for Nation Building.* Uppsala: Uppsala University, Uppsala Reports on Education no.29, 1990.

Teshome G. Wagaw. *Education in Ethiopia.* Ann Arbor: University of Michigan Press, 1979.

Teshome G. Wagaw. *Education in Ethiopia.* Ann Arbor: University of Michigan Press, 1979.

Teshome Wagaw. *Education in Ethiopia, Prospect and Retrospect.* Ann Arbor: University of Michigan Press 1979.

Tezeta. Ethiopiques Collection # 10, Paris, Non-dated

Thomson, Blair. *Ethiopia: The Country that Cut Off Its Head.* London: Robson Books, 1975.

Thuo, M. and United Nations Fund for Population Activities. Country Support Team Addis Ababa. *Media advocacy strategy: making a difference in population and development interventions.* Addis Ababa, Ethiopia, UNFPA CST. 2003.

Thuo, M., United Nations Fund for Population Activities. Country Support Team Addis Ababa., et al. *Enter-educate using print media: making a difference in population and development interventions.* Addis Ababa, Ethiopia, UNFPA CST. 2003.

Tirussew, T. *Disability in Ethiopia: issues, insights, and implications.* Addis Ababa, Addis Ababa University Print. Press. 2005.

Tokiomi, Kaigo. *Japanese Education: Its Past and Present.* Tokyo: Kokusai Bunka Shinkokai, 1968.

Transitional Government of Ethiopia, *Education and Training Policy*, Addis Ababa, 1994.

Trudeau, Edouard. "Higher Education in Ethiopia." Ed.D. research, Columbia University 1964.

Turton, David. 'The Politician, the Priest, and the Anthropologist: Living Beyond Conflict in Southwestern Ethiopia," *Ethnos* 68, No. 1 2003: 5-26.

U.S. Embassy in Addis Ababa, Commission for Educational Exchange between Ethiopia and the United States. Addis Ababa, 1963.

U.S. Operation Mission to Ethiopia. Progress Report: Point IV Report to Ethiopia on Ten Years of Joint Technical and Economic Co-operation between the United States and the Imperial Ethiopian Government. Addis Ababa: Communications Media Centre, 1961.

U.S. Operations Mission in Ethiopia. *Progress Report: Point IV.* Addis Ababa, 1961.

U.S. Security Agreements and Commitments Abroad: Ethiopia. Washington, D.C.,June 1, 1970.

Ullendorff, Edward. *The Ethiopians: An Introduction to Country and People.*3rd ed. London: Oxford University Press, 1973. trans.

Ullendorff, Edward. Translator's Preface. *The Autobiography of Emperor Haile Selassie, 1891–1937.* London: Oxford University Press, 1976.

UNDP, *Human Development Report 2005.* UN Plaza, New York, New York, 10017,USA, 2005.

UNESCO, *Introduction: Learning: The Treasure Within. International Commission on Education for the Twenty-first Century. Paris,* 1996.

United Nations Human Settlements Programme. Human values in water education: creating a new water-use ethic in African cities. Nairobi, Kenya, United Nations Human Settlements Programme, UN-Habitat. 2001.

United Nations Millennium Development Goals, 2000.

United Nations. "Report to the Ethiopian Ministry of Education and Fine Arts." December 20, 1969.

United Nations. *Demographic Yearbook.* New York: United Nations Publications, 1949–1985.

United Nations. Economic Commission for Africa. Economic and Social Policy Division. *Non-formal and distance education in Ethiopia: lessons and experiences.* Addis Ababa, The Division, Economic Commission for Africa. 1997.

United Nations. Economic Commission for Africa. Public Administration Human Resources and Social Development Division. *Public expenditure patterns in selected African countries: impact on health and education Ethiopia.* Addis Ababa, The Division. 1993.

United Nations. Economic Commission for Africa. Public Administration Human Resources and Social Development *Division, A review and analysis of past attempts towards curricula reform for socio-economic development in Africa: Ad Hoc Experts Group Meeting on Assessment of Confidence Building Factors in School Curricula: 18-21 October 1993, Addis Ababa,* Ethiopia. Addis Ababa

United Nations. Economic Commission for Africa. Public Administration Human Resources and Social Development Division. *The way forward in curriculum development for socio-economic recovery and transformation in Africa.* Addis Ababa, The Division. 1993.

United Nations. UNESCO-ECA. *Final Report.* UNESCO, E.D./181/1961.

United Nations. UNESCO-ECA. *Statistical Yearbook.* Paris: United Nations Publications, 1963–1985.

University College of Addis Ababa, Student Union. *News and Views.* Addis Ababa, 1960–1966.

University of Utah. "Survey of Higher Education in Ethiopia, 1959–1960." Addis Ababa, 1960.

Vaughan, Sarah. *Ethnicity and Power in Ethiopia. Ph.D Dissertation,* University of Edinburgh. 2003.

Verwimp, Philip. "Measuring the Quality of Education at Two Levels: A Case Study of Primary Schools in Rural Ethiopia" *International Review of Education* 45, 2, 1999: 167-196

Von Massow, F. *Access to health and education services in Ethiopia: supply, demand, and government policy.* Oxford, Herndon, VA, Oxfam. 2001.

von Massow, Fra. "International development targets, poverty, and gender in Ethiopia". *Gender and Development* vol 8.No 1, March 2000: 45-54.

Wartenberg, D. and W. Mayrhofer Education in Ethiopia. Hamburg, Kova*c. 2001.

Whitton, J. B. and S. L. Gwynn *The sanctity of treaties Pacta sunt servanda.* New York,, Carnegie Endowment for International Peace. 1935.

Woldehanna, T. and Young Lives Project *Child labour, gender inequality and rural/urban disparities: how can Ethiopia's national development strategies be revised to address negative spill-over impacts on child education and wellbeing?* London, Young Lives, Save the Children UK. 2005.

Woldehanna, T. and Young Lives Project *Education choices in Ethiopia: what determines whether poor households send their children to school?* London, Young Lives, Save the Children UK. 2005.

Woldehanna, T., N. Jones, et al *Children's educational completion rates and achievement: implications for Ethiopia's second poverty reduction strategy 2006-10.* London, Young Lives, Save the Children UK.. 2005.

Woldehanna, T., N. Jones, et al. *How pro-poor is Ethiopia's education expansion?: a benefit incident analysis of education since 1995/96.* London, Young Lives, Save the Children UK. 2006.

Woldehanna, T., N. Jones, et al. *How pro-poor is Ethiopia's education expansion?: a benefit incident analysis of education since 1995/96.* London, Young Lives, Save the Children UK. 2006.

Wolf, E.. *Europe and the People without History.* Berkeley: University of California Press, 1982.

World Bank, "Education in Ethiopia: Strengthening the Foundation for Sustainable Progress, AFTH 3", *Human Development Department, Africa Region,* 2004:107-10.

World Bank. *Education in Ethiopia: Strengthening the Foundation for Sustainable Progress.* Washington, D.C. 20433, U.S.A. 2005.

World Bank. *Education in Ethiopia: strengthening the foundation for sustainable progress.* Washington, D.C., U.S.A., World Bank. 2005.

World Bank. *Ethiopia: social sector report.* Washington, D.C., World Bank. 1998.

World Bank. *Higher Education Development for Ethiopia:* Pursuing the Vision. Washington, D.C. 20433, U.S.A.2003.

World Bank. *Lessons learned from abolishing school fees in Ethiopia, Ghana, Kenya, Malawi and Mozambique.* Washington DC, World Bank. 2008.

World Wide Federation of Ethiopian Students. *Challenge.* 13 August 1973: 1–20.

World Wide Union of Ethiopian Students. *Democratic Revolution in Ethiopia."* October 1, 1972: 1–97.

Yalew, E. and W. Almaz *Academic achievements, drop out, and repetition rates of female students in some selected schools of Addis Ababa.* Addis Ababa, Forum on Street Children Ethiopia. 1997.

Yalew, E. and W. Almaz *Academic achievements, drop out, and repetition rates of female students in some selected schools of Addis Ababa.* Addis Ababa, Forum on Street Children Ethiopia. 1997.

Ye Etiopia Seb'awi Mebtoch Guba'e *The impact of federalization on education in Ethiopia 1991-1998.* Addis Ababa, Ethiopian Human Rights Council. 2001.

Year book of graduating students from Kotabe College of Teacher Education. Kotabé mamheran tem*hert kolé*g. Graduates bulletin. Addis Ababa, The College: v. 1996.

Yelfign, W., Forum for African Women Educationalists., et al. *Study on primary school female participation and performance in Chaha District.* Addis Ababa, Forum for African Women Educationalists: Ministry of Education. 1995.

Yelfign, W., Forum for African Women Educationalists., et al. *Study on primary school female participation and performance in Chaha District.* Addis Ababa, Forum for African Women Educationalists: Ministry of Education. 1995.

Yemin Heywat Naw" What a Life. Pamphlet distributed in Addis Ababa, February 19, 1974.

Yeshitla Mengistu. "History of Meserete Krestos Church." Senior essay, Makana Yesus Seminary, 1984

Yoseph Kidane Wolde. "The History of the Pentecostal Movement in Addis Abab." Senior essay, Haile Sellassie I University, 1976.

Contributors Bio:

Paulos Milkias, Ph.D., is Professor of Humanities and Political Science at Marianopolis College/Concordia University in Montreal Canada. He earned his Ph.D. from McGill University. His major publications include *Ethiopia: A Comprehensive Bibliography* (G.K. Hall/Macmillan, 1989); *The Battle of Adwa: the Historic Victory of Ethiopian over European Colonialism,* [Coedited] (Algora Publishing, 2005); and *Haile Selassie, Western Education and Political Revolution in Ethiopia.* He was also an Associate Editor of Nelson's *New Christian Dictionary* (Thomas Nelson, 2001), and a contributor to *Encyclopaedia Aethiopica,* (University of Hamburg 2006) *ABC-CLIO* Schools Project 2008, and *World Education Encyclopedia,* (Facts on File Publications, 1988). He is currently, *inter alia,* Co-Editor of *North-East-African Studies,* (Michigan State University), and Associate Editor of *Horn of Africa Journal,* (Rutgers University), Dr. Milkias has published numerous articles that appeared in prestigious scholarly journals.

Messay Kebede, Ph.D., is an Ethiopian professor who teaches philosophy at the University of Dayton, Ohio. He obtained his Ph.D. from the University of Grenoble in France. He has previously taught philosophy at Addis Ababa University (Ethiopia). He is the author of four books, *Meaning and Development* (1994), *Survival and Modernization* (1999), *Africa's Quest for a Philosophy of Decolonization* (2004), and *Radicalism and Cultural Dislocation in Ethiopia, 1960-1974* (2008). He has also published numerous articles in professional journals.

Maimire Mennasemay, Ph.D., teaches in the Humanities/Philosophy Department, Dawson College, Montreal, Qc. Canada. His research interests are in Ethiopian studies, political philosophy, and African political thought. His publications have appeared in the *Canadian Journal of African Studies, Journal of Modern African Studies* (co-author), *Northeast African Studies, Horn of Africa* (guest editor for a special on Federalism in the Horn), and he is the senior editor of the *International Journal of Ethiopian Studies.* He is also on the editorial board of a number of academic journals.

Eva Poluha, Ph.D., is associate professor in social anthropology from Dalarna University in Sweden. Her recent main interests are the anthropology of children, political anthropology and gender studies. In 2004 Poluha published the monograph *The Power of Continuity, Ethiopia Through the Eyes of its Children,* with the Nordic Africa Institute, and in 2002 Poluha and Rosendahl co-edited *Contesting Good Governance, Cross-cultural Perspectives on Representation, Accountability and Public Space,* published by Routledge Curzon. In 2002 Poluha also published Beyond the Silence of Women in Ethiopian Politics in M. Cowen and L. Laakso (eds) *Multi-party Elections in Africa.* Oxford: James Currey Ltd.

Tekeste Negash, Ph.D., is a professor of History at Dalarna University. He is a visiting professor at the Universities of Bahir Dar and Mekelle and Bologna. He is the author of *Italian Colonialism in Eritrea* (1987); *Eritrea and Ethiopia: The Federal Experience* (1997); Co-author of *Brothers at War: Making Sense of the Eritrean-Ethiopian War* (2000); *The Crisis of Ethiopian Education: Implications for Nation-building* (1990); and *Education in Ethiopia: from Crisis to the Brink of Collapse* (2006).

Data Dea, Ph.D., is assistant professor of Anthropology/International Studies at University of Northern British Columbia. He taught as a visiting lecturer at McGill University. He also worked for Alemaya University (Ethiopia), the Institute of Development Studies at the University of Sussex (UK), and Max Planck Institute for Social Anthropology (Germany). He has published extensively on contemporary issues in Ethiopia including rural livelihoods, indigenous knowledge, social inequality, election, conflict, religion and civil society. His monograph *Rural Livelihoods and Social Stratification among the Dawro, Southern Ethiopia* (2007) was published by the Department of Sociology and Social Anthropology, Addis Ababa University.

Tibebe Eshete, Ph.D., is an adjuct professor in the department of Religious Studies in Michigan State University. He has taught as an assistant professor of African History at Calvin College, Michigan State University and Missouri State University. He has also taught at Alemaya College, Asmara University, Addis Ababa University and Kotebe College of Teacher Education. He had published extensively on the Horn of Africa as it pertains to Ethio-Somali relations and on issues relating to New Religious Movements in Ethiopia. His recent research interests focus on social/culture changes and youth movements and the like. His publications include, *The Silent Revolution* (World Vision, 2001) and *The Evangelical Movement in Ethiopia: Reisistance and Resilience* (Baylor Press, 2009), which has been considered by scholars as ground-breaking work on a little studied yet important religious phenomenon in Ethiopia.

Judith Narrowe, Ph.D., is an American long-time resident in Stockholm, Sweden received her BA degree from Barnard College, Columbia University in British Studies and a Ph.D. from Stockholm University in Social Anthropology. She has taught a variety of courses in social anthropology at both Stockholm University and more recently at Dalarna University College in Falun, Sweden. She has participated in several evaluations of Swedish development co-operation projects in Ethiopian and has recently completed an ethnographic study of social life at an Ethiopian.

Bekele Haile-Selassie Tomas, J.S.D., holds the degrees of Doctor of Juridical Science and Masters of Laws from the University of Wisconsin Law School. He received the degree of Bachelor of laws from Addis Ababa University Law School and a Diploma from Lund University's Raoul Wallenberg Institute in Advanced International Programs on Human Rights. In May 1993, he was a visiting scholar at the headquarters of the International Committee of The Red Cross, (ICRC). His work experience spans nearly three decades and includes over fifteen years of teaching and research both at the University of Wisconsin Law School and at the Addis Ababa University Law School. Dr. Bekele has presented many papers on various topics dealing with Africa and Ethiopia at scholarly seminars and conferences. He has also authored several articles in the Journal of Ethiopian Law. Currently, Dr. Bekele is engaged in a private research activity.

Index

Academic, xi, 10, 11, 17, 20, 31, 32, 60, 61, 69, 104, 111, 144, 169, 171, 187, 194, 197, 203
Acculturation, 22
Achievement, 16, 95-96, 113, 186, 194, 202
Addis Ababa University, 184, 187, 192-193, 195, 197, 201
Addis Zemen. 100-01, 107-08, 111-114
Admissions, 197
Adwa, 22, 68, 74-76, 174, 176, 198
Afan-Oromo, 10, 17, 19, 21, 23-24, 197
Africa, 1-2, 9, 18-19, 21, 30, 32, 34-35, 40, 48-49, 52-53, 68-69, 73, 118-119, 162, 165-170, 172-173, 175-179, 181-183, 185-186, 188-190, 192-203
Agew, 81
Agriculture, 12-13, 31, 43, 60, 102, 169
Aklilu Habte, 170-171,192
Alemaya, 102, 111
Alienation, 34-36, 46-48, 52-53, 55, 68, 91, 112, 169, 182, 195
Alphabetization, 170
Ambo, 107, 111
Amharic, 4, 10, 13-14, 17, 19, 21-24, 26, 35, 40, 59, 63, 86-87, 112, 120, 122, 140, 142, 170, 172-175, 182, 184, 190, 192-197, 199
Anatomy, 40-42, 45, 168-170, 181, 189, 199
Anthropology, ix, 73, 148, 183, 185, 188-189, 194, 197
Apartheid, 2
Apostolic, 113
Aptitude, 55, 60
Archaeology, 184, 197
Aristocracy, 11, 52, 58
Aristotle, 1, 26
Armenia, 50
Arsi, 107, 134, 136-137, 180, 185, 187
Arts, 16, 49, 60, 111, 170, 172, 195, 202
Assessment, 9, 19, 29, 31, 112, 197, 202
Awasa, 102, 104-106, 177-179, 193

Bag-Making, 140
Bekele Haile-Selassie Tomas, vi, ix, 5, 57
Biology, 18
Books 1, 3, 13-14, 22, 26-27, 32, 35, 46, 86, 103, 108-109, 122-123, 154, 158, 160, 161, 168-171, 174, 177, 181-182, 184, 189, 191, 198-199, 200-203
Boys, 16, 108, 130, 135, 142-144, 154-156, 161
Brain Drain, 69, 78, 88, 173, 192, 201
Britain, 31, 42, 52, 59, 160, 194
Business, iv, 12, 50, 70, 111, 179, 194

Canada, ix, 168, 171, 200
Capitalism, 5, 46, 175
Catholic, 32, 100, 183
Centralization, 52
Certificate, 31, 59-60, 197
Children, viii, 1, 34, 7-8, 11, 15-16, 28, 39, 47, 54, 62, 68-71, 73, 88, 110, 123, 135, 137, 139-140, 147-149, 153-156, 158, 160-161, 163, 175, 186, 188-189, 200-203
Christian, x-xii, 1, 9, 27-28, 32, 34, 47, 100-105, 107, 113-114, 125, 154, 166, 172, 176-179, 182-183, 194, 197-198, 200
Church, vi-vii, 2, 4, 6, 21, 26-30, 34, 39, 47, 51, 68, 70-71, 74, 80-81, 95, 100-101, 104-114, 150, 154, 166-167, 173, 176-183, 190, 194-198, 201, 203
Civic, 5, 18, 24, 61-62, 64-65, 170
Class, 2-3, 13, 16-19, 26, 30, 36-37, 40, 43-46, 53-54
Clinic, 137
Cognition, 154, 188
College, viii-xi, 2, 7, 10, 15, 20, 31, 60, 102, 110-111, 129-130, 135-137, 141-145, 165-168, 183, 185, 192-193, 198-200, 202-203
Colonial, 2, 11, 22, 32, 67, 71, 73, 132, 175
Commercial, 61, 103

Communication, 10-11, 22-23, 40, 45, 50, 63, 125, 156, 196, 202
Communism, 177
Competition, 25, 157, 182, 187
Conscientization, 47
Conservatism, 29, 32
Cooperation, 129
Counter-Culture, 113
Coup d'etat, 40, 53, 113
Courses, 28, 31-33, 59-61, 139-140
Creativity, 28, 73, 84-85
Criteria, 5, 67, 121-22, 147, 154, 157
Critic, 17, 28, 34
Culture, 12, 19, 20-23, 28-29, 31-36, 45, 47, 61-62, 70-71, 73-77, 79, 86, 92-93, 95-96, 108-109, 112-13, 122, 124, 127, 135-36, 142-45, 148-49, 173, 175-76, 184-89, 194, 197-98, 200

Dabtara, 2-4, 25, 27-28, 36, 51, 53, 80-83, 85, 90, 93-94, 174, 190
Dangla, 150, 190
Daro, 138
Data Dea, 6, 183-84, 193-94, 197
Deacons, 26-27
Deaf, 88
Debate, 7, 21, 24, 32, 57, 71, 83, 91, 129, 162
Decentralization, 24, 121
Degree, 2, 16-17, 33, 45, 50, 51-52, 58, 69, 124, 148-49, 155
Demographic, 41-42, 202
De-Schooling, 170
Desk, 160-61
Dessie, 179
Dewey, John, 175
Dialectic, 49, 67, 87, 94, 96, 175, 198
Dialogue, 97, 108, 132, 187
Diaspora, 20, 179-180
Diploma, 12, 15-17
Dire-Dawa, 102, 180
Disability,136, 201
Discipline, 3, 45, 47, 52, 73, 110
Discrimination, 63, 124, 134, 141, 185-86, 199
Dismissal, 28, 36, 54, 126
Doctrine, 27-28, 105, 158
Dogma, 28, 32
Dormitory, 130, 136, 179

Dorze, 183, 201
Drama, 106, 112
Drawing, 5, 86, 175
Dropout, 31, 70
Drought, 1

ECA, 170, 202
Eclecticism, 71, 92
Ecology, 188-89
Ecumenical, 106
Education, 1-7, 9-19
Elementary, 26, 31, 35, 52, 59-60, 62, 110-11, 123-25, 187, 192
Elite, 2-5, 23, 25-26, 28-29, 34-36, 39, 40-41, 45, 48-53, 55, 67, 76-77, 99, 107, 109, 111-112, 119, 121-22, 126, 147, 16668, 170, 175, 181, 200
Employment, 3, 11, 17, 41, 165, 198
English, 3-4, 9-19, 21-24, 59, 62, 101, 111, 142, 165, 171, 173-174
Enrolment, 4, 11, 14-16, 19-20, 30, 68
Entrance, 67, 142
Entrepreneurship, 198
EPRDF, 3, 6-7, 14-15, 69, 71, 90, 94, 121, 124-126, 150-52, 162-163
Eritrea, 30, 40, 107, 123, 151, 172, 180, 184
Essay, 22, 153, 168-69, 173, 194, 201, 203
Estefanites, 112
ESUNA, 171
Ethics, 35, 190
Ethiocentric, 26
Ethiopia, 1-7, 9-36, 39-41, 45, 48-65, 67-97, 99-114, 117-121, 123-124, 126-131, 133-137, 139, 141-145, 147-148, 151-152, 154, 156-157, 159-161, 163, 165-168, 170-203
Ethiopic, 14, 27, 175, 193
Ethnicity, 24, 37, 55-56, 75, 77, 96, 118, 121, 126, 166, 184-85, 192, 202
Ethnology, 63
Eurocentrism, 167, 199
Evaluation, 7, 13-14, 28-29, 60, 93, 129-130, 137, 139, 187
Examination, 9, 16, 45, 59-60, 62, 155, 197
Exercise, 50, 64, 80, 85, 93, 103, 110, 114, 154, 160-61, 178
Expatriate, 30, 32, 34, 36, 61-62, 64, 111

Expenditure, 30, 52, 54, 202
Experience, 6-8, 10, 15, 17, 19, 35, 42, 44,
61, 63, 67, 86-87, 92-94, 99-104, 107,
109, 112, 114, 117-118, 126, 128,
130-131, 147-154, 157-159, 163, 170,
174, 176-178, 180-181, 184, 193,
195, 199, 202
Expertise, 13, 62
Expression, 7, 36, 75, 82, 86, 96-97, 100,
107, 114, 129, 158, 189
Expulsion, 2, 28, 35, 109, 171
Extension, 27, 78, 185
External, 14-15, 21, 31, 36, 43, 70, 89-90,
94-95, 101, 109, 114, 132, 134

Factories, 54
Faculty, 113, 171, 197
Failure, 1, 5, 20, 22, 26, 29, 42, 45, 52, 54,
61, 69-72, 85, 89-91, 97, 113, 126-
128, 170, 183, 186
Famine, 3, 42, 54, 199-200
Farmers, 63, 124-126, 151
Fascist, 2, 52, 59, 171
Fellowship, 104-105, 178-179
Females, 7, 15-16, 20, 123, 129-130, 134,
141-142, 156, 160, 187, 193, 203
Feteha Negast, 27, 190
Feudal, 3, 5, 40-42, 46, 49-54, 120, 140,
171, 200
Fieldwork, 136, 150, 153, 183
Finance, 14, 16, 40, 183, 195, 199
Fitness, 60
Folklore, 62
Food, 10, 63, 69, 109, 139, 150, 152, 155
Foreigners, 59, 61
Formative, 70, 121, 181, 198
Formula, 36
Foucault, 4, 10, 128, 170, 196
Freedom, 5, 6, 24, 28, 36, 68, 73, 77-78,
88, 90, 92, 94, 97, 101, 108, 150, 175
Freud, Sigmund, 175
Friere, 47, 170
Funding, 9, 13-15, 18, 153, 197, 201

Gada, 21, 70, 72, 74, 95, 119, 183, 193
Gambella, 184
Gamo, 7, 81, 119-120, 122, 128, 159, 183,
184

Ge'ez, 1, 26, 28
Gender, 1, 16, 69-70, 77, 83, 87, 95, 130-
36, 141-43, 145, 147-48, 154-56, 173,
185-87, 193, 199-200, 202
Geography, 22, 33
Girls, 16, 68, 108, 130, 133, 135-136, 141-
143, 154-156, 160-61, 186, 189
Globalization, 7, 39, 55, 129-130, 192
Gofa, 119-122, 183-184
Gojjam, 7, 68, 101, 107, 135, 147-148,
162-163, 176, 180, 186, 188
Gondar, 68, 77, 111, 174
Gore, 68
Gospel, 6, 36, 105-107, 109, 114, 176,
178-180, 182, 191, 193, 197
Grade, 9, 11, 13, 16-18, 20, 22-23, 32, 59-
62, 68-69, 76, 97, 101, 153, 165, 176
Gragn, Ahmed, 75
Gramsci, 46, 94, 170
Gurage, 178

Hadiya, 81
Haile Selassie, 2, 4-7, 10, 26, 29-34, 36,
39-40, 46, 49-54, 57-65, 68, 99, 102,
104, 109-111, 119, 150-151, 167-168,
170-172, 176, 179, 181-182, 184,
190, 193-194, 196-202
Handbook, 169-170, 196
Harar, 2, 96, 102-104, 111, 123, 177-178,
180
Health, 62, 69, 111, 137, 155, 166, 173,
192, 196, 199, 201-202
Heritage: 1, 5, 11, 28, 33-36, 61-62, 64,
70, 115
Hierarchy, 7-8, 27, 51, 130-131, 135, 154-
156, 158-159, 164, 184, 194
Historiography, 167-168, 199
History, 1-2, 4-7, 12, 14, 21, 23, 26-27,
32-33, 36, 39, 51, 53, 55, 57, 60, 62,
64, 67, 71-79, 81, 84-97, 99-100,
104-106, 109, 119, 127, 148, 154,
156-157, 165-166, 168-170, 172-179,
182-184, 189, 191, 193-195, 197-203
HIV-AIDS, 141
Housework, 143
Humanities, 168
Hypothesis, 3, 44, 165

Ideology 4-7, 12, 14, 24, 31, 33, 36, 39,
    46, 53, 106, 137, 140, 143, 152, 153,
    156, 170, 185
Idiom, 6, 35
Illich, Ivan, 47, 170
Illiteracy, 9, 11
Illubabor, 107, 180, 197
Imitation, 5, 30, 35, 84, 88, 90-91
Imperialism, 40
Improvization, 70
Income, 11, 19, 68, 130, 133-134, 136,
    139, 141, 144
Indigenous, 1, 3, 21, 27, 36, 41, 50, 62,
    104, 111, 114, 119, 165, 179-180
Individual, 5-7, 9, 15, 27, 48, 55-56, 58,
    62, 83, 89, 95, 106, 111, 113-114,
    121, 127, 129, 131, 133-134, 136,
    138-139, 144, 147-153, 155-156, 158-
    159, 160, 162-163, 175, 182, 185
Indoctrination, 12, 45
Industrialization, 43, 50, 132
Infrastructure, 12, 23, 46, 139
Initiative, 59, 63, 114, 135, 139, 150, 153,
    155, 172
Innovation, 84, 91, 149, 173, 188, 198
Inquiry, 58, 77, 155
Insight, 1, 41, 80, 105, 158, 166, 172, 195,
    201
Inspiration, 15, 33, 109, 112, 178, 185
Institutional, 16, 47, 92, 159, 181, 186
Instrument, 4, 6, 10, 14, 25, 46, 83, 88-89,
    92-94, 107, 128, 131, 175, 184
Intelligentsia, 3, 5, 25, 29, 37, 39, 49, 51-
    54, 57-58, 68, 168, 192
International, 11-12, 15, 31, 41, 43, 48-49,
    60, 88, 92-93, 108, 121, 123, 129,
    131-132, 165-170, 173-174, 179, 180-
    181, 183-185, 187, 192-195, 197-200,
    202
Intervention, 28, 131, 152, 168, 171, 180,
    193, 198, 201
Introductory, 181
Isomorphism, 159

Jijjiga, 68, 67, 180
Jimma, 68, 77, 107, 111, 119, 130, 176,
    183, 192, 198
Jobs, 10, 31, 41, 49, 131, 133-134, 136-
    139, 141, 144-145, 151, 157, 194

Judgment, 20, 29, 58, 78, 81, 110
Junior, 13, 17, 60
Justice, 61-63, 68, 76-78, 81-83, 88, 90,
    92, 94, 96, 97, 108, 123, 175

Kaffa, 119-120
Kebra-Nagast, 27
Konta, 119-122
Koranic, 1
Kotabe, 141, 143-144, 203

Laboratory, 10, 71, 189
Lalibela, 75, 166, 172, 200
Language, 3-4, 6-7, 9-14, 17, 19, 21-24,
    26-28, 35-36, 40, 59, 63, 73, 96-97,
    101, 117-125, 127-128, 148-149, 151,
    153, 165-166, 169, 172, 184, 186,
    188-189, 191-192, 194, 197, 200
Latin, 14, 176, 191, 199
Law, 26-28, 33, 47, 61-63, 81-83, 108,
    171-172, 180, 186, 190
Laymen, 82
Leadership, 4, 32, 103, 105, 106, 121, 150-
    152, 162, 173, 179-180, 182, 192, 197
Lecture, 18-19, 105, 136, 183
Left, 11, 21, 23, 36-37, 41, 54, 56, 64, 68,
    69, 87, 101, 103, 106, 127, 128, 140,
    158
Legal, 45, 61, 106, 114, 134-135, 186
Legend, 27, 56
Lesson, 1, 17-18, 59, 63, 85, 155, 172,
    202-203
Level, 2, 4, 10, 12, 18, 23, 26-28, 30-33,
    35-36, 40, 52-53, 59, 60-62, 69, 70,
    83, 90, 96, 105, 108, 109-113, 120-
    121, 123-124, 128, 131, 133, 135-
    136, 139, 152, 157, 170, 173, 176,
    190, 202
Liberal, 5, 32, 39, 45, 49, 54-55, 60-61, 88,
    97, 132, 179
Liberation, 3, 14, 73, 75, 97, 129, 134,
    169, 182, 186
Library, 33, 105, 180
Lingua Franca, 1, 63, 172
Linguistic, 35, 63-65, 97, 117, 119-120,
    122, 128, 168, 183, 184, 194, 197
Liq, 27, 190
Literacy, 3, 9, 14, 17, 47, 68-70, 80, 89,
    93-94, 138, 187, 200

Literature, 40, 41, 45, 47, 49, 58, 60, 63, 71, 73, 102-103, 112-113, 157, 173, 177, 199
Liturgy, 26
Logic, 15, 43, 89, 154, 188
Low-Income, 68
Lyrics, 87, 175

Maimire, Mennasemay, 5-6,67, 166, 174, 176, 188, 198
Makalle, 77
Makana Yasus, 101, 176-178, 180, 195, 201, 203
Males, 16, 20, 45, 52, 121, 141-142, 156, 187
Malnutrition, 201
Manpower, 13, 41, 49, 165, 198-199
Manual, 2, 63
Manuscript, 26, 170
Manze, 188
Map, 119-120, 177, 185, 187
Marginalization, 23, 34, 84, 166
Marks, 99, 142-143, 160-161
Marx, Karl, 20, 44-45, 169-170, 174, 176-177, 179, 199-200
Marxism-Leninism, 4-5, 25, 26, 36
Masafint, 63, 191
Maskal, 171
Materialism, 55
Mathemathics, 18, 160-161, 165
Maturation, 96
Meles Zenawi, 175
Memorization, 30, 73, 80, 95, 155
Menelik, 1-2, 27, 30, 49, 50, 51, 59, 63, 67, 93, 104, 119, 142, 165, 175
Menen, 59
Mengistu, Haile Mariam, 3
Mental, 44, 55, 73, 79, 149, 158, 162
Meritocracy, 50
Merkato, 102-103
Mesfin, 179
Mesqel, 170
Messay Kebede, 1, 4, 20-23, 25, 110, 166-167, 175, 188, 198-199
Messianic, 105, 109, 113
Methodology, 113
Metsahaf, 26, 191
Metsahafe-Falasfa Tabiban, 26, 191
Miaphysite, 2

Military, 3, 5, 14, 24, 25, 32, 39, 40, 42-43, 49, 52-54, 102, 151, 157, 160, 163, 169, 171, 180, 190, 196
Millennium, 15, 51, 165-166, 192, 202
Mind, 1, 28-29, 35, 41, 44, 48, 51, 55, 57, 109, 113, 130, 156
Ministry, 3, 13-14, 20, 31, 59, 60-62, 105, 122, 170, 178-179, 181, 193-196, 198-199, 202-203
Minor, 106, 150
Minorities, 131, 184, 193, 196, 200
Misappropriation, 153
Misconceptions, 29
Misconduct, 108, 125, 127
Mismanagement, 126
Missionary, 53, 101-102, 107, 114, 176-179
Mobility, 42, 44, 168
Model, 32, 41, 50, 70, 90, 106, 113, 137, 148, 169, 179, 188
Moderation, 32
Modernization, 4, 11, 20-24, 28-29, 33-36, 39, 40-43, 49, 50, 57, 70, 72, 89, 90, 92-93, 95, 97, 99, 108-112, 132, 166-167, 171, 175-176, 181, 186, 188, 197-199
Monastic, 26
Morale, 54
Moslem, 27, 108-109, 119, 154, 172, 179-180
Mosque, 21, 70, 72, 74, 95, 154
Motivation, 7, 149
Multidisciplinary, 3
Multi-Ethnic, 128, 198
Multilingual, 176, 194
Museum, 33
Music, 26, 85-87, 107, 174, 180, 184, 191, 193
Mussolini, 2
Myth, 40, 47, 172, 188

Nagarit Gazetta, 196
Narrative, 7, 63, 77, 107, 129
Narrowe, Judith, 7, 129, 185, 187, 188
Nationalism, 6, 56, 64-65, 95, 166, 168, 184, 199
Nationalities, 14, 59, 61, 118, 120-121, 168, 184, 192, 195
Nazareth, 102-104, 107, 193

Neo-Liberal, 88, 97, 132
Neo-Marxist, 46
Neqemte, 68
News, 127, 163, 178, 180, 184, 202
NGO, 132, 183
Nihilism, 89
Nobility, 30, 110
Norm, 27, 29, 36-37, 58, 64, 113, 131,
    148-149, 156, 161-162
Normative, 48, 112, 134, 145, 159
North-East-Africa, 1, 182, 185, 189, 192,
    194
Norway, 167, 183, 194, 198
Norwegian, 189
Notebooks, 170, 197
Novel, 3, 6, 28, 85

Obedience, 73, 82, 147, 154, 155, 157-158
Objective, 4, 12, 13-14, 24, 31, 33-34, 44-
    45, 53-54, 58, 60, 64, 86, 89, 93, 96,
    124, 128, 168, 173, 177, 186, 197
Objectivity, 46
Obligation, 158
Occupation, 2, 11, 30, 41, 52, 63, 101,
    121-122, 147, 193
Ogaden, 174
Ometo, 120-122, 183-184, 197
Omission, 32, 64
Omo, 6-7, 117-122, 124-126, 128, 183,
    194, 196
Opinion, 14, 19, 21, 24, 103-104, 108, 127,
    143, 152, 182, 186
Oppression, 44, 71, 75-78, 87, 88-90, 92,
    94, 96, 134, 140
Organic, 81, 94
Organization, 3, 4, 10, 14, 24, 26, 31, 36,
    43, 59, 91, 105, 122, 124-125, 131-
    135, 137, 139, 144, 149-150, 157,
    158, 159, 165, 169-171, 177, 178,
    181, 186, 188, 197-201
Orientation, 4, 26, 31, 33, 36, 45, 90, 111,
    140
Oromia, 118
Oromo, 4, 10, 14, 16-17, 19, 21-24, 40, 77,
    119, 168, 183, 191, 193, 197-198
Orphan, 194
Orthodox, 2, 6, 26, 28, 32, 56, 81, 100,
    102, 107-109, 113-114, 166, 173,
    176-178, 181, 194

Ossification, 28
Outreach, 106, 177-179
Overcrowding, 13, 30, 55
Overlap, 78
Overseer, 178
Oxfam, 202

Painting, 26, 87, 90
Pamphlet, 32, 203
Pandemics, 175
Pankhurst, Sylvia, 27
Pantheon, 196
Paper, 4, 10, 18-19, 23, 25, 34, 58, 79, 86,
    93, 108, 117, 119, 125, 133, 139, 144,
    147-148, 158, 165-168, 171, 173-174,
    182-185, 189, 193-194, 197-201
Paradox, 32, 39, 48, 112, 139, 168, 183,
    201
Parents, 11, 15, 17, 23-24, 28, 31, 34, 110,
    147-149, 154, 156, 197, 199
Parliament, 63, 123, 124, 162
Parochialism, 3, 65
Participation, 69, 83, 106, 110, 133, 135,
    140, 144, 163, 178, 187, 189, 193,
    203
Partnership, 200
Pass, 29, 159-161, 171
Pastoralist, 77
Patriotism, 62, 71,108
Patron, viii, 8, 31, 147-148, 156-157, 164,
    188-189
Paulos, Milkias, iii, iv, vi, ix, xi, 1, 4, 6,
    39, 166, 167, 168, 170-171, 174, 181,
    193, 198, 200
Pausewang, Siegfried, 184, 186, 189, 200
Pay, 11, 54, 103, 106, 149, 151, 154, 199
Peace, 12, 31, 57, 61, 91, 121, 125, 151,
    156-157, 172, 180, 183, 198, 202
Peasant, viiii, x, 3, 7, 43, 50, 54, 77, 86-87,
    121, 124-126, 134, 137, 139, 147-
    148, 150-153, 157-158, 160, 162-164,
    169, 174-175, 187-189, 201
Pedagogy, 19, 53, 67, 72, 74, 170
Pen, 51, 154, 196
Pentecost, vii, x, 6, 56, 99-109, 112-114,
    176-183, 195, 198, 203
Perception, 5, 7, 39, 41, 44, 48, 53, 106,
    109-110, 129, 132-133, 135, 148, 185

Personality, 23, 45, 105, 136, 141, 144-145, 170
Pharmacy, 179
Philosophy, ix, xi, 26, 35, 59, 107, 73, 174, 190, 194, 201
Phonemes, 122, 183
Phonetic, 2
Phrasing, 83
Physician, 69
Physics, 18
Physiography, 121
Placement, 14, 194
Plan, 3, 58, 138, 155, 165, 179, 195-196, 199
Plant, 175
Plasma, 18-19
Platform, 3, 53
Plato, 26, 79, 89
Playground, 32
Pluralism, 29
Poetry, 26-28, 62, 80, 175, 190-191
Polemic, 16
Police, 53, 108, 122-123, 156-157, 160, 162, 180
Policy, v, vi, 3-7, 10-12, 14-15, 17, 21-24, 29, 31-34, 36-37, 39, 43, 50, 53, 57, 60, 69, 111, 117-118, 120, 126-129, 131-144, 165, 185-186, 196-197, 201-202
Politicization, 24, 189
Politics, iv, vii, 5, 23, 39, 43, 45, 47, 71, 75, 78, 89, 90, 91, 97, 105-106, 113, 117, 127-128, 156-157, 166, 168-170, 182-186, 188-189, 192, 194, 198
Poluha, Eva, viii, ix, xi, 7-8, 135-136, 147, 166, 185, 187-189, 200
Polyphonic, 75
Post-Colonial, 132,
Post-Modernism, 185
Post-Secondary, 20
Postulates, 58
Postwar, 167, 181, 199
Potentialities, 85, 186
Poverty, 9, 14-15, 19-21, 71-78, 87-89, 91-92, 94, 97, 130, 132-133, 142, 173-175, 202
Pragmatism, 89
Precepts, 35, 55
Prerequisite, 78, 96

Prescriptive, 95
Priest, 26-28, 82, 101, 154, 176, 178, 184, 201
Primary, 9, 11-12, 14-15, 16-17, 19-20, 30-31, 35-36, 47, 59-60, 64, 68-70, 88, 96-97, 122, 140, 173, 192, 193-194, 199-200, 202-203
Primers, 11
Print, 182, 201
Priorities, 42, 150
Procedure, 137, 139, 151, 159, 163, 180
Profession, 8, 50, 67, 192, 199
Professor, ix, xi, 107, 112-113, 158, 168, 177, 179, 182
Program, xi, 13, 16, 18, 31, 34, 49, 60-61, 68-70, 101, 104, 105-106, 110, 130-134, 136-137, 139, 141-142, 144, 162-163, 165, 171, 178, 181-182, 185-187, 192-194, 197-198, 200, 202
Progressive, 13, 22, 52, 55, 73, 79
Promotion, 3, 19, 37, 109
Propaganda, 34, 94, 122, 195
Protest, 3, 6, 32, 100, 109, 118, 122-127, 169, 184
Protestant, 32, 100, 109, 125
Psychology, 41, 168, 170
Publication, iv, 23, 107, 170, 184, 189, 192, 200, 202
Punishment, 150, 155, 184
Pupil, 2, 3, 12-13, 16, 28, 59, 68, 70, 162, 194, 199

Qené, 70, 80, 191
Qualitative, 75, 77-78, 81, 89, 136
Quantitative, 33
Qubé, 14, 191
Quota, 151-152

Race, 2, 166, 168, 186, 196
Radicalism, v, 32, 34, 36, 57, 182
Rahel, Getachew, xi, 174, 181, 198
Rank, 27, 29-30, 49, 51, 53, 101, 112, 125, 154, 165, 178
Rates, 16, 68, 132, 202-203
Ratio, (Teacher-Student) 12-14, 16, 68-70
Readers, 23, 198
Reasoning, 57, 83, 85
Rebellion, 44-45, 48, 52, 87, 123, 165, 169, 188

Reciprocity, 156
Recolonization, 172
Recording, iv, 107
Recruitment, 13, 151, 172
Reference, 33, 61, 112, 149, 157, 170, 180,
    197
Reflection, 46, 68, 71, 81, 83, 85, 88, 95,
    126, 138, 144, 163, 168, 177, 183,
    185-188, 192, 194
Reform, 20, 26, 35, 52, 68, 88, 90, 92, 109,
    114, 120, 150, 167, 171, 177, 181,
    192, 199, 202
Rejection, 28, 84-85, 175
Relapse, 126
Relativism, 91
Relevance, 9, 17, 74, 85, 91, 113, 197
Religion, 1-2, 27, 29, 32, 73, 87, 100, 107-
    108, 110, 113-114, 149, 154, 176,
    183-184, 186, 188, 190-191, 197
Renaissance, 6, 198
Renewal, 37, 109, 114, 181, 183
Reorientation, 33
Reparative, 121
Repeat, 18, 33, 124, 142, 150, 161,
Repetition, 73, 80, 84, 88, 156, 158, 203
Replacement, 14, 19, 21, 23, 171
Report, 31, 61-62, 69, 101, 108, 114, 123,
    139, 155, 165, 170, 172-173, 176-
    181, 184, 186-187, 189, 192-196,
    200-203
Research, iv, vii, ix, 3, 5, 12, 24, 33, 35,
    40-41, 48, 84, 113, 118, 121, 131,
    134-137, 148, 153, 168, 170, 182-
    184, 186-188, 191-195, 197-200
Resourcefulness, 80
Revolution, vi, x, 3, 4, 5, 12, 14-16, 21, 25-
    26, 36, 39-45, 47-55, 57-58, 90-91,
    99, 106-107, 111, 115, 120, 134, 151,
    166-171, 176-177, 179-180, 184, 189,
    192, 194-197, 199-200, 203
REWA, x, 134-135, 137, 139, 186
Reward, 48-49, 155, 159, 161, 164
REYA, x, 137
Rights, iv, 27, 50, 82, 117-118, 121, 123,
    127, 133-135, 141, 158, 184-186,
    189, 196, 203

Sabaean, 167
Salary, 13, 138, 145

SAPC, 182, 198
Scarcity, 30, 70
Schism, 103
Scholar, xi, 1-2, 21, 26-27, 31, 34-35, 40-
    41, 44-45, 47-48, 100, 105, 110-111,
    176, 182-183, 190
School, viii, 1-7, 9-12, 15-19, 21-23,
    24-31, 34-36, 39-40, 45-47, 51-57,
    59-62, 64-67, 69-70, 90, 93, 101-104,
    110, 117, 122-125, 127-128, 135, 137,
    138, 142, 147-148, 154-156, 158,
    160-162, 165, 167-168, 170-173, 176,
    182-183, 187-188, 190-195, 197, 199,
    200, 202-203
Science, ix, xi, 12, 16, 28, 35, 40-41, 45,
    49, 52, 60, 73, 105, 111, 113, 165,
    168-169, 170-172, 174, 177, 182,
    188, 197, 199, 200-201
Scientific, 12, 23, 28-29, 175
    Scientist, 3, 125
Script, 14, 191
Secondary, 9-20, 26, 30, 36, 59-62, 68,
    96-97, 103, 111, 165, 171, 187, 195,
    197, 199
Secularization, 111-112
Self, 19, 21, 23-24, 52, 55, 60, 68, 71-73,
    75, 76, 80, 88, 90, 93-97, 106-107,
    109, 110, 114, 123, 131-133, 135,
    141-142, 144-145, 150, 154, 168,
    182, 191
Semantic, 92
Seminar, 19, 106, 192, 199
Seminary, 177-180, 195, 197, 201, 203
Semitic, 167
Seniority, 183, 201
SEPDF, x, 126
Sexism, 92
Shakespeare, 60
Shelter, 56
Shepherd, 138
Shoa, 96, 119, 168
Shortcoming, 4, 13-14, 28, 31, 33-34, 41,
    69, 70, 89
Shum-Shir, 157
SIDA, 14, 137, 185-187, 189, 193
Sidama, 184, 192
Sidamo, 96, 119
Simen, 102
Similarities, 12, 84, 156

Skill, viii, x, xi, 5, 33-34, 50, 63, 67, 70, 80, 84, 89, 111, 114, 130-131, 133-134, 136, 139, 141, 144-145, 147, 191, 200
Slides, 90
Slogan, 6, 107, 151, 172, 178
Smart, 163
Soap-Making, 140
Social, i, iii, iv, vii, xii, 3-5, 7, 9-12, 21, 23, 27-28, 30, 35-36, 40-49, 52-55, 58, 60-61, 63, 67, 69-76, 78-79, 81-82, 84, 87-97, 99-100, 106, 108, 111-112, 114, 123-125, 127, 129-131, 133-136, 141-142, 144-145, 147-148, 150, 154, 156, 159, 165-170, 173-174, 177, 181-189, 192-195, 197-198, 200-203
Socialism, 12, 14, 22-23, 71, 90, 184, 195
Socialization, vi, 5, 45-47, 55-59, 61, 64, 111, 135, 170, 189
Societal, 50, 165
Society, x, 3, 6-7, 10, 12-16, 20-24, 27, 29, 31, 36, 42, 44-50, 58, 62, 64, 68, 70-72, 75-78, 83-101, 104, 107, 109-110, 117-118, 124, 127-128, 131, 133-135, 144, 148, 156, 158, 160, 166, 168, 170, 172, 179, 183, 188, 193, 194, 198, 200
Sociology, 168-169
Soddo, 122-127, 184
Solomonian Dynasty, 27
Solution, 18, 26, 32, 128, 150, 163, 172
Songs, 62, 87, 107, 115, 174-175, 180, 191, 197
Sophist, 80
Sovereignty, 80, 89
Soviet Union, 12, 49
Speech, 31, 33-34, 36, 63, 82, 108, 150, 154, 162, 167, 197
Spirit, 27, 29, 33, 58, 85, 100-103, 105, 107, 175-178, 183
Spiritual, 1-2, 6, 28, 63, 73, 93, 104-107, 112-114, 150, 177-178, 183
Spoken, 18, 130
Sponsor, 67, 122
Staff, 30-32, 34, 60-62, 69, 111
Standard, 5, 30, 48, 120, 124, 132, 139, 150-151, 158, 179
Statistics, 20, 49, 170, 195
Status, 7, 16-17, 27, 32, 35, 41-42, 44-45, 47-49, 51-53, 67, 72, 119-120, 123, 129, 134-135, 141, 144, 147, 154-156, 184, 186, 198
Stephanites, 190
Stigma, 124
Stimulus, 49-50
Stories, 27, 136, 153, 195
Stratification, 45, 47, 121, 124, 169, 184, 188
Stream, vii, 53, 102-105
Structural, 110, 132, 141, 155, 169
Student, vii, x, 2, 4, 6, 7, 9-13, 15-20, 24-28, 30-36, 39-40, 46, 49, 52-54, 59-62, 64, 68-72, 77, 80, 85, 87, 93-96, 102-107, 109-113, 122-125, 130, 135-137, 141-142, 144-145, 153-155, 160-161, 165-167, 170-172, 176-179, 181-182, 186-187, 193-197, 199, 202-203
Sub-Groups, 148
Subject, xi, 9-10, 12-14, 17-18, 22-23, 26-27, 40, 57-58, 60, 62, 72, 74, 77, 81, 83, 91, 95-96, 125, 171-172, 188
Subjective, vi, 45, 53, 60, 74
Subjectivity, 77-78
Subordination, 154
Sub-Regional, 165, 198
Sub-Sahara, 68-69, 186
Subsistence, 58, 188
Sub-Systems, 42
Subversive, 35, 73, 75-76, 170
Sudan, 68, 111
Summerskill, 182, 201
Supernatural, 102
Super-structure, 46
Supervision, 5, 64
Supplies, 59-60
Survey, 1, 14, 18, 31, 45, 110, 136, 172, 173, 183, 194-198, 202
Sustenance, 82
Sweden, ix, xi, 168, 185-187, 199-200
Symbols, 57, 95, 110, 175
Symposium, 197
Synergy, 105
Synthesis, 198
Syria, 185
System-Maintenance, 89

Taboos, 109

Tabot, 178
Tabula Rasa, 4, 29, 68, 95
Talent, 107, 114, 180
Target, 11, 83, 129, 144, 173, 180, 202
Task, 3, 11, 20-22, 26, 29, 33-36, 40, 59, 61-62, 65, 68, 78-80, 89, 93, 96, 97, 106, 111, 122, 129, 142, 151
Tax, 152
Teaching, 9, 17-18, 56, 62, 130, 179, 185, 187
Team work, 31, 122, 139, 179, 184, 197, 201
Technical, 10, 13, 31, 33, 49, 52, 59-61, 69, 120, 131, 194-195, 202
Technology, 2, 12-13, 18, 22, 28, 35, 41, 138-139, 144, 158, 166, 187
Tekeste, Negash, v, ix, xi, 3-4, 9, 36, 70, 89, 165, 167-168, 173, 175, 179, 185-186, 188, 201
Television, 88, 110
Telos, 83
Tertiary, 15, 60-61, 69
Teshome Wagaw, 20, 28, 111, 167, 171, 181-182, 195, 201,
Tewahdo, 2, 6
Tewodros, 2, 51, 63, 75, 172
Texts, 13, 14, 26-28, 122,180, 191
Theatre, 110, 121
Theology, 26, 110, 182
Theory, vi, 4, 6, 22, 41, 45, 67, 74, 79, 81, 85-86, 93, 95-97, 159, 166, 168-170, 174, 176, 184, 186, 188-189, 198
Thesis, 5, 22, 57, 100, 167, 184, 194, 197, 199
Thinking, 20, 23, 79, 85-86, 92-93, 100-112, 127, 148, 156-157
Tibebe Eshete vii, ix, 6, 99, 183
Tigray, x, 3, 81, 165, 168, 198
Tigrigna, 14, 17, 175, 197
Totalitarianism, 175
TPLF, x, 30, 126,
Trade, 43, 50, 54, 63, 77
Tradition, v, 2, 7, 17, 20, 22, 29, 33-36, 41, 45, 50, 57-58, 61, 63-64, 67, 73-74, 79-80, 91, 95, 100, 109-110, 112-113, 127, 129, 134-135, 139, 143, 172-173, 183, 186, 188, 198-199
Training, 1, 2, 63, 134, 136, 139, 145, 177, 188

Transcendental, 6
Transition, 2, 6, 12, 23, 30, 71, 96, 114, 119, 165, 167, 183, 194, 199, 201
Translation, 1, 23, 167, 174, 188
Transmission, 35, 70, 74, 80, 94
Transnational, 176
Trauma, 81, 84, 127
Travel, 62, 95, 172
TV, 127, 149, 158

U.S.A., 172, 203
UCAA, x, 111
Undergraduate, 15
Understanding, xii, 7, 13, 28-29, 33, 42, 48, 63, 71, 73-79, 82-86, 88, 90-93, 95-96, 108, 144, 148-149, 153-155, 182-188
UNDP, 172, 202
Unemployment, 31, 54, 165
UNESCO, 14, 20, 31, 170, 176, 202
UNFPA, 201
UNICEF, 193, 200
Uniform, 13-15, 45, 161, 176
University, iv, vii, ix-xii, 2, 3, 10, 13, 16, 31-34, 60, 102-107, 109-112, 125, 145, 165, 167-177, 179, 181-189, 192-203
Unrest, 53, 58
Upgrade, 60
Urban, 7, 12, 15, 16, 23, 30, 35, 41-43, 55, 69, 88-89, 105, 125, 129, 135-136, 144, 162, 175, 196, 198, 202
USUAA, 179
Utilitarian, 5, 35
Utopia, vi, 5, 74-75, 79-81, 84-88, 90, 93, 95

Vanguard, 49
Vietnam, 43, 189
Villagization, 137
Violence, 85, 91, 151, 168-169
VOA, 184
Vocation, 10, 13, 60-61, 168, 192, 194, 197
Voluntary, 112
Volunteer, 61, 104, 106, 172, 183

Wage, 44, 54, 169
Walaita, 183
Wallaga, 77, 96, 107

Wallo, 77, 96, 165, 174
War, 3, 9, 12, 24, 20, 42, 55, 109, 123, 132,
    151, 167, 169, 181, 184, 189, 198-
    199, 201
Water, viii, 58, 84, 130, 134, 136-139, 144-
    145, 180, 182, 185, 187, 202
Wealth, 44, 132
Western, 2-6, 12, 21-22, 25, 28-29, 31-32,
    25, 36, 39, 40-41, 45, 47, 49-56, 60-
    61, 67-68, 72-73, 90-92, 107, 109,
    110-111, 114, 132, 135, 162, 166-168,
    170-171, 175, 197, 200
Wisdom, 29, 67, 70, 73, 99, 114, 176, 187,
    191
Withdrawal, 13
Woldegiorgis, xi
Women, vii-viii, x, 7, 15-16, 33, 59, 62,
    69, 82-83, 86, 89, 107, 129-145, 150-
    151, 154, 156, 172, 178, 185-188,
    197-198, 200, 103

Woyanes, 55-56
Writers, 174, 198

Yasteseriyal, 175
Yem, 120
Youth, vi, x, 1, 3- 4, 6, 17, 20, 53-55, 61,
    64, 77, 95, 100, 103-105, 107-114,
    137, 165-166, 168, 170, 178, 181-
    182, 194, 198, 200

Zara Ya'qob, 82, 112
Zema, 26, 28, 191
Zemecha, 196, 200
Zikre Neger: 170

www.ingramcontent.com/pod-product-compliance
Lightning Source LLC
Chambersburg PA
CBHW070906270326
41927CB00011B/2476